City of Islands

CARIBBEAN
STUDIES
SERIES

Anton L. Allahar and Natasha Barnes
Series Editors

City of Islands

Caribbean Intellectuals in New York

TAMMY L. BROWN

University Press of Mississippi / Jackson

www.upress.state.ms.us

The University Press of Mississippi is a member
of the Association of American University Presses.

First printing 2015
∞
Library of Congress Cataloging-in-Publication Data

Brown, Tammy L., 1976–
City of islands : Caribbean intellectuals in New York / Tammy L. Brown.
pages cm. — (Caribbean studies series)
Includes bibliographical references and index.
ISBN 978-1-62846-226-5 (cloth : alkaline paper) — ISBN 978-1-62674-639-8 (ebook) 1. West
Indian Americans—New York (State)—New York—Intellectual life. 2. West Indian Ameri-
cans—New York (State)—New York—Politics and government. 3. Intellectuals—New York
(State)—New York—Biography. 4. Immigrants—New York (State)—New York—Biography.
5. New York (N.Y.)—Intellectual life. 6. New York (N.Y.)—Emigration and immigration—His-
tory. 7. New York (N.Y.)—Race relations—History. 8. Social justice—New York (State)—New
York—History. 9. West Indies—Emigration and immigration—History. 10. New York (N.Y.)—
Emigration and immigration—History. I. Title.
F128.9.W54B76 2015
305.896'9729074710922—dc23   2015006780

British Library Cataloging-in-Publication Data available

For Stephen, Marion, Darren, Lamont,
and Charnée Brown
With love and gratitude—always.

Contents

Abbreviations

AME	African Methodist Episcopal Church
ANLC	American Negro Labor Congress
AUA	American Unitarian Association
ABB	African Blood Brotherhood
AWILAD	American West Indian Ladies Aid Society
BAA	Barbadian American Association
CLC	Cosmo Letter Company
CNN	Cable News Network
CORE	Congress of Racial Equality
CP, CPUSA	Communist Party USA
FBI	Federal Bureau of Investigation
HCC	Harlem Community Church
HUAC	House of Un-American Activities Committee
ILD	International Labor Defense
IQ	Intelligent Quotient
JBA	Jamaica Benevolent Association
JPL	Jamaica Progressive League
KKK	Ku Klux Klan
NAACP	National Association for the Advancement of Colored People
NBFO	National Black Feminist Organization
NOI	Nation of Islam
NOW	National Organization of Women
NYPL	New York Public Library
TED	Technology, Education, and Design
TEDx	Technology, Education, and Design—Independently organized
UBW	Urban Bush Women
UNIA	Universal Negro Improvement Association
UUA	Unitarian Universalist Archives
WPA	Works Progress Administration
YCL	Young Communist League
YMCA	Young Men's Christian Association

Prologue: An Autobiography of the Biographer

> Finding out and writing about people, living or dead, is tricky work. It is
> necessary to balance intimacy with distance while at the same time being
> inquisitive to the point of invasiveness. Getting too close to your subject is
> a major danger, but not getting to know her well enough is just as likely.[1]
> **—JILL LEPORE**

This book is about the power of biography and the complex cultural landscapes that are formed and transformed through the struggles and triumphs
of an individual's life. I use the life stories of Caribbean intellectuals as "windows" into the dynamic history of immigration in New York and the long
battle for racial equality in modern America, from the time of the New Negro
through the post-civil rights era. The historical subjects that I've selected,
Ethelred Brown, Richard B. Moore, Pearl Primus, Shirley Chisholm, and Paule
Marshall, show how black immigrant intellectuals leveraged their African
diasporic identities to both challenge racism and to push for the reform of
American democracy during four important political movements: the era of
racial uplift, anti-colonialism, the civil rights movement, and third-wave feminism. In each case, personality, cultural upbringing, and historical context
shaped the intellectual's chosen mode of resistance. These life stories prove
that the personal is political and the political is personal. The public and private realms of each life are inextricable, and the very process of telling these
life stories is a personal and political endeavor for me as the author.

In presenting the delicate balance between the personal and political
meanings of a life story, the biographer takes center stage alongside her historical subjects. No matter how objective a writer claims to be, the author's
personal and political views dictate the substance, shape, and tenor of the
story told. Yes, historical "objectivity" is a myth—a fact that impressed me so
much as a freshman at Harvard University in my first reading assignment for
a course called "The History of Modern Africa." I still recall the provocative
quote from British historian Edward Carr's seminal text *What is History?*:
"The facts of history never come to us 'pure.' . . . They are always refracted
through the mind of the recorder."[2] It follows that, to understand the meaning
of any historical narrative, we also must understand the life story and cultural

perspective of the author. This mandate might sound like the words of an anthropologist in the mouth of a historian, but instead of an act of ventriloquism, I consider it sage advice.

The author's identity is fundamental because her worldview determines which stories she deems worthy of being told. Historian David Levering Lewis, known for his epic accounts of celebrated black (male) intellectuals, including W. E. B. Du Bois and Martin Luther King Jr., underscored this point in his keynote address titled "The Autobiography of Biography," which he delivered at the sixth annual Leon Levy Biography lecture at the City University of New York in September 2013. In his meditation on the relationship between the biographer to the chosen subject, Lewis attributed his own success as an author to his privileged upbringing in an upper-middle class, stable family that valued education and his training at two of the world's premier institutions of higher learning, Columbia University and the London School of Economics. Referencing Du Bois's classic vision of racial uplift, Lewis's description of himself as a newly "minted... pure [member of the]'talented tenth'" reveals a productive self-awareness that is characteristic of exceptional writers, but it also suggests a tacit acceptance of elitist norms that influences his sole focus on highly educated black men.[3] Lewis's familial and educational background laid the foundation for his award-winning writing, but he also recognizes the role that curiosity and serendipity played in shaping his intellectual success. Scholars should do this more often—that is, reveal their own idiosyncrasies and humanity behind their academic methodology. After all, the intellectual path of even the most circumspect scholar has a few twists and turns. This is especially pertinent in the genre of biography. By fully acknowledging her own jagged edges, the biographer awakens her own humanity and the life stories that she tells are better for it.

It follows that all skilled biographers recognize the perils of their own biases when writing a life story. Historian Barbara Ransby is a prime example. In her award-winning biography of civil rights activist Ella Baker, Ransby cautioned "Feminist biographers and scholar-activists like [herself]" against the danger of "imposing . . . contemporary dilemmas and expectations on a generation of women who spoke a different language, moved at a different rhythm, and juggled a different set of concerns."[4] I share this sentiment. Scholars are often tempted, especially those who are socially conscious, politically astute, and passionate about the subject at hand, to apply current-day reality to issues of the past. This tendency to time travel is especially prevalent when writing about issues of race and cultural identity, because these concepts are fundamentally modern creations. Because academic and popular discussions of race and cultural identity can lend themselves to an anachronistic "slippery slope," I have provided close readings of primary sources—including speeches, sermons, poetry, novels, and even choreography—in order to ground my analysis in the local cultural and historical context in which these documents were produced. At every turn, my methodology brings us back to the life witness of each historical actor as testimony to the lived experience of black immigrant and African diasporic peoples in twentieth-century New York.

I share Ransby and Lewis's belief that authors should be fully forthcoming about how their own political ideals determine which stories they choose to tell and the manner in which they render them. In other words, my argument that the personal is political also applies to the author herself. So, to fully appreciate this book, you must first understand my own life story. I am, unapologetically, a feminist and humanist, and I've decided to tell the stories of lesser-known Caribbean intellectuals, especially women artist-activists, because I find value in telling stories that have not been told.

I was born and raised in Cincinnati, Ohio. My interest in social justice and understudied events in black history dates back to my preteen years in the mid-1980s when my mother's interest in African American history and quasi-radical politics encouraged me to devour classic texts such as Carter G. Woodson's *The Mis-Education of the Negro*, Lerone Bennett's *Before the Mayflower: A History of Black America*, and Alex Haley's *Autobiography of Malcolm X*. A decade before I was born, the racial politics of the time sparked riots in Cincinnati that prevented my mother from enjoying a formal graduation ceremony from Hughes High School in 1967 and forever changed the neighborhood in which she grew up, Avondale. (Two decades later, at age eleven, I would attend my mother's twentieth class reunion in the format of the graduation ceremony that they never had.) I cannot count the number of times I've heard my mom talk about the black- and white-owned businesses that were ransacked that summer. Usually, in that melancholy recollection, my mother also reminisces about the social and economic class diversity of the all-black neighborhood of her youth. Avondale was a neighborhood made up of single-family houses and modest apartment buildings with well-manicured lawns, and homes in which famous black baseball players, including Frankie Robinson and Vada Pinson, lived alongside working-class families like my mom's. My maternal grandfather Clifford Wills did hard manual labor at a sweltering steel-casting factory while my grandmother Clara took on domestic work, doing laundry and cleaning houses. To earn extra money, Clifford and Clara together painted and mounted wallpaper in other folks' homes. This was more than a decade before the civil rights movement effectively ended segregation throughout the nation and upwardly mobile blacks could move to more prosperous suburbs. My mother describes interaction among the members of the all-black neighborhood of her youth, even across class lines, as not only friendly but uplifting. These are the roots of my mother's community-based black consciousness that helped shape my own racial and intellectual identity .

During my adolescent years, I had a strong interest in African history, stemming from my father's travels to Central and Southern Africa as a non-denominational Christian pastor preaching and supporting the development of Christian congregations abroad, but I did not have any first-hand knowledge of black immigrants in America. As I came of age in a middle-class suburb west of Cincinnati called Mt. Healthy during the 1980s, most of my neighbors were either black or white and born in the United States. The majority of Cincinnati-born blacks were descendants of what scholar Cornel West has called "post-Negros,"[5] or post-slavery American-born blacks who trekked from the South to the North in hope of finding better jobs. My family is no exception. Towards the end of this period known as the Great Migration, my maternal grandparents moved from Millers Ferry and Mobile by way of Selma, Alabama, to Cincinnati. My paternal grandmother moved with her mother from Cannonsburg by way of Jackson, Mississippi to Cincinnati. My family, like most black Cincinnatians, is American-born black through and through. More than a half century later, this demographic made up most of the congregation of the church that my father founded in 1981 and still pastors, Abundant Life Faith Fellowship. The congregation is 99 percent black, and all but one of its members are American-born, with both parents and grandparents born in the US. The binary of American-born blacks and American-born whites that I encountered from the 1980s through the 1990s resembled that experienced by many Americans in the Midwest and the South at the time.

My first-hand knowledge of black immigrants in America began as an undergraduate at Harvard University in the mid-1990s. Moving from my hometown of Cincinnati to Cambridge, Massachusetts, brought an intellectual and social transition very much tied to the major theme of this book—"diversity within blackness." At Harvard, one of my classmates would occasionally look around the room and declare, "We're the only JBs here!" When she noticed my quizzical expression, she explained, "JB means just black, born here."[6] She was right. Her words made me realize that not only was I the only JB in my small group of friends, I was also the only non-Nigerian. My experience was representative—I discovered later that the majority of black undergraduates at Harvard in the late 1990s were first- or second-generation immigrants from the Caribbean and Western Africa; Ivy League schools aggressively recruited students from preparatory high schools in the

Northeastern United States, the region with the highest concentration of black immigrants in the country.

During my time at Harvard, one Nigerian student's stereotyping of American-born blacks as "shiftless" and unwilling to take advantage of opportunities deepened my understanding of the cultural divisions between black immigrants and American-born blacks. Several years later, as a graduate student at Princeton University, my study of Caribbean immigration to the United States revealed that such cultural clashes were not new, but dated back to the early twentieth century when the first wave of African Caribbean immigrants, mainly from Jamaica, Trinidad, and Barbados, arrived at Ellis Island and other American coastal outposts, hoping to follow their own unique American dreams by hard work and good luck. Even as African Caribbean new immigrants found common ground with American-born blacks in their allied fight against northern-style Jim Crow, Caribbean political leaders such as Unitarian minister Ethelred Brown seized every opportunity to criticize American-born black leaders, especially New Negro Christian ministers who supposedly led their congregations astray by promising prosperity in the by-and-by instead of social justice in the here-and-now. Brown's criticism of American-born black religious leaders was very much rooted in negative stereotypes of black American culture and his own striving for upper-middle class social status.

As in Ethelred Brown's time, competitive striving to reach upper-middle class status still fuels cultural clashes between black immigrants and American-born blacks. At the turn of the twenty-first century, these conflicts centered on competition for admission into America's top-tier institutions of higher learning. Because black immigrants and children of immigrants outnumber American-born black students at Ivy League universities by 2:1, scholars and admission officers have debated whether the self-selecting group of middle-upper class black immigrants should disproportionately benefit from Affirmative Action policies that American-born blacks (along with civil rights allies from various cultural backgrounds) worked so hard to achieve. This question of black inter-ethnic equality is so controversial that when Harvard African American Studies scholar Henry Louis Gates and esteemed law professor Lani Guinier broached the topic at a Harvard black alumni reunion in June 2004, heated debates ensued. A *New York Times* article titled "Top Colleges Take More Blacks, but Which Ones?," contextualized Gates's and Guinier's concerns: "In the high-stakes world of admissions to the most selective colleges—and with it, entry into the country's inner circles of power, wealth and influence—African-American students whose families have been in America for generations [are] being left behind."[7] I agree; this is cause for concern.

Although, over the past decade, the practice of Affirmative Action has been phased out of the admissions process at numerous high-ranking universities (based on the argument that it's no longer needed), I still contend that cross-cultural diversity *and* black intraracial diversity are politically necessary values in the college admissions process. Unfortunately, many black immigrants and children of immigrants have interpreted this argument as a threat to their own success. My disagreement with a Trinidadian-born Harvard Business School student underscores this point. In spring 2005, I joined a party at an upscale restaurant in midtown Manhattan to celebrate the graduation of a mutual friend and Ghanaian immigrant. After the introduction of guests and standard exchange of pleasantries, an intense debate began over the *New York Times* article published one year prior. The newly minted Harvard MBA graduate from Trinidad argued that Gates's and Guinier's promotion of black intraracial diversity in the college admissions process hinders the progress of black immigrants in America, claiming that Caribbean immigrants, like himself, simply outperformed American-born blacks and that the system should remain strictly merit-based. As the conversation became increasingly antagonistic, I noticed that, once again, I was the only "JB" at the table. I pointed out that the civil rights activism of American-born blacks was central to the passage of the 1965 Immigration Act that allowed immigrants, like himself, to enter the country and that American-born blacks paved the way for access to quality education and jobs irrespective of race. I concluded that black intraracial diversity in university settings is not only politically necessary, but it is also historically expedient.

The youthful "Afrocentric" black-consciousness that had inspired me to keep my hair natural, wear dashikis, and travel to St. Croix[8] and South Africa[9] to learn and write about these African diasporic cultures enabled me to see commonalities among black folk; but by the turn of the twenty-first century, my personal biography reflected a shift from *Songs of Innocence* to *Songs of Experience*.[10] During my undergraduate and graduate-school days, I began to see, like never before, the deep-rooted animosity between foreign-born and American-born blacks. My exchange with the Trinidadian business school graduate is one example in the long history and ongoing antagonism between Caribbean immigrants and American-born blacks, which I historicize through the life stories that follow.

Academic studies of Caribbean New York, especially in the discipline of sociology, provide quantitative and qualitative evidence that supports my own observations of cultural clashes between black immigrants and

American-born blacks. A number of scholars have suggested that black immigrants' negative stereotypes of American-born blacks come from the media and from the poor black neighborhoods in which the immigrants often settle.[11] In a study by sociologist Mary Waters, with whom I took a course as an undergraduate at Harvard, a Guyanese schoolteacher observed in an interview, "They [West Indians] think black Americans are lazy, they don't want to work," and "they want to be on welfare." This forty-eight-year-old Caribbean teacher attributed such negative stereotypes to Caribbean immigrants' settlement in poor, urban environments in which they "meet the worst people. . . . [They] see these people just sitting around, drinking, hanging out on the street, and from there [they] build [their] stereotypes."[12] In contrast, sociologist Milton Vickerman has observed a decrease in negative stereotypes held by second-generation Caribbean Americans. Vickerman suggests that second-generation Jamaicans "feel a closer identification with African Americans than their immigrant parents because they are American by birth and because they have assimilated into the African American community." Still, "This assimilation is not tension free, since Jamaican immigrants, seeking to counter anti-black stereotypes, try to transmit their own emphasis on achievement and pride in their ethnic identity to their American-born children."[13] These black immigrants show us that black identity is neither uniform nor static. Or as I often tell my students at Miami University of Ohio, "All black people are not alike!"

All of this considered, the intellectual path between my personal experience and the publication of this book is not direct. I did not set out to historicize current-day cultural clashes between American-born blacks and Caribbean immigrants by writing a series of biographical accounts of Caribbean intellectuals who contributed to the battle for racial equality in America. Much broader questions about black racial identity motivated my initial research.

My research began with my fascination with the historically determined but ever-shifting racial categories of "black" and "white." As a graduate student, while preparing for the comprehensive exams in my masters program, I was drawn to the growing body of literature in the field of "whiteness studies." I immersed myself in books such as David Roediger's *The Wages of Whiteness*, Noel Ignatiev's *How the Irish Became White*, and Matthew Frye Jacobson's *Whiteness of a Different Color*.[14] (I had already met one of these authors, David Roediger, because we co-organized a labor history conference at the Minnesota Historical Society, where I worked in the education department between my undergraduate and graduate studies.) These books by "whiteness studies" scholars fascinated me because they were my first encounter with thoroughly researched, historical accounts of how Irish, Jewish, Italian, Polish, and other immigrants from Eastern and Southern Europe were not considered "white" when they arrived in the United States at the turn of the twentieth century. I learned about the elaborate ways in which white racial identity was constructed, using alleged black inferiority as its foil, over the course of the early twentieth century. After reading these books, I began to wonder how black immigrants, who also arrived in New York at the turn of the twentieth century, understood their own racial and cultural identities. Did they privilege their immigrant identity over their racial identity? Did they become black American? How did they reconcile their hopes for a better life in a new land with the brutal reality of American racism?

While I was asking these broad questions about race, ethnicity, and identity, my sources led me to the specific life stories that make up this book. Based on conversations with scholars in the fields of African diasporic and American studies, and with archivists at the Schomburg Center for Research in Black Culture, I discovered the personal papers and sermons of Jamaican-born Unitarian minister Ethelred Brown; the letters, speeches, and poetry of communist and anti-colonial activist Richard B. Moore, born in Barbados; the performance art, scholarly writing, and diary of Trinidadian-born choreographer and dancer Pearl Primus; the brilliant oratory and teacherly personal style of Barbadian-American politician Shirley Chisholm; and the rich novels and short stories of Barbadian-American writer Paule Marshall. While the majority of these source materials are housed at the Schomburg, I also relied on source materials at the New York Public Library for the Performing Arts, Brooklyn College, the Andover-Harvard Theological Library, Emory University, Rutgers University, and the American Dance Festival archives at Duke University.

For me, these primary sources provided details of real lived experience that made the abstract categories of "race" and "culture" come alive. These letters, sermons, speeches, poems, short stories, novels, diaries, and choreography became the focus of my intellectual inquiry, and I progressed from broad questions about how Caribbean immigrants contributed to black racial identity in America to detailed studies of these individuals, of how their family histories, personalities, and cultural upbringing shaped their resistance to racism in New York from the 1920s to the present.

All of this said, taking into account my own intellectual and artistic personality, family history, and diverse cultural biography, I recognize my own intellectual and creative biases. After living with these subjects for nearly a decade, I have developed a profound respect and admiration for each person's courage and proactive resistance to racism, class oppression, sexism, and the myriad psychological and emotional challenges that conspired to hamper the very "life, liberty, and pursuit of happiness" they had traveled so many miles to obtain. Still, I have tried my best to avoid hagiography. In my conversation with these historical actors, I offer explanations and criticisms of their actions that are intended to deepen our understanding of the historical context and the political concerns of Caribbean intellectuals in twentieth-century America. Still, even as I write this, I understand that my own rendering of these life stories is both personal and political.

City of Islands

The Personal Is Political: An Introduction

I use lives as windows to a period and its issues.[1]
—DAVID LEVERING LEWIS

The story of an individual life, no matter how famous or obscure, is both intensely personal and political. No one stands in isolation, but everyone is, instead, embedded in local, regional, national and even global communities. Careful attention to personal biographies reveals tensions between the individual's definitions of self and societal forces that conspire to limit her freedom—racism, sexism, and classism—to name a few. For the Caribbean intellectuals in this book, their personal biographies determined their chosen mode of resistance in the long battle for racial equality in modern America; their political engagement also impacted their private lives. Even the manner in which they talked, dressed, and ran their households may be read as a political statement. I am not the first to make this argument. Feminists such as Carol Hanisch, Audre Lorde, and Gloria Steinem popularized the concept that the personal is political and the political is personal during the late 1960s and early 1970s—a time when private interactions between men and women were scrutinized as instances of sexist oppression. Contemporary Black Power activists also embraced the power of personal politics as they picked out their Afros and donned dashikis to express their Black Pride. In turn, I contend that the lived experiences of Caribbean intellectuals prove that the political meanings of personal lives were relevant long before the feminist and Black Power identity politics of the 1960s and 1970s and are still relevant today.

Personal lives serve as windows into the broader political landscape of any given time and place. The best biographers not only recognize this truth, they embrace it. The power of this approach lies in the movement beyond that which is overtly political into the murkier realm of personal politics. Equally important, in my opinion, is that writing about the idiosyncrasies of a personality transforms otherwise stodgy historical actors into exquisitely flawed human beings. By using individual lives as "windows to a [historical] period and its issues,"[2] and through this process of humanizing life stories, skilled biographers accomplish a feat elusive for many scholars: the production of well-researched and informative prose that also captivates a public audience.[3]

3

The individuals in this book are no exception—in the lives of the Caribbean intellectuals that I've selected, the personal was political, and the political was personal. Ethelred Brown, Richard B. Moore, Pearl Primus, Shirley Chisholm, and Paule Marshall, replete with personal foibles and idiosyncrasies, all drew on their own cultural upbringing and individual personalities to advance the cause of racial equality. Consider how Ethelred Brown's precociously religious youth in Jamaica paved the way for his use decades later of Unitarianism as a liberation theology to counter British colonialism and as a vehicle for racial uplift in Harlem. Richard B. Moore's witness of his father's communal, socialist politics in Barbados, combined with his own interest in black history, informed his communist fair-housing campaigns on behalf of black residents in Harlem, as well as his activism for the end of European colonial rule throughout the English-speaking Caribbean. Pearl Primus's family folklore, centering on her native Trinidad and her West African lineage, provided the source material for her artistic activism, especially her efforts to defy negative stereotypes of blackness during the height of the civil rights movement. Shirley Chisholm made history as the first black woman to win a seat in Congress and the first to seriously run for president—accomplishments that she attributed to her rigorous primary education under the tutelage of teachers in Barbados and to the influence of her politically astute father, a staunch follower of Marcus Garvey. And Marshall's coming-of-age in Brooklyn, watching the beautiful struggle of Barbadian immigrant women, inspired her to record their experiences in novels and short stories. All of these intellectuals found political power and moral authority in their own life stories.

While the trajectories of the lives of these intellectuals might appear straightforward, this is not a story about straight lines. This book is about intersecting spheres. All of the historical actors in this book transformed and were transformed by major political movements and contributed to institutions, including those of Unitarianism, socialism, communism, the civil rights movement, and third-wave feminism. These intellectuals were writers, agitators, creative thinkers, and above all else, they were human. At times their stories are idiosyncratic, because their lives were idiosyncratic. Still, the common denominator in each chapter is that studying the biographies of Caribbean intellectuals shows how the story of America is as dynamic and varied as its inhabitants.

To understand the recursive nature of the personal and political lives of the subjects at hand, we must begin by recognizing their commonalities and differences. What do these historical actors have in common? They are all black, and they are immigrants or descendants of immigrants from the

English-speaking Caribbean, who lived in New York and produced intellectual work in the cause of racial equality in the twentieth century. Two are men, Ethelred Brown and Richard B. Moore, who were born in Jamaica and Barbados respectively and immigrated to Harlem during early to mid-adulthood. Moore started his political career in Harlem at the young age of sixteen after his arrival in the black metropolis in 1909. Brown was forty-four years old when he arrived in Harlem, his wife and two children in tow, in 1920, more than a decade after Moore's arrival. Three are women, of whom one, Pearl Primus, emigrated from Trinidad to New York in early childhood at the start of the Harlem Renaissance. Because of her young age, Primus did not participate in that classic arts movement, but she was a beneficiary of its radical ideals and New Negro aesthetic when she was mentored by Harlem Renaissance poet Langston Hughes and encouraged by other black American luminaries such as Paul Robeson and Billie Holiday. Primus took the world of modern dance by storm at the age of twenty-one. The other two women, Shirley Chisholm and Paule Marshall, were born in Brooklyn to parents from Barbados. Brooklyn was a fertile ground for the cultural and intellectual development of both Chisholm and Marshall. Marshall was thirty years old upon her entrance into the literary world with the publication of her first novel, *Brown Girl, Brownstones*, at the height of the civil rights movement, while Chisholm was forty-four when she became the first black woman to serve in Congress in 1968—a model of progress for both black Americans and women of all races at the dawn of third-wave Feminism. Marshall was born at the start of the Great Depression, and she drew on her personal experience in writing *Brown Girl, Brownstones*, which also takes place during the Great Depression. Like Selina, the main character of her novel, Marshall resisted the safe vocational paths that her mother had urged her to pursue—to work with the telephone company or as a nurse—and forged her own selfhood through the more unconventional path of becoming a writer. For Chisholm, her work in American politics was a second career; she had already made a name for herself as a teacher and daycare center supervisor. She used her educational and organizational background as well as her personal and professional networks in Brooklyn to launch her political career. All of these historical actors drew on their individual personal and professional experiences as they used the written, spoken, and performed word in the battle for racial equality.

Why are these details important? They are important because each life story shows us how myriad factors beyond the scholarly trinity of race, class, and gender shaped black immigrant experiences throughout the twentieth century in America. Birthplace, age at the time of immigration, family history, education, chosen vocation, stage of career, personality, and historical context are all factors that shaped each individual's experience. By comparing and contrasting how the life stories of these intellectuals influenced their cultural production, I will show that their work in the cause of social justice was both personal and political, historical and situational, public and private; and that their diverse modes of civic engagement reflect the "life witness" of each.

The value of my multi-biographical approach is in the synergy of comparison, which makes this book not only a useful teaching resource but also a dynamic story. Although recent scholarship has shown a newfound interest in some of my historical actors—mainly Ethelred Brown, Pearl Primus, and Shirley Chisholm[4]—*City of Islands* is unique in content and format, as it compares and contrasts the personal and political meanings of multiple life stories. I put these intellectuals in conversation with contemporary thinkers as well as in conversation with myself to show how Caribbean intellectuals used their cultural production, their sermons, speeches, literature, and even dance, to engage national and international audiences in a conversation about the need for racial equality in America and throughout the African diaspora. These life stories reveal the complex historical, social, psychological, and emotional forces behind the public face of Caribbean intellectualism.

Biography as Methodology

What is the value of biography? What sort of analytical work does this category of analysis accomplish in the context of Caribbean immigrants in New York, or any other historical study for that matter? There is a major body of literature in the disciplines of history and the social sciences on the usefulness of biography as a methodological approach. The literature is so vast that it is not possible to engage each theorist in this text, so I reference the scholarship and popular debates that resonate most with my work.

Surveying the life stories in the chapters that follow requires a meta-discussion about the *process* of analyzing autobiographical sources and the self-reflective nature of writing biography, or any historical account for that matter, which inevitably turns into an intellectual debate about subjectivity and truth. Even at the young age of twelve, I was drawn to the question of how the worldview of a storyteller shapes the narrative that she renders, when a classmate gave me a cassette tape of reggae music, and I played and replayed, again and again, the lyrics, "There are many stories, both old and new, what is true?"[5] In the song "What's True?" Jamaican-born Ziggy Marley and the Melody Makers, the children of legendary reggae artist Bob Marley, draw the listener's attention to the inaccuracy of colonial accounts of conquest, when, in an incredulous yet harmonic tone, they sing, "Christopher Columbus discovered whom?"[6] The implied answer is, of course, no one. The vocal harmony and upbeat tempo mock the audacity of such a claim, as all conscious people of the Marley ilk are aware that long before the arrival of European colonizers, native Americans inhabited the land the colonizers called the "New World." While Ziggy and his siblings, like so many profound reggae artists who came before them, pointed out the fallacy of white supremacy, more recently, Nigerian-American writer Chimamanda Adichie reminds us that black skin does not make one exempt from the pitfalls of prejudgment. In her popular lecture "The Danger of a Single Story," Adichie offers a nuanced account of her own intraracial misconceptions based on class differences. She recounts a story about her childhood in Nigeria and her interactions with her family's "houseboy," Fide—a youth from the neighboring rural area who was paid to help her family with domestic chores. Because the Adichie family always talked about Fide's poverty and charitably gave him food and old clothes, young Chimamanda was surprised to see a "beautifully patterned basket, made of dyed raffia" that Fide's brother had made by hand, because "it had not occurred to [her] that anybody in his family could actually make something."[7] She had defined Fide's family solely by their poverty, which hindered her own recognition of the multidimentionality of their humanity.[8] Like the Marleys and Adichie, I recognize the complex forces that conspired to constrain the freedom and humanity of my historical actors. I also recognize that the stories that they told about themselves and the times and places in which these stories were produced are inextricably linked to their personal evaluations of self in tension with the constraints of socially constructed categories of race, ethnicity, class, and gender. .

I contend that Caribbean immigrants' constructions of their own personal and political identities were individual and contextual. Their definitions of self were multilayered, as Caribbean intellectuals simultaneously held island-specific, regional, racial, class, gender, vocational, and personal identities. They privileged one category over the others depending on the political context—a process that I term "life witness." This term differs from concepts like double consciousness, dual-citizenship, intersectionality, and transnationalism previously advanced by scholars of immigration history, philosophy, and critical race theory, because it emphasizes historical context—especially an individual's intellectual evolution over a lifetime. While the other concepts center on political and cultural constructions of the state, personhood, or nationalism, "life witness" captures the psychosocial vicissitudes in between.[9]

In each of the following chapters, I focus on the individual lived experience of each intellectual, because categories of identity such as "West Indian," "immigrant," and "black" do not completely convey the sense of selfhood and agency that each individual exercised. I am not the first writer to recognize the limitations of such categories when writing a biography. In the instructive study *Telling Stories: The Use of Personal Narratives in the Social Sciences and History*, the authors argue that when biographers rely solely on broad categories of identity, "social actors are treated as if they had little or no individual history, no feelings or ambivalences, no self-knowledge—in short, no individuality."[10] In other words, the character, personality, and style of the individual are lost. Such details are important because they make up the core of multidimensional protagonists, who might otherwise seem flat and two-dimensional. Biographer Annette Gordon-Reed makes a similar observation in her Pulitzer Prize-winning biography of the controversial historical figure Sally Hemings, an enslaved black woman with whom President Thomas Jefferson fathered six children. "For Hemings lived in her own skin, and cannot simply be defined through the enumerated experiences of the group – enslaved black feminists."[11] Likewise, the lives of Caribbean intellectuals should not be reduced to any combination of socially constructed categories. Each lived experience functions as a "life witness" of the historical moment and as a validation of the individual self.

Given the reflective and introspective nature of autobiographical sources and biographical writing, these life stories dwell in a realm of dichotomies. They are simultaneously private and public, personal and political, complex but unified by the writer's lived experience. As a writer, I embrace these dichotomies, and I acknowledge the dangers of taking a historical subject's word at face value without donning the cap of scholarly skepticism.

Numerous scholars have expressed a profound skepticism regarding the quest for "truth" when analyzing autobiographical sources and writing biographical work. Accordingly, Arnold Rampersad, acclaimed biographer of Langston Hughes, Ralph Ellison, and Jackie Robinson, to name a few, has characterized biography as an "art precisely to the extent that we recognize that what a biographer hopes to recapture is impossible to recapture absolutely—that is, the spirit and the truth of his or her subject's life."[12] In this regard, Rampersad hints at the mystery and complexity of human experience. In the June 2009 volume of the *American Historical Review*, prominent scholars debated the usefulness of biography as a methodological approach to understanding cultural phenomena beyond the limited scope of an individual life. The historian Alice Kessler-Harris expressed her caution in less mystical, albeit still hopeful terms: "Like many historians, I am skeptical about whether there is a 'truth' to be found in the past, but I resist the notion that we are therefore engaged in our own form of fiction writing."[13] In the realm of arts and letters, biography, as a genre, has endured intense scrutiny, but still has managed to survive as one of the most captivating forms of intellectual inquiry. Scholars continue to question the blurred lines between literary and historical writing when analyzing autobiographical sources.

I contend that each historical actor's personal "truth" is contextual and ever evolving. I am not interested in the concept of Truth with a capital "T"— meaning one grand, unified narrative of American history on which we all agree. What is true for any historical figure is based on her personal experience and historical context.

Analysis of the cultural production of an intellectual is paramount to understanding his or her personal "truth." While David Levering Lewis admits that "biography remains an art with few rules," the one rule he suggests all biographers must abide by is to allow the historical actors to speak for themselves. According to Lewis, "Until the protagonist reveals his/her character-his/her inner self to the biographer, what the biographer produces is less a life than a report, an autopsy rather than a séance."[14] In this assessment, Lewis echoes Arnold Rampersad's argument that biographers must capture the spirit of the historical subject. In turn, in the chapters that follow, the cultural production of each intellectual is paramount because I argue that these primary sources reveal each intellectual's character and concerns.

In the interest of privileging the voices of my historical actors, I primarily engage with archival and primary source materials in the body of the text, while I reserve most of my engagement with historiographical debates for the endnotes. I offer close readings of the primary sources—including sermons, speeches, poetry, short stories, novels, and filmed choreography—to provide insights into each individual's personality and intellectual development. I address relevant scholarship on analyzing autobiographical sources, biography as a methodological approach, and the history of Caribbean immigration to New York in the introductory chapters of the book. In contrast, in the biographical chapters on Ethelred Brown, Richard B. Moore, Pearl Primus, Shirley Chisholm, and Paule Marshall, my decision to limit secondary sources is a deliberate methodological choice to allow the voices of my historical actors to be heard loud and clear.

The many forms of autobiographical sources that I analyze provide a deeper understanding of individual interpretations of broader political movements. Historian Jochen Hellbeck makes a similar observation while analyzing diaries written during the Russian Revolution. According to Hellbeck, "The individual operates like a clearing house where ideology is unpacked and personalized, and in the process the individual remakes himself into a subject with distinct and meaningful biographical features."[15] Although the historical and cultural context of Caribbean immigrants in twentieth-century New York is drastically different from the totalitarian Russian regime about which Hellbeck writes, his point is still well taken. Life stories provided individualized human meaning of more abstract phenomena. For the historical actors in this book, Ethelred Brown provides insights into the black immigrant lived experience as a Unitarian and member of the Socialist Party, Richard B. Moore sheds light on the experience of black members of the Communist Party, Pearl Primus deepens our understanding of Caribbean immigrant women's artistic activism during the civil rights movement, Shirley Chisholm's life provides a window into cultural collaborations and clashes among contributors to third-wave feminism, and Paule Marshall's life and literature offer snapshots of the dynamic and still evolving sense of agency among black immigrant women.

Of course, not all academics agree on the usefulness of biography as a methodological approach to understanding broader historical context. On one hand, historian Jill Lepore argues that biography enhances our understanding of history by adding an element of humanity, but she is circumspect in drawing broad conclusions about history and society based on the lived experience of one person.[16] Lepore makes a strong case for writing a balanced account of the historical subject at hand; however, I lean toward interjecting more of my own opinion into the text than Lepore, in the interest of engaging the reader. Still, such self-conscious thinking is imperative when writing any historical account, especially given the humanistic lure inherent to the genre of biography. On the other hand, historians Nell Painter, Annette Gordon-Reed, and Laurel Ulrich, with whom I took a historical methodology class as an undergraduate at Harvard, have all written seminal biographies of women historical figures—Sojourner Truth, Sally Hemings, and Martha Ballard respectively—from whom they draw broader conclusions about the history of gender relations and race in America.[17] I value this approach.

In pondering the power of life stories, I return to an observation by biographer David Levering Lewis as a touchstone. Lewis has argued that the power of telling a life story lies in the more difficult task of showing how "biography mediates and shapes the nation's image of its many selves."[18] I agree. Because the individual self is at the center of any biography, the fundamental nature of the genre lends itself to proving that the project of American democracy has been an ever-evolving and culturally collaborative endeavor. Documenting the myriad stories of America in all of its diversity is important, because contrary to the Great Man theory of history that still pervades the genre of academic and popular biography,[19] charismatic white men are not the sole progenitors of political change. The title of "change agent" also belongs to both known and lesser-known black intellectuals, American-born and immigrant, men and women alike.

The process of stretching the academic landscape to include more biographies of people of color and women of all races has been an ongoing process that began in earnest during the cultural wars of the 1960s. One scholar has marveled, "Remember when all big biographies were of famous, scrupulously straight white men?"[20] Much progress has been made in the diversity of stories being told. I am grateful for the "revolution" in biography that has taken place over the past four decades, and I am writing within that tradition. As a researcher, writer, and as a woman of color, I understand that I am indebted to a long line of writers. I credit African American studies scholars, feminist academics, labor historians, and those who inhabit overlapping fields of study that have been traditionally considered "marginalized," for clearing the brush and paving such varied roads of intellectual inquiry that a book about Caribbean intellectuals, such as my own, is possible.

Caribbean Intellectualism

These life stories function as windows into the long history of Caribbean intellectualism and activism in New York, which spans the entire twentieth century. Caribbean immigrants have made their mark on American politics and culture dating back to the turn of the twentieth century.[21] The majority of the 150,000 immigrants of African descent who arrived in the United States during the first-wave of Caribbean immigration to New York hailed from the English-speaking Caribbean—mainly Jamaica, Barbados, and Trinidad.[22] A significant number of African Caribbean immigrants also hailed from Spanish-speaking islands, and a small portion immigrated from West and Northern Africa. I could have written about African as well as African Caribbean immigrants from the Spanish and French-speaking islands in this book; however, I deliberately choose to focus on immigrants from the English-speaking Caribbean because they constituted the majority of black immigrants during the first wave of *voluntary* immigration to the United States. This permits me to track changes within a single demographic over time.

Arriving at the height of the Second Industrial Revolution and a new era in black culture and progress, classically called the New Negro movement, these black immigrants dreamed of a more prosperous future. But a deep-rooted dilemma hampered their dreams. I call this issue America's favorite four-letter word: race. More famously and eloquently, in 1903 African American philosopher W. E. B. Du Bois declared, "The problem of the Twentieth

Century is the problem of the color-line."[23] From the first wave of Caribbean immigration to New York starting in the 1880s through the third wave in the post-civil rights era, the myriad manifestations of white supremacy that Caribbean New Yorkers endured and challenged have proved Du Bois's assertion true.

As an African diasporic Mecca and a center of American culture, New York's social climate was progressive in many ways, but black immigrants quickly learned that northern-style Jim Crow hindered their upward social mobility. In response, as members and descendants of the most highly educated group of immigrants to enter the country during the opening decades of the twentieth century, Caribbean intellectuals delivered speeches and sermons, wrote poetry and novels, and created performance art that challenged the very racism that impeded their success. Consistent with the adage "the pen is mightier than the sword," they wielded the written, spoken, and performed word as weapons in their battle against racism in New York. In the pulpit of Ethelred Brown's Harlem Community Church and in Richard B. Moore's fiery speeches on Harlem street corners during the age of the New Negro; in Pearl Primus's declaration that "dance is a weapon for social change" on stages at Café Society and on Broadway during the long civil rights movement; in Shirley Chisholm's representation of women and working-class Americans in the House of Representatives at the height of the feminist movement; and in novelist Paule Marshall's insistence that black immigrant women be seen and heard in American arts and letters at the advent of "multiculturalism" in American schools, the wide-ranging styles of Caribbean campaigns for social justice reflect the expansive imaginations and life stories of each intellectual. In addition to deepening our understanding of the long battle for racial equality in America, these life stories reveal the powerful interplay between personal and public politics. In turn, the protagonists of this book prove my argument that the personal is political and the political is personal.

Early on, black journalists and scholars recognized the significant role that Caribbean immigrants played in the cultural metamorphosis of black New York. Drawing on early studies of 1920s–1940s Harlem by scholars such as Ira Reid, James Weldon Johnson, and Roi Ottley, and contemporary scholarship on Caribbean New York in the first three decades of the twentieth century,[24] this book spans the 1920s through the present. My chronology highlights the recursive nature of black identity politics in modern America, from Jamaican Marcus Garvey's black consciousness movement of the 1920s to the demand for Black Power by activist Stokely Carmichael during the late 1960s and Paule Marshall's current-day insistence that black immigrant women in literature be seen and heard.[25] I am indebted to both historical and social scientific scholarship that focuses on Caribbean immigration and assimilation into New York's racial politics from the 1960s to the present.[26] One major current in this scholarship is the comparison between the social and economic statuses of Caribbean immigrants and American-born blacks. Scholars are still responding to economist Thomas Sowell's 1975 thesis that African Caribbean immigrants outperform their American-born black counterparts because of a superior work ethic.[27] Most recent scholarship suggests that over time, Caribbean immigrants do not necessarily surpass the accomplishments of American-born black *migrants*. This is a more accurate assessment, because such studies compare movers to movers (i.e. Caribbean immigrants who move to the US and American-born blacks who move within the US). My study contributes to these debates by exploring the long history of cultural clashes and antagonisms between Caribbean- and American-born blacks that have framed such debates.

Other scholars focus on how Caribbean intellectuals transformed and were transformed by New York City. A relatively small cohort of early twentieth-century African Caribbean immigrants had wide-reaching political and cultural impact on Harlem and broader society. Between 1900 and 1930, about forty thousand black immigrants, including those of African and Caribbean origin, settled in the burgeoning black community of Harlem. By 1932, over thirty-six thousand immigrants from the non-Hispanic Caribbean lived in New York City and made up a quarter of Harlem's black population.[28] The majority of these newcomers hailed from the British West Indies—mainly Jamaica, Barbados, and Trinidad. Prominent Caribbean émigrés such as Jamaican-born Harlem Renaissance writer Claude McKay, and political activists Wilfred A. Domingo (Jamaica) and Claudia Jones (Trinidad), contributed to the social, political, and intellectual milieu. During the same period, Harlem became the headquarters of one of the most influential figures in the development of black consciousness, Marcus Mosiah Garvey, and his Universal Negro Improvement Association (UNIA). Garvey's promotion of Pan-Africanism and his black nationalist "Back to Africa" mission reshaped dialogue about blackness by providing a message of bold self-sufficiency that other black organizations subsequently embraced.

The impact of Caribbean immigrants on American culture was not only intellectual. Their presence also transformed the material culture of black New York. In his 1943 publication *New World A-Coming: Inside Black America*, journalist Roi Ottley compared racial politics in black immigrants' islands of origin with *de facto* and *de jure* racism in the United States. Ottley paid careful attention to how New York was transformed by Caribbean immigrants. "Much of . . . West Indians' culture eventually filtered into Harlem life.

Besides adding the zombies, jumbies, and obeah men to the gallery of voo-doo characters," Ottley detailed, "a number of tropical items found their way to the tables of American Negroes—like imported yams, eddoes, mangoes, pawpaws, ginger roots, avocados, and plantains."[29] Caribbean intellectuals not only brought their ideas to their new American homes, but also carried with them foodstuffs, medicine, and spiritual practices that contributed to the cul-tural diversity within black New York.

Caribbean immigration coincided with the arrival of new immigrants from Eastern, Central, and Southern Europe. Whiteness studies scholars have explored how Irish, Polish, and Italian immigrants became white through a process of distancing themselves from American-born blacks.[30] This study poses similar questions of identity construction with reference to African Caribbean immigrants from the English-speaking islands.[31] Did Caribbean intellectuals identify as black American? What was the role of British colonial-ism and institutionalized racism in the United States in shaping black racial consciousness, pan-Caribbean identity, and African diasporic consciousness? The answers to these questions varied depending on the individual, but for the most part, Caribbean immigrants saw themselves as *both* Caribbean and black American. All of the historical actors in this study were motivated by pride, a quest for dignity, and an intense disdain for white supremacy, whether from Britain or the US, and they mobilized themselves and others to disman-tle racism.

Of course, African Caribbean immigrants could not "become white," because their skin color relegated them to the lower rungs of society. In con-trast to light-skinned European "New Immigrants," who used racial slurs in factory courtyards and exploited widespread negative stereotypes of blackness on vaudeville stages in efforts to prove their solidarity with American-born whites, black immigrants could not stage similar dramas or enjoy the same social and material luxuries of white privilege. In response to racism, Carib-bean intellectuals worked hard to transform negative stereotypes of black-ness. This process required intense interactions with black immigrants from other islands and with American-born blacks through efforts to forge racial solidarity during the early twentieth century. The late twentieth century was characterized by intraracial cultural conflicts. Alignment of Caribbean and American racial identities has long been complex, as Caribbean intellectuals created distinctions that emphasized the more "acceptable" aspects of their immigrant identities in contrast with American-born black culture.

Just as black-American racial-identity construction took numerous turns, the locus of Caribbean political power in New York shifted from Harlem to Brooklyn during the 1940s and 1950s. By the 1960s, Brooklyn had become the epicenter of intense cultural production by Caribbean intellectuals. The significant rise in Caribbean immigration to the US after World War II pushed black New Yorkers to expand beyond Harlem. Novelist Paule Marshall and politician Shirley Chisholm were both born in Brooklyn to parents from Barbados. As will be discussed in chapter five, a large part of Chisholm's success as a politician may be attributed to her strong rapport with the culturally diverse, multilingual denizens of Brooklyn, and as explored in chapter six, Marshall's literature captures the distinctive cadences of Barbadian immigrants. Jamaican-American writer June Jordan also epitomized this shift in the geographical locus of Caribbean intellectualism during the 1940s, because she was born in Harlem and moved to Bedford-Stuyvesant at age five with her family. Brooklyn became home to the West Indian Day Parade, the largest celebration of Caribbean Carnival outside of the Caribbean islands, from 1947 to the present. Thus, the cultural environments of Harlem, Brooklyn, and various rural and evolving urban areas in the English-speaking Caribbean laid the foundation for the development of Caribbean intellectuals' political engagement.

Layout of the Book

The historical actors in this book journeyed along singular psychological, emotional, and spiritual paths. As they moved beyond the classic sense of double consciousness as members of black American culture and of American culture writ large, they are best understood within a framework of multidimensional identity. As seen through the lives and work of Brown, Moore, Primus, Chisholm, and Marshall, Caribbean immigrant identities are lodged in historical contexts and a discerning and deliberate perception of their intended audience.

In each chapter, I begin by showing how individual biography lays a foundation for understanding the "process and condition"[32] of African diasporic identity, arguing that black Intellectualism is first cultivated in families and emerges in the context of local communities. Second, I explore how the social, political and cultural milieu of particular locales in the Caribbean and in New York shaped black immigrant intellectuals' understanding of blackness and determined their mode of civic engagement from the era of "racial uplift" through the advent of "Black Power." Third, I analyze how Caribbean immigrants transformed the nature of civic engagement and black intellectual thought in modern America. By drawing on distinct perspectives forged in local communities at particular historical moments, Caribbean intellectuals articulated a mission of racial solidarity during the early twentieth century, anticolonial and civil rights activism during the mid century, and a celebration of intraracial, cultural differences (*i.e.*, cultural pluralism) during the late twentieth century.

The chapters that follow provide windows into the interior lives of black intellectuals who worked to dismantle and transcend racism while managing their own personal, familial and financial challenges and triumphs.

In Chapter 1, I use the intellectual biography of Jazz-pianist Hazel Scott to provide an overview of African Caribbean immigration to New York throughout the twentieth century. Chapters 2 and 3 explore the vital role of religion and spirituality in shaping New Negro visions of racial equality as revealed through the intellectual biographies of Unitarian minister Ethelred Brown and political activist Richard B. Moore.[33] By taking a new approach to the "politics of respectability in the cause of "uplifting the race," Brown used his ministry to challenge racism and redefine blackness in affirmative terms.[34] His faith-based initiative added a Caribbean cultural slant on progress in the here-and-now. Brown's embrace of Unitarianism was integrally tied to his status as a British colonial subject because he relied heavily on sponsorship from the British Unitarian Association. Brown's congregation offered an alternative vehicle of social and political advancement for black Harlemites in contrast to the racial uplift efforts of more common Christian denominations led by American-born blacks in the Abyssinian Baptist Church in Harlem or the African Methodist Episcopal (AME) Church. Brown's Harlem Community Church (HCC) established that there were other "games in town" and challenged the dominance of organizations led by better-known Caribbean political leaders such as Marcus Garvey's Universal Negro Improvement Association (UNIA) or Cyril Briggs's African Blood Brotherhood (ABB).

In Chapter 3, I argue that communist activist Richard B. Moore's (Barbados) vision of pan-Caribbean identity was a product of his immigrant status. During the height of anti-colonialism campaigns in the 1940s and 1950s, Moore developed a sense of pan-Caribbean identity after years of working alongside political activists from various islands in New York. Although Moore's work for the Communist Party and the African Blood Brotherhood from the 1920s through the 1930s has been discussed at great length in prior publications,[35] *City of Islands* presents Moore in a new light by centering on his efforts to transcend island-specific stereotypes and his vision of Caribbean independence from British colonial rule, and political unity among the governmental structures of all of the English-speaking islands.

While Caribbean male voices were heard loud and clear during the era of the New Negro, Caribbean women intellectuals assumed center stage in the cultural battle against white supremacy from the 1940s through the 1980s.[36] In

Chapter 4, I analyze how Trinidad-born choreographer and dancer Pearl Primus used the theatrical stage in the campaign for civil rights. By the late 1930s, Primus alongside other Caribbean women literary and performance artists such as musician and actress Hazel Scott, dancer Beryl McBurnie, and playwright Amy Ashwood Garvey, were forging novel paths in the entertainment industry. They leveraged their respective Trinidadian and Jamaican cultural identities and celebrity status to gain a sense of personal and political power throughout their careers. Primus's focus on the beauty and dignity of African peoples foreshadowed the identity politics of "Black Pride" of the 1960s civil rights era. Their lives epitomized the personal and political power of black immigrant, cultural identity in the long battle for racial equality.

In Chapter 5, I analyze how politician Shirley Chisholm leveraged her Barbadian-American identity to gain constituents among Brooklyn's polyglot immigrant communities during her campaign for Congress in the 1960s and during her 1972 bid to become the presidential candidate of the Democratic Party. Chisholm's legacy as the first black woman to seriously run for president is part of the rich history leading to the election of America's first black president (with immigrant roots) Barack Obama. The historical and political context of the civil rights movement and third-wave feminism provided an increasingly open landscape in which Caribbean women intellectuals felt empowered to express themselves and assume civic leadership roles. I focus on how Shirley Chisholm's conception of a "new era in American political history"[37] was shaped by a progressively vocal female constituency and the increasingly culturally diverse face of New York during from the 1960s through the 1970s. The 1965 Hart-Cellar Immigration and Nationality Act, a byproduct of the civil rights movement, opened United States borders to a larger number of immigrants from the Caribbean, Latin America, African countries, and Asia. At the same time, women of all races and ethnic backgrounds took to the streets and election polls to exercise their newly found political power. Chisholm stood at the crossroads of these vibrant movements, and she gained a sense of personal and political power by articulating her translocal identity throughout her campaigns for Congress and her 1972 bid for the presidency of the United States.

In Chapter 6, I explore the biography of Barbadian-American novelist Paule Marshall's career as a literary artist. As such, Chapter 6 presents a biographer of her career through her literary work. I analyze how Marshall created a self-defined African diasporic identity through a series of critically acclaimed novels and short stories. For Marshall, "language is a homeland," and the Bajun dialect that Barbadian immigrant women spoke in Brooklyn allows them to remember the best parts of their birthplace and to carve out new realms of personal power in the context of their new American home. Marshall intended to empower her readers through the depiction of strong, black immigrant women characters in a series of critically acclaimed novels and short stories from the 1960s through the 1980s. Marshall is the only person I write about who is still alive; her work continues to reveal how the interplay of gender, race, and immigrant cultural identities shape interpersonal relationships today.

A Note on Terminology

Throughout this book, I interchangeably use the terms "Caribbean," "African Caribbean" and "black Caribbean" to refer to people of African descent who were born in the English-speaking Caribbean—mainly Jamaica, Trinidad and Barbados. Historically, the term "West Indian" has been used to refer to the English-speaking Caribbean; however, most contemporary scholars now consider that term to be politically incorrect. I also occasionally use the term "Caribbean" to refer to people of African descent who were born on various islands across linguistic barriers and colonial histories including the English-speaking, French-speaking, Spanish-speaking, and all of the attendant patois and creole languages of the Caribbean. I use the term "American-born black" to refer to people of African descent who were born and raised in the United States. I use the term "foreign-born black" and "black immigrants" interchangeably to refer to people of African descent who were born outside of the United States but moved to America after birth. I use "black" as a descriptor to refer to people of African descent who were born in any locale throughout the African diaspora—including the United States, the Caribbean and various African countries. I use island-specific hyphenated descriptors such as Barbadian-American and Jamaican-American to refer to people of African descent who were born in the United States to parents who emigrated from the island listed.

I am aware of the current academic turn toward using the term "Caribbean" to describe immigrants from the islands covered in this book[38] because the etymology of the term "West Indian" is mired in the racialized colonial history of Spanish-sponsored explorer Christopher Columbus who mistook the Caribbean for islands southwest of India. Keeping this in mind, my occasional use of the term "West Indian" in no way condones the racist politics of the colonial misnomer, but I use the term solely as a descriptor for immigrants from the English-speaking Caribbean when it is relevant to the historical context. Based on conversations with and publications by other scholars such as anthropologist Oneka LaBennett, I have decided that my occasional use of the term "West Indian" to refer to black immigrants from the English-speaking Caribbean is nettlesome but justified.[39] As an anthropologist, LaBennett notes the importance of recording how people self-identify and describes the dynamic, teenaged girls in her book *She's Mad Real* as "West Indian" because that is the term that they preferred themselves. I also privilege the voices of my historical subjects and use the terminology that they used to describe themselves throughout the book.

As I write this note on terminology, I am struck by a sense of *déjà vu* considering one of the major historical actors in this book, Richard B. Moore, tackled a similar issue regarding his 1960s campaign to abolish the term "Negro" because he considered it a misnomer and a degrading holdover from America's racist past. Moore settled on the term "Afro American" over "African American" because he felt that the former rolled off the tongue with greater ease. Likewise, my use of the term "Caribbean" instead of "British Caribbean" is a political and stylistic choice.

A Note on Chronology and Content

The book proceeds in chronological and thematic order, there is a temporal overlap in many of the chapters. Each chapter centers on a period in each intellectual's life to show how historical context interacts with personality, intellect, and talent to shape Caribbean intellectuals' political activism in the cause of racial equality. Because all of the intellectuals in this book lived full and prolific lives, I've found the overlapping chronological scope from chapter to chapter to be an asset and not a detriment. The layering of the lived experiences of these historical actors is intentional because it augments the fundamental, comparative methodological approach of the. In addition to the explicit comparisons that I draw, the reader is invited to draw conclusions of her own regarding the efficacy of each intellectual's method to civic engagement.

Because each historical actor is worthy of a stand-alone, book-length biography in his or her own right, the chapters in this book should not be read as complete biographies. The segments of the life stories told function as windows into how Caribbean intellectuals used their cultural production to challenge racism in America throughout the twentieth century. In this exploration of the personal and political meanings of the lives of Caribbean immigrants, let us begin with the life story of Trinidadian-born, performance artist Hazel Scott.

Tammy L. Brown, *From Calypso to Harlem Boogie Woogie: Hazel Scott*, Mixed Media, 2014.

CHAPTER 1

Caribbean New York

It is so stupid and idiotic—the jealousies, rivalries and
discords between West Indian and American Negro[s].[1]
—CLAUDE MCKAY, 1932

On August 1, 1945, Café Society Uptown was abuzz. The offshoot of a successful Greenwich Village club run by Barney Josephson, and long a center of cross-cultural bohemia, the uptown location provided yet another venue for black and white intellectuals to mix and mingle. On that August day, a crowd of some three thousand well-wishers awaited the arrival of the beloved newlyweds Hazel Scott and Adam Clayton Powell, Jr.[2] The bride, a twenty-five-year-old ingénue and jazz pianist, and the groom, a handsome thirty-six-year-old New York congressman, had wed earlier that day in a private ceremony officiated by the groom's father, Reverend Adam Clayton Powell Sr., at the Bethel African Methodist Episcopal Church in Stamford, Connecticut. Always elegant, the bride wore a tea-length Chantilly lace gown and carried a bouquet of gardenias and white orchids. Powell wore pinstriped pants and a box-cut black suit jacket with a white gardenia on his lapel. In photographs, the couple appears happy, albeit a bit overwhelmed. By 1945, Scott's celebrity had reached an international audience, and Powell's political cache had expanded beyond black New York as he worked to establish a reputation as a national civil rights leader. By the mid-1940s, Scott also was known as a champion of civil rights in her own right.

In many ways, the marriage of the Trinidadian-born starlet Scott to the American-born politician Powell provides a glimpse into the close—and sometimes fractious—social and political relationships that Caribbean immigrants and American-born blacks formed during the early decades of the twentieth century. What made the "New Negro," a term popularized by philosopher Alain Locke, so new was the synergy and diversity of cultural ideals and intellectual influences among Caribbean immigrants and American-born blacks mixing and mingling in the world's premier black metropolis.[3]

21

Although many Caribbean immigrants held on to their island-specific cultural identities by way of neighborhood settlement patterns and mutual-aid societies, the strictures of American racism forged shifting political alliances, friendships, and even romantic partnerships among Caribbean immigrants and American-born blacks. And New York City was the epicenter of this African diasporic cultural exchange.

The sheer volume of black migrants from southern states intermingling with black immigrants, especially from the English-speaking Caribbean, fostered a climate ripe for black cultural reinvention. In 1910, the black population in New York totaled 91,709. By 1920 it had increased by two-thirds, to 152,367.[4] Dramatic push and pull factors fueled the Great Migration of blacks from the South to states in the North, Midwest, and later the West. Racial violence, disenfranchisement, crop failure due to the boll weevil scourge, and economic underdevelopment and isolation pushed blacks out of the South toward industrializing cities such as Philadelphia, Pittsburgh, Indianapolis, Cincinnati, and Chicago. Between 1900 and 1930, more than five hundred thousand southern blacks moved from rural areas to cities, and to the North, Midwest, and West.[5]

The biblical Exodus narrative in which Moses led the children of Israel out of slavery in Pharaoh's Egypt and into freedom in Canaan, which dominated the imaginations of enslaved Africans in antebellum America, continued to resonate for blacks during the Great Migration.[6] Just as African slaves followed the North Star along the Underground Railroad to freedom in a "promised land," the North maintained its allure as a place of tremendous opportunity for black migrants invested in individual and collective racial uplift in the aftermath of failed Reconstruction at the turn of the twentieth century. News of better-paying jobs and less stringent racial politics in the North reached black southerners via the black press and word of mouth. The *Amsterdam News* and the *Chicago Defender,* black-run newspapers, published testimonials by migrants who were thriving in northern cities; companies sent representatives to the South to aggressively recruit new employees; and migrants sent letters to family members full of details about job opportunities, housing arrangements, and social life. Some families, like that of Harlem Renaissance painter Jacob Lawrence, gradually moved northward along the Eastern Seaboard. Although Lawrence's father was from South Carolina, his mother came from Virginia, and he was born in Atlantic City, New Jersey. Harlem brownstones, streets, and city folk were central images in Lawrence's visual vocabulary, because he had moved to the black mecca with his family at age thirteen.[7]

Likewise, African Caribbean immigrants came in droves to New York City during the opening decades of the twentieth century. The forces driving the immigration were in some ways similar to those pushing American blacks northward. British colonial oppression, the declining price of sugar, and natural disasters—hurricanes, floods, droughts, and earthquakes— pushed immigrants out of the Caribbean toward better job opportunities in the United States.[8] In New York, social networks established between families and through churches, fraternities, and mutual-aid societies informed immigrants' family and friends in the Caribbean about city life and the jobs awaiting for them in the carpentry and garment industries. On arriving in New York, many black immigrants found skilled-labor hard to come by, and worked in white homes as domestic workers or in restaurants and buildings as bellhops, elevator operators, and waiters.[9]

Beyond the pragmatic pull of jobs, more intangible matters of the spirit and heart also attracted some to New York. One of those moved by the heart was Amy Ashwood, who would later become the wife of Jamaican-born black consciousness leader Marcus Garvey. Garvey and Ashwood would become the center of a racial uplift movement in both Jamaica and New York. The two had met in Jamaica and cofounded the Jamaican branch of the Universal Negro Improvement Association in 1914, and were secretly engaged in 1915. Two years later, frustrated by the long engagement, Ashwood wrote to Garvey from Panama, stating her plans to take the *Royal Mail* boat to New York to be reunited with him.[10] She was a woman of her word. She arrived in 1918 and married Garvey in 1919. Although the marriage was short-lived, it began Amy Ashwood's long love affair with the city of New York.[11]

By 1932, the total number of Caribbean immigrants living in the United States was eighty-eight thousand, of whom thirty-six thousand lived in New York City.[12] Although many Caribbean immigrants were laborers, New York was the ideal place for members of the professional class.[13] Caribbean intellectuals, like Ashwood, Garvey, Ethelred Brown, and jazz pianist Hazel Scott, found New York to be a wellspring of inspiration and opportunity. Brown deemed Harlem's multi-ethnic, liberal, and cosmopolitan environment the best milieu in which to advance his racial uplift mission through his Unitarian ministry, which had floundered in Jamaica. Manhattan also was the ideal location in which Scott thrived artistically; young Hazel was admitted into the prestigious Juilliard School of music when she was only eight years old. Scott's Trinidadian heritage combined with the cross-cultural newness of New York inspired her musical compositions—ranging from Harlem stride piano Jazz to Calypso. Ashwood, Garvey, Brown and Scott transformed the meanings of blackness through the very process of their intellectual endeavors. Historian Gilbert Osofsky captured this new "melting pot" in his book on Harlem:

> There were ten times as many foreign-born Negroes in New York City as in any other American urban area. In 1930, 54,754 foreign Negroes lived in the city—39,833 of whom resided in Manhattan. Miami, the next largest American city in terms of immigrant Negroes, was settled by only 5,512 people; Boston ranked third with 3,287 Caribbeans. About 25 per cent of Harlem's population in the twenties was foreign-born. Harlem was America's largest Negro melting pot.[14]

Osofsky's deliberate use of the term "melting pot" underscores the very important but underanalyzed phenomenon of "diversity within blackness."[15] As discussed in the following chapters, black New Yorkers were diverse in every way imaginable; birthplace, age at time of migration to New York, family background, gender, class, and individual personality were significant categories that marked the cultural and intellectual diversity among black New Yorkers. Osofsky recognized these factors that constitute diversity within blackness when he articulated his idea of Harlem as a "melting pot." While the term "melting pot" usually applies to America as a whole, and particularly during the surge of European immigration at the turn of the twentieth century, Osofsky conjures the same metaphor to describe the intraracial cultural diversity of Harlem—a city within the city—teeming with multiethnic, black denizens from North Carolina, Georgia, Alabama, Jamaica, Trinidad, Barbados, Puerto Rico, and other locales throughout the African diaspora. And just as American-born whites tried to make sense of where immigrants from southern and eastern Europe fit in America's racial hierarchy, American-born blacks and black immigrants also danced a dance of political alliances and betrayals as they grappled with the meanings of blackness in attempts to elevate their own social and economic status in modern America. This battle of cultures, black immigrant versus American-born black cultural ideals, was intensely felt in New York City.

New York, NY

New York has dominated modern reality and mythology as a center of American cultural capital and as the leading site of cultural production throughout the world for the greater part of the twentieth century. The city that poet Emma Lazarus, the daughter of Jewish immigrants from Portugal, wrote about in her famous sonnet "The New Colossus," held different meanings for its diverse denizens. Written in 1883 and engraved on a bronze plaque at the foot of the Statue of Liberty in 1903, the poem calls Lady Liberty a "Mother of Exiles": "From her beacon-hand/ Glows world-wide welcome."[16] For impoverished immigrants from southern and eastern Europe, Lazarus's description of "huddled masses" and "wretched refuse" who "yearn to breathe free" was more apt. But for educated immigrants of a professional class, including Hazel Scott's family and other Caribbean immigrants, New York was a voluntary "exile," with promises of better opportunities in America's industrializing, cultural capital compared to the largely agricultural economies of the Caribbean islands.

Members of the first-wave of Caribbean immigration to New York, from the 1880s through the 1920s, were by far more highly educated than European new immigrants who arrived in New York at the same time. According to historian Winston James, the "most remarkable feature of the social and economic profile of the early [West Indian] migrants is the high proportion who, in their country of origin, held professional, white collar, and skilled jobs."[17] More than a half century earlier, scholar Roi Ottley made a similar observation when he wrote, "many of them were skilled workers—carpenters, masons, bricklayers, tailors, printers—in trades which American Negroes lost when the race was excluded from the trade unions in the last century."[18] Indeed, the first wave of highly educated, predominantly upper-middle-class Caribbean immigrants cut a different figure upon arrival in New York.

Yet, while they moved to the United States with high hopes for good paying jobs that better fit their skills, Caribbean immigrants quickly learned first-hand about northern-style Jim Crow racism. Consider the life of Jamaican-born minister Ethelred Brown who wanted to put his theological training to good use in full-time ministry. Yet he was only able to pursue his ministry part-time because he also had to work as an elevator operator in order to pay the bills.[19] Brown blamed the all-white leadership of the American Unitarian Association (AUA) for denying him funding to run his ministry fulltime. When he considered the AUA's generous fiscal support of his white counterparts, Brown felt slighted. Stories like this appear so frequently in novels about the Caribbean immigrant experience that it is safe to assume that the frustrations of fictional characters reflect this reality of American dreams deferred.[20] Black immigrants navigated a new, complex, terrain of racial politics, bringing prior knowledge of British colonial oppression into conversation with northern-style Jim Crow laws, challenging both and re-envisioning blackness through this process of self-definition and reinvention.

That reinvention of black cultural identity was taking place amid a city reinventing itself at the time. In the opening decades of the twentieth century,

Caribbean New Yorkers became part of a city under construction, literally and figuratively. In the literal sense, new edifices sprang up throughout the city, ranging from overcrowded, predominantly European immigrant tenements on the Lower East Side to gargantuan skyscrapers in downtown proper. Historian Richard Plunz notes that, "By 1900 more than 80,000 tenements were built in greater New York City. These buildings housed a population of 2.3 million, out of a total city population of 3,369,898."[21] In 1931, the Empire State Building was completed, built at the intersection of Fifth Avenue and West 34th Street and towering 1,250 feet over the blooming cityscape. America's own Eiffel Tower, the Empire State Building represented modernity, industrial capitalism, and newfound power in an age of steel, brawn, and intellectual might.

As the buildings were going up, families were sorting themselves in new ways. Whites were moving out of Harlem and into Brooklyn and Long Island, leaving real estate that black entrepreneurs such as Philip A. Payton Jr. could afford to purchase. Other cramped apartments were owned by whites but represented by black agents. Bridges, tunnels, and the new subway better linked the five boroughs of New York.

Although racism was less overt than in the South, northern-style Jim Crow and racially segregated neighborhoods still made Caribbean immigrants feel like they inhabited islands within the city. Many New Yorkers, especially during the early twentieth century, lived and worked in the same neighborhood and rarely ventured into other boroughs for work or play. For Caribbean immigrants, it was not uncommon to live in Harlem and commute to Manhattan to work as doormen in high-rise residential and office buildings or to Brooklyn to work as domestics in white homes. The divisions between the white worlds of Manhattan and Brooklyn and the black world of Harlem during the early twentieth century were so distinct that I consider such movement between boroughs a kind of "island hopping," similar to that in the mid- to late nineteenth century in the Caribbean, when islanders moved to other islands in search of jobs.[22] Chain migration and island-specific settlement patterns made New York a big city, but a small world. And Harlem symbolized a sort of black utopia.

The New Negro

It is not surprising that Harlem emerged as the mecca of African diasporic intellectual and cultural exchange in the first decades of the century. The combination of people and ideas was explosive, providing the undeniable intellect and attitude that fueled the birth of the New Negro.[23] This new, bold, cosmopolitan, and fiercely intelligent cadre of black intellectuals walked the streets of Harlem with a literal and figurative swagger. In 1925, leading black American intellectual James Weldon Johnson proclaimed, "Harlem is indeed the great mecca for the sight-seer, the pleasure-seeker, the curious, the adventurous, the enterprising, the ambitious and the talented of the whole Negro world; for the lure of it has reached down to every island of the Carib Sea and penetrated even into Africa."[24] Philadelphia-born black intellectual Alain Locke echoed Johnson's assessment. In 1925, Locke called Harlem not only the "largest Negro community in the world," but also the "first concentration in history of so many *diverse elements of Negro life*."[25] Indeed, Locke located Harlem's promise in the cultural, intellectual, professional, and moral diversity among foreign-born and American-born black New Yorkers. Harlem enjoyed a sense of cosmopolitanism and trans-local identity. As Locke observed, the "Negro of the North and the Negro of the South, the man from the city and the man from the town and village," all contributed to Harlem's dynamic social and political milieu. It was this collaboration among foreign-born and American-born black Americans, Locke maintained, that made the burgeoning black metropolis so distinctive. Their greatest experience, Locke argued, "has been the finding of one another."[26], Activists Hazel Scott and Adam Clayton Powell Jr. were indeed happy to find each other, and such romantic and professional alliances among Caribbean immigrants and American-born blacks proved to be fruitful in advancing the cause of racial uplift and civil rights.

In the 1920s and 1930s, Harlem became the gathering place for influential Caribbean émigrés such as Jamaican-born Harlem Renaissance writers Claude McKay and Amy Jacques Garvey. Of political activists there were many, among them Universal Negro Improvement Association leader Marcus Garvey and his first wife Amy Ashwood Garvey, both from Jamaica; Nevis-born communist activist and founder of the African Blood Brotherhood Cyril Briggs; Jamaican-born Wilfred A. Domingo, who was a journalist and member of the Socialist Party of America; Trinidadian-born communist activist Claudia Jones; and Jamaican-born journalist Joel A. Rogers. Caribbean immigrants also made their presence known in New York by making strong claims to public space. Marcus Garvey's elaborate UNIA parades, in which men in military regalia and women in nurses' uniforms proudly marched throughout the streets of Harlem, were internationally known. Caribbean immigrants also brought the celebration of carnival to New York. In 1928, Trinidadian immigrant Rufus Gorin established carnival as a small outdoor festival in Harlem.[27] Caribbean immigrants continued to demonstrate a sense of cultural nationalism through carnivalesque parades in New York from the 1950s through the present.[28]

The city would serve not only as the artistic paradise of black and white bohemia, but also as a battlefield of culture and ideas for black intellectuals who transformed the meaning of blackness in modern America through the power of their own voices. Such verbal sparring among black intellectuals took place on street corners in Harlem, around kitchen tables in Brooklyn, in Manhattan cafés, and in cigar shops in Queens. Marcus Garvey's favored platform was a stepladder at the corner of 135th Street and Lennox Avenue, or alternately the stage of Lafayette Hall on 131st Street and Seventh Avenue in Harlem. Garvey's passion and oratorical finesse infused his July 8, 1917, speech in response to the horrendous East St. Louis race riot that began six days prior, during which more than one hundred black people lost their lives. Garvey called the riot a "massacre" and declared, "This is no time for fine words, but a time to lift one's voice against the savagery of a people who claim to be the dispensers of democracy."[29] Richard B. Moore is also a prime example of the Caribbean intelligentsia in 1920s Harlem. As a member of the Communist Party, Richard B. Moore lobbied for fair and safe housing for black New Yorkers in the 1920s and 1930s. He called exploitive landlords "rent-hogs" and demanded they lower rent and repair dilapidated tenement buildings. Although Moore is mainly known for his anticolonialism and fiery radical speeches about racial uplift in New York, in his poetry he expresses love for his Caribbean heritage and his African ancestry. Black Jewish religious leader Rabbi Wentworth Matthew also used the power of his voice to challenge racism and uplift black people. When Matthew declared, "The colored man was a great man as long as he could hold on to his true religion"[30] in 1936, he evoked Biblical scripture and historicity to argue that Judaism was the most viable path for blacks to obtain the peace and prosperity that all Americans desired. Moore, Matthew, and their compatriot intellectuals wielded words as weapons in their battle against racism in the US and abroad.[31] In this battle of words and ideas, Matthew and Moore competed with other New Negro leaders such as Marcus Garvey, Father Divine, and Ethelred Brown as they attempted to persuade black New Yorkers that their respective philosophies should be the racial-uplift vehicle of choice. In contrast to the male-dominated arena of Harlem street-corner orations and racial uplift politics, jazz pianist and actress Hazel Scott commanded the theatrical stage at Café Society, Carnegie Hall, and other vital performance arts venues as her political platform to challenge racism and reform American democracy.

City of Islands

For Hazel Scott, New York was the place to be. It provided the ideal locale for the Caribbean immigrant entertainer and her American-born black clergy husband to rise to new heights during wartime America. Hazel Scott flourished in the cross-cultural bohemian environment of the original Café Society—the heart and soul of New York's multicultural bohemia. Café Society Uptown, which opened on October 8, 1940, at 128 East 58th Street, made it possible to hear jazz greats such as Mary Lou Williams on piano and mingle with Lena Horne and Paul Robeson on the same night. On the nights that Hazel Scott played, the Golden Gate Quartet often opened for her, and Jewish actor Jack Gilford served as the emcee. By the mid-1940s, Scott had become Café Society's *grande vedette*, a place previously held by famous jazz vocalist Billie Holiday. Adam Clayton Powell Jr. frequented Café Society Uptown and was captivated by Scott's musical genius and style. The breathtaking excitement of the time and place infused Powell's assessment of his favorite nightclub: "There was nothing like Café Society and there has been nothing like it since."[32] And the excitement of the time and place undoubtedly stoked the embers of his affection for his favorite performer at the club, Scott herself.

Scott moved among "islands in the city" that included the progressive, cross-cultural environment of Café Society, her tightly knit Trinidadian family in Harlem, the all-black Abyssinian Baptist Church pastored by Adam Clayton Powell Jr., and her own suburban dwelling in White Plains, New York. While navigating the cultural politics of these places, Scott aggressively maintained her Trinidadian identity. She saw herself as Caribbean, black, and American, and saw no contradiction in simultaneously holding each of these identities. Scott's sense of Trinidadian cultural pride, which had been nurtured by her family and friends throughout her youth, reflects a broader trend in black cultural-identity formation as Caribbean immigrants participated in island-specific mutual-aid societies as well as political organizations founded by American-born blacks.

Scott's mother and extended family created a "Little Trinidad" in 1920s Harlem. When four-year-old Scott moved from Port of Spain, Trinidad, with her mother Alma to join her maternal grandmother, Margaret Long, in Harlem in 1924, she developed an intimate knowledge of the language and cultural values of Trinidad. The Long clan was large and sprawling. As family members frequently visited from Trinidad and more came to settle in Harlem, the Long family was its own "island in the city," in a three-story brownstone at West 118th Street where Hazel spent a good deal of her childhood living with her mother, aunt, uncle, cousins, and more distant kin.[33] Hazel Scott's biographer Karen Chilton noted the importance of food in maintaining their Trinidadian cultural identity for the Long family: after working a long day, mainly as a domestic servant in white homes in on Intervale Avenue in the Bronx, Margaret "expected her daughters to make sure that the scents of home met her at the door. Island tradition called for spicy and sweet combinations, dishes made with brown sugar, coconut milk and lime, garlic, curry, and Scotch bonnet peppers."[34] Sunday breakfast was most extravagant and often included sumptuous chocolates from Trinidad and baked ham spiced with cloves. Powell, as well as their son, Adam Clayton "Skipper" Powell III, also recalled manifestations of Scott's Trinidadian heritage in culinary terms. In Hazel Scott's "lovely home high on a hill in North White Plains," Powell nostalgically recalled, "[Hazel's] mother cooked tingly, peppery West Indian dishes," food so delectable and inviting that he "practically moved in,"[35] despite the fact he was still married to his first wife, actress and Cotton Club notable Isabel Washington. The suburban setting of Scott's home, combined with savory, exotic, home-cooked meals, made 25 Monroe Place in White Plains a refuge for the busy politician from the bustling comings and goings of Manhattan.

Scott's Trinidadian heritage shaped her music. Scholars have focused on black American influences in Scott's musical career, which encouraged her proclivity for "jazzing the classics," but it is important to draw attention to manifestations of Scott's Trinidadian background that were expressed through her appreciation of Calypso music. While still living in Port of Spain, at the tender age of three, "Hazel was [already] performing in small gatherings. She played by ear, duplicating the popular Calypsos performed by live bands in the streets of Trinidad during the pre-Lenten carnival celebration."[36] Hazel carried this love for music and the limelight with her when she immigrated to New York. As the story goes, during the voyage aboard the *Maraval* from Port of Spain to New York on June 11, 1924, Hazel's fourth birthday, young Hazel slipped away from her cabin while her mother slept and "played several calypsos for the captain and a small crowd of delighted passengers, reveling in the spotlight."[37] The musical feat by the child-prodigy Hazel is plausible enough; escaping the watchful eye of her mother Alma seems less likely. Young Hazel and Alma Long carried with them the sights, sounds, tastes, and rhythms of their native Trinidad to their new home in New York City. After arriving, Alma quickly established a firm regimen for Hazel, teaching her sight reading, scales, and proper fingering. In her unpublished memoir, Scott would recall that she often rebelled against her mother's discipline and "would break into 'Hold 'em Joe—Me Donkey Want Water!' [because] calypso was much more fun than Every-Good-Boy-Does-Fine."[38] When relatives from Trinidad visited the Long family in New York, they would prod young Hazel to play popular calypsos. Such experiences—a Trinidadian family gathered around a piano, listening to calypso music while enjoying Trinidadian chocolate—demonstrate the importance of leisure-time cultural enjoyments to immigrants in maintaining their Caribbean identity after moving to New York.

The Long family represented an island of Trinidadian culture within the borough of Harlem. From the outside Harlem might have appeared to be an undifferentiated sea of blackness, but an insider would know better. *De facto* and *de jure* segregation zoned and redlined Caribbean immigrants, regardless of class, into black neighborhoods—mainly Harlem, the Tenderloin, and Sugar Hill. However, immigrants did not instantly relinquish their cultural identities and disappear into a monolith of African American culture. Caribbean immigrants maintained cultural ties to home by establishing "Little Jamaica," "Little Barbados," and "Little Trinidad" in New York.

Mutual Aid

They were helped in establishing themselves in the new city by mutual aid societies, fraternal orders, and social clubs. Historian Irma Watkins Owens has emphasized the importance of such organizations because they "added interest and vitality to community activity while bringing together influential people to mediate community problems and advance its goals."[39] For instance, the Bermuda Benevolent Association (BBA) founded in 1897 provided participants with a support network, both financially and socially. Members met monthly at the home of Rosinia Campbell at 250 West 17th Street, and the admissions process was so selective that membership never rose above 250 compatriots. In contrast, the Grenada Mutual Association boasted 425 members.[40] Other organizations restricted membership to males only, so women's auxiliary branches emerged. The American West Indian Ladies Aid Society (AWILAD) was founded by immigrants from the Virgin Islands in 1915 with an organizational mission of "love, fraternity and benevolence among all women of the Virgin Islands."[41] Like most benevolent associations, AWILAD stepped in if one of its members fell sick or died, offering financial assistance and home visits with food and spiritual support. The organizations also sponsored social activities and gathering spaces for its members to congregate, gossip, make new friends and even meet one's future husband or wife.

Cricket matches, basketball games, dances, and dinners provided opportunities for Caribbean immigrants to nurture their cultural identities while living miles from home. The West Indian-sAmerican newspaper is a useful barometer of the social life for Caribbean New Yorkers. Small's Paradise, owned by Edwin A. Smalls and located at 2294½ 7th Avenue near 135th Street advertised itself as "The House of Fun"—a site for "dining and dancing" that featured local jazz musicians and "6 beautiful Chorus Girls."[42] While some conservative black intellectuals viewed nightclubs as bastions of immoral

activity, other intellectuals extolled Harlem nightclubs as progressive, democratic spaces. In her essay "Night Clubs of New York: Moral Turpitude?" Sara
Edwin Jenkins wrote, "The Harlem Night Club, even the 'high class' night
club, is a highly democratic enterprise. There are no specially reserved pews,
there are no box seats, there is no grandstand."[43] Acutely aware of rampant
intraracial classism that threatened ethnic and racial solidarity during this
time of racial uplift, Jenkins celebrated the mixture of elite, "plain folk," and
even smooth-talking con artists who frequented Harlem nightclubs, because
she considered this social intermixing a broader reflection of an egalitarian
impulse in black New York.

Sports events also afforded countless opportunities for Caribbean immigrants to forge a sense of ethnic solidarity that transcended class. Cricket was
of special interest to Caribbean immigrants who longed to recreate a bit of
home in the midst of the hustle and bustle of New York. The newspaper the
West Indian American covered cricket matches extensively, including those in
New York as well as the Caribbean. On October 29, 1927, the Cosmopolitan
Cricket League of New York held its annual presentation and dance, where
trophies were presented to the league's most valuable players.[44] Members
of the Sussex branch were awarded "The Mc Dermon Trophy, the crowning
glory of New York cricket" for the third year in a row.[45] Such sports teams
grew out of island-specific social clubs, and such events sponsored by Caribbean business owners fostered new commercial networks.

Caribbean owned businesses also reflect Caribbean immigrants' commitment to ethnic solidarity and social and economic uplift. In a 1911 study of
black businesses in New York, sociologist George Edmund Haynes found that
19.7 percent of businesses in Harlem were owned and operated by Caribbean
immigrants.[46] Most of these entrepreneurs had arrived in New York City
with educational backgrounds and vocational training that prepared them
for skilled labor, were connected to church and fraternal order networks,
had lived in New York for at least ten years and were naturalized citizens.[47]
The majority of the businesses advertised in the West Indian American were
owned and operated by immigrants from the English-speaking Caribbean.
Scotland & Osborne on Edgecombe Avenue, near 140th Street sold ice cream,
"West Indian candies" and "brown and white sugar cakes." These petite cakes
"made in small balls of the size of chocolate candies" cost thirty cents per
pound.[48] Music was a significant part of Caribbean culture in New York
because numerous music stores advertised their wares and services in popular Caribbean publications. Zellman's Music Store on Lenox Avenue near 127th
Street sold instruments and sheet music, which included "a full line of West
Indian rolls always in stock."[49] The Morris Music Store, located at 659 Lenox

Avenue, took out a full, front-page advertisement in the November 1927 edition of the newspaper. Individual instructors such as Eulalie Domingo also advertised lessons in piano, violin and vocal training. According to Domingo, she had earned her music certification from the Royal Academy and the Royal College of Music in London.[50] The Valentine Laundry located at 2572 Seventh Avenue near 139th Street, also extensively advertised its business in the *West Indian American*. Perhaps W. E. B. Du Bois had some of these businesses in mind, given his emphasis on business ownership as an effective means of racial uplift, when he expressed his hope that Caribbean immigrants would lead the way toward black social and economic progress in America.

Cultural Collaborations

American-born black intellectuals had high hopes for learning strategies to overcome racism from black immigrants, and Caribbean intellectuals shared their hopes. Both groups were products of a common history of forced migration and brutal enslavement, and Caribbean immigrants represented a fierce determination to improve their lives in spite of it, evidenced by their decision to immigrate to the US.[51] Perhaps the most famously enthusiastic endorsement of Caribbean intellect and ability was W. E. B. Du Bois's statement in the September 1920 edition of the *Crisis* literary magazine: "It is not beyond possibility that this new Ethiopia of the Isles may yet stretch out hands of helpfulness to the 12 million black men of America."[52] Du Bois tapped into the popular language of black solidarity used by New Negro leaders by referencing Psalms 68:31, "Princes shall come out of Egypt; Ethiopia shall soon stretch out her hands unto God."[53] Du Bois's own Caribbean ancestry—his paternal grandfather was Bahamian and his father was born in Haiti[54]—might have fueled his optimism.

Du Bois was writing, in the 1920s, at a time when the New Negro leaders in New York were still struggling to define the best path toward racial uplift and searching for their twentieth-century Moses. For some, Jamaican-born Marcus Garvey would assume that mantle. It is not surprising that many American-born blacks looked to the Caribbean intellectuals, and Garvey in particular, for guidance, because Jamaica's history of slave revolts and maroon societies reinforced its symbolism as an "Ethiopia of the Isles." The Haitian Revolution also loomed large in the black imagination as an exemplar of a successful liberation struggle against European colonial rule. Such robust mythology surrounding black Caribbean resistance to white supremacy influenced American-born black intellectuals' positive views of Caribbean immigrants. In 1939, sociologist Ira De Augustine Reid wrote a glowing assessment of Caribbean chutzpah in the cause of black nationalism and independence: "Haiti became the first Latin-American country in the new world to achieve its independence. The Jamaicans rose against the British and the Spanish time and time again, and secured for themselves a greater measure of independence. . . . The West Indian Negro has developed into a spirited, aggressive culture-type, whose program and principle of accommodation has been singularly different from that of the American Negro."[55]

Although Reid's assessment of Caribbean character was often tinged with notions of Caribbean cultural superiority and exceptionalism, his views reflected beliefs held by both American-born black intellectuals and black immigrants at the time. While some American-born black intellectuals believed that Caribbean immigrants' prior knowledge of and resistance to racial oppression in their islands of origin might offer American-born blacks insight into how to deal with their own race problem in the US, Caribbean intellectuals also believed their educational background and skill sets would be put to similarly good use as they struggled to break through professional color barriers on their arrival in New York. In his famous 1925 essay "Gift of the Tropics," Jamaican-born writer W. A. Domingo wrote, "Skilled at various trades and having a contempt for body service and menial work, many of the immigrants apply for positions that the average American Negro has been schooled to regard as restricted to white men only, with the result that through their persistence and doggedness in fighting white labor, West Indian immigrants have in many cases been pioneers and shock troops to open a way for Negroes into new fields."[56] Domingo certainly harbored cultural pride, as is evident in his depiction of Caribbean immigrants as trailblazers and teachers in the cause of civil rights, as well as his implication that Caribbean immigrants possessed more intellect and gumption than their American-born black counterparts. The *West Indian American* repeatedly expressed a similar sentiment: "It is therefore interesting to page the volume and become familiar with the foreign born, particularly those born in the British West Indies, and see what they have done to advance the cause of the Negro in America."[57] Writers for the *West Indian American* were unabashed in their positive representations of Caribbean immigrants. Such articles served the dual function of motivating its Caribbean readership to excel to in the new land and convincing American-born blacks of Caribbean immigrants' worthiness as newcomers to their communities.

Occasionally American-born black intellectuals would agree with positive stereotypes of Caribbean intellect and work ethic. In 1930, based on anecdotal evidence, James Weldon Johnson put forth an image of Caribbean exceptionalism in his classic text *Black Manhattan*, in which he wrote, "Those from the British West Indies average high in intelligence and efficiency. . . . They are characteristically sober-minded and have something of a genius for business, differing almost totally, in these respects, from the average rural Negro of the South."[58] Johnson, like many Harlem intellectuals, accepted positive stereotypes of Caribbean New Yorkers as truth. But the underbelly of such positive stereotypes also cast an ominous shadow and fueled cultural clashes between foreign-born and American-born blacks, as affirmative views of Caribbean immigrants often implied to whites and blacks a sense of American-born black intellectual and cultural inferiority.

While American-born black intellectuals espoused the virtues of Caribbean immigrants, Caribbean intellectuals celebrated the good example that American-born blacks had set in fighting for the cause of civil rights and racial solidarity. One staff writer for the *West Indian American* declared, "A study of the Negro in America since emancipation to the present day will reveal the advance of a people unparallel [sic] in recorded history. We know of no similar achievement by any people anywhere on earth in so brief a space of time."[59] Thus the respect and admiration between Caribbean and American-born black "race leaders" was mutual. Many Caribbean émigrés saw themselves as united with American-born blacks in the battle against white supremacy not only in America, but also throughout the African diaspora. In turn, W. A. Domingo declared, "Just as the West Indian has been a sort of leaven in the American loaf, so the American Negro is beginning to play a reciprocal role in the life of the foreign Negro communities, as for instance, the recent championing of the rights of Haiti and Liberia and the Virgin Islands."[60] In this historical moment, the perception of white supremacy as a shared source of oppression united American-born and foreign-born blacks in spite of their cultural differences.

Caribbean immigrants also joined racial uplift institutions such as the National Association for the Advancement of Colored People (NAACP), the Universal Negro Improvement Association (UNIA), and the African Blood Brotherhood (ABB). These organizations provided countless opportunities for black immigrants to work side-by-side with American-born blacks in the cause of racial equality, black nationalism, and social and economic progress. Their joint efforts also spurred a far-reaching debate about race and class in America.

The collaborations that emerged were political and personal. For example, in 1895, Puerto Rican-born writer and bibliophile Arturo Schomburg, whose mother was from St. Croix and whose father was of mixed German and Puerto

Rican ancestry, married a black American woman, Elizabeth Hatcher, from Staunton, Virginia.[61] Hatcher helped Schomburg forge bonds with American-born black New Yorkers, as would his second wife, Elizabeth Morrow Taylor, whom he married following Hatcher's untimely death. Schomburg also was great friends with black American journalist Wendell P. Dabney, and he forged a professional alliance with Maryland-born writer and activist John E. Bruce, with whom he cofounded the Negro Society for Historical Research in New York in 1911.

Other institutional alliances among black immigrants and American-born blacks appeared, disappeared, and reemerged, and New York provided a singularly ideal intellectual environment in which new ideas took root and flourished. Historian Winston James notes in his account of African Caribbean radical politics in early twentieth-century America that, "even when there were different party allegiances, in the early 1920s there was considerable co-operation among the black radicals of the left."[62] One case in point is the *Messenger* literary magazine, founded in New York City in 1917 by North Carolina-born writer Chandler Owen and Florida-born activist A. Philip Randolph. The magazine would often feature articles by Caribbean intellectuals such as W. A. Domingo, who would later become a major contributing editor of the journal.

This exchange of cultural practices and ideas continued throughout the twentieth century in myriad formal and informal ways. Missouri-born Harlem Renaissance writer Langston Hughes was an intellectual comrade and generous mentor to Trinidadian-born choreographer and dancer Pearl Primus and Barbadian-American novelist Paule Marshall. Both Primus and Marshall incorporated elements of Hughes's distinctive lyrical style into their own work. In 1944, Primus danced to "The Negro Speaks of Rivers," a poem by Hughes first published in *Crisis* in 1921, and Marshall adopted the same metaphor of African diasporic waterways in her memoir *Triangular Road*.[63] Broadway actor, intellectual, and activist Paul Robeson, born in New Jersey, was especially fond of Primus. Robeson was one of Primus's most influential advocates at the start of her career. Primus also enjoyed a synergistic, creative partnership with American-born black guitarist and folksinger Joshua Daniel White (known as Josh White), most notably in their antipoverty song-dance collaboration "Hard Time Blues." These are several examples of the many collaborations of cultural production among Caribbean and American-born black intellectuals and artists.

Just as Du Bois believed that political alliances were possible between black immigrants and American-born blacks, Adam Clayton Powell Jr. considered Hazel Scott's immigrant background an asset rather than a barrier.

The political dimensions of Scott's Caribbean identity were profound. Hazel Scott's popularity and keen ability to mobilize Caribbean voters on Powell's behalf contributed to his successful 1945 bid to represent Harlem in the US House of Representatives. Because the Powell dynasty was so well known and respected throughout black New York, especially among the ten-thousand strong, predominantly American-born black congregation of the Abyssinian Baptist Church in Harlem, and because Powell was already a celebrity in his own right, sometimes the magnitude of Hazel Scott's political influence went unnoticed. Powell's biographer Will Haygood observes, "Not many in New York City realized how much Hazel Scott had contributed to [Powell's] success. As a native West Indian, she drew West Indian votes into his camp."[64]

Perhaps the Afro-Cuban heritage of Democratic journalist Louis Martin helped him realize the significance of Scott's Caribbean identity as a rallying point for black immigrant voters during Powell's 1945 congressional campaign when he noted a "bloc of West Indian voters in Harlem . . . had a better turnout record than American blacks, 75 percent against 50 percent," which propelled Powell to victory.[65] Powell had already won a position in New York's City Council in November 1941 with help from his Abyssinian Baptist Church congregation, the American Labor Party, and the grassroots efforts of the People's Committee, but with his hopes set on higher goals, he needed to gain an even broader constituency. Scott leveraged her Trinidadian identity as a kind of political cache that allowed her to tap into the electoral power of Caribbean New Yorkers and contributed to his successful run for the House of Representatives. Scott and Powell's marriage eight months later was both a natural progression of their friendship and a fruitful political alliance. Even the couple's wedding cake, a towering, edible replica of the White House with furnished rooms inside that required four men to carefully hoist from a delivery truck to place it among the Café Society reception guests, reflects the excitement surrounding the romantic and political merger of Scott and Powell as their nuptials conveniently coincided with the beginning of Powell's tenure in Congress on behalf of the "newly established twenty-second district of New York."[66]

Scott and Powell were true comrades in the struggle against white supremacy in America. Such alliances among Caribbean immigrants and American-born blacks took place on a political level as well as on a private level. The lives and work of New York's leading black intellectuals demonstrate this truth. The personal dimensions of Scott and Powell's relationship inspired Powell to gushingly describe Scott, in his autobiography, as a "West Indian, born in Trinidad, Hazel is, without doubt, one of the most intriguing women living."[67] Powell's adoration for Scott and general love of Caribbean culture were somewhat romanticized and indulgent, since they were usually expressed as appreciation for spicy cuisine and a wry approval of Scott's "West Indian stubbornness." Still, the point remains that Powell considered Scott's Trinidadian heritage to be an asset. Scott also attributed her own tenacity and professional success to an idealized Caribbean sense of self.[68] Scott and Powell's relationship reflects broader attempts to define and redefine the political and cultural interactions among Caribbean immigrants and American-born blacks.

Cultural Clashes

Not all relationships were smooth, however. As time went on, the clash between American-born blacks and Caribbean immigrants began to spark. Caribbean immigrants, like most of their European counterparts, tended to stick together and help one another in finding jobs, creating a kind of ethnic solidarity that sometimes left American-born blacks feeling boxed out. In 1939, sociologist Ira Reid observed this tension. "For in the Negro community the foreign-born Negro is viewed as a threat to the native-born Negro's status. In New York the native complains that he can no longer get work because the West Indians are so 'clannish' that once one gets work he proceeds to bring in a full crew of West Indians."[69]

Just as white racial identity was in flux in early modern America and the presence of poor, European immigrants forced American-born whites to reconfigure notions of whiteness, so too did the presence of highly educated black immigrants force American-born blacks to revise the meanings of black racial identity in America. While Irish, Italian, and Polish immigrants attempted to prove their white racial solidarity by using racial slurs like "nigger" in factory yards, American-born blacks used pejorative terms like "monkey chaser" to describe Caribbean immigrants in an effort to shore up their own status as more American than their black immigrant counterparts. According to Reid, "[The American-born black] complains that he cannot secure work-relief because of those 'damn monkey-chasers'; that 'they' have ruined the Baptist Church, captured the Episcopal Church and monopolized politics. The West Indians in turn are defensively resentful, constantly looking for insults, discrimination, and evidence of segregation."[70] One popular early twentieth-century rhyme captures the hatred that some American-born blacks felt toward Caribbean immigrants:

When a monkey chaser dies
Don't need no undertaker

Just throw him in de Harlem River
He'll float back to Jamaica.[71]

The backward, primitive, "just off the boat" persona that the limerick conjures puts Caribbean immigrants in direct contrast to the cosmopolitanism
of American-born blacks in Harlem.

Tensions emerged in other arenas as well. Jamaican-born writer and poet
Claude McKay's debut novel, *Home to Harlem* (1928), was an affront to many
in the American-born black intellectual circles for its bawdy depictions of
Harlem. McKay deliberately chose to explore the underbelly of Harlem—the
lives of everyday people, which included prostitutes, pimps, and the unedu-
cated underclasses—in stark contrast to the coterie of New Negro intellectuals who were focused on black nationalism, racial uplift, and civil rights
activism. One critic indignantly asked of McKay, "What right have you, a West
Indian ... got writing about Harlem?" When Harlem socialite Hugh Jackman
relayed this message to McKay, Jackman delivered a cutting blow by stating
that this same critic had called McKay a "monkey chaser."[72] Du Bois also took
umbrage at McKay's lusty portrayal of Harlem. In a 1928 editorial in *Crisis*,
Du Bois declared that McKay's *Home to Harlem* made him feel nauseous, and
after reading the "dirtier parts of its filth" he felt "distinctly like taking a bath."[73]
McKay was so hurt by Du Bois's review that he in turn accused Du Bois of
being "holy-clean and righteous-pure."[74] McKay was especially dismayed
because the criticism from American-born black intellectuals depicted him
as a race traitor and amplified any perception of his outsider status as an
immigrant.[75]

Personality politics came to the fore as the 1920s progressed. While in 1920
Du Bois had praised Caribbean immigrants for the good example they might
offer American-born blacks, by the mid-1920s his view was less glowing, as
is evidenced by his vehement criticism of Marcus Garvey. Du Bois was one
of many who considered Garvey's steamshipping business, the Black Star
Line, and his "back to Africa" movement to be ill-planned scams. Sometimes
American-born black intellectuals expanded their disdain for Garvey into a
broader disapproval of black immigrants as outsiders and interlopers. In turn,
Caribbean intellectuals such as W. A. Domingo and Ethelred Brown made it
clear that they also disapproved of the racial uplift strategies of their compatriot Garvey—hence ethnic solidarity did not trump good sense.

For many American-born and foreign-born black intellectuals, Garvey's
radical black-nationalist politics represented a threat to sober-minded progress. At one point, Du Bois called Garvey "a little, fat black man; ugly, but with
intelligent eyes and a big head."[76] Du Bois's criticism reflected a broader class

conflict that often overlapped with skin tone—Garvey was a dark-skinned populist and Du Bois a light-skinned elitist. "Fat, black, and ugly" also harks back to the "monkey chaser" slurs. Yet Du Bois still recognized Garvey's tremendous ability to "move a crowd" and inspire black consciousness and pride; he offered Garvey a degree of respect that explains his positive description of Garvey's "intelligent eyes."

In response to these negative stereotypes of black immigrants and ethnic slurs, some Caribbean immigrants would argue their intellectual and cultural superiority to American-born blacks, while others would appeal to a sense of racial solidarity with calls to rise above their cultural differences in order to form a united front against the scourge of Jim Crow. From the early 1900s through the late 1950s, the political strength of Caribbean immigrants was indeed rooted in political alliances with American-born blacks. In 1927, one writer for the *West Indian American* recognized this truth and expressed a sense of frustration and optimism regarding social interactions between Caribbean immigrants and American-born blacks:

> There has been a noticeable improvement during the past twenty years in the relationship of colored people of American and West Indian origin residing in the city. This has been possible despite the activities of certain elements of West Indian blatherskites and American nincompoops, from whom we too frequently encounter an emission of mucient effluvia. Too dumb to comprehend the axiomatic truth relation to the whole and its parts, they never miss an opportunity to hurl a monkey wrench into the delicate machinery. Were it possible to muzzle this type of people, a disgusting menace to the welfare of the community would be removed. Fortunately, their influence must continue to wane under the relentless pressure of decent people who understand the significance of *common origin* and *common purpose*.[77]

The histrionic language reflects the depth of the writer's discontent with divisive language and behavior and underscores the commonalities among black immigrants and American-born blacks—their shared African ancestry and experience with racial oppression—to promote racial unity. Many other black immigrants expressed a similar sentiment. In 1928, another writer for the *West Indian American,* James H. Hubert, declared, "If by some hook or crook, we could be driven to realize that Negroes of all complexions, nationalities and social rank are indissoluably [sic] bound together and that the misfortune of the one is the common concern of all, we would begin to get ready to arrive."[78]

Hubert, like so many other Caribbean intellectuals, was eloquent in his promotion of racial solidarity; but there was often a gap between rhetoric and action. While lofty ideals of black unity sounded good in print and speeches, its proponents often neglected to outline a specific strategy by which that unity could be achieved.

In addition to efforts to bridge the cultural gap between American-born and foreign-born blacks, from the 1930s through the 1960s many Caribbean intellectuals also took up the cause of Caribbean political federation and independence from British colonial rule. Such anticolonial campaigns complemented their activism for fair and decent housing, a living wage, and general revision of negative stereotypes of blackness in the United States, as Caribbean immigrants combatted racism on two fronts—in New York and in their island homelands. Richard B. Moore's political biography is a case in point. Moore was the "sole U.S. black radical" to attend the International Congress against Colonial Oppression in Brussels in February 1927.[79] Moore continued his anticolonial campaign throughout the 1940s and 1950s.

Caribbean intellectuals also made strides in the arena of New York politics. In 1953, Hulan Jack was elected to serve as the president of the borough of Manhattan. Jack was born in St. Lucia and grew up in British Guiana. He would later become a mentor to Barbadian-American politician Shirley Chisholm. Prior to his election as president of Manhattan, Jack had built a solid track record as a legislator in Harlem. By the 1940s, he was one among many black activists who were outspoken advocates of the "Double V" campaign for victory against fascism in Europe and racism in the US.[80] Jack used his position in public office as a platform for challenging racism in the US and colonialism abroad. He inspired his compatriots to remain committed to their individual and collective uplift missions; in a 1959 issue of the *West Indian American* he declared, "West Indians everywhere are on the alert to keep in step with progress."[81]

Post-World War II

Despite the racism that festered in the US during the war years, Hazel Scott traveled to Europe as a performer to boost the morale of American troops. While US soldiers abroad waged wars for democracy during the first and second world wars, the wars of culture and ideas that raged within American borders laid the foundation for the civil rights movement. In postwar America, black New York was a hotbed of ideas, cultures, and people. Hazel Scott was one among many Caribbean émigrés energized by civil rights advancement. Scott's talent, intellect, blending of musical traditions, and unique cultural background appealed to a diverse cross section of black and white New Yorkers. For instance, she embraced the black American tradition of jazz and European classical music while still holding on to her love of Trinidadian calypso. She crossed social boundaries easily, mingling with black working-class people on the streets of Harlem black and white bohemians and the black elite, much as members of Harlem's intelligentsia did. In 1950, she earned the distinction of being the first African American woman to host her own television show. The same year, Scott's celebrity and her outspokenness as a civil rights advocate earned her a hearing before the House Un-American Activities Committee (HUAC). At the height of McCarthyism, she agitated for the chance to stand before HUAC, prompting her husband Adam Clayton Powell to jokingly attribute her persistence to Caribbean stubbornness. In a public declaration, Scott concluded by requesting that the committee "protect those Americans who have honestly, wholesomely, and unselfishly tried to perfect this country and make the guarantee in our Constitution live."[82]

Caribbean immigrants played an important role in the cultural battle against white supremacy in modern America by drawing on their foreign-born status and prior travel experiences to provide diversified and more complicated views of blackness. Hazel Scott, for example, invoked her cultural identities as a Caribbean immigrant, a woman, an artist, and a black American to advance her career as a professional musician and to promote the political career of her husband. She leveraged these cultural identities to appeal to a broader audience and to create a politics of alignment among contemporary civil rights activists. Scott's intellectual acumen and creative abilities empowered her to become a crucial actor in a deeply engaged northern civil rights movement that began in earnest in the mid-1940s.[83]

Scott's life and legacy point to the cross-cultural fertilization of ideas and talent that black immigrants and American-born blacks enjoyed during the first half of the twentieth century. Scott and Powell's partnership epitomized the merger of religious, political, and creative power so important to black intellectuals in post-World War I America. Scott often felt the greatest sense of personal freedom while onstage, but her personality and intellectual development motivated her to pursue broader causes of freedom. Scott not only bridged the cultures of Caribbean and American-born black New York, but also linked her artistic endeavors to a radical political platform.

Hazel Scott's life and work demonstrate the enduring power of cultural production during the postwar American civil rights struggle. When Scott claimed the stage at Café Society or Carnegie Hall she executed a difficult

repertoire with confidence and used her talent to challenge negative stereotypes of blackness. Scott was living proof that black artists could not only
make a living but thrive in New York City.

There was great enthusiasm surrounding Scott and Powell's wedding day.
The throng of onlookers and black and white paparazzi that strained to catch
a glimpse of the couple behind Café Society's doors attest to the fact that the
couple was well loved and an inspiration to a growing public. Scott and Powell were Harlem royalty in the days when black artistic, religious, and political leaders walked hand in hand. The couple's fusion of celebrity style with
civil rights activism attracted a following among Caribbean New Yorkers,
American-born blacks, and white liberals. They epitomized the fierce intellect, talent, and upward social mobility of cosmopolitan African American
elites who showed strong interest in the lives of working-class blacks. Further,
as inheritors of the passion and fury of the New Negro leaders and symbols
of the creativity, courage, and charisma of a new black internationalist civil
rights vanguard, they bridged two generations of black intellectual activists.

Scott and Powell relished their accomplishments but serving as paragons
of racial progress was no easy task. In many ways, they represented black
privilege, still, living in the spotlight sometimes overwhelmed the couple. For
instance, on the day of their wedding, Scott felt pressured to please the crowd
of well-wishers at Café Society Uptown. She grew so exhausted from smil-
ing, shaking hands, and kissing cheeks that she fainted. Once she came to,
however, she freshened up and continued to greet her guests. In her careers as
both an entertainer and a civil rights activist, Scott ensured the show always
went on. But her showbiz persona was no match for the challenges of real life.
Public pressures and personal conflicts ultimately led to the demise of her
fifteen-year marriage to Powell.

In happier days, Hazel Scott enjoyed her post-war prosperity. With fame
came financial wealth. At the time of her marriage, Scott's record sales and
concerts earned her a salary of $75,000 a year, while Powell's salary as a pastor
of Abyssinian Baptist Church in Harlem was $20,000.[84] Their annual house-
hold income of $95,000 in the late 1940s is the equivalent of nearly $900,000
today. With this wealth, they traveled freely and invested in rental properties.
In 1946, Scott and Powell purchased a ten-story apartment building in Harlem at 706 Riverside Drive and 148th Street valued at $345,000 for $228,000
in cash.[85] In a family photo taken in London in 1951, Scott appears relaxed
and happy alongside her husband Powell and their young son Adam Clayton Powell III—affectionately nicknamed Skipper.[86] Later photographs show
Scott with longtime friends and famous artistic collaborators Lena Horne,
Dizzy Gillespie, and James Baldwin in France. Another photo that ran in *Jet*

magazine in 1953 shows Powell kissing Scott's temple as Skipper embraces his mother to welcome her home after a four-month tour throughout Europe, Africa, and the Middle East.[87]

Scott knew how to strike the pose and play the role of a powerful "race woman" who had it all—a distinguished career, political clout, and a beautiful family. But her real life was not as pretty. The hectic pace of stardom, the demands of public intellectualism, and Powell's infidelity strained the marriage, and the two were divorced in 1960. Still, for a decade and a half, Scott and Powell served as a black "power couple" and their inspirational image remained indelible in the minds of black America. This partnership and dissolution between the Trinidadian-born starlet and American-born clergyman function as a metaphor for the productive but often contentious relationship between Caribbean and American-born blacks in New York.

Just as the Powell's marriage had its ups and downs,[88] the relationship between black immigrants and American-born black intellectuals also experienced its fair share of twists and turns throughout the long twentieth century. While Jim Crow politics compelled political collaborations between Caribbean immigrants and American-born blacks during the early decades of the century, the opening of educational and employment opportunities for black Americans during the latter half of the century has fueled antagonisms between them. Increased competition for jobs, educational opportunities, and status meant black immigrants and American-born blacks have toed a thin line between love and hate since the 1960s. I contend that studying the biographies of Caribbean intellectuals deepens our understanding of intraracial conflicts and collaboration among black intellectuals who fought for the cause of racial equality in America.

To fully understand the magnitude of the careers of Hazel Scott and other Caribbean intellectuals who challenged racism and reimagined blackness on a national and international stage in postwar America, we must return to the historical context that led her to black internationalist politics. We must begin with the birth of the New Negro as understood through the life and times of Unitarian minister Ethelred Brown.

CHAPTER 2

Ethelred Brown and the
Character of New Negro Leadership

[The Harlem Community Church] is a church-forum where the honey-
in-heaven and harassment-in-Hades type of religion is not tolerated.
There are no "amen corners" in this church, and no "sob sister bench."[1]
—ETHELRED BROWN, 1934

At a Sunday evening church service in Harlem on January 8, 1928, Jamaican-
born Unitarian minister Ethelred Brown denounced Marcus Garvey as a
fraudulent political leader and applauded his 1927 deportation from New York
to Jamaica. Ousted by the United States government on charges of mail fraud
and exiled in London, Garvey's larger-than-life political persona still haunted
Harlem a year after his departure and for years to come. Garvey's ghost hovered over the congregation at the Harlem Community Church on that winter
night, when one of Garvey's loyal supporters interpreted Brown's disparaging
remarks as "fighting words." He attacked Brown on the spot, hitting him so
hard that he drew blood.[2] The following morning, a newspaper headline read,
"Harlem Preacher Hit on Head at Sunday Service."[3] Brown detailed this alter-
cation in a letter to American Unitarian Association officials: "Last night I was
viciously attacked. . . . I had to be rushed to the hospital." He gladly reported
that the "wound inflicted is not serious," then, in a tone of righteous indigna-
tion, complained that his "eye-glasses [had] been smashed and [his] clothes
ruined."[4] Toeing the line of what historian Evelyn Higginbotham has termed
the "politics of respectability," Brown understood the value of a polished and
dignified self-presentation as a sign of one's status as a New Negro committed to the cause of racial uplift. In a time when race leaders preached that the
behavior and attire of one individual could reflect favorably or poorly on the
image of the entire black race, Brown proudly donned the uniform of gentil-
ity—eyeglasses and the best clothes he could afford. Thus, from Brown's point
of view, his dramatic encounter with the aggressive Garveyite was more than

Tammy L. Brown, *Mould Thine Own Destiny: Ethelred Brown*, Mixed Media, 2014.

an attack on his physical person, it was an assault on the stature to which he aspired—a public intellectual and respectable man of God.[5]

Battles for political power and influence among New Negro intellectuals were so intense that they sometimes resulted in material and corporal damage: shattered spectacles, disheveled clothing, and even death. Radical political activist Richard B. Moore recounted the same incident of this Garveyite's violent reaction to what he described as Brown's attempts to "constructively criticize" Garvey's Universal Negro Improvement Association (UNIA), noting similarly violent run-ins with "fanatical followers" of Garvey. In one instance, Moore was speaking at the corner of Seventh Avenue and West 138th Street, when several Garveyites "rushed the ladder from which he was speaking." The quick thinking and action of an audience member who "brandished a weapon against the attackers" rescued Moore from "who knows what evil or fatal consequences."[6] As a former member of Brown's church and survivor of an attempted assault himself, Moore could not hide his bias.

He aligned himself with a calm, cool and collected manner of leadership, in line with Brown's Unitarian-based message of a "sober-minded" approach to racial uplift, in contrast with the aggressive methods of Garveyites whom he depicted as brutal and Machiavellian. Although Moore was an impartial witness, his account still revealed an unfortunate truth—such use of violence to intimidate and even eliminate political rivals was not uncommon among Garvey's followers. For instance, W. E. B. Du Bois received a series of death threats from devout Garveyites. In response, Du Bois declared that Garvey was not interested in attacking white prejudice, but only in attacking "men of his own race who [were] striving for freedom."[7]

Brown, Moore, and Du Bois's violent encounters with aggressive Garveyites reveal the central role of personality and political rivalry in the formation of racial uplift ideologies during the New Negro movement. In this chapter, I use Ethelred Brown's biography to show how the battle for power among black leaders was local, cultural, and personal. I begin with the foundation of Brown's intellectual development: his upbringing in Jamaica, his African Methodist Episcopalian religious roots, and the peculiarities of his conversion to Unitarianism. I discuss then Brown's "pilgrimage of faith" from Kingston to Harlem, the founding of the Harlem Community Church, and Brown's leadership roles in radical Jamaican-nationalist groups in New York, including the Jamaican Progressive League, the foremost organization in the campaign for Jamaican independence from British colonial rule. In this regard, as a black immigrant living in America, Brown simultaneously pursued racial equality in both the United States and the Caribbean. Brown retained his Jamaican cultural identity, and after his arrival in New York, developed a pan-Caribbean sense of identity, which I argue was a product of Harlem's singular intraracial and cultural diversity. Interwoven throughout each section is my argument that Brown's ambitious personality and Caribbean cultural identity shaped his use of Unitarianism as a theology of liberation to uplift and inspire hope in the liberation of Jamaicans from the tyranny of British colonial rule and black Americans from the albatross of Jim Crow racism—and in the process, to make a name for himself.

Brown's biography is important because it shows how race as a social construct in tension with immigrant cultural identity and individual personality influenced the politics of black leadership during the age of racial uplift. Although Brown was one man with limited influence—at its height the Harlem Community Church boasted no more than seventy members—as founder of the first black Unitarian church in Harlem, a member of the Socialist Party, and a leading figure in several Jamaican nationalist organizations, Brown stood at the vanguard of radical leftist politics.[8] Historian Irma

Watkins-Owens describes Brown as a "Harlem radical, a stepladder Socialist, and a major figure in the Jamaican independence movement in New York."[9] Through his Unitarianism-based liberation theology, Brown confronted American racism and British imperialism head on. As a Jamaican immigrant, he leveraged his status as a British colonial subject to gain financial support for his ministry and to challenge racism within the Unitarian church in both Jamaica and the US. In all of these endeavors, Brown used his personal biography and Caribbean identity as a kind of cultural capital to further his mission of racial uplift and anticolonialism.

Brown's mission was political *and* personal. Although Unitarianism, like all Christian denominations, promoted the practice of humility and service for the greater good of society, Brown was still a man with a substantial ego. His ambition to establish himself as a powerful leader sometimes overshadowed his desire to uplift his fellow Harlemites. Personal honor and public prestige weighed heavily on Brown's conscience. In one instance, he bitterly complained about being forced to take on odd jobs to make ends meet during his early years in Harlem, including work as an elevator operator, which he called "distasteful and incongruous work" for a man of his stature.[10] "This deprived me of that *prestige* so necessary to the leader of a radical religious movement," Brown complained, "and also robbed the church of much of my time."[11] Acutely aware of the image of success that he wished to portray, Brown blamed the failures of his ministry on white Unitarian officials whom he believed too racist to support his cause. In turn, Brown was a controversial figure. Many members of the British and American Unitarian associations considered him a menace and a shameless beggar, while Brown believed he was exercising his God-given and institutionally ordained right to petition these institutions for fiscal and moral support.

Social progress never assumed the form of a well-oiled machine, because people push progress and the matter of humanity can be messy. Despite Brown's persistence, the extenuating circumstances of life relentlessly intervened in his plans for professional success. Brown's wife Ella suffered from mental illness throughout the majority of her life in Harlem, which, according to Ethelred Brown, was brought on by the emotional strain of fighting racism within the Unitarian church. To add misery upon misfortune, Brown's unemployed, eldest son committed suicide during the Great Depression.[12] These personal tragedies were exacerbated by the family's financial woes. As a man of God, well versed in the patriarchal expectations of his time, Brown staggered under the weight of supporting his family while achieving his own professional dreams.[13] Brown's unabashed idealism—in spite of his meager resources—conjures the image of a marble palace perched on wooden stilts.

With matters of money, power, and respect on his mind, it is not surprising that Brown questioned the criteria of professional success. In his case, this elusive goal was most often measured by the size of a minister's congregation and the money in church coffers. Because Brown came up lacking in both regards, a strong, defensive tone pervades his literary record. Brown was a proud man and well aware that critics might box him into a category marked "failure."

My account challenges this simplistic interpretation of Brown's life by showing how his biography holds a key to understanding the broader, complex interplay of race, class and immigrant cultural identities in shaping New Negro leadership. For Brown, Caribbean cultural identity vested him with a degree of social and political capital. So, in utterly ironic fashion, Brown's struggles reveal the fault lines in positive stereotypes of Caribbean immigrants as "model minorities" of social and economic success. Brown's example also challenges overly romantic portrayals of the New Negro as triumphantly bold, cosmopolitan, brilliant thinkers who took the world by storm. It's important to remember that New Negro intellectuals, like all political leaders, were human, with strengths and weaknesses, with dreams fulfilled and deferred.[14] Yet, even in the midst of heartache and financial hardship, Brown labored to keep the faith. Armed with an immigrant's ambition and a willingness to wield his Caribbean cultural identity for political gain, Brown pursued his vocation as a God-ordained calling, which began even in his youth.

Jamaican Upbringing and Spiritual Conversion

Egbert Ethelred Brown was born in Falmouth, Jamaica, on July 11, 1875; he was the eldest among four siblings. Brown's father worked as an auctioneer, and his mother shouldered the brunt of domestic responsibilities. Brown's youngest brother, Walter Launcelot Brown, heeded the call to ministry as a young adult, and he traveled throughout Africa as a Christian missionary. His example inspired his older brother to pursue a career in ecclesiastical affairs.[15]

Brown believed his destiny as a man of faith was an inevitable outcome of his curiously devout youth. As a boy growing up in rural Jamaica, one of his favorite pastimes was delivering sermons. He would wrangle his siblings and neighborhood playmates into an open-air congregation to witness his impromptu lectures.[16] Quite a precociously devout hobby for a preadolescent boy, this sort of hagiography is a common trope in the autobiographies of religious leaders. But when considering Brown's fifty years of service as a Unitarian minister, it is quite possible that young Ethelred felt compelled to seek out an audience. After all, every messenger needs addressees.

As an adult, Brown fondly summoned childhood memories of singing his favorite hymn, "O Paradise 'tis Weary Waiting Here" and that as he uttered the melancholy lyrics, his "face was bathed in tears." Even in middle age, Brown was baffled by the keen sense of spirituality that dominated his youth as he wondered aloud: "Why should a boy have chosen a hymn so other-worldly?"[17] Ethelred's penchant for public speaking as a youth and self-described "abnormally religious temperament"[18] augured work and struggles to come as the founder and pastor of the first black Unitarian church in Jamaica and Harlem.

Brown's conversion from the African Methodist Episcopal (AME) faith of his parents to embrace the Unitarian doctrine of rational thought and radical, racial equality marked a pivotal moment in Brown's intellectual development. As a boy, Ethelred attended a small AME church with his family on Sundays. Then, one day, upon his own volition, he converted to Unitarianism at a young age.[19] He took great pride in his embrace of a doctrine that espoused rationality and intellectualism over emotionalism and mystery. Brown framed the disavowal of his childhood AME doctrine and the acceptance of Unitarianism as a movement from darkness to light and from ignorance to truth. He thanked serendipity for his introduction to his Unitarian faith through a pamphlet he found at his uncle's house in Montego Bay. Unitarianism was so uncommon on the island of Jamaica that even his uncle's possession of the pamphlet was somewhat odd. Brown took this odd occurrence as a favorable sign. Shortly thereafter, he experienced a spiritual awakening. In his words: "I was a choir boy of Montego Bay Episcopal Church when the first ray of light broke through my Trinitarianism. The strangeness of the Trinitarian arithmetic struck me forcibly—so forcibly that I decided then and there to sever my connection with the church which enunciated so impossible a proposition."[20] In other words, young Ethelred rejected the spiritual principle that God the Father, his son Jesus, and the Holy Spirit are one in the same. Brown's description of his teenaged doctrinal revelation bore an uncanny resemblance to the Biblical narrative of Saul who was struck down by a blinding light on the road to Damascus. After this spiritual revelation, Saul turned from his sinful past, changed his name to Paul, and moved forward along a religiously devout path. In true form of a budding intellectual, Brown's sense of rationalism trumped the appeal of spiritual mysticism. Because we only have Brown's account, in his own words, written in mature hindsight, it is impossible to know whether his conversion experience was indeed saturated in sun rays, as he described. Memory can be a misleading muse. Even if his revelation emerged in subtler fashion, the point remains that through the act of disavowing the Trinity, young Ethelred took the first steps in defining himself as a spiritually astute young man, capable and courageous enough to engage in critical, independent thought. His self-fashioning as a rational, respectable and reserved Christian was in line with the characteristics of racial uplift ideology held among many New Negro intellectuals decades later.

Personal circumstances and serendipity determined Brown's spiritual development, and his detailed account of the twists and turns of his individual path of faith reveal his penchant for the melodramatic turn of phrase. Because, at the time of his conversion experience, Brown was too young to launch out and start at Unitarian church on his own, he continued to work as a pianist and lyricist for a local AME and Lutheran church, and pushed his revelation regarding the improbability of Trinitarianism to the margins of his psyche. However, once he came of age to lead his own congregation, his conscience would not allow him to continue in the same denomination. Brown was offered a ministerial position at an AME church, but "had not well posted his letter of application when [his] outraged conscience violently protested." Brown used metaphors of struggle to describe his spiritual battle with internal and external forces. Metaphorically speaking, the "devil" lurking over his shoulder was the allure of a stable job at a well-respected church, versus the "angel" option, the pursuit of a more righteous, untraveled road. He recalled, "Four days later another letter was posted, strangely addressed— 'To any Unitarian Minister in New York City,' seeking information as to the possibility of entering the Unitarian ministry." Brown confronted his moral dilemma: Should he accept the AME church position with the benefits of starting immediately or take the more challenging route, which required years of training in Unitarianism with no guarantee that he would ever lead his own congregation? He pondered, "If I did enter the ministry I was under moral and spiritual compulsion to be a minister only of that church in which I would be absolutely honest." Brown declined the job as an AME minister began pursuing Unitarianism in earnest as he continued his correspondence with white Unitarian official Franklin Southworth.[21]

As a young adult, Brown publicly declared his break from his Methodist roots at a gathering of the Wesleyan Methodist Church in Montego Bay, which he later described as the "first public Unitarian pronouncement in the Island of Jamaica." Extending the metaphor of spiritual enlightenment, he declared, "The candle of Unitarianism was lighted—lighted, I hope, never to be put out." Assuming the mantle of the messenger, Brown's preacherly penchant for the dramatic turn of phrase energized his account of his proselytizing mission, which, in his words, was message that "fell like a bomb on the quiet community, and men and women were amazed at 'this strange teaching.'"[22] Despite the obvious use of hyperbole, Brown's "light" infused conversion experience set up Unitarianism as a doctrine of hope and truth, which had particular resonance for politically oppressed peoples of African descent. In addition to pointing to the newness of his Unitarian message of racial uplift in a land dominated by the Anglican and Methodist denominational faiths, Brown's use of the word "bomb" indexed the transformative power of Unitarianism to uplift his compatriots, even in the context of British colonial oppression.

Freedom on Shaky Ground: The First Unitarian Church in Jamaica

Over the course of two decades, Ethelred Brown led Unitarian uplift efforts based in Montego Bay and Kingston Jamaica that prefigured black liberation theology, the tradition in which black Christians used the Bible to not only refute white supremacy but to argue that, like the children of Israel, black people were chosen and favored by God.[23] At age thirty-two, Brown founded the first black Unitarian church in Jamaica in 1907. Brown's Unitarian message took on unique political import on an island where white supremacy assumed the form of British colonial rule. James Cone, preeminent scholar who coined the phrase "black liberation theology" during the height of civil rights movement half a century later, has argued that "In a society where persons are oppressed because they are *black*, Christian theology must become *black theology*, a theology that is unreservedly identified with the goals of the oppressed and seeks to interpret the divine character of their struggle for liberation."[24] In the context of British imperialism in Jamaica, which spanned from the mid seventeenth century until Jamaica won its independence in 1962, Brown's message of hope and progress endowed black Unitarians with moral authority. Brown's emphasis on optimism and rational thought was rooted in the philosophical tradition of humanism. Because religious humanism designates the first-hand, lived experience with the Divine as paramount, its eschewal of religious hierarchy in favor of individual insight echoes the fundamental premise of liberation theology. In other words, black Jamaicans did not need white colonial authorities to interpret scriptures on their behalf because their own suffering and survival was the ultimate testimony to God's power. This individual and personalized interpretation of scripture favors the politically oppressed.

Although white Unitarians were overwhelmingly silent on the issue of slavery and colonialism in Jamaica as unethical, exploitative institutions, Unitarianism in Brown's hands became spiritual ammunition for black empowerment. Scholar Juan M. Floyd-Thomas has argued that Brown's greatest power grew out of his embrace of "black humanism" as a philosophical tool to combat racism and class oppression.[25] Floyd-Thomas observed that although black humanism, like European humanism, has a "shared focus on individual human action, emphasis on free will, moral agency, the centrality of reason, and the appeal of democratic self-governance, etc., Black humanism functions in vastly divergent ways than its white counterpart because it has different obstacles to overcome and different objectives to obtain."[26] In the context of white supremacy in America, the most glaring obstacle to black humanism was the history of chattel slavery that designated blacks as property—alleging that people of African descent were more animal-like than human—and continued racial violence and discrimination after the abolition of slavery. Thus the suffering of black Americans was different from the condition of white Americans, and Brown's assertion of the humanity, dignity, and equality of black people held particular political import in a society still mired in racism and racial violence.[27] Indeed, Brown attempted a precarious balancing act between presenting a straightforward, pragmatic message that faith in God and hard work would bring success, and a more dramatic message of encouragement through his own poetic, rhetorical style. While black Baptist, Methodist, and Episcopalian ministers expressed this message of liberation through the rhetorical jeremiad, which linked black people's suffering to the last suffering of Christ, Brown used Unitarian tenets of humanism and rationalism to put forth an equally radical, albeit more subtle argument for racial equality. Brown's belief in spiritual equality, regardless of race, undermined the fundamental white supremacist ideology of British colonial rule.

Given the historical context—British imperial rule on an island with a strong history of slave rebellion and Maroonage—Brown's mission of uplift was complex and at times contradictory. It can be argued that, as a black colonial subject, his missionary efforts both challenged and supported British imperialism in Jamaica. On one hand, white Unitarian fiscal support of his all-black congregation fit the spirit of British "civilizing missions," which stressed moral uplift of colonial subjects mired by "sloth and heathen Folly."[28] This interpretation of Brown as a co-conspirator in British colonial upkeep calls to mind the poignant question that Grenadian-born poet Audre Lorde raised decades later, during the convergence of the civil rights movement and third-wave feminism: Is it possible to use the master's tools to dismantle the master's house?[29] Although Lorde concluded that this is impossible, Brown's life presents a more nuanced story.

On the other hand, we may read Brown's persistent requests for financial support from white Unitarians paired with his radical message of black social progress as a counter narrative to British imperial power. His letters to Unitarian officials convey a remarkable sense of entitlement.[30] In this regard,

Brown's religious diasporic ties to England refigured and redirected the "triangular trade" of transatlantic slave trade history. Instead of human cargo moving from West and Central Africa to the "New World" to grow raw materials to ship to Europe to produce manufactured goods, Brown's intrafaith trade moved money from white Unitarians in England to the West Indies to spiritually and materially uplift black Unitarians. Brown's message and method undermined the very premise of racialized colonial rule because of its fundamental message of spiritual equality, regardless of race, culture, and gender.

In spite of the liberatory potential of his message, Brown's efforts to spread the gospel of Unitarianism met great resistance from some Jamaicans who deemed it blasphemous. Brown viewed this antagonism as a trial inherent to his vocation. Instead of giving up in despair, he decided to pursue education and formal training in America that would help him make a more persuasive case for Unitarianism as a vehicle of racial uplift in Jamaica. Shortly after founding his church in Montego Bay, he sailed to Baltimore, Maryland, on a fruit boat, hoping to make his way to Pennsylvania to attend the Meadville Theological School. This image of Brown as a lone pilgrim who was willing to step out on faith to further his career in America bolstered Brown's narrative of his spiritual authority gained through personal sacrifice.

Brown's path to Meadville was difficult and winding. He planned to do accounting work for a small black-owned business in Richmond, Virginia, for one month and then continue on to Pennsylvania to enroll at the seminary. To Brown's dismay, immigration officials in Maryland ordered that he be deported because of insufficient documentation. After one more failed attempt, he finally arrived at Meadville Theological School and enrolled as a special student in September 1910. Over a decade later, Unitarian official Louis Cornish recalled the opposition that Brown endured during this educational endeavor: "Strong effort was made to dissuade him because it seemed so uncertain whether or not he could ever find a parish, but against all counsel he went to Meadville."[31] Consistent with his grand ambition and tenacious character, Brown ignored the naysayers and carried on with his professional vision.

Brown impressed his instructors at Meadville. A Mr. Stallworthy (his first name is unknown to us) relayed the professors' high regard for his ability: "He speaks clearly, writes well, is a skilled musician and both he and his wife are attractive solo singers."[32] Such a glowing assessment of Brown's intelligence and talents written by a reputable, white American Unitarian official bolstered Brown's own sense of prestige during the early critical years in his mission to be the first black Jamaican Unitarian minister in a practically all-white denomination. Such positive reviews helped Brown raise money for his congregation in Jamaica and paved the way for his later immigration to New York.

After completing his studies a Meadville Theological School, Brown returned to Montego Bay in 1912. In 1913 his persistence paid off, and he secured $500 per annum from the British Unitarian Association to support his ministry in Jamaica for the next three years. Despite Brown's optimism and sincere hope for spiritual equality with his white brethren, he discovered that racism was a many-headed beast. He repeatedly felt the sting of benevolent paternalism and outright racism from the British, rooted in a long, gnarled history of Darwinian racial hierarchy that dated back to the Enlightenment in Europe. So it is not surprising that racist reasoning permeated British views for (out of pity) or against (out of contempt) Brown's ministry in Jamaica.

One assessment of his Montego Bay congregation by British Unitarian official Hilary Bygrave reveals how Brown's interactions with white Unitarians ran the spectrum from outright racism to benevolent paternalism to occasional good will. Bygrave wrote, "If we want to do a bit of *genuine humanitarian work* for a quite intelligent class of distinctively colored people, seventy-five years removed from slavery, but still quite poorly paid in the matter of wage, with no thought of ever getting anything but love and respect in return, I urge that in some way, the cause there be given this further impetus to a more assured success."[33] In this passage, Bygrave struck a middle ground between compassion and condescension. He complimented Jamaicans by calling them intelligent, but implicitly suggested Jamaicans were sinful enough to warrant the "civilizing" support of British Unitarians. In other accounts, Bygrave depicted Jamaicans as licentious and incapable of self-control. Ironically, he offered a backhanded compliment by calling Jamaicans a "quite sober people," while also providing a list of their "great vices," which included "sexual irregularities, nay sexual excesses."[34] Just as a photograph emerges gradually in a bath of chemicals in a dark room, the full extent of Bygrave's racism revealed itself by the end of his written assessment of Brown's ministry. He proclaimed that Brown was "pronouncedly black . . . a handicap to him in his work," invoking an early twentieth-century discourse of racial hierarchy, but he still appealed to "any members of our household of faith who are . . . interested in [a] social uplift effort" to financially support Brown's ministry in Jamaica.[35]

The Brown family recognized the racist underpinnings of white Unitarian charity and answered it with a spiritual appeal to their shared humanity. Even in dire straits, the Brown family maintained their dignity by emphasizing their moral rectitude and spiritual equality with their patrons in letters written to white Unitarian officials. This is best illustrated by a scathing letter in which Brown's eldest daughter, Dorice, addressed Unitarian officials: "None of you know Jamaica, and so you seem to think we are a sort of savages; but we are not. We are the same as you, and we only require a little time and we shall pay you in the best way for all your trouble."[36] In this regard, Dorice used her Unitarian faith as a sort of liberation theology on her family's behalf. She personalized the church's message of racial equality to argue that the family was worthy of financial aid. This rhetorical strategy chiseled away at the white supremacist hierarchies where the powerful colonizer governs the lowly colonized, by placing both groups on the same spiritual level.

In addition to Brown's fraught relationship of economic dependence on British Unitarians, Brown recieved greater monetary and moral support from white American Unitarians. One of his American Unitarian allies, Stallworthy, visited Brown's Kingston congregation and sent a report to England, which was published in a 1915 issue of *Christian Life*. Stallworthy praised Brown's theological acumen and leadership skills, calling him a "zealous, able, and well educated man of color, [who is] supported by the American Unitarian Association." While links to white Unitarians in England were rooted in the history of colonialism, Brown's more successful relationship with white American Unitarians grew out of a sense of spiritual diaspora as well as perceptions of the United States as brimming with untapped educational and job opportunities. Brown strategically leveraged his religious affiliation to transform racially oppressive and materially exploitive relationships into lucrative alliances that better suited his local mission of social justice.

Although Stallworthy issued a favorable report, over the course of Brown's fifty years in ministry, numerous British and American Unitarian officials criticized Brown for alleged financial mismanagement and poor leadership skills. Ironically, Brown possessed the very same weakness for which he would criticize Marcus Garvey—insufficient bureaucratic skills. The British and Federation of Unitarian Americans decided that Brown was too irresponsible to be trusted with the mission of spreading Unitarianism in Jamaica. The AUA terminated funding in 1915, but gave Brown $100 to soften the financial blow while he got back on his feet, recommending that he return to work as an accountant.

Brown's spiritual idealism, the idea of the unity of spirits that transcended race, repeatedly clashed with the historical reality of British racism. Brown continued his ministry in spite of the British Unitarian Association's withdrawal of fiscal support. Brown felt betrayed by his white Unitarian brethren in England; years later, he expressed his disappointment: "I gave up a good position on this understanding and [after] 3.5 years I was deserted and left in a large city disillusioned and discredited. For a little over two years I struggled on against great odds and then decided to come to this country."[37] Considering the power imbalance between British Unitarians and Brown's

small congregation in Jamaican, it is not surprising that British Unitarian officials did not deem Brown's church worthy of support. In 1918, Dorice wrote
the British Unitarian association about her family's financial difficulties. "My
father owes now about $150 for our schooling and for rent. He will be sued
for these as the people will not wait much longer. Now I am asking you as
sympathetic Christian people to send him that amount. I do not think you
will miss it, and it will be a great deal to him."[38] Dorice's appeal on behalf
of her family assumed a tone similar to that of her father's previous letters.
She also based her request on shared faith that emphasized charity. Astutely
aware of the historical and racial power imbalance in this relationship, she
also attempted to shame the AUA board members by implying mere stingi-
ness would be the only hindrance to granting her family's plea for financial
aid. According to Dorice, when the requested money never arrived, Brown
remedied the family's financial strain by "borrowing" money from the trea-
sury at his civil service job. When Brown's supervisors discovered the missing
money, Brown's father and older brother repaid his debt, but he still lost his
job. Brown's spiritual and financial struggles persisted, but his commitment to
his calling propelled him to try his luck in Harlem.

Given Brown's inability to attract a significant following in Montego Bay
and Kingston, his move to Harlem to promote an unfamiliar doctrine and
start a church in a new city was a high stakes gamble. In a letter to white Unitarian official Louis C. Cornish, written in January 1920, one month before
his immigration to Harlem, Brown revealed how much he believed was "on
the line" regarding this move: "After two years of vain effort to get my feet
back on the commercial ladder, and after frantic efforts to make ends meet,
I am now practically a bankrupt—owing nearly 120 pounds, and am at this
moment facing public disgrace and ruin... My *salvation* is to leave for New
York as early as possible. My health, my reputation, my future usefulness all
demand this."[39] In his characteristic, melodramatic style, Brown expressed the
enormous spiritual and financial toll that his foray into uncharted territory
as the first black Unitarian minister in Jamaica had taken on him. But, in
this passage, Brown's sole focus on himself begs the question: *Did his personal ambition, to make a name for himself as a religious pioneer, eclipse the
practical needs of the very souls whom he had hoped to uplift?* Perhaps Brown
would have been more effective as a non-sectarian, anti-colonial activist. Notwithstanding this counterfactual, the life of a visionary is difficult. Brown had
endured enough pricks of rejection at the hands of his compatriots and white
Unitarians, but he held onto hope that Harlem might be the path leading
toward redemption.

"A Pilgrimage of Faith": From Montego Bay to Harlem

Reverend Ethelred Brown chose Harlem as fertile ground to grow his Unitarian ministry because he had faith in Harlem's large, bustling, cosmopolitan black population and New York's general atmosphere of intellectual liberalism. He and his wife Ella emigrated from Kingston to Harlem in February 1920. For Brown, Harlem represented a modern-day Canaan—an escape from public disgrace in Jamaica and from dire financial straits—in which to begin anew, in the fastest growing cultural metropolis in the world, New York. Years later, he preached a sermon titled "From Montego Bay to Harlem: A Pilgrimage of Faith," in which he recounted that he had arrived in New York during a "fierce snow storm." This metaphor foregrounds Brown's depiction of himself as a black pioneer in the Unitarian church willing to confront challenges and succeed against the odds. Perhaps the snow storm also foreshadowed greater challenges to come after his arrival in New York.

After arriving in New York, Brown did not waste time in furthering his Unitarian proselytizing mission, which resonated with other Caribbean immigrants who worked at the forefront of black political radicalism. At a meeting in March 1920, a group of attendees agreed to establish Brown's church, and nine individuals signed the declaration as charter members.[40] Although Brown viewed his congregation as the first black Unitarian church established in America, William W. C. Carter had him beat by two years when he founded "the Church of the Unitarian Brotherhood" in Cincinnati in 1918.[41] However, the multi-ethnic diversity and intellectually liberal message of Brown's church made it unique. Among Brown's fledgling congregation was a group of Caribbean religious and political radicals including: Caribbean American Grace Campbell, W. A. Domingo from Jamaica, Richard B. Moore from Barbados and Frank Crosswaith from St. Croix, all whom had played some role in Communist or Socialist Party politics at the time.[42] Moore, Domingo, and Brown all served as active members of the New York Socialist Party during overlapping years from the 1920s through the 1930s.[43] These Caribbean intellectuals considered the HCC an organic extension of the Socialist Party's mission of racial equality. Brown's congregation was overwhelmingly male and its cultural makeup mirrored the intraracial diversity of Harlem at the time.

Brown's church had three different names over its life—first the Harlem Community Church, then the Hubert Harrison Memorial Church in 1928,[44] and finally, the Harlem Unitarian Church in 1937, after its official association with the AUA.[45] The congregation numbered forty-five members in 1937.

As a Caribbean immigrant, Brown believed his cultural values and Unitarian faith imbued him with a singular sort of spiritual and intellectual enlightenment that could benefit the diverse denizens of black New York. In such, he framed his church as a beacon of light in the midst of Harlem's throng of misguided souls. Brown used metaphors such as "light," "candle," and "shine" interchangeably to describe the transformative power of his faith. He believed that Unitarianism could bring black New Yorkers out of the "darkness" of overly emotional and impractical denominations such as the AME, Baptist, and Pentecostal churches and into the "light" of sober-mindedness. Although he never explicitly outlined cultural differences amongst Caribbean and American-born blacks, his rebuke of American-born black Christians' devotional practices intimated his broader disapproval of American-born black cultural practices. Brown certainly saw himself as a missionary to save blacks in America.

In a bulletin inviting fellow Harlemites to visit his new church, Brown appealed to the progressive sensibility of black New Yorkers: "It is generally believed that conservatism in religion is characteristic of Negroes. The fact is, nevertheless, that in this regard we are not essentially different from other races. Here in Harlem the percentage of religious liberals and anti-religionists among Negroes is, we believe, as large as in any white community."[46] Brown believed black New Yorkers were just as open-minded as their white counterparts. Echoing the prevailing discourse on what made the New Negro so new was the embrace of progressive political thought and the abandonment of old-time religion, Brown replaced his concept of a black collective cultural identity with a description of the culture of Harlem, whose inhabitants had diverse values, hopes, and dreams. This focus on black Americans as culturally diverse contrasted sharply with "outsider" perceptions of black homogeneity. Accordingly, in one sermon, Brown observed, "I found very soon that in Harlem there were not so much Negroes as plain human beings," but instead, Harlem was defined by the intellectual and political diversity among black "conservatives, liberals, radicals, men and women who had long since intellectually and ethnically outgrown the fundamental teachings of the other churches."[47] In its cosmopolitan diversity, Harlem provided a stark contrast to the agrarian cultures of Montego Bay and Kingston. Perception is within the eye of the beholder. Likewise, from the vantage point of 1920s-1950s era American-born whites and European immigrants, Harlem was a sea of undifferentiated blackness,[48] but for an insider like Brown, Harlem was an ecosystem unto itself, teeming with variegated minds, souls, and skin tones.

In the personal and political drama of battles for political power among New Negro leaders, immigrant cultural identity played such a central role that it might be argued that the presence of Caribbean culture, as a counter-point to American-born blackness, served as a political actor in its own right. In Brown's case, he presented an idealized image of Caribbean immigrants as a professional class of disciplined, rational thinkers in contrast to the stereotype of black Americans as passive and overly emotional, more concerned with salvation in the sweet by and by than with social progress in the here and now. From Brown's point of view, Caribbean immigrants were living, breathing proof of the New Negro's progressive and cosmopolitan *esprit de corps*, while American-born blacks still languished in the irrational ways of the "Old Negro"—an unwelcome relic from plantation time. This perception was more myth than reality since Harlem was home to some of the most powerful social-progress ministries led by American-born blacks, most notably Adam Clayton Powell Sr. and Adam Clayton Powell Jr.'s Abyssinian Baptist Church, which boasted more than ten thousand members. Founded in 1808, Abyssinian Baptist was full of American-born black elite and politically engaged members. Powell's formidable congregation relocated from lower Manhattan to Harlem in 1920, the same year Brown immigrated to Harlem, so he was certainly aware of Abyssinian Baptist as a bastion of American-born black religious progressivism. Still, Brown described his own ministry as a mission to "emancipate [black Americans] from the emotionalism and superstition and other worldliness of old time religion."[49] While the Powell's were progressive, the very fact that their denominational affiliation was Baptist meant they had not reached the same level of rational, enlightenment as Brown. Of course, Brown's rivalry with Marcus Garvey is an exception to this rule, but, Caribbean identity still factored strongly in this case, because their shared Jamaican heritage fueled the vehemence behind Brown's denunciation of Garvey as an incompetent leader because Brown feared that Garvey might give Caribbean immigrants, like himself, a bad name. In this regard, the issue of black immigrant cultural identity took on a life of its own. Brown believed his immigrant status held political cache and he was determined to use his Caribbean culture to his advantage.

For some Caribbean intellectuals, negative stereotypes of American-born blacks served as a foil to make a case for black immigrants' allegedly superior intellect and character. Brown's friend and colleague W. A. Domingo relied on this trope. Domingo believed that Harlemites were in great need of spiritual guidance from a sober-minded, Caribbean religious leader like Brown. In 1925, Doming wrote, "There is a diametrical difference between American and West Indian Negroes in their worship. While large sections of the former are inclined to indulge in displays of emotionalism that border on hysteria, the latter, in their Wesleyan Methodist and Baptist churches maintain in the face of the assumption that people from the tropics are necessarily emotional, all the punctilious

emotional restrain characteristic of their English background. In religious radicalism the foreign-born are again pioneers and propagandists."[50] In this case,
Domingo used his position as a British colonial subject to put forth the case
of polished character. Domingo and Brown took great pride in their embrace
of sober-mindedness and restraint within religious and secular contexts. They
believed that Caribbean intellectuals like themselves, formally educated and
well versed in British customs, would lead their fellow Harlemites into a progressive, and more dignified future. However, I contend that these values also
resonated with American-born blacks who made the politics of respectability
a central element in defining the New Negro as different from the "old Negro"
epitomized by the image of the powerless slave of plantations past.

Brown's sense of propriety, decorum, and rationality had deep roots in
British colonial mores. In 1926, Brown emphasized the need for "a church of
this type" especially "in this district of the city in which the 'colored churches'
are mostly *homes of fanaticism and superstition*, and where so many men and
women have intellectually outgrown the teachings of orthodoxy, and because I
know that worked under proper conditions it will develop into a strong influential liberal church."[51] Brown described the Harlem Community Church as "a
church-forum where the honey-in-heaven and harassment-in-Hades type of
religion is not tolerated. There are no 'amen corners' in this church, and no 'sob
sister bench.'"[52] Although Brown drew sharp lines in the sand with his catego-
rization of American-born black Christian styles of worship as overly emotional versus the reserved style of his Unitarian practice, we must understand
the intellectual common ground among black immigrant and American-born
black intellectuals who were middle and upper class members or aspirants.
Although Brown used broad brush strokes to paint American-born blacks as
lowbrow, American-born religious leaders such as the black Baptist women
in Evelyn Higginbotham's *Righteous Discontent* would be quick to argue in
favor of his values—such as his belief that a clean appearance and orderly
behavior reflected well on the black race as a whole. Nonetheless, Brown not
only imported the doctrine of Unitarianism when he arrived in Harlem, but
also brought a bias toward British conservatism in speech, hymnal form and
content, and movement (or lack thereof) in style of religious worship.

Church Forum

The Harlem Community Church held political forums every week, then
monthly, but finally returned to its weekly meetings.[53] Brown described the
HCC as a "'temple and a forum' in which we worship the true and good and
beautiful, and receive inspiration to live a life of service; a forum whereas

mind sharpens mind as we strive to plumb the depths, span the breadth, and scale the heights of knowledge."[54] Brown intended to uplift his fellow Harlemites through the power of rational thought; however, his belief in a dispassionate and reserved style of devotional practice did not always sit well with all of his congregants.

Despite Brown's determination to uphold the humanist and rationalist principles of Unitarian practice, tensions between emotionalism and rationalism shaped debates about whether the church should have a primarily political or spiritual mission. Some congregants believed that Brown's investment in rationalism had made the church into a political institution at the expense of spiritual uplift. In 1930, for example, a Mr. Asbury suggested that Brown was too concerned with worldly things and not sufficiently invested in the salvation of souls. Brown's ministry was quite successful as a political forum, but complaints such as these prompted him to incorporate more music into the Sunday morning agenda. However, he soon found himself in a no-win situation when other congregants complained that the time devoted to musical devotion detracted from the church's political mission.[55] In trying to mediate his diverse congregants' interests in spiritual and political progress, Brown was engaged in a precarious balancing act. One member of the congregation observed, "The Harlem Unitarian Church lost ground, so far as attendance is concerned, when 2 years ago the nature of the service was changed, and the forums abandoned. Mr. Brown felt, mistakenly, that this was necessary in order to secure support from the American Unitarian Association."[56] The old adage, you can't please all the people all the time, might be cliché, but still rang true for Brown.

Over the course of three decades, the Harlem Community Church moved several times. Members met at the Lafayette Hall from 1920 until 1921, and then it moved to the Lodge Rooms at the American West Indian Association, located at 149 West 136th Street. Again, the cultural affiliation of this meeting place is a relocation that demonstrates the social and spatial connectedness of the HCC to Caribbean communities in Harlem. Near the end of Brown's career, he fondly remembered this gathering place: "we made local history in this small hall where we remained for seventeen years."[57] In 1938, his congregation moved to Room 101 of the Harlem YWCA, where they met for the next eight years. In 1946, the Harlem Unitarian Church made its last move to the YMCA Chapel at 180 West 135th Street.[58]

Brown self-consciously framed his professional and spiritual narrative as a triumph against the odds when he wrote that "in the face of many handicaps" he and his congregants "did creditable work" at their longest-standing location, the Harlem YMCA. Brown did not detail the "handicaps" in this document, but sources reveal that Brown continued to struggle financially while contemporaneous religious leaders enjoyed a degree of material success. In contrast to contemporaneous religious leaders such as Rabbi Wentworth Matthew and Father Divine who purchased real estate in Long Island and moved to larger buildings to accommodate their growing membership, Brown's relocations sprang from necessity and serendipity. Throughout the life of his Harlem church, the congregants' personal and professional networks determined the next meeting place when the HCC's lease proved unrenewable. Cultural affiliation and immigration status shaped these networks, which were crucial parts of Caribbean New York at the time.

Brother's Keeper: Jamaican Mutual Aid and Pan-Caribbean Identity

While living in New York, Brown still understood Unitarianism as a liberation theology that could help his compatriots back in Jamaica. Brown's embrace of Unitarianism and participation in black radical politics inspired him to fuse his religious faith with his socialist politics and his continued commitment to the wellbeing of Caribbean immigrants, especially Jamaicans living in New York or abroad. In addition to his former membership in the UNIA and work as secretary for the Socialist Party, Brown also served as chairperson for the Jamaican Benevolent Association, vice president for the Federation of Jamaican Organizations, cofounder and president of the Jamaican Progressive League (JPL), and fundraiser for the People's Nationalist Party (PNP) in Jamaica.[59] Upon achieving independence from British colonial rule, Jamaica's Prime Minister Norman Manley extended an invitation to Brown to serve as an official member of his cabinet.[60] It goes without saying that Brown was a busy man, a truly engaged public intellectual; but the most important thing that these institutional affiliations reveal is his retention of this Jamaican cultural identity after his immigration to Harlem.

While celebrating the success of Jamaicans living in New York, Brown advocated for the economic uplift and political independence of Jamaica. He drew on his musical talents as the lyricist and composer of anthems for the JPL. In 1937, he penned a ballad called "Ode: 'Jamaica,'" which he sang at the JPL's thirtieth anniversary celebration:

> Move on to sovereignty;
> Mould thine own destiny—
> A nation free.
> . . . .
> That though a living State
> At length wilt be.[61]

Brown's devotion to his homeland shone through the lyrics. The rhyme scheme and imagery bear an uncanny resemblance to James Weldon Johnson's "Lift Every Voice and Sing," which became the official anthem of the National Association for the Advancement of Colored People in 1900.[62] Though Brown would have sung Johnson's "Negro national anthem" with pride, he felt compelled to write a national hymn that conveyed the unique political concerns and geographic specificities of his birthplace Jamaica. Brown lived the through complex evolution of black cultural identity in America, as he held onto his Jamaican-ness while confronting American racism.

Brown was not alone in his commitment to translocal identity—meaning a sense of cultural ownership and belonging based on his first-hand participation in political communities in Montego Bay, Kingston and in Harlem. Another JPL member, W. Adolphe Roberts, wrote a song titled "Exiles' Hymn" for the same anniversary celebration. Roberts expressed a similar loyalty to Jamaica and a desire for independence from British colonial rule, but in his foregrounding of Jamaica's natural resources, he rendered a romanticized portrait of his birthplace that oozed nostalgia:

Jamaica, *glorious homeland*, we turn again to you.
We hail you and remember your sky's eternal blue,
Your sunshine ever golden on forest, hill and plain,
Your rich, red earth that ripens the coffee and the cane.[63]

This robust depiction of Jamaica's topography is reminiscent of Langston Hughes's "The Negro Speaks of Rivers" and Countee Cullen's "Heritage." It is very likely that Roberts had encountered both poems by these American-born black poets, since Hughes's "Rivers" first appeared in the June 1921 issue of the *Crisis*, and Cullen first published "Heritage" in his 1925 volume of poetry titled *Color*. If so, Brown and Robert's poems put their own homeland on the map, per se, as their presence made Jamaica a cultural island within the borough of Harlem. Even if Hughes, Cullen, Brown, and Roberts were unaware of each other's work, Harlem's ethos of artistic and intellectual exchange most likely inspired the cultural production of these Jamaican immigrants.

Brown and Roberts's lyrics demonstrate their continued attachment to their island birthplace, its people, and its political future. While Langston Hughes represented the class and race struggles of American-born blacks in the muck and glory of diasporic rivers, from the Mississippi Delta to the Nile River basin, Roberts painted a more idyllic picture of Jamaica's enslaved past, colonial present, and political future by extolling its cash crops and lush landscape. He recognized the intrinsic value of the island's raw materials, especially coffee and sugar, which inextricably linked Jamaica's present agricultural economy to the history of black enslavement and the triangulated cultural clashes and collaboration of the Caribbean, Western African and European people. But Roberts's idyllic portrait begs the question: *What next?* Beautiful words and nostalgic memories only buoy the spirit to a certain point. In the face of continued colonial oppression in Jamaica and northern-style Jim Crow in New York, proactive resolution is required.

Brown understood the power of rhetoric, and, to the best of his abilities, he matched his political idealism with action. Even in furthering his Unitarian, altruistic agenda in Harlem, Brown still took special care when Jamaicans at home and abroad were in need. In one instance, he rushed to aid survivors of the 1944 hurricane in Jamaica by rallying fiscal support from his Unitarian congregation as well as Jamaica Progressive League (JPL) members. The JPL functioned as a mutual-aid society whose members pooled financial and human resources to help one another purchase property, send students to college, and pay for funeral and burial services.

In November 1944, Brown preached a sermon titled "The Dreamer Dreameth" in which he prayed for "aid of the hurricane stricken people of the island of Jamaica."[64] Brown's sense of diasporic ties and moral obligation remained intact as he linked the plight of "a stricken people across the sea" to Jamaicans living in Harlem—the burgeoning black metropolis that he described as "a large city of sympathetic and generous souls."[65] Although the gathering was small, Brown raised $250 for the hurricane relief effort, publicly applauding a large donation from a "small West Indian lodge."[66] Because Brown did not specify the ethnicity of the lodge's owners and members, one may read this as a semantic attempt to underscore pan–Caribbean political unity.

Brown carried this theme of pan-Caribbean solidarity in later speeches. In October 1947, in his keynote address for the Jamaica Benevolent Association's (JBA) thirtieth anniversary, Brown commended members for their hard work and cooperative spirit. Because Unitarianism extolled the unity of all people, regardless of race, ethnicity, gender, and class, Brown emphasized how the JBA benefited non-Jamaicans as well as its immediate members. He acknowledged the benefits of national pride, but countered ethnocentrism: "But this love of country, this getting together as Jamaicans did not make us insular or narrow. Our love of our own land created in us a love for others."[67] Brown stressed the JBA's broad outreach agenda, which included anyone in need, regardless of ethnicity. In this respect, he constantly merged his secular, political leadership with his Unitarian faith.

The Jamaica Benevolent Association's political agenda reveal a burgeoning pan-Caribbean identity in Harlem. Brown praised JBA members for befriending other Caribbean mutual-aid societies. He declared, "Our hands were open—not only to our members, not only to Jamaicans . . . but to all whose need made them our neighbors and our brothers." He continued: "We gave our strength to serve our brother in his need—We took to us our sorrowing brother for our guest and shared with him our bread of blessing. And we did it all, because we realized that when our hearts enfold a brother, God is there."[68] Once again, Brown's Unitarian faith shone through his words—even during a secular gathering. In fact, the word "secular" inadequately captures the strong overlap of black politics and religion during the opening decades of the twentieth century. For example, the Jamaica Benevolent Association was ostensibly a political organization, but Brown freely mixed his faith and socialist politics. In the spirit and rhetoric of Unitarianism, he beseeched anniversary celebration attendees to make their "alms-giving a sacrament of love."[69] He acknowledged current-day social struggles such as unemployment, sickness, and funeral expenses, but also emphasized the biblical principle, "Man doth not live by bread alone."[70] Brown preached that JBA members who helped others, JPL affiliates, and nonaffiliates would reap abundant spiritual rewards. For Brown, the realms of spirituality and politics were inextricable.

Brown vs. Marcus Garvey

Although Brown developed a sense of Pan-Caribbean consciousness after his emigration from Jamaica to Harlem, his solidarity with fellow Jamaicans could not overcome his animosity toward his compatriot, political leader Marcus Garvey. Thus, the disagreement that transpired between Reverend Brown and the Garvey supporter on that Sunday evening at the Harlem Community Church in 1928 was more than a mere tussle between political rivals, but is instead an apt demonstration of a broader contest of ideas among black intellectuals regarding the most viable path toward "racial uplift" for American-born blacks, only forty years removed from slavery, and for Caribbean immigrants fleeing British colonial oppression in their islands of origin and chasing their own uniquely Caribbean immigrant "American dreams." The competition for political power among black intellectuals during this age of the New Negro was particularly intense. Garvey's black-nationalist vision conflicted with Brown's progressive, integrationist vision of racial uplift.[71]

Ethelred Brown, born in Falmouth, Jamaica in 1875, and Marcus Mosiah Garvey, born two years later and thirty miles away in St Ann's Bay, Jamaica, on August 7, 1877, shared a similar cultural upbringing; however, their intellectual trajectories took very different paths. After wayfaring throughout Central

America and living in London, Garvey moved to New York in 1916—with a black nationalist, Back-to-Africa agenda, while Brown emigrated from Kingston, Jamaica, to Harlem, New York, on February 27, 1920—with a mission to spread the gospel of Unitarianism, a doctrine that advocated for racial integration instead of separation. Their common cultural background may have even heightened Brown's animosity towards Garvey, because it was clear that Brown thought Garvey was not only giving New Negro leaders a bad name but he feared that his fellow countryman might sully the reputation of Caribbean immigrants, broadly speaking. Hence, Brown was careful to note that it was not only American-born black intellectuals who opposed Garvey but that he and Jamaican-born writer W. A. Domingo were two of the first most vocal critics of their own compatriot.

Ethelred Brown was one among many black intellectuals who criticized Marcus Garvey's back-to-Africa "racial uplift" mission, his bombastic personality, and imperious leadership style, and Garvey returned the rancor of his critics, tit-for-tat. Most famously, Garvey criticized the elitism of leading civil rights organizations such as the National Association for the Advancement of Colored People (NAACP), by sarcastically alleging that the "C" in the organization's acronym stood for "Certain People" (*i.e.* light-skinned, middle and upper class blacks), part and parcel of the Du Bois's presumed elitism. It is well known that Garvey was stuck on this issue of skin color as a barometer of New Negro leaders' commitment to everyday, working-class black people, when he criticized Nevis-born, radical political leader Cyril Briggs of being white and questioned the intentions of American-born black intellectual W. E. B. Du Bois because he thought his fair skin and Ivy League pedigree was the root of Du Bois's elitism. In turn, Briggs sued Garvey for defamation of character and Du Bois described Garvey as a "a little, fat black man, ugly, but with intelligent eyes and a big head."[72] Such disagreements among foreign-born and American-born black intellectuals suggest that contrary to popular opinion racial solidarity was not a seamless endeavor in 1920s New York. Racial unification was a *process*, not a given outcome. Furthermore, the process remained incomplete. Cultural and intellectual differences had to be worked through and transcended in order to press forward with a mission of racial solidarity, and Brown's criticism of his compatriot Marcus Garvey is a case in point that although all black intellectuals did not agree about the best strategies toward progress as a race, they still worked within a similar framework and used the popular language of the time regarding racial unity.

While the animosity between Garvey and American-born black intellectuals (such as W. E. B. Du Bois) has dominated the debate regarding the personality politics of New Negro leaders, Jamaican-born intellectuals such as Ethelred Brown and W. A. Domingo demonstrate intra-cultural conflicts among Caribbean intellectuals because they made a conscious effort to underscore the fact that their shared Jamaican-ness did not exempt Garvey from criticism. In 1925, W. A. Domingo wrote, "It has been asserted that the movement headed by the most-advertised of all West Indians, Marcus Garvey, absentee 'president' of the continent of Africa, represents the attempt of West Indian peasants to solve the American race problem."[73] Domingo's wry sense of humor and ironic tone is not lost on this reader; he hints at Garvey's sense of self-righteousness and bombastic ego by suggesting he is the self-proclaimed "president of Africa," ruler of an entire continent, not a state, and most importantly of a land in which he was neither born nor fully understands. Domingo's disdain for Garvey blasted black American perceptions of Caribbean solidarity, demonstrating yet another level of intraracial and intracultural clashes. Domingo continued, "The support given Garvey by a certain type of his countrymen is partly explained by their group reaction to attacks made upon him because of his nationality. On the other hand, the earliest and most persistent exposures of Garvey's multitudinous schemes were initiated by West Indians in New York like Cyril Briggs and the writer."[74] The competition to win over the hearts and minds of Harlem's New Negroes was intense, and the stakes were high. Given the historical moment, failed reconstruction, the migration of freed slaves to northern cities and westward lands, combined with the arrival of hopeful black immigrants from the English-speaking Caribbean, 1920s New York was the perfect storm for the flourishing of black cultural production. W. A. Domingo, Richard B. Moore, Cyril Briggs, Reverend Ethelred Brown, and others took to the streets and the pulpit to declare their own visions of progress. Such examples of New Negro intra-cultural conflicts pervade Reverend Brown's sermons and letters written from the 1910s through the 1950s—demonstrating the complexity of Caribbean immigrant cultural identity.[75] Brown's sermons reveal his personal understandings of racial, ethnic and religious identities and also suggest a degree of disdain for American-born blacks—mainly expressed as an intense dismay regarding black American Christian emotionally-demonstrative devotional practices. Brown's British colonial background played a major role in how he interacted with American-born blacks as well as Caribbean immigrants whom he grouped to be among a class lower than himself.[76]

Conclusion

Through his membership in Jamaican nationalist organizations, the Socialist Party, and the Harlem Community Church, Ethelred Brown joined the strong current of black radicalism during the age of racial uplift. However, he worked hard to distinguish himself as a peculiarly enlightened public intellectual through his Unitarian based ideology of social progress. The political ideals promoted at his church-forums reflected the ethos of the time—the principles of intellectual liberalism, self help, and cultural reinvention.

Brown's personality and cultural identity shaped Brown's style of political leadership. His inability to navigate organizational bureaucracy, exemplified by his ineffective, albeit persistent, fundraising efforts, hampered his efficacy as a minister. He also exerted a good deal of energy fighting political opponents, when that time and effort would have been better spent further developing his own ideology of social progress and leveraging professional alliances with Jamaican mutual-aid societies or Socialist Party to build his church membership. Still, Brown's life encourages us to rethink the role of religion and political rivalry in determining the trajectory of New Negro leadership.

Personal circumstances and political context influenced Brown's use of Unitarianism as liberation theology in both Jamaica and New York. During his thirty-six years of residence in Harlem, he challenged institutional and quotidian racism through his faith and political practice. Brown died on February 17, 1956, at age eighty, still hoping that Unitarianism would find a greater voice among Harlemites. Brown's comrade and fellow founding member of the Harlem Community Church, Barbadian-born, radical political activist Richard B. Moore, would continue to fight similar battles against institutionalized racism while remaining committed to the progress of the compatriots whom they had left behind in the English-speaking Caribbean.

CHAPTER 3

Richard B. Moore and Pan-Caribbean Consciousness

I am a Caribbean now—a Caribbean American.[1]

—**RICHARD B. MOORE**

While Ethelred Brown's Unitarian ministry explicitly doubled as a political forum and spiritual gathering place in the cause of racial uplift in Harlem and black political empowerment in Jamaica, communist and anticolonial activist Richard B. Moore's life represents a broader and more complex ebb and flow of members and ideas among Caribbean-led political and religious institutions. Moore's devoutly Christian upbringing in Barbados combined with his recognition that the church was one of the most effective institutions for reaching the masses of working-class blacks in New York inspired him to join Brown's Harlem Community Church (HCC) as one of the founding members.[2] In the face of orthodox communists who frowned upon his association with the small Unitarian congregation because the Communist Party's official platform condemned religion as an "opiate of the masses" that distracted workers from the urgency of pragmatic change in the here-and-now, Moore's singular cultural biography laid the foundation for a reconciliation between his Christian values and radical politics. While attending the HCC, Moore would begin to question the role of religion in political progress. Historian Joyce Moore Turner has duly noted that although Moore eventually became a "staunch atheist," the HCC—where sermons such as "Jesus and Marx" and "The Church and the Negro Problem" were preached, provided Moore with the ideal forum to express his radical, socialist ideas.[3] Still, even after his distancing from organized religion, I contend that Christian ideals of human dignity and unity continued to undergird Moore's political platform.

Moore also shared common ground with Reverend Brown regarding their continued interest in and support for their islands of origin, long after they had immigrated to New York. While Brown's solidarity with his compatriots

Tammy L. Brown, *Becoming Caribbean American: Richard B. Moore*, Mixed Media, 2014.

mainly took the form of philanthropic fundraisers during times of need, such as in the case of natural disasters and his membership in the Jamaican Progressive League, Jamaican Benevolent Association, and the People's Nationalist Party, Moore's political efforts in the Caribbean centered on ending British colonial rule and forging a unified, all-black government among the English-speaking islands. Moore was a stalwart orator who attacked British colonialism at its root—the ideology of white supremacy.

If Richard B. Moore were alive today, he would be the sort of politician who "reaches across the aisle" in an effort to bridge philosophical and cultural differences and move forward for the greater good of the community. In a spirit of harmony, comparable to Reverend Ethelred Brown's attempts to transcend racial barriers between black and white Unitarians, Moore worked to transcend island-specific allegiances and negative stereotypes that conspired to divide Caribbean New Yorkers. As such, this chapter centers on Moore's development of a pan-Caribbean consciousness, as well as Moore's campaigns for Caribbean independence from British rule and unity among the governing bodies of the English-speaking islands. I argue that the fierce spirit of political solidarity that inspired Moore to declare, "I am a Caribbean American"[4] during the height of anti-imperialism, was an expansion of his communist and socialist activism during his early political career in Harlem. Throughout the entirety of his prolific career as a public intellectual from the 1920s through the 1970s, Moore remained true to his fundamental commitment to improving the plight of politically oppressed people.

Moore's primary development over time pertained to his political strategy, as he progressed from pragmatic concerns like advocating for fair and safe housing for black New Yorkers during the 1920s to ideological pursuits of dignity in his "Afro-American" name campaign during the 1960s. Several books deal with the life and times of Caribbean communist intellectuals such as Moore and his comrades, British Guiana–born Hermina Dumont and Dutch Guiana–born Otto Huiswoud,[5] and most focus on political work. In this chapter, the discussion instead centers on Moore's Caribbean identity: his relentless campaigns for freedom from British colonial rule and for political federation for the English-speaking Caribbean as an intellectual progression and expansion of his communist activism during his early political career in Harlem. Despite being ousted from the Communist Party in 1942 because of his race consciousness, Moore continued to merge radical politics with his commitment to black racial progress. His anticolonial activism and campaigns for Caribbean political federation were natural extensions of his fundamental commitment to improving the plight of socioeconomically and politically oppressed people. Because Moore's religious, communist, and pan-Caribbean identities were so intertwined, the concepts of internationalism, diaspora, and transnationalism do not fully capture his political commitments. Moore's personality and interpersonal and professional relationships forged the link among his diverse political affiliations.

Moore's Formative Years

As an adolescent growing up in Barbados, Richard was extremely religious. His parents had left the Anglican Church to join a small Christian denomination called The Brethren, in which his father served as a lay minister. Young Richard soon followed suit, but as a member of the Barbadian Evangelical Christian Mission. He was so moved by the fire-and-brimstone sermon delivered by a visiting white evangelist from Knoxville, Tennessee, that he joined the church and began preaching the gospel of Jesus Christ with other young converts. Although his zeal and commitment to the Christian faith was undeniable, when fifteen-year-old Richard posed for the Christian Mission group portrait, his facial expression and body language hinted at a degree of cynicism concerning religious matters, which manifested itself, ironically, after he became a member of Ethelred Brown's Unitarian congregation in Harlem. Richard's tilted chin, unbuttoned blazer, and firmly clasped hands confidently resting on one knee suggested a self-assured, intelligently debonair, and even skeptical quality that seemed to belie his youth.[6] Young Richard's passion for existential transformation and just causes coupled with his impressive oratorical skills would bode well for a far-reaching political career to come.

Richard Benjamin Moore was born on August 9, 1893, in Hastings, Christ Church, Barbados. He was named after his father, a prominent building contractor who supervised construction throughout the island. Richard Moore, Sr. was known for his generosity and commitment to his local community. His practice of selling a loaf of bread for four cents instead of the standard six cents inspired a catchy rhyme that could be heard throughout the neighborhood: "R. H. Moore, six for four, / Keep starvation from the door."[7] Moore wrote that his father's commitment to community helped shape his own sense of moral obligation to improve the plight of working-class people, and indeed, his father, though a successful businessman, preferred to share his wealth with his neighbors rather than accumulate it for himself.

Financial hardship propelled Moore's immigration to New York, just as a declining economy would also push novelist Paule Marshall's parents out of Barbados toward Ellis Island twenty years later. With the hope of better jobs and opportunities, Richard was just a few months shy of his sixteenth birthday when he moved with his stepmother to New York City on July 4, 1909. Like many male Caribbean immigrants, he worked many odd jobs as an office assistant, elevator operator, and hotel bellhop until he found a job in a field that better suited his intellectual interests and talents.

While working odd jobs in New York City, Richard used his lunch hour to discover new books and to hear prominent black political orators in Madison Square Garden. Moore cut his teeth on radical speeches delivered by other Caribbean socialists, including St. Croix–born political activist Hubert Harrison, who would later become a mentor to Moore and to his colleague Otto Huiswoud.[8]

Harlem provided the ideal cultural milieu for Moore to nurture his socialist and communist affiliations. He engaged in dialogue with Caribbean and

American-born black intellectuals such as Cyril Briggs, Ethelred Brown, Chandler Owen, W. A. Domingo, Arturo Schomburg, A. Philip Randolph, and Harold Cruse. He worked alongside Nevis-born Cyril Briggs in the African Blood Brotherhood (ABB), a radical organization that advocated armed self-defense against racial violence from its founding in 1918 until its dissolution in 1925. After the ABB disbanded, most of its members joined the Communist Party. The ferment of radical politics spurred by the influx of Caribbean intellectuals in conversation with American-born black political leaders set the stage for Moore to become a prominent soapbox orator, socialist activist, and Communist Party leader.

Moore was only twenty-three years old when his interests in local politics and black culture coalesced in the form of a modest Caribbean-owned publishing company in Harlem. He formed a partnership with Isaac Newton Braithwaite, Orlando M. Thompson, and a few other Caribbean intellectuals to found the Cosmo Letter Company (CLC) in 1916. The CLC introduced the first multigraph machine to Harlem, and, as the Cosmo Printing Company, brought the first linotype machine to the district. The establishment of this small printing press reflected and fueled Moore's passion for political expression via the published word.

Moore had received a rigorous formal education in Barbados, and he continued in the English tradition of self-discovery, self-improvement, and education after his arrival in the United States. He read all of the classics and dabbled in various genres of writing, including speeches, academic essays, and poetry. His daughter Joyce Moore Turner would later recall that her father was always reading late at night and that books filled their New York apartment.[9]

The American tradition and rhetoric of self-made men also informed Moore's philosophical and social justice agenda. Frederick Douglass was one of the most influential intellectual role models for Moore. His autobiography, *The Life and Times of Frederick Douglass*, greatly inspired Moore nearly a half century after the book's first publication. Given Moore's love of literature—he was a bibliophile who left an expansive library collection in Barbados when he died[10]—he would have relished the revolutionary implications of how as a slave in colonial America young Frederick learned to read under the tutelage of the mistress of the house, much to the chagrin of his master. When Douglass observed the outrage of his master, who chastized his wife with a long lecture on the importance of keeping slaves illiterate and docile, the bold-faced expression of white supremacy spurred Douglass to learn even more.[11] Douglass wrote:

His iron sentences, cold and harsh, sunk like heavy weights deep into my heart, and stirred up within me a rebellion not soon to be allayed.... from that moment I understood the direct path from slavery to freedom.[12]

Like Douglass, Moore viewed education as a pathway to freedom. For Douglass, the context was American slavery; for Moore, it was fair housing for black New Yorkers and liberation from British colonial oppression in the Caribbean. Although the trajectory between education and freedom might not be as direct as Douglass suggested, the psychological empowerment that he gained by his mastery of the written and spoken word cannot be measured. His talents themselves challenged the fundamental ideology of white supremacy that undergirded the institution of slavery.

In this tradition of literacy as a pathway to freedom, Moore founded an educational center in Harlem in 1940 and named it the Frederick Douglass Historical and Cultural League in homage to his political and intellectual hero. Two years later, with the help of his good friend Loddie Briggs—who would later become his wife,[13] Moore opened a bookstore called the Douglass Book Center. He stocked the shelves with classic literature on African diasporic history and philosophy, and this Harlem institution thrived as an important intellectual center until a fire destroyed the building and its contents in 1968.

Moore's interest in sharing his knowledge and preserving the history of African diasporic peoples through institution-building calls to mind the fastidiousness of Puerto Rican-born writer and bibliophile Arturo Schomburg, whose extensive collection of African diasporic literature and artifacts endures today as one of the preeminent archives of black culture in the world. Moore would have agreed with the fundamental premise of Schomburg's classic essay "The Negro Digs Up His Past," in which Schomburg declared, "The American Negro must remake his past in order to make his future.... For him, a group tradition must supply compensation for persecution, and pride of race the antidote for prejudice. History must restore what slavery took away."[14] As a meticulous researcher, prolific writer, and voracious collector of books and material culture pertaining to African diasporic people, Moore shared Shomburg's commitment to education and preservation. In the latter years of his life, Moore also would bequeath his personal library to an educational institution for the benefit of future generations—the Library of the Centre for Multi-Racial Studies at the Cave Hill campus of the University of the West Indies in Barbados.[15] Moore's faith in education as a means of black empowerment was an extension of his radical politics.

Postwar Radicalism and the "Negro Masses"

When Moore arrived in New York City, he quickly immersed himself in Harlem's vibrant intellectual communities. Moore came of age during the height of early twentieth-century black radicalism in Harlem. He was one of the first black militants to join the Communist Party (CPUSA) in the late 1920s.[16] In 1925, the CPUSA started the American Negro Labor Congress (ANLC); most of its leaders were former African Blood Brotherhood (ABB) members. Moore represented the CPUSA as he lobbied for fair and safe housing for black New Yorkers from the 1920s through the 1930s. Moore argued that it was fundamentally unacceptable for citizens in the richest state in the wealthiest country in the world to be forced to live in such squalor.[17] In 1928, he delivered a "Statement on Housing" before the New York State Legislature, declaring, "Rent profiteering, overcrowding, unsanitary and *beastly conditions* are at their worst in the segregated districts where Negroes are compelled to live."[18] He called exploitive landlords "rent-hogs" and demanded repair of dilapidated tenements and lower rent for tenants. Moore recognized the compounded pressures of race and class as he represented the Communist Party by advocating for fair housing for the denizens of Harlem.

Like many Caribbean New Yorkers who pursued Communist Party membership, Moore joined the Harlem branch of the organization, the Workers Party, sometime in the late 1920s or early 1930s. In October 1925, he attended the American Negro Labor Congress (ANLC) in Chicago and served as editor for the ANLC's publication, the *Negro Champion*. Moore also served as president of the CPUSA's Harlem Tenants League, as an executive member of the Harlem Educational Forum, and as the New England organizer for the International Labor Defense (ILD).

Richard B. Moore was front and center during those heady days when Marcus Garvey stood on a Harlem stepladder so impassioned in speech that he forgot to take a break to eat and fainted from exhaustion. He emigrated from Barbados to New York in 1909, and soon after his arrival he joined the ranks of outspoken Harlem intellectuals. One of his comrades, Hermina Dumont Huiswoud, would later recall, "Dick had the capacity to speak as eloquently to an audience of two as two thousand."[19] Celebrated Harlem Renaissance poet Claude McKay was so inspired by Moore's forceful oratorical skills, that he dedicated a poem to him titled "You are the Thunder."[20] The admiration between these Caribbean intellectuals was reciprocal, because Moore often carried with him a copy of McKay's famous poem, "If We Must Die."[21] Published in 1919, in response to lynchings and race riots that raged across America, McKay's fiery words ignited a sense of determination among radical activists. Moore even incorporated this poem into some of his speeches. As his voiced reached a crescendo reciting the words, "Like men we'll face the murderous, cowardly pack / Pressed to the wall, dying, but fighting back!," the audience would erupt.[22]

Moore's Caribbean identity shaped his radical politics. He shared common ground with Ethelred Brown regarding their continued interest in and support for their islands of origin, long after they had immigrated to New York. While Brown's solidarity with his compatriots mainly took the form of philanthropic fundraisers during times of need, such as in the case of natural disasters and his membership in the Jamaican Progressive League, Jamaican Benevolent Association, and the People's Nationalist Party, Moore's political efforts in the Caribbean centered on ending British colonial rule and forging a unified, all-black government among the English-speaking islands. Moore was a stalwart orator who attacked British colonialism at its root—the ideology of white supremacy.

Anti-Imperialism

From the 1930s through the 1950s, Moore campaigned for Caribbean and African independence from colonial rule by challenging white supremacist notions of civilization and progress. In 1927, he appeared at the Congress of the League Against Imperialism and for National Independence. His speech before the Berlin congress took the form of a jeremiad. He suggested that European imperialists were devising "a new world war" that pitted race against race—a war that could wreak "devastation . . . far worse than the last World War."[23] Considering Moore delivered this speech only nine years after the end of World War I, the jeremiad was an apt rhetorical strategy because it capitalized on the prevalent fear of another Great War. "It is conceivable that the despised Negro peoples will be instrumental in tipping the scale of freedom," Moore admonished, "in favor of the oppressed classes against the imperialistic oppressors in the event of a war between the oppressed and the exploiters." Like many of his internationally minded foreign-born and American-born black colleagues, Moore linked the black Americans' social and economically oppressed status to that of colonized people in Africa and the Caribbean. Moore attempted to arouse fear as he urged white elites to think strategically by suggesting that their concession of a degree of political power to the lower social classes sooner might prevent their complete loss of political control later.

But Moore offered more than apocalyptic diatribes regarding the fate of the world if the working-class masses were not granted freedom and full citizenship rights; he also proposed resolutions. In his 1927 appeal for the liberation of African and Caribbean colonies, he called for the abolition of colonialism and the formation of independent black-run governments, and for the elimination of forced labor and unfair taxes, and he demanded freedom of speech and movement as well as the right to have access to quality education and to organize labor unions. Moore believed that the establishment of black workers' unions and cooperatives was the best means to achieve these objectives. He also emphasized the interconnectedness of liberation struggles throughout the world. Moore recommended the coordination of freedom movements throughout the African diaspora and demanded that workers of all races unite in the "fight against imperialist ideology: Chauvinism, fascism, kukluxism, and race prejudice." Although Moore's anticolonial activism centered on the islands of the Caribbean, his Communist Party training still pressed him to conceive of international political coalitions that transcended racial and cultural differences.

Moore went on to challenge European notions of civilization by depicting imperialism as the epitome of barbarity.[24] "Civilization is endangered by the *monstrosity* of world imperialism which is *mauling* all people in its *deadly claws*," he declared. By portraying European colonizers as destructive and indiscriminate beasts, Moore stressed the contradictions inherent in imperialism as an institution that allegedly reflected a nation's political progress but instead measured its moral depravity. Moore turned white supremacist ideology on its head as his "monster" metaphor suggested that European imperialists were guilty of the very same savage behavior of which they accused their colonial subjects. He depicted the European "Scramble for Africa" and colonial possessions in the Caribbean as the exemplification of social and moral backwardness and barbarity, instead of cultural and political progress as European imperialists professed. In addition to promoting international black racial solidarity, Moore also called for the union of "European workers with the workers in the colonies for a *common fight* against this *monster*." Thus, the actualization of full citizenship rights for European workers was inextricably linked to the liberation of colonized peoples in Africa and the Caribbean. Once again Moore's communist underpinning percolated through his language of anti-imperial protest.

Although Moore eloquently advanced his anticolonial agenda, his scathing critique of European imperialism was peppered with contradictions. He oscillated between depicting people of African descent as noble and accomplished or as somewhat unfortunate and "downtrodden" people due to no fault of their own. In a 1940 address, Moore called imperialism a "device of tyrants" who "seek to justify their predatory domination over these down-trodden peoples by declaring them to be unfit to "govern themselves." This is an astute observation regarding the contradictory psychology that propped up white supremacist "civilizing missions." However, Moore's portrait of the black and dispossessed was written from the position of victimhood—a status that Moore would later eschew in his 1960s essays that celebrated African intellectual and cultural accomplishments. But Moore rightly challenged the widespread belief that the industrial revolutions of European civilizations epitomized scientific, social, and political progress. "The whole specious theory of modern Empire," Moore continued, "of spurious trusteeship, and indeed of fascist domination, is founded upon this false and *monstrous denial of the fitness and ability of people to govern themselves.*"[25] After underscoring the hollowness of white supremacy, Moore proposed the right of "self-determination and self-government to the West Indian peoples" and reiterated the threat of war if European imperialists failed to heed his request. Moore called it "unquestionably necessary to remove this major danger of war from the Western Hemisphere."[26] In Moore's political matrix, the only way to avoid the catastrophe of a massive upspring of colonized people of color was the abolition of imperialism.

"The fight against imperialism," Moore declared, "is first of all an incessant struggle against imperialistic *ideology.*" He delivered this statement on behalf of the American Negro Labor Congress (ANLC) and the Universal Negro Improvement Association (UNIA) at The Congress of the League Against Imperialism and for National Independence in Brussels in February 1927. Like his contemporaries Ethelred Brown, Claudia Jones, and Marcus Garvey, black intellectual comrades and foes alike, Moore's most effective weapon to combat racism in the United States and European imperialism throughout the Caribbean was the power of his own words. "We must fight fascism," Moore continued, "the Ku-Klux-Klan, chauvinism and the *doctrine of the supremacy of the white race.*"[27] Moore linked the political struggles against fascism in Europe with the battle for social justice in the United States—more specifically, freedom from racialized violence—by identifying an iconic institution of white supremacy, the KKK. Such Double-V protests resembled those of other Caribbean intellectuals like Trinidadian-born Marxist political activist C. L. R. James, who vigorously condemned the US government's hypocritical stance regarding the realization of democracy at home and abroad. James was quite cynical in his criticism of America's democratic rhetoric during World War II as he wondered aloud why any black American should participate in a war against fascism abroad when he suffered such social injustices at home. Written in a voice inspired by Richard Wright's *Native Son* (1940), James posed a sardonically rhetorical question: "Tell me, Mr. President, what democracy do I defend by going to fight Hitler? Hitler is a vile criminal and should be driven off the face of the earth. But I have no democracy and the democracy I haven't got Hitler didn't take from me."[28] Richard B. Moore, Ethelred Brown, and Pearl Primus expressed similar sentiments.

Caribbean Federation

Numerous academic discussions of African diasporic anticolonial struggles have highlighted the interconnectedness of civil rights activism against Jim Crow racism in the United States with international communities of color who waged comparable liberation struggles against European colonial oppression. In contrast, Moore's is a unique connectedness to the plight of English-speaking Caribbean islanders as a Caribbean New Yorker who considered it his moral obligation to aid his "brothers in the Caribbean."[29] I suggest that this sense of solidarity was different from that of American-born blacks who imagined greater political empowerment via Pan-African political coalitions, because Moore's understanding of Caribbean brotherhood was rooted in experiential knowledge. The distance of geographic space and time spent away from his birthplace of Barbados gave Moore's quest for Caribbean freedom and Caribbean unity a particularly empathetic tenor.

Moore often wrote about Caribbean federation and anti-imperialism as one and the same because a politically united Caribbean implied independence from colonial rule. Although he used the terms "Caribbean Unity" and "Caribbean Freedom," his mission to politically mobilize his birthplace and neighboring islands centered on the Anglophone Caribbean and did not include the French or Spanish-speaking islands. This linguistic distinction was important in Moore's proposal for a pan–Caribbean identity as he underscored cultural commonalities shared among Caribbean islanders to construct a new and broader sense of nationalism. In 1947, Moore wrote that all Caribbean people "inhabit territories in a *common* Caribbean zone; they speak a *common* language; they already engage in some respects in a *common* economic life which is possible of far greater development; their culture is common in its fundamental patterns." Because of these linguistic and cultural commonalities, he concluded, "These people thus possess the characteristics of developing nationality and should now be encouraged by the British government and people to federate voluntarily in a free Caribbean Commonwealth with full control over their internal and external affairs."[30] The reiteration of the word "common" demonstrated Moore's fervent belief in the political potential of a united West Indies.

Like many writers for the *West Indian American* newspaper, Moore depicted Caribbean people as staunch upholders of democracy and deserving of political autonomy. By stressing Caribbean contributions to American society broadly and to the Allied forces during World War II in particular, Moore constructed an image of Caribbean loyalty and upstanding character in spite of colonial oppression, traits that deserved to be acknowledged and rewarded. Exploiting the military context, Moore described the Caribbean islands as a "curving *shield* around the Panama Canal" which served as "outposts to the approaches to the Americans."[31] Framing the Caribbean as the first line of defense during World War II was comparable to Moore's discussion of Crispus Attucks, a black merchant seaman who was the first person slain in the Boston Massacre. Moore quoted Irish poet John Boyle O'Reilly's praise poem for Attucks:

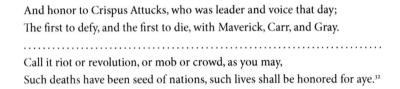

And honor to Crispus Attucks, who was leader and voice that day;
The first to defy, and the first to die, with Maverick, Carr, and Gray.
. . . .
Call it riot or revolution, or mob or crowd, as you may,
Such deaths have been seed of nations, such lives shall be honored for aye.[32]

In Moore's mind, Attucks exemplified honor and dedication to democratic ideals as he paved the way for American victory against British rule. "The resistance of Crispus Attucks," Moore suggested, "heightened the demand of various classes for freedom from British exactions and colonial domination."[33]

Moore further underscored the geopolitical significance of the Caribbean during World War II, adding, "The attack of German submarines upon Aruba brought the war directly to American soil and the Caribbean people suffered the first casualties in the hemisphere in that crucial conflict to preserve democracy." That is to say, Caribbean soldiers' willingness to take a bullet in the name of democracy should be worth something. In this context Moore did not mention his early reluctance to see Caribbean military men serve on behalf of imperial Britain because that detail might sully the image of Caribbean peoples' commitment to democracy. Nonetheless, Moore's initial reservations really implied the opposite—a dedication to unmasking all forms of political and social and economic oppression as he drew attention to the hypocrisy of European imperialists waging a war for democracy in Europe while they oppressed people politically in the Caribbean and across the African continent. In a similar vein, Trinidadian-born New York communist activist Claudia Jones wrote, "Democracy has been a farce to some 500,000,000 enslaved colonials under the domination of English rule." Jones's

1940 pamphlet, aptly titled "Jim Crow in Uniform," thoroughly denounced the double standard regarding the failure of democracy within the borders of the United States even as the nation waged a war under the banner of democracy abroad. She stressed black Americans' need for decent employment and fair wages as well as black soldiers' right to be treated as existential equals to their white counterparts. "Stories of Jim-Crow treatment of Negro men in arms seep through even the most conservative journals," Jones observed, and she also exploited the iconic image of black American mothers mourning over the loss of their sons.[34] The irony and sadness of this image called attention to the broad gap between American democratic rhetoric and practice.

Moore's commitment to the English-speaking islands' political future is particularly compelling when considering that he had lived in New York for more than three decades by the time of the publication of his appeal for "Caribbean Unity and Freedom" in 1947. This was more time than he had spent in his country of origin, Barbados, as he had moved to New York at age fifteen. Yet, Moore's construction of a pan–Caribbean identity was influenced by his New York experience. As he collaborated with Caribbean intellectuals such as Hubert Harrison from St. Croix, Otto Huiswoud from Dutch Guiana, and Ethelred Brown from Jamaica, the geographical and temporal distance from his birthplace helped to broaden his political imagination. Therefore, New York City provided a unique vantage point from which to imagine the political unity of Caribbean peoples abroad, as a degree of pan–Caribbean political solidarity had already been achieved via political coalitions in New York City.

Pan–Caribbean sentiments, however, surfaced long before the 1940s. Numerous Caribbean New Yorkers had expressed such hopes for pan–Caribbean solidarity during the first issues of the *West Indian American* newspaper in 1927. Although Moore never wrote for the paper, he was connected to its pan–Caribbean and black racial solidarity political agenda via friends and colleagues like W. A. Domingo, a Jamaican-born political activist and entrepreneur who contributed to the publication. In the second issue of the paper, published in November 1927, Thomas Bowen's letter to the editor expressed "hope that this periodical will be instrumental in effecting a better understanding between the people of colour in this land and the West Indies."[35] In the spirit of black racial solidarity, Domingo hoped the paper would serve as a vehicle of communication, education, and unification among American-born and foreign-born black New Yorkers. Domingo wrote a letter to the editor wishing the publication a long life and expressing hope that the paper would "serve as a medium for educating West Indians about islands other than their own, and Americans about all the islands, thus educating both groups at one and the same time and helping to dispel the ignorance and prejudice which is the greatest obstacle to inter-insular and interracial rapprochement."[36] Like Benedict Anderson's classic argument for the importance of print culture in fostering national identity,[37] Domingo believed the *West Indian American* would not only promote a sense of pride among Caribbean New Yorkers but also cultivate a black racial solidarity that transcended island-specific, cultural identities and American-born status.

This sustained sense of loyalty to the people and affairs of one's island of origin took numerous forms, and Caribbean New Yorkers even gleaned inspiration from the example of their European counterparts. One writer for the *West Indian American* urged readers to look to Irish immigrants as role models to better understand how Caribbean New Yorkers might improve the social, economic and political plight of family and friends whom they had left behind in the islands: "West Indians in America, mindful of the part Irish-Americans have played in the fight for Irish freedom, must do all in their power to aid the folks back home to better their condition."[38] During the early twentieth century, Caribbean intellectuals such as Ethelred Brown and Richard B. Moore would eloquently express and act upon a continued sense of allegiance to the inhabitants of their islands of origin in the form of fiscal aid in times of need and political activism in the cause of Caribbean independence.

Writers and readers of the *West Indian American* newspaper hoped the articles might foster pan–Caribbean consciousness and racial solidarity among American-born and foreign-born black New Yorkers. Staff writers like Clyde Jemmott reasoned that such political cohesion was necessary to confront racism in America as well as abroad. An article titled "All for One," which appeared in the first issue of the *West Indian American*, summed up this point. One reader noted, "If you live up to your professions as implied in the editorial article 'One for All, etc.,' I can see no reason why every man, regardless of his source of origin, should not consider it his duty to support the enterprise."[39] Pan-Caribbean consciousness was on the rise in Harlem, and the *West Indian American* newspaper fostered a sense of unity among Caribbean New Yorkers from the English-speaking islands.

Nostalgia and Interethnic Conflict

Although Moore became a naturalized citizen in 1921 and was committed to the fight for social justice within American borders, he also demonstrated a longing toward a somewhat idyllic and romanticized Caribbean. Unlike the father figure in Paule Marshall's *Brown Girl, Brownstones*, Deighton Boyce, Moore did not express a desire to return immediately to his birthplace after "catching his hand" in New York, but Moore's 1966 return to Barbados after his second wife's death did demonstrate a longing to return home after more than fifty years of residence in New York. In many ways, his homecoming to a free and independent Barbados was the culmination of over forty years of anti-imperial activism.

Although Moore was often evenhanded in his scholarly discussions of African diasporic history, he did not restrain his love for his birthplace and the Caribbean in general, and he often used effusive language to describe them. In 1947, Moore advocated freedom of the "several islands and areas washed by the waters of the *beautiful* Caribbean."[40] In another essay titled "Caribbean Unity and Freedom," Moore characterized the Caribbean as a "glittering and golden empire" for European imperialists. Such visual imagery conveyed the geographical and cultural richness of the islands. Moore's love of poetry is evidenced by his use of alliteration; the repetition of the "g" sound in "glittering and golden" depicted his Caribbean heritage in terms of unbounded wealth and cultural value. Moore's sense of nostalgia for an idyllic Caribbean shone in his image of an otherwise impeccably beautiful woman blighted by the history of racialized slavery that sowed political and cultural discord among its inhabitants. "For centuries," Moore lamented, "disunity and slavery have *disfigured the natural beauty* of [the] area."[41] This metaphor transformed the Caribbean's political landscape into a physical entity. Moore might have imagined a politically federated Caribbean that functioned with such a high level of cooperation and smoothness that it would rival Europe or the United States in its scope of political and economic power. But by the time Moore wrote this essay in 1964, his hope for Caribbean unity was being leveled by Jamaica's withdrawal from the West Indies Federation. Jamaica backed out of the political union once the nation achieved independence from British colonial rule in 1962, and Trinidad soon followed in 1963.

History loomed large in Moore's interpretation of the main hindrances to Caribbean unitiy and black racial solidarity in general. He identified "fratricidal division" rooted in the legacy of racialized slavery and colonialism as the culprits responsible for the lack of political cohesion among islanders. He urged Caribbean New Yorkers and those living abroad to transcend the "*crippling heritage* of varied division and manifold slavery, as the indispensable condition for freedom."[42] Perhaps Moore imagined the English-speaking Caribbean islands as a flawlessly functioning human body and each island was an organ that served its designated function; no thought was needed for digestion, blood circulation, transpiration, or even mobility because these functions were automatic. But because of the psycho-historical trauma of slavery and colonialism, this would-be-perfect body was instead "crippled." For Moore, chattel slavery and colonialism bred interethnic conflicts and stereotypes that often hindered political unity. He deemed this sort of long-standing antagonism manufactured by white supremacist ideology to be so pernicious that he compared it to a pathogen. He stressed the "urgent necessity of overcoming the virus" of ethnic divisiveness and the "*mental enslavement* which is all too dominant still in the Caribbean body politic."[43] Moore used the word "overcome" so many times that his entreaty for Caribbean unity and political autonomy echoed the steadfast optimism of American civil rights activists captured by the anthem "We Shall Overcome."

Moore revisited the topic of how the history of racialized slavery and colonialism hindered current Caribbean political mobilization. He suggested that "present difficulties appear then to stem largely from the conflict inherent in an order set up by adventurers, sea rovers, traders, plantation owners, and imperial rulers."[44] Moore blamed white supremacist slaveholders and colonists but failed to acknowledge African and African Caribbean elite collaborators in the oppression of other peoples of African descent. Although historical injustices and oppression certainly have created dysfunctional futures, one must also acknowledge the ability of formerly subaltern groups to transform their own political situations. This is where Moore walked a slippery slope. He failed to acknowledge the role that various African and African Caribbean elites played in contributing to the slave trade and the maintenance of colonialism. Just as Moore eloquently insisted that African and "Afro-American" history predated European contact with the continent and racialized slavery, he also should have applied the same historical periodization to interethnic political conflict among people of African descent, in light of the fact that interethnic warfare in Western and central Africa preceded European colonialism in the continent. Moore concluded that "the legacy of the Caribbean past still weighs like a mountain upon the living present."[45] Thus, Moore used the metaphors of malfunction, disease, and mountains to describe the psychosocial obstacles to Caribbean political unity, but he remained optimistic that Caribbean peoples would transcend the interethnic strife wrought by slavery and colonialism.

Masculinity and Cultural Conflicts

Moore was in many ways a "race man," but his collaboration with working-class whites demonstrated an existential and political longing to transcend the rigid racial constraints of Jim Crow America. He successfully worked across racial lines during his early Communist Party activism; however, gender divisions proved to be more impervious. Although Moore considered his first and second wives, Kathleen James and Loddie Biggs, to be comrades in the struggle for social justice and he worked alongside other Caribbean women intellectuals, the time and place in which he lived lent a raucously masculine tone to black intellectualism.

Even Moore's repeated recitation of Claude McKay's poem "If We Must Die"[46] was a markedly masculine endeavor. It is worth quoting the sonnet to illustrate this point:

> If we must die, O let us nobly die
> ....
> What though before us lies the open grave?
> Like men we'll face the murderous, cowardly pack,
> Pressed to the wall, dying, but fighting back!

To say the tone of this poem is militant and masculine would be an understatement. Written in response to the violence that ravaged the nation during the race riots of Red Summer 1919, McKay understood that the threat of death was a reality for black Americans, especially black men—from New York to New Orleans.

On one hand, the macho tenor of "If We Must Die" is understandable considering black men made up the majority of injuries and fatalies that dreadful summer. On the other hand, the blatant appeal to black manhood fails to acknowledge the powerful role that black women intellectual-activists, American-born and immigrant alike, played in the battle against racism and racial violence at the time. For instance, when the courageous, anti-lynching activist Ida B. Wells learned of the notorious race riot in East St. Louis, she immediately took a train from Chicago to the devastated city to see how she could help. In her autobiography titled *Crusade for Justice,* Wells documented how she served as a witness to the destruction of black-owned property and as an advocate for blacks who were unlawfully imprisoned.[47] In addition to the proactive efforts of such individuals, black women used social clubs to mobilize against racial violence. In August 1919, the Northeastern Federation of Colored Women's Clubs appealed to President Woodrow Wilson to put an end to the race riots in Chicago and requested that "all people, regardless of race, creed or color be protected from mob violence."[48] These are just two examples among many that demonstrate black women's contributions to social justice at the time. Thus, Claude McKay and Richard B. Moore's conflation between manhood and political activism at the time did not recognize the efforts of black women intellectuals.

Furthermore, Moore's membership in the African Blood Brotherhood, his work for the predominantly male Communisty Party, and his intense intellectual debates with American-born black male intellectuals such as A. Philip Randolph and Harold Cruse also reflect the markedly masculine nature of public intellectualism among Caribbean immigrants during the early twentieth century. Even the *West Indian American* newspaper's depiction of Caribbean federation, independence, and progress was personified by male figures. In one illustration, the West Indian "Federated Son" is a middle-aged black man who looks both dignified and devout, dressed in a black suit and posed on bended knee in the outstretched hand of God, implying the divine ordination of Caribbean independence from British colonial rule.[49] He is holding a large flag with a circle at the center, framed by horizontal wavy stripes. This flag, ruffled by the wind, represents the political union of the English-speaking islands. The caption under the illustration, which reads: "Let us pray for guidance"[50] juxtaposed with the kneeling "Federated Son" in the outstretched hand of God amid cumulus clouds calls to mind artist Michelangelo Buonarroti's famous depiction of the creation of man painted on the ceiling of the Sistine Chapel in Italy. Just as Michelangelo rendered Adam's muscular physique with an outstretched arm—reaching to touch the hand of an older but also muscular God—in his masculinist depiction of the Biblical narrative of the origin of humankind, the editors and illustrators for the *West Indian American* newspaper considered the difficult diplomatic negotiations required to achieve Caribbean federation to be divinely appointed men's work.

In another illustration celebrating the one-year anniversary of West Indian Federation, a cherubic, black baby boy in a diaper smiles in the foreground, while multiculural leaders from around the globe welcome the unification of the islands.[51] Although this male child is only a year old, he is strong enough to hoist a sphere larger than his one body over his head. The sphere lists all of the members of the federation: Antigua, Barbados, Dominica, Grenada, Jamaica, Montserrat, St. Christopher-Nevis Anguilla, St. Lucia, St. Vincent, and Trinidad and Tobago. As the dark-skinned baby stands atop the world, he is surrounded by all-male, adult figures who represent their respective countries through posture and style of dress. The illustration suggests that the United States, China, England, Canada, France, Japan, India, Russia, and Ghana all recognized and supported the union of the English-speaking islands. The caption under the illustration reads, "Amid internal strife and disunity I am walking erect with my eyes to the future and my trust in God. I will overcome, as others before me, the roadblocks, etc. I shall then look back, not in anger, but with pride, because I once suffered inescapable anguish from which I learned a valuable lesson."[52] Once again, the editors and illustrators for the *West Indian American* invoked their Christian God and their own maleness in asserting their faith in Caribbean solidarity.

Still another illustration on the front page of the *West Indian American* depicts two brawny, shirtless men pushing a gigantic wheel while being supervised by an equally brawny man, dark and handsome, who is dressed in a crisp white shirt and striped tie with his sleeves rolled up.[53] The caption under the man in the shirt and tie reads "America," while "West Indian Federation" is inscribed on the gigantic wheel that the two shirtless men are pushing. The open space to the right of the wheel reads "PROGRESS" in all capital letters. The bulging muscles of the men in this illustration parallel the muscular nature of political debates dominated by Caribbean male intellectuals throughout the early twentieth century. On the left-hand side, the backdrop behind the Caribbean American man is filled with skyscrapers, at the center behind the two burly Caribbean laborers is a lone palm tree leaning toward the right, while the right-hand side of the illustration is untilled, agricultural land. The composition of this drawing reflects the powerful role that Caribbean immigrants in America played in the battle to achieve political unity among the English-speaking islands. Richard B. Moore is a prime example of the Pan-Caribbean consciousness that Caribbean immigrants gained through working side-by-side with immigrants from other islands while in New York. This experiential knowledge lent an added authority in re-envisioning blackness and the destiny of the Caribbean.

Although these robust, hypermasculine images reflected the overwhelmingly male public face of Caribbean intellectualism at the time, women such as the Trinidadian Claudia Jones and Grace Caribbean American Campbell were exceptions to this rule by valiantly serving as members of the Communist Party USA. Still, after poring over letters and speeches penned by prominent political leaders throughout Moore's career, I am left with the distinct impression that many cultural clashes between Caribbean and American-born black intellectuals grew out of personality conflicts between men with big egos. Moore's contentious relationship with Harold Cruse is a case in point.

Moore versus Harold Cruse

Like all good public intellectuals, Richard B. Moore had a nemesis: American-born black political activist and scholar Harold Cruse. Cruse's disdain for Moore mirrored the political rivalry between Jamaican-born Ethelred Brown and American-born black religious leader Father Divine. Cruse accused Moore of being arrogant, "very superficial, evasive and a little bit dishonest,"[54] just as Brown portrayed Divine as a fraudulent leader who distracted black Harlemites from pragmatic political concerns.[55] The conflict between Moore and Cruse is particularly compelling because it highlights prevalent cultural clashes among native-born and foreign-born blacks that many black intellectuals preferred to ignore in the interest of racial solidarity. But like a wound that festers into a sore without a salve, turning blind eye to cultural clashes among American-born and foreign-born black New Yorkers certainly did not make the problem go away. Even 1970s Barbadian-American political leader Shirley Chisholm felt the sharp sting of outsider status, since her foreignness caused some American-born black intellectuals to shun her as an inadequate representative of her Brooklyn constituents. American-born black politicians, most often male, often insinuated that Chisholm's Caribbean background hindered her understanding of the difficult plight of blacks in America. "There is a strong undercurrent of resentment, at least in New York, where most of the islanders migrated," Chisholm observed, "It has never come out in the open against me, but sometimes I sense it."[56] Harold Cruse similarly emphasized his own American-born status to present himself as a more authentic political representative of black American political concerns compared to foreign-born New York intellectuals such as Moore.

Harold Cruse was born in Petersburg, Virginia, on March 8, 1916. The son of a railway porter, Cruse attended City College of New York but did not graduate. Although Moore left the Communist Party during the 1940s, Cruse—who briefly joined the party during the late 1940s—was most likely familiar with his prior service for the CPUSA and International Labor Defense. Cruse is best known for his controversial 1967 publication *The Crisis of the Negro Intellectual*, in which he devoted a full chapter to lambasting Richard B. Moore's Afrocentric politics, especially his campaign to abolish the use of the term "Negro." Cruse had most likely met Caribbean New Yorkers who gave the impression of feeling intellectually and culturally superiority to American-born blacks, because he placed Moore in a generalized category of pompous, pro-British West Indian immigrant. Although Moore took the moral high ground by refraining from publicly challenging or ridiculing Cruse, his nemesis's scathing assessment of his intellectual shortcomings undoubtedly stirred his ire. Moore's daughter, Joyce Moore Turner, would later recall that her father "felt the less you could say about Cruse the better."[57] Although *The Crisis of the Negro Intellectual* was accepted in many political circles as a definitive work on mid- to late twentieth-century black, Cruse's negative perceptions of Moore did not muffle his intellectual rival's voice. Moore still moved forward with his mission to upend general negative stereotypes of peoples of African descent by focusing on the power of names.

Cruse interpreted Moore's "obsession" with the battle over proper names to be a mere ploy to remain in the fray of influential voices among black political leadership. But given Moore's longstanding career as a political activist committed to controversial ideas, this is not a fair assessment. Cruse's attack on Moore was more than intellectual; it was personal, as evidenced by a 1963 letter he penned after debating Moore at a social gathering in New York. Cruse opened the letter: "My reasons for writing you are, (1) to take strong objections to certain attitudes you exhibited towards me . . . (2) To attempt to settle and resolve certain ideological differences."[58] Cruse took particular offense at any statement that Moore "presented with the prefatory admonition . . . '*I don't want you to forget them*.'" The tone and content of Cruse's letter suggested that he was more interested in defending his own intellectual ego than settling "ideological differences" between himself and Moore. Cruse took such personal offense at Moore's manner during the previous social gathering that he concluded that Moore considered himself to be intellectually superior to Cruse. Cruse went to great lengths to set Moore straight. He informed Moore that he did not posses a "monopoly on what is called in many quarters 'race consciousness' or awareness of the meaning of 'African heritage,'" and that numerous American-born black intellectuals held diverse and legitimate views on the issue of the most politically empowering proper name to ascribe to black Americans.

Cruse's letter caustically and eloquently captured prevalent cultural clashes between foreign-born and American-born blacks. He alleged, "There are many people from both the West Indies and from Africa who have the impression every American Negro grows up in this society in a complete vacuum where nothing is ever learned experienced or suffered that influences or alerts their views. As for myself, I believe that my experiences in the U.S. (north and south) Europe, North Africa and Latin America have taught me many things." Cruse defended the intellectual and cultural honor of American-born blacks by presenting himself as a shining example of homebred pride and intellectual accomplishment. He emphasized his personal travel experiences to suggest that foreign-born black New Yorkers did not possess a monopoly on *savoir faire* or cosmopolitanism. Although Cruse accused Moore of intellectual arrogance, his own counter argument to Moore's "Afro-American" name campaign suggested a degree of territorialism regarding issues of race in the United States, since Cruse boasted greater personal and historical experience with such matters: "When you discuss racial matters with me, *I don't want you to forget* that you are not talking to an unknowledgeable child. I am a *black person* of African descent, now past 40, born and reared in Virginia."[59] As if any doubt remained, Cruse concluded his letter with a tone of unequivocal resignation: "As for me, I no longer care to hear this argument over the word 'Negro' any longer and will avoid any involvement in it."

Cruse revisited this issue of cultural clashes among American-born and foreign-born blacks four years later in *The Crisis of the Negro Intellectual*. "This same motivational conflict between West Indians and American Negroes can be seen behind Moore's present semantic campaign," Cruse complained, "Today, the term *Afro-American* suggests and designates the Negro's African background; but it is also another way of expressing non-identification with the American Negro qua American Negro and his social status in America." Perhaps part of Cruse's ire stemmed from the fact that he and Moore had too much in common—mainly an intellectual fervor for revisionist history and a desire to set the record straight. Cruse was determined to have the last word in the proper name debate, saying,

> For many years there was another trend that favored *Colored-American* over *Negro* but who would object to being "Africanized" as an *Afro-American*. There is now a faction in Harlem who wants to dispense with *Afro-American* as too "moderate"—in favor of *African-American*. Then there is the ultimate integrationist trend that prefers simply *American*, without hyphenated qualifications (not to speak of those extreme nationalists who maintain that they have never ceased to be Africans despite centuries of separation from that continent).[60]

Even if Cruse overheard Moore utter an insinuation of Caribbean superiority, the undisputed fact remains that Moore demonstrated a solid track record regarding political commitment to causes for all black Americans. Given Cruse's opportunistic tendencies, he would have directly quoted Moore if such a pro–Caribbean stereotype had escaped his lips. Thus it appears that Cruse merely interpreted Moore's tone to imply a degree of cultural divisiveness. Unfortunately, Cruse made sweeping generalizations that stemmed from his own personal biases when he placed Moore in a box of supercilious Caribbean intellectual offenders.

Although Moore and Cruse did not get along, to say the least, Moore still was dedicated to overcoming cultural antagonism among Caribbean and American-born blacks, as evidenced by his diplomatic handling of the "Garvey Must Go" campaign supported by his colleagues Cyril Briggs and A. Philip Randolph. During the heat of the campaign during the mid-1920s, Moore refrained from any public condemnation of Marcus Garvey or personal collaboration with United States governmental entities that pressed for his

deportation. However, once the issues racial equality and black rule throughout the English-Caribbean had been legislatively settled, Moore roundly
criticized Garvey's main failure as a political leader: his lack of respect for
American-born blacks' unique political plight and a lack of respect for his
fellow Caribbean political leaders. "Marcus Garvey and many of the potential Afro-American leaders allowed themselves to fall into the most bitter
opposition to each other," Moore lamented, "and to engage in fratricidal and
destructive conflict. Due recognition of this basic and fatal error now appears
in retrospect to be the chief lesson of the rise and decline of the UNIA and
the leadership of Marcus Garvey."[61] Moore's analysis of the failure of black
political leadership in New York echoed the language he used to discuss the
major threat to Caribbean unity abroad. The adjective "fratricidal" implied
that Garvey and his American-born and foreign-born black political rivals
were brothers in the same family. Moore pinpointed Garvey's enormous ego
as the main hindrance to the achievement of a grand black political solidarity
that he so desperately wanted. In this context, the potentially successful family relationship turned into a dysfunctional and even murderous affair akin to
Cain and Abel.

Richard B. Moore's Communist Party activism, anti-colonial campaigns,
promotion of a pan-Caribbean identity among New Yorkers as well as Caribbean political federation abroad, along with his work in Africa-centered,
revisionist histories demonstrate the complexity of Moore's translocal self
identity and political voice. Although he worked as a Caribbean American
and Pan-Africanist, he still argued for a Communist inspired class consciousness that transcended race.

Conclusion

In addition to his attempts to bridge the worlds of religion and politics, Moore
also worked hard to transcend cultural differences and ethnocentric biases
held among Caribbean immigrants. In dramatic fashion, Moore demonstrated his New York-inspired, Pan-Caribbean cultural identity at a political
meeting among his compatriots during the latter years of his political career
in New York. At this meeting, Reginald Pierrepointe, a Barbadian-born trans-
plant to New York and journalist for the *West Indies News Service*, reported
that Prime Minister Sir Grantley Herbert Adams of the newly established
West Indies Federation "gave as enlightening a discourse on the ebb and flow
of the tides of West Indian affairs as could be expected" and that the prime
minister optimistically promised a successful "future unity of the embryo

nation." Adams addressed an "overflow audience" that included "some of the most important persons in American and West Indian affairs in New York" at the Carnegie Endowment Auditorium. Adams also thanked Pierrepointe and Barbadian-born political activist Richard B. Moore for urging Adams's first visit to Barbados to foster pan–Caribbean political mobilization; W. A. Domingo for writing part of the declaration that he delivered at the American Foreign Ministers conference in Havana Cuba in 1940; and Daisy Brooks-Johnson for generously offering her apartment as a meeting place during a New York City visit by the prime minister of Jamaica, Norman W. Manley. It was during this visit that they planned to found the Caribbean League of America, Inc., "in the early morning hours." Adams concluded by applauding the efforts of "men and women like these who dedicated themselves to the cause of West Indian Nationhood."[62]

The celebratory tone undoubtedly turned a bit sour when Moore posed a pointed question: "How can you, as Prime Minister, foster the development of Federal National Consciousness when you make such insular and provincial comparisons as: 'The Barbadians are the most intelligent and industrious in the West Indies'; 'The average Trinidadian would rather sing Calypso than do any hard work'"; and he sarcastically added: "A super-dynamic personality being a Barbadian, etc.'"[63] Adams attempted to defuse the tension as he gestured toward Moore and jokingly stated, "You wouldn't think that he is a Barbadian." Adams implied that Moore's intensely outspoken nature contradicted popular stereotypes of Barbadians as acutely dignified and reserved, but Adam's sarcastic tone also insinuated that Moore should welcome the positive stereotypes of uniquely high intellect associated with his own Barbadian ethnic group. However, Moore's political ethics would not allow him to accept the backhanded compliment. He retorted, "I am a Caribbean now—a Caribbean American."[64] Adams did not back down, but instead repeated the inter-island stereotypes: "Now, really, do you know any Trinidadian who wouldn't rather sing a Calypso than do any hard work?" Moore replied, "Yes I do. There is one right there—Mr. Clouden—and I know many others." Adams responded, "Would you deprive a man of the right to make a little joke?"[65]

For Moore, stereotypes were no laughing matter. If he were alive today, Moore would agree with the observations of Nigerian, feminist novelist Chimamanda Ngozi Adichie who stated during her famous talk at the convention for Technology, Entertainment and Design (TED): "The single story creates stereotypes, and the problem with stereotypes is not that they are untrue, but that they are incomplete. They make one story become the only story."[66] In other words, although the island of Trinidad is known for its Calypso music and its elaborate celebration of Carnival, there are countless other factors that also define Trinidadian culture—including its production of towering intellectuals such as C. L. R. James, Hazel Scott, Pearl Primus and Stokely Carmichael. For Moore, the celebration of black intellectual achievement, instead of frivolity, fostered a sort of cultural dignity that united the islands of the Caribbean.

The political union of the English-speaking Caribbean islands was finally achieved in 1958, after over thirty years of prodding by Caribbean political activists like Moore. He devoted his entire political career to bridging cultural divisions in the interest of political mobilization against class-based oppression, Jim Crow racism, and European imperialism. He articulated his translocal identities by working with myriad socialist, communist, and pan–Caribbean organizations while also acting independently, most often as a guest lecturer on labor relations in the United States, African history, and "Afro-American" history.[67] Whether working for the International Labor Defense (ILD) during the 1920s or on behalf of the West Indies National Emergency Committee, which he founded in 1958, Moore unflinchingly spoke out against social and political injustice. Moore worked hard to elevate the status and image of blacks in America, and during the 1950s, the broader political landscape pushed him to mainly focus on the issue of pan-Caribbean identity in New York and Caribbean federation. During an age of imperialism, Moore re-envisioned blackness by imagining a Caribbean occupied, owned, and operated by all blacks—free of British colonial rule. Moore's exceptional oratorical and writing skills were put to good work in this mission to uplift blacks in New York and abroad.

While Ethelred Brown embraced British colonial precepts of respectability, Richard B. Moore's translocal consciousness included class-based, racial, and ethnic political identities, which he expressed in speeches, articles, and poetry written from the 1930s through the 1970s.[68] Moore's intellectual biography demonstrates the complexity of Caribbean intellectuals' translocal identity as he juggled and combined sundry political agendas.

Unlike many black nationalists at the time, Moore did not advocate for a separate geographical state within the United States to be reserved for citizens of African descent, nor did he argue for the relocation of black Americans to land outside the country. He instead worked to help black Americans obtain full citizenship rights within United States borders. He lobbied for fair wages, improved housing, and for the abolition of social injustice, as demonstrated in his contributions to the legal and public defense in the famous Scottsboro Case. These examples illustrate the varied political strategies that Moore employed to improve the social and economic standing of the working classes—especially people of African descent. Richard B. Moore as a case study enriches the understanding of how wide-ranging and deeply contested black identity politics were throughout his political career from the 1920s through the 1970s.

Moore's Caribbean identity and immigrant status also influenced his formulation of black identity and political power, while his keen sense of displacement and dissatisfaction with the depressed social and economic reality of blacks in America compelled him to take action. Such political activism coupled with his writings on African diasporic history was motivated by a search for identity and an "Afrocentric" resolve that people of African descent should name themselves and write their own history, instead of leaving such vital tasks to European imperialists. Richard B. Moore was a self-taught historian and political commentator who loved to get the facts right and to set people straight.

Regardless of the chosen vehicle or venue, Moore was steadfast in his mission. He advocated for the rights of the working poor within the United States and for members of lower social and economic classes around the world—especially peoples of African descent. In his speeches and essays, he maintained that the legacy of racialized slavery in the Americas and colonialism in Africa and the Caribbean fueled contemporary assaults on humanity by way of limited educational opportunities for peoples of African descent, unemployment, low-wage jobs, unhealthy living conditions, and ethnic stereotyping. A proud and vigorous resident of Harlem all his adult life, Moore died in Barbados on August 18, 1978, just nine days after his eighty-fifth birthday.

Moore passed away the same year that Trinidadian-born choreographer and dancer Pearl Primus finally finished her dissertation to earn her PhD in Anthropology from New York University. Moore and Primus shared a great deal of intellectual common ground, epitomized by the Africa-centered consciousness that Moore articulated in the latter years of his career. Primus would have appreciated the fact that Moore discussed African and Caribbean independence as one in the same, grouping them under the rubric of freedom from white European colonial oppression. She also would have valued Moore's writing on the topic of ancient African civilizations with an emphasis on documenting the history of black philosophical and architectural accomplishments such as the construction of the pyramids in Egypt. For Moore, African history predated European contact with the continent and black American history started long before the arrival of slave ships at New England ports in colonial America.[69] Everything and everyone started in Africa, which he would later call the "Matrix of Mankind."[70] Black Power activist Stokely Carmichael also echoed this sentiment: "Although I was born in Trinidad, in a real sense it would be inaccurate—actually *incomplete* would be a better word—to call me Trinidadian. Ultimately our roots are in Africa, but in a more immediate and recent sense they truly are pan-Caribbean."[71] Pearl Primus and novelist Paule Marshall shared a similar Africa-centered consciousness.

Likewise, Richard B. Moore would have appreciated Primus's focus on African, Caribbean, and black American history as a means to uplift people of African descent in the US and around the world. Like Moore, Primus stressed the centrality of Africa as the birthplace of all civilizations, and she worked hard to counter negative stereotypes of blackness. For Primus, commitment to revisionist history was a divinely appointed mission. "I think it was really a mandate from the ancestors," Primus explained. "From early on, I wanted to speak in dance of the beauty, the strength and dignity in the heritage of peoples of African ancestry. But I also always felt strongly and still do that African dance is for everyone—the heritage of one people is the heritage of all."[72] With this humanistic philosophy, Primus led the way as Caribbean women artists-activists assumed center stage in the battle for civil rights.

CHAPTER 4

Pearl Primus and the Performance of African Diasporic Identities

Dignity in my past; hope in my future; I fight among fighters
for a new world; That will blossom in a bright new spring.[1]

—PEARL PRIMUS

In contrast to the predominantly male Caribbean intelligentsia that dominated the opening decades of the twentieth century, choreographer and dancer Pearl Primus's entrance into New York's artistic and intellectual limelight during the 1930s reflects a changing tide in Caribbean intellectualism, which was increasingly creative and noticeably female. Primus, alongside fellow Trinidadian-American jazz virtuoso Hazel Scott, stood at the vanguard of early civil rights artistic activism, and these two laid the foundation for other women to come, including writers such as Caribbean American poet and essayist Audre Lorde, Trinidadian-born novelist and playwright Rosa Guy, and Barbadian-American novelist Paule Marshall. Given this lineage of Caribbean women artists committed to the cause of social justice, it is important to remember that religious and secular New Negro racial uplift organizations led by Caribbean male intellectuals such as Ethelred Brown and Richard B. Moore set the stage for Caribbean women intellectuals' creative approach to battling racism in America and beyond.

Throughout World War II and post-war America, Caribbean women artist-activists created provocative literary and performance art to confront America's race problem head on. They used the theatrical stage to educate white audiences about African diasporic cultures—with the hope of engendering a sense of respect for and appreciation of the broad spectrum of philosophical traditions and cultural practices of black people in the United States and around the world. These women were warriors for social justice. I use this militaristic metaphor to draw attention to the ways in which black women writers, musicians, dancers, and actors framed their own artistic activism as a

Tammy L. Brown, *Omowale-Daughter Returned Home: Pearl Primus*, Mixed Media, 2014.

sort of political and moral warfare against the perils of white supremacy in all
of its soul-crushing forms, from Jim Crow in the United States to European
colonial oppression in Africa and the Caribbean. This notion of wielding art
as a weapon against racial injustice was particularly poignant in the historical moment. In an age when African American soldiers fought to prove their

manhood and patriotism on battlefields throughout Europe more than a half century before women of any race were allowed to engage in military combat, Caribbean women artist-activists waged their own local and national wars for democracy through theatrical performances at community centers, speakeasies, and concert halls.

From the 1940s through the 1950s, Pearl Primus was at the forefront of this artistic civil rights movement, which I term a campaign of "artistic democracy." While most scholars have used the term "modernism" to categorize this age of experimentation and marked movement away from realism and linear narrative form, especially in the realms of visual and literary art, I define this time as an era of artistic democracy because of the ground-breaking work produced by black writers, musicians, actors, and dancers who used their art to imagine a better world—a world free from racism and class oppression.[2] Democratic ideals also defined this time as black artists worked to dismantle racial segregation by joining multiracial performance art collectives and by protesting for the desegregation of venues where they performed. From Primus's choreographic renditions before integrated audiences at Café Society in Manhattan, to Baltimore-born actress Anne Brown's one-woman protest against segregated audiences at the National Theater in Washington, DC, Caribbean women joined American-born blacks in a creative and concerted effort to stamp out racism, both legally and in the practice of everyday life. Pearl Primus's life and work best illustrate this point. Although conservative political scientists might not recognize the political import of Primus's work because she did not shout her message from a stepladder on Harlem street corners or lobby for legislative changes like Richard B. Moore, I argue that Caribbean women artists turned the theatrical stage and the literary page into sites of political protest in their own right.

I contend that Pearl Primus's use of dance as a mode of political protest in Jim Crow America was particularly powerful because at a time when black bodies were criminalized, demonized, mocked and physically attacked, Primus used physical movement to reclaim the sanctity and dignity of the black body. Let us consider the terrifying context. According to the *Chicago Tribune* newspaper, between the years 1882 and 1918, 3,337 people were lynched in the United States, the majority of whom were black men.[3] Historical figures such as anti-lynching activist Ida B. Wells and contemporary scholars such as Crystal Feimster also have written about the under-reported and under-analyzed issue of rape as an act of terror against black women.[4] Although scholars are still debating the actual number of incidents of racial violence against black men and women at the hands of white perpetrators, the overwhelming reality that the safety of black bodies was in jeopardy cannot be overstated. Scholars of African diasporic studies, including Toni Morrison and Houston Baker, have written about the inadequacy of standard English to express the unspeakable horror of slavery and subsequent forms of racial and sexual violence. In a lecture titled "Unspeakable things Unspoken," Toni Morrison stated:

> My choices of language . . . my reliance for full comprehension on codes embedded in black culture, my effort to effect immediate co-conspiracy and intimacy . . . as well as my (failed) attempt to shape a silence while breaking it are attempts (many unsatisfactory) to transfigure the complexity and wealth of Afro-American culture into a language worthy of the culture.[5]

Thus, Toni Morrison understands the failures of the written, spoken and heard word in capturing the unspeakable trauma of racial oppression, and she attempts to address this issue by creating silences in the text. Scholar Houston Baker has described such efforts in Morrison's novel *Love* as a "discursive system replete with both dread silences, and 'broken word' narratives of resilience, spiritual retention, and miraculous survival."[6] I agree with Baker's assessment regarding Toni Morrison's mastery of ephemeral space and time in the way she uses literary devices such as non-linear narratives and magic realism as a multidimensional spiral that takes the reader closer and closer to the heart of a character's suffering. In contrast, Pearl Primus used the kinesthetic vocabulary of dance to bring her viewers closer and closer to understanding the physical, spiritual and psychological trauma of racism.

While Ida B. Wells used the written and spoken word as a weapon against racial violence and Billie Holiday belted blue notes in protest of lynching, Pearl Primus's use of dance as a "weapon for social change" added depth and power to civil rights activism during this era of artistic democracy. Through the visual and visceral vocabulary of bodily movement, she captured the psychological, spiritual and physical torment of the time and a longing for racial equality that was so intense, it could not be fully expressed in words. Primus understood the symbolic work of her movements as the dance connected her, as an individual, to a broader multiracial America struggling to find common ground. "I dance not to entertain but to help people understand each other," Primus stated, "Because through dance I have experienced the worldless joy of freedom, I seek it more fully now for my people and for <u>all</u> people everywhere."[7] In this context of rampant disregard and contempt toward the black body, Primus reclaimed and reframed the black body as a thing of beauty and intelligence. Given Primus's life-long promotion of mutual cultural respect as a democratic value, Primus's presentation of the black body and African diasporic cultures in positive terms was an effort that not only benefited black Americans, but it benefited the nation as a whole. Primus's vision of a better America required strategic collaborations with white and black artist-activists.

In 1941, Primus made history as the first black dancer to join the New Dance Group—a radical performance art collective founded by white leftists a decade earlier. Wholeheartedly embracing the troupe's guiding mantra: "Dance is a weapon for social change," Primus approached the theatrical stage with a radical, political mission—to shine light on the hypocrisy of American democracy by speaking the truth about the nation's race problem at home while it waged its "war for democracy" abroad.[8] Her choreographic protest against racial violence, "Strange Fruit," best illustrates this point. At the same time, Primus revolutionized the world of modern dance as one of the first choreographers to bring West African and Caribbean dance forms to American audiences. The titles of her early work, including "Yanvaloo," the Haitian "snake dance"—a dance of supplication, and "Fanga," the Ghanaian dance of welcome, which most likely greeted Primus upon her first visit to the country that she considered her spiritual and ancestral motherland, reflect the diversity of African diasporic cultural influences that inspired Primus's choreography.[9] The way that Primus's cultural identity constituted a mode of artistic activism is best captured by a pride-filled declaration that she made during one of her early performances as a solo artist: "Dignity in my past; hope in my future; I fight among fighters for a new world; That will blossom in a bright new spring."[10] The "new world" that Primus struggled to achieve was undeniably optimistic and idealistic because she dreamed of a world that was not only free of racism, but a world that affirmed the intelligence and dignity of all black people. In this regard, Primus was both a lover and a fighter. Armed with knowledge of African, Caribbean, and black American cultures, gained through self-directed study and academic training, combined with her own family folklore, Primus used her love for black people and black culture as ammunition in her fight against racism.

Primus's distinctive style of presenting Caribbean and West African dance in their most "authentic" forms to American audiences was a radical political statement, in and of itself, forged by her personal biography and the historical moment. As a young immigrant immersed in the rich intellectual and cultural climate of Harlem's African diasporic artistic flourishing, the avant-garde experimentation of cross-cultural bohemia, and the resounding revival of American folk art sponsored by the Works Progress Administration (WPA) of President Franklin Roosevelt's monumental New Deal, Primus inhabited an intellectually charged, and, I argue, an unprecedentedly egalitarian time in the history of modern American performance art. Through her choreography, poetry, interviews, and academic writing, Primus worked to kill the seeds of white supremacy by challenging the fundamental idea of black inferiority, which had philosophical roots dating back to the age of European Enlightenment. Given Primus's understanding of performance art as a kind of creative warfare against racial injustice and class oppression, we should understand Primus's no-holds-barred criticism of the failures of American democracy as her strategy of attack; whereas her proactive celebration of the diversity of African diasporic people and cultures constituted her strategy of artistic defense against Jim and Jane Crow attacks on black human dignity.

I want to reintroduce Pearl Primus because little scholarship exists on Primus's work, especially how her personal biography shaped her theatrical, political protest. Dance critics John Martin and Doris Hering have discussed Primus's explosive entrance on the New York dance scene in the early 1940s, but they do not take a long-view of her life and legacy, placing them in historical context. Primus's longtime friend and colleague Peggy Schwartz recently published a book-length biography of Primus, but it is more descriptive than analytical. Most recently, African American studies scholar Farah Jasmine Griffin published a brilliant chapter on Primus in *Harlem Nocturne: Women Artists and Progressive Politics During World War II,* in which she observes, "Modern dance had been ensconced in radical politics since its formation; traditional African dance sought to give expression to the community's history and aspirations. In creating a dialogue between these two forms, Primus helped to introduce a new context for the marriage of black aesthetics and politics."[11] Griffin's astute observation of the forward-looking synergy between Primus's kinesthetic vocabularies of modern dance and West African based polyrhythmic movement eloquently captures Primus's political and educational mission as an artist and activist. Because Griffin does such an exceptional job in covering the historical and political context that produced Primus's political protest, my treatment of Primus, in contrast, centers on how she leveraged her personality and immigrant cultural identity in the cause of civil rights. My discussion takes into account these studies of Primus in the realms of modern dance and African American studies, as I present both a personal and political portrait of the legendary choreographer, dancer, and scholar.

Pearl Primus was part of a broader movement of artist-activists who used the theatrical stage to fight for civil rights. By the 1940s, She and Trinidadian-born Jazz pianist Hazel Scott were forging new paths in the entertainment industry and public intellectualism, and Café Society in Harlem became one of the most notable sites of artistic activism. Both Primus and

Scott emphasized their Trinidadian cultural identity, in their personal lives, on stage, and in the public sphere, as a source of political power. While Scott drew upon her extensive Caribbean social networks to gain support for her husband Adam Clayton Powell's political campaigns, Primus developed her network of Trinidadian performance artists—including drummer Percival Borde, whom she would eventually marry—to better understand the history and cultural meanings of dance in the land of her birth. Such relationships enhanced the content of her choreography and subsequently bolstered her credibility as an anthropologist, artist, and educator. She also forged extensive artistic and academic networks throughout Western Africa to obtain source material for her choreography, and through the process of performance, she hoped to improve public perception of people of African descent. We've explored the example of Hazel Scott's career in the introductory chapter; so, now let us turn our attention to the life and work of Pearl Primus.

I argue that Primus's career as an artist-activist, from the 1940s through the 1950s, should be seen as a theoretical bridge between two of the most significant movements in the history of modern American art: the Harlem Renaissance and the Black Arts Movement. Through Africa-centered anthropological research and choreographic practice, Primus built upon the literary legacy of "Africa" in the imagination of Harlem Renaissance writers and extended the tradition of New Negro anthropologist-artists such as Zora Neale Hurston and choreographer and dancer Katherine Dunham. Like Dunham, Primus's positive vision of African diasporic peoples and cultures prefigured the "Black Pride" campaign of the 1960s Black Power movement by nearly two decades. How might we explain such political foresight? I contend that Primus's immigrant experience, bold personality, and participation in New York's avant-garde artistic communities endowed her with the cultural capital to advance such a pro-black message during this era of artistic activism. This is important because Primus's biography shows the power of family history and cultural identity in shaping the creative vision and political message of Caribbean women artist-activists during World War II and the postwar years.

Just as there are two sides to every coin, the flipside of Primus's boldly creative personality was a tendency towards irritability. Numerous diary entries testify to this truth. For instance, during one of her sojourns to western Africa, she wrote, "[I] feel better today—apologized for bad behavior the day before—work on itinerary—sleep—wash hair."[12] Her inclusion of "bad behavior" in a list of otherwise mundane tasks, such as sleeping and washing her hair, suggests that Primus desired to downplay her emotional idiosyncrasies, but she still felt compelled to include the detail, perhaps as a confession of sorts, to ease her own conscience. In this regard, we must remember that the fundamental nature of autobiography is usually to present the author in her best light. So, is it safe to assume that Primus's "bad behavior" was much worse than she documented? Copious interviews with people who knew her well can only illumine this point; however, we also could read her inclusion of "bad behavior" on a list of routine tasks as a Freudian slip suggesting that such behavior was common for her. Regardless, while Primus neglected to mention the nature or details of her "bad behavior," the point remains that at least she possessed the humility and self-awareness to apologize for whatever emotional harm she might have inflicted. In Primus's defense, her journal entries reveal she was devotedly self-reflective regarding this matter. Thus, she was not an unrepentant narcissist, although her interpersonal interactions sometimes reinforced the stereotype of the black, woman artist as "diva."

In her personal life, Primus also was brilliant, complex, and moody. For instance, the same "Afrocentrist" who found the love in her heart to embrace an entire people—black folk around the globe— sometimes could not demonstrate the same acceptance on a personal level. Her stepdaughter, Cheryl Borde, who lived with Primus and her father Percival Borde after they married in 1961, would later complain that she felt isolated in their home, confined to her basement bedroom, not allowed to join the rest of the family upstairs.[13] According to Cheryl, Primus's interactions with her were just as chilly as Cheryl's literal surroundings while living in the dank basement of her father and stepmother's apartment—amid costumes and theatrical props.[14] Although the "wicked stepmother" is a common trope in fictitious narratives of blended families, that image has endured because at its core is a grain of truth. Given Primus's diary confessions of her fickle temperament, I am inclined to believe Cheryl's account. Such personal recollections provide us with a multilayered understanding of Primus's interior self. I contend that exploring the interior lives of performance artists is especially important to more fully understand the humanity of the person beyond the stage lights. Primus's ability to leap and hang in the air, as if time were suspended, and her mastery of certain elements of emotional intelligence and performance that made her so adroit at "moving a crowd," sometimes made her seem superhuman. But accounts of her mercurial personality, such as stories relayed by Cheryl Borde and self-disclosures in Primus's own diary, reveal that she was just as human as anyone else. In turn, Primus felt great emotional distress during the time she was married to her first husband, Yael Woll, while having an affair with Percival Borde (who was also married), especially worrying about her public perception when she became pregnant with their son Onwin.[15]

Primus also felt sensitive at times regarding her media reception, sometimes feeling utterly vexed by the fact that white critics did not fully understand the intellectual rigor behind her kinesthetic expertise. Like Hazel Scott, Primus willingly assumed the role of an international civil rights activist; although she undertook this role with much verve and élan, it did not make the burden of race any easier to carry. During the height of Primus's career, she also endured the stress brought on by constant surveillance by the Federal Bureau of Investigation, which included her on a list of potential Communists or Communist sympathizers as her work for the New Dance Group, Workers Children's Camp (Wo-Chi-Ca), and other friendships with leftist artists and organizers spurred the FBI's suspicions. Primus still labored tirelessly to achieve her artistic and education visions of spreading knowledge and increasing appreciation of African peoples and cultures—a mission that her family nurtured even during her earliest years as a young girl in Trinidad.

From Port of Spain, Trinidad, to New York

Pearl Eileene Primus was born on July 1, 1919—though, for reasons of her own, she would incorrectly claim November as her birth month—in Port of Spain, Trinidad. Her father Edward was a merchant seaman, and her mother Emily Jackson worked as a domestic off and on. Although Pearl lived in Trinidad for only three years before moving to New York, three distinct memories of her birthplace remained etched in her memory. She recalled "bending down in the soft earth" as a young girl and playing with a "nest of coral snakes" that she had mistaken for beautiful coral beads. She remembered tightly hugging her father's neck as he dove deep into the Caribbean Sea, spying some kind of sea urchin that frightened her into letting go, sinking, then feeling her father's reach and rescue. Emily was so angry with Edward after this near-drowning incident that she did not speak to him for weeks. Primus concluded, "Maybe that's one of the things that influenced my fear of water."[16]

Primus also called to mind a "carnival creature" that leapt over the tall fence surrounding her yard, "terrifying [her] to pieces." Her mother reinforced this memory by telling and retelling this story throughout her youth.[17] The masked creature was a colorfully theatrical participant in Trinidad's annual carnival and inspired Primus's dissertation topic at New York University more than forty years later as she studied the educational use of masks among the Mano of Liberia. Primus's fascination with naturalistic imagery—earth, water, masks, and spirits—started with such rich childhood cultural experiences. Primus's fascination with nature is also evidenced in her diaries, which include countless doodles of trees, birds, lakes and other bodies of water as well as poems about the natural flora and fauna of Caribbean islands and African countries that she visited. Primus's early memories of Trinidad intermingled with family folklore and an idyllic Africa in her mind's eye to shape a language of power and protest throughout her career.

Young Pearl moved with her family from Port of Spain to New York in 1921, during the first wave of Caribbean immigration to the United States, which coincided with the height of the Harlem Renaissance. She grew up in a tightly knit Caribbean community in New York City, ran track and field in high school, and became interested in modern dance as a teenager. In an interesting twist of fate, Richard B. Moore's daughter, Joyce, and Pearl Primus were classmates at Hunter College, but they only knew each other in passing. Joyce Moore Turner recalled that she was merely taking the dance class for fun and to fulfill a gym requirement, whereas Primus was so intensely focused on the dance as an art form that she did not bother much with her classmates.

When Pearl Primus first moved to New York she lived with her family at 69th Street and Broadway. Her father was the janitor for the building, much as Trinidadian-born activist Claudia Jones's father found work as a maintenance man. Between the years of 1930 or 1931 the family moved to Hell's Kitchen, then several years later they found a building at 536 Madison Avenue in the Williamsburg neighborhood in Manhattan. The Primus family still owns this property today. When young Pearl was six years old, she attended PS 94 at 68th Street and Amsterdam Avenue. She and her childhood friend Sophie Johnson would wait for the bus after school on Wednesdays to take them to church on 65th Street and Central Park West for Bible study.[18]

Like Barbadian-American novelist Paule Marshall, Primus's sense of space and time was fundamentally nonlinear. History was always present as she sculpted her personal family folklore, travel experiences, and anthropological studies of West and Central Africa and Caribbean dance styles into performance pieces and lectures to present to American audiences. Her definition of "progress" was also nonlinear as it resembled the *adinkra* West African symbol *sankofa*—a bird craning her neck backward until her body becomes a full circle. Likewise, Primus proposed a historical and metaphysical return to one's African roots in order to move forward into a brighter and more confident future. Going backward meant revising narratives of American history that omitted the accomplishments of peoples of African descent. This process of return and revision would transport black and white Americans into a better, more inclusive, democratic future.

Pearl Primus's interest in dance and anthropology alike grew out of her own African diasporic cultural heritage. In the introduction to her dissertation, Primus called herself "a product of multi-cultures" and emphasized that she was reared by a "proud African mother in a strictly West Indian home within an American community."[19] Her views of cultural identity and difference echoed that of prominent cultural studies scholars, for she defined herself in contrast to a proximate other. Scholar Ann Pellegrini has observed, "Racial difference, like sexual difference, provides one of the instituting conditions of subjectivity. It helps to set limits between self and other, precariously identifying where the 'I' ends and unknowable other begins . . . the 'I' knows itself by what it is not. . . . But it is a self-identity that must always look anxiously outside for its confirmation, disavowing any relation between inside and outside, self and mirroring image."[20] Although most scholarly discussions of othering pertain to socially constructed categories of race, Primus mainly defined otherness in cultural terms. Like Jamaican-born Unitarian minister Ethelred Brown, she recognized intraracial diversity. Pellegrini's discussion of racial difference is instructive when thinking about Primus's understanding of ethnic differences. She viewed her household as distinctly Africa-centered and Trinidadian in contrast to her non-Caribbean New York neighbors.

Family folklore and ideas of cultural retention infused Primus's language of self-identity. She frequently discussed her maternal African ancestry. Her father and uncles were expert storytellers who recounted the sights, sounds, and textures of family travel experiences throughout the Caribbean and West Africa. As a young girl, Pearl especially enjoyed hearing stories about her maternal grandfather, nicknamed Lassio, who was a renowned herbalist and healer in West Africa.[21] Lassio rooted his medicinal practice in the worship of ancestor spirits called Orishas. In the popular black periodical, *Ebony* magazine, one journalist observed the strong influence of family folklore on Primus's performance, art, and intellectual pursuits: "One of her grandfathers was a voodoo doctor, an impressive gentleman whose feats are still recounted in the Primus household in Brooklyn."[22] Like novelist Paule Marshall's family friends, whom she affectionately nicknamed "the Poets in the Kitchen," for their preservation of Barbadian idioms and wit, Primus also found artistic inspiration through her own family's West African and Trinidadian oral traditions.

For Primus, this family lore provided an alternative, non-European vision of "civilization" and "progress." This worldview sharply contrasted with white supremacist images of Africa and its descendants depicted through vaudeville minstrel shows and World Fairs. While Irish and Jewish immigrants performed in blackface to mock African Americans and demonstrate racial solidarity with American-born whites and World Fairs presented Pygmies as spectacularly underdeveloped, both mentally and physically, Primus arrested these negative stereotypes and turned them on their head.[23]

Although her mother was born in Trinidad, Primus's Africa-centered cosmologies informed her description of her mother as "African." Primus's parents deliberately made African and Afro-Trinidadian cultural retention a priority via storytelling, dance, and food. In many ways, they recreated Trinidadian island life to the best of their abilities in New York, which led Primus to conclude: "Cultural differences were very obvious between life outside and inside the home."[24] Like novelist Paule Marshall, Primus emphasized the importance of growing up in a tightly knit Caribbean community in New York that shielded her from racism and bolstered her self-esteem. In an April 1946 interview, Primus recalled her parents' negotiation of the racial politics of their new home: "When my parents came to this country, they made the adjustment by isolating themselves. I was raised in a narrow circle that embraced church, school, and home."[25]

In 1946, Primus similarly recalled, "I guess I was fortunate in that race prejudice struck me late, about the time I graduated from high school. By then I knew enough and was grown up enough to adjust myself to it without becoming bitter."[26] This strategy allowed the Primus children to enjoy the material and social benefits of both worlds; their parents earned more money in New York and the family maintained many Trinidadian cultural values that were reinforced by social participation in New York's burgeoning Caribbean communities.

In a 1946 article, Primus further outlined the differences between racial discrimination in the United States and class-based divisions in the Caribbean. She said, "I was born in the West Indies and did not run into race discrimination until late in life. In the Indies there is no color system, but a class system. A black person with money and prestige is in the top brackets. A white peddler remains a white peddler."[27] Although Trinidad's class-based social hierarchy teemed with its own unique set of injustices, the Primuses still preferred Trinidad's allegedly "race-blind" classism to the race-based prejudice that they encountered in the United States. So, Primus's parents tried to recreate this notion of the lesser of two evils by keeping Pearl and her siblings close to home. Unlike Paule Marshall, Primus neglected to acknowledge that although Caribbean populations were mainly black, members of the upper social and economic classes were quite light-skinned. Thus, although a blatant binary system of white versus black racism did not exist in the Caribbean, the political economy still revealed intense suffering due to the legacy of racialized

slavery and colonialism that produced a broad spectrum of skin color grada-
tions overlapping with class and upheld by light skinned Caribbean elites.

But Primus also was sure to note that although her family abhorred white
supremacy, they still remained open-minded. "My parents taught me not
to indict the whole white group if one white person discriminated against
me. It was a valuable lesson,"[28] Primus recalled. Her first visit to the southern United States to study the movements of sharecroppers left her feeling
"licked." "Everything looked ugly to me there—the Negroes because of their
hunger and feeling of inferiority, the whites because of their fear and hunger."
Although her encounters with racism and intense poverty left her feeling "an
absolute hollowness . . . for months" after her return to New York, Primus
would later recall several kind deeds proffered by white southerners, which
stirred her memory of her parents' advice to resist the temptation to group all
whites in the same category.[29]

Primus mingled with well-known American-born and foreign-born black
entertainers and political activists, including Paul Robeson, Hazel Scott, and
Billie Holiday. A mature Primus would later humorously recall the humiliat-
ingly dramatic start to her performance career as a solo artist. She was barely
nineteen when she approached one of the programmers at Café Society in
Greenwich Village to audition, and he was not at all impressed by her appearance. Her simple skirt and bobby socks conjured an image of drab naïveté
rather than the fabulously dynamic personality and talent needed to impress
Café Society goers. But Primus insisted that she be given a chance, and she
danced with such skill and enthusiasm at her audition that she earned a cov-
eted slot as a Café Society entertainer. Primus reminisced: "My first night at
Café Society Downtown, my music failed. I was brand new, so I used records.
Eddie Heywood put one on, and I counted to three and jumped on. Silence.
The third time I tried, I dissolved in tears, and this huge man emerged from
the audience. "Aren't you the person who broke up my home?' he asked. It was
Paul Robeson. I'd taught his son to do the Lindy Hop at camp and the child
had gone home and smashed up all the furniture dancing. But Robeson made
me get up and keep dancing that night."[30] Jazz luminary Billie Holiday also
was present that night. She shouted encouragement from the back of the jam-
packed room, and Primus danced and danced. She performed three shows
each night for ten months. When music lovers came to hear famed guitarist
and songwriter Josh White and Trinidadian-born pianist Hazel Scott, they
also would have the pleasure of witnessing one of Primus's dance concerts.
Primus inherited the energy and synergy of Harlem Renaissance greats such
as Paul Robeson and Billie Holiday, took up the mantle of artistic activism,
and carried it throughout the remainder of her career.

The Harlem Renaissance and Beyond

In many ways, Pearl Primus is a daughter of the Harlem Renaissance. When she moved to New York City as a toddler, New Negro declarations of black intelligence, sophistication, and cosmopolitanism as expressed through poetry, music, and the visual arts was in full swing. As a up-and-coming performance artist and intellectual in her own right, Primus "cut her teeth" on the poetry of Langston Hughes, the Jazz renderings of Billie Holiday, and the theatrical work and radical example of legendary scholar-athlete, actor, and activist Paul Robeson. Her creative vision, kinesthetic vocabulary, and choreographic ability expanded under the tutelage of American-born blacks, African immigrants (*e.g.*, Asadata Dafora), Caribbean and white American instructors. As a young adult, Primus took dance lessons with famed Trinidadian-born choreographer Beryl McBurnie, and performed alongside compatriot Jazz pianist Hazel Scott at Café Society. Primus also took dance lessons with groundbreaking white choreographers of modern dance such as Martha Graham, Doris Humphrey, and Charles Weidman. She gleaned inspiration from New York's vibrant artistic communities, her own family folklore, and Trinidadian cultural roots to create work that pushed the boundaries of modern dance and the social strictures of race and class in pre-Civil Rights era America. Examples? Primus used her artistic vision and her African diasporic cultural identity as ammunition in the battle for civil rights.

Pearl Primus's African-inspired performance art was not spontaneously generated in a vacuum. She came of age during the wake of the Harlem Renaissance, and her incorporation of imagined African dance elements into her choreography was a practice that many at the time termed "primitivism." Primus frequently mythologized Africa in ways comparable to poet Countee Cullen, whose poem "Heritage" begins:

> What is Africa to me
> Copper sun or scarlet sea
> Jungle star or jungle track
> Strong bronzed men, or regal black.[31]

Cullen used colors like "copper," "scarlet," and "bronzed" to paint a sultry and idyllic portrait of the African landscape and to sensually describe its inhabitants, more specifically, African men. The words "jungle," "strong," and "regal" depict Africa as a land where naturally rugged royalty thrived. Primus similarly extolled a monolithic "Africa" in her professional debut, "African Ceremonial" (1943). Her costume and stylized movements suggested an exoticized gaze. Primus could have performed "African Ceremonial" in everyday West African women's attire like an oversized top, sarong skirt, and head-wrap or varied her costume, but she wore a sleeveless black leotard, midriff exposed, and layered with a short raffia skirt. This costume was a variation on the same theme of scantily clad "primitivists" like Tarzan in Edgar Rice Burroughs's 1912 novel. Primus also used props like spears and beaded gourds to conjure the sights and sounds of "Africa." Although she claimed to represent African dance in its most authentic form, she exaggerated jumps and turns for dramatic purposes. Harlem was a transformative locale in shaping Primus's civil rights activism, which paradoxically included this mythologized view of African people and cultures.

Primus's proximity to Harlem Renaissance artistic production wasn't the sole impetus behind "primitivist" choreography like "African Ceremonial;" the broader modern dance scene in New York also shaped her work. Leading choreographers and dancers like Martha Graham, Jane Dudley, and Asadata Dafora began performing "primitivist" choreography in the 1930s. Although the latter part of Primus's career focused on West and Central African and Caribbean dance forms almost exclusively, Primus still squarely placed herself in the midst of the early modern dance movement in New York City. She reminded her audience: "My dances aren't all African and Caribbean inspired," she said. "Aside from the Ruth Benedicts and the Franz Boases, I've studied with Graham, Humphrey, Weidman and Holm. When they had four people in their class I was there."[32] Indeed Primus's expression of her civil rights activism through the power of dance was rooted in anthropological vocabularies learned under the tutelage of scholar Franz Boas during her studies at Columbia University as well as in a kinesthetic vocabulary learned during intensive study with leading modern dance instructors.

The New York worlds of performance and literary art were synergistic as artists in both realms took on African-inspired themes, but Primus's view of her African heritage was more affirmative than most of her contemporaries. Although poet Countee Cullen romanticized the African topography, culture, and people, he also implied that Africa was a spiritually backward continent. At this juncture, Primus strongly dissented, for she never condemned any African religion, social structure, or political system. By stressing the sanctity of non-Westernized African cultures, she contested white supremacist notions of the uncivilized "other" and constructed new black identities based on Africa-centered consciousness, mutual cultural respect, and humanism.

Insular and vibrant artistic communities in Manhattan and Harlem also shaped Primus's civil rights activism. While holding on to her Trinidadian heritage, she embraced the world of multi-racial, leftist intellectualism at Café

Society in Greenwich Village as well as Café Society Uptown in Harlem. She grew as an artist-activist-intellectual in the company of like-minded souls at Hunter College, the 92nd Street YMCA, and even a leftist summer camp called Worker's Children Camp, better known as Wo-Chi-Ca.

Primus's work as a principal dancer with the integrated New Dance Group and as a counselor and dance instructor at Wo-Chi-Ca Camp, founded in New Jersey during the Great Depression, placed her at the center of leftist artistic projects at a very young age. Wo-Chi-Ca Camp photos of black and white children playing, dancing, talking and learning from a multiracial staff echo the same spirit of racial equality and mutual respect seen in photographs of Primus with white classmates at Hunter College and fellow performers of the New Dance Group. These experiences laid the foundation for Primus's role as "cultural ambassador" to the New York Public Schools where she would later, from the 1970s through the mid-1990s, assume responsibilities as instructor and demonstrator.

Primus grew up in a household filled with music, and in numerous interviews throughout her performance career she thanked her mother for instilling in her the love of dance. Famed Harlem Renaissance poet Langston Hughes was one of Primus's mentors, and her later solo work throughout the 1940s reflected her rich personal experience—coming of age as a performer and woman in the midst of such vibrantly diverse intellectual expression and cultural production. To say Hughes was a fan of Primus would be an understatement. He understood Primus's importance as a singular, kinesthetic complement to the written and spoken intellectualism of the Harlem Renaissance when he observed, "Every time she leaped, folks felt like shouting. Some did. Some hollered out loud."[33] Hughes's witness to the visceral affect that Primus had on her audiences is both poignant and insightful. While political speeches, poetry, and jazz music dominates popular and academic discussions regarding the political import of the New Negro and the civil rights movement, I, like Hughes, cannot emphasize enough the power of Primus's singular presence as a dancer. In other words, in addition to Marcus Garvey's legendary marches throughout 1920s Harlem that displayed black consciousness, power, and solidarity, Primus's choreography powerfully presented these same themes on the theatrical stage from the late 1940s onward.

Primus's Solo Career

By the mid 1940s, Primus stood poised—ready to pursue her career as a solo choreographer and dancer. She enthusiastically donned the mantle of a radical, artist activist among a vanguard of Caribbean women literary and performance artists centered in the battle for civil rights. On Wednesday October 4, 1944, Primus made her debut at the Belasco Theatre in midtown Manhattan. She had already earned critical acclaim as a principal dancer in the New Dance Group, but this Broadway showcase signaled her arrival as solo artist and principal choreographer. For the greater part of the soiree, Primus took full command of the stage—expressing a unique vision of her own African diasporic identity in motion. Alternately accompanied by a quintet of male dancers and a five-piece jazz band, Primus explored the rites and rituals of the Belgian Congo in "African Ceremonial" and riffed off of her own Caribbean roots in a Vodun-inspired piece titled "Yanvaloo," a ritualistic dance of the snake or spirit Damballah that literally means "I beg of You." Perhaps this dance of supplication was a direct plea to the white audience of well-to-do theatergoers to acknowledge the intelligence, beauty, and diversity of black cultural experiences in America and throughout the world. Primus's presence on that stage not only marked her personal achievement as a gifted dancer and budding intellectual, but it also reflected the changing times in a nation close to winning a "war for democracy" abroad, while racial injustices persisted at home. The United States was a nation in love with things considered "primitive." The undulating motions of West African-based dances such as the "Yanvaloo" conjured faraway lands of exotic peoples who still fit the hierarchy of American empire and alleged African inferiority, but Primus's individual training with the racially integrated New Dance Group, whose motto was "Dance is a weapon for social change," her solo dance protests of racial violence in America, and her work documenting the triumphs and trials of black Americans in the south, demonstrate her commitment to tell the truth about America's race problem. Her mission to revision blackness in positive terms, such as in the Belasco Theater performance, suggests a degree of openness, especially among white liberals, to hear Primus's message of reform.

Although Primus was only twenty-five years old when she made her Broadway debut, the confidence she drew from her own cultural identity gave her wisdom beyond her years. On the Belasco stage, Primus did not hold back; her repertoire was expansive and ambitious as it followed the contours of her literal and imagined travels throughout Africa, the Caribbean, and the southern states of America. Primus danced to the soul-wrenching sounds of South Carolina–born guitarist and folksinger Josh White, whom Primus met after he moved to New York in 1931, and she danced to music composed by master pianist Mary Lou Williams in a piece titled "Study in Nothing." All of these artistic collaborations demonstrate Primus's keen ability to incorporate the culture of her Trinidadian heritage, her family's West African folklore, and her own independent studies of African, Caribbean, and black American cultures. In typical Primus style, she incorporated the spoken word into her dance performance as she declared, "Dignity in my past; hope in my future; I fight among fighters for a new world; That will blossom in a bright new spring."[34] The "new world" that Primus envisioned was one free of *de facto* and *de jure* racism, a social environment that affirmed the dignity of black people in the United States and abroad.

Dance critic John Martin wrote in the *New York Times* the following day that Primus's Broadway debut was "all fine and authentic in spirit, well composed and danced with great technical skill as well as dramatic power."[35] He was put off, however, by Primus's use of a narrative voice, performed by New York-born, black actor Gordon Heath, between choreographic sets in order to "tie the various numbers together into a kind of over-all picture of the Negro." I, however, contend that Primus's incorporation of a narrative voice was appropriate and speaks volumes regarding her ambitious historical scope and educational mission.

Building upon the vocabularies of West African art, Trinidadian carnival, and the movements of American-born black agricultural workers, Pearl Primus used the language of dance to combat racism and revise negative stereotypes of blackness. She articulated her "civil rights activism" through dance and scholarly writing based on her anthropological research. Primus embraced West African spiritual practices of the worship of multiple deities called Orishas, and believed that her ancestors spoke to her in her dreams. While most scholarly studies of the New Negro have focused on the literature of the Harlem Renaissance and predominantly male, radical public intellectuals, black women intellectuals, artists, and activists re-envisioned blackness in affirmative terms in the midst of continued white supremacist attacks on black folk's humanity.[36]

"Strange Fruit"

More than a year before her performance at the Belasco, Primus had arrested the attention of the arts world with her radical interpretation of the song "Strange Fruit." On February 14, 1943, Pearl Primus commanded the stage at the 92nd Street YMCA in Manhattan—performing solely to the words of the famous protest song for the first time. Written by Abel Meeropol (a.k.a. Lewis Allen) and popularized by Billie Holiday, "Strange Fruit" is arguably the best-known example of anti-lynching artistic activism in the history of the United States.[37] Primus deliberately chose a lyrical soundtrack for her choreography that already carried moral weight in the context of political protest of racism in America. She choreographed a thoroughly modern dance solo and performed it to the poem's words alone—without the accompaniment of instrumental music. Its awed and radicalizing reception was comparable to when Billie Holliday first sang the haunting lyrics before an integrated audience at Café Society in Greenwich Village, NY, in 1939.[38]

I contend that Primus's choreographic rendering of "Strange Fruit" in contrast to Billie Holiday's vocal performance, struck a chord with viewers on a visceral level. In place of music, Primus used the pounding, percussive sounds of her body, as she literally through herself onto the floor, to punctuate the spoken words. This dance differed from her prior repertoire in both form and content. In contrast to the uplifting tenor of "Yanvaloo," "Fanga," and "African Ceremonial," in which Primus celebrated the Africa of her imagination, "Strange Fruit" was stark, contorted, and traumatic. Scholar Farah Jasmine Griffin described Primus's choreography to "Strange Fruit" as follows:

> Gone were the leaps. In their place, there is a body on the floor, a writhing, distraught human figure, reaching to the tree one moment, fallen down in twists and turns the next. And running but getting nowhere: running in a circle.[39]

Contrary to popular belief, the perspective of the dancer is of a white man or woman who participated in the lynching of a black person (most likely a man). The dance is set after the lynch mob has dispersed, and a sole viewer or executioner reflects on the horror of what just occurred. Primus's contorted and violent movements reflected the psychological and emotional torment of the white viewer or executioner.[40] This was an interesting perspective to portray because most civil rights activism focused on the violence Jim Crow inflicted on black Americans, but Primus also stressed how white supremacy and racial violence damaged its perpetrators.[41] In a 1944 article, Primus explained, "In mobs, you have the mass mind to treat . . . my dance shows a member of the mob as he leaves the scene of the crime. He looks back at the black body hanging by its neck and reviles himself for what he has done. It is not a beautiful dance."[42] Primus's radical interpretation of "Strange Fruit" encouraged passionate and renewed critiques of racial violence in the United States.

Primus's adaptation of "Strange Fruit" was one among many interesting and intimate collaborations with New York Jews. Although most of us are only aware of Primus's marriage to Trinidadian-born drummer and actor Percival Borde, Primus had been married before. In 1950, she married her first husband, Yael Woll, the son of Russian Jews who had immigrated to New

York. Woll's father was principal of the Downtown Talmud Torah School, where he also taught Hebrew, and "his mother was the daughter of a rabbi." Pearl and Yael met during the early 1940s in New York because they ran in overlapping artistic, leftist circles. When the couple announced their marriage plans, Yael's family was opposed, but the Primuses were more accepting. Yael would later recall, "They did the best they could with a white face in the house and in time they got more and more used to it." During the early years of their partnership and marriage, Yael Woll assisted Pearl Primus in lighting design and stage management. He handled logistical details, including transportation for Primus and her small band of dancers."[43]

According to Pearl Primus, she also had a genealogical connection to Jewish culture because her paternal grandfather was Jewish. Her son, Onwin Borde, later claimed that his grandfather "Herr Primus was a rabbi, a very upper-class, Ashkenazi Jew. I know all about Yom Kippur. I had a Jewish grandfather."[44] Whether this bit of family folklore was myth or reality, the point remained that Primus had close personal and professional relationships with New York Jews within the vibrant, cross-cultural artistic and intellectual life of the city at the time.

Primus's performance of "Strange Fruit" catapulted her into the pantheon of black women artist-activists. Primus's radical performance also attracted the attention of the House of Un-American Activity Committee, which listed her as a potential Communist although she was never a member of the party. Unlike fellow Trinidadian pianist and actress Hazel Scott, HUAC never required Primus to formally appear in a court trial before the committee. Despite FBI surveillance, Primus continued to work within a radical political paradigm. Her civil rights activism was nurtured through interactions with members of New York's intelligentsia because their progressive politics provided the vocabulary and intellectual space for Primus to fully express her own multi-cultural identity.

"Hard Time Blues"

Although it took years for Pearl Primus to acquire enough funding to travel abroad to conduct anthropological research, as World War II neared its close, Primus traveled extensively throughout the southern United States and found inspiration in the mundane. In the summer of 1944, she conducted intense ethnographic research in rural black communities in Georgia, Alabama, and South Carolina. As an anthropologist and "participant observer," she assumed the role of an anonymous migrant worker. When asked why it was necessary

to travel to the South instead of observing black Christian devotional practices in New York churches such as Abyssinian Baptist, Primus responded
that she could go to the Clayton Powell's church because he "follow[ed] the
revival pattern," but she was leery of this cosmopolitan context because she
believed Powell's intellectualism might hinder the authenticity of the church
service. Primus continued, "I could go to other churches where there is even
less intellectual development, but [the service] may be diluted."[45] Primus's
self-taught and formally learned anthropological underpinnings led her to
embrace this interpretation of rural cultures as more authentic, dignified, and
static compared to the cultures of fast-paced urban areas. So, like anthropologist Zora Neale Hurston and prominent black gay professional dancer
Bill T. Jones who came after her,[46] Primus traveled throughout the South and
immersed herself in the religious and work cultures of rural folk to inform
her choreography. During the week, she worked alongside black laborers toil-
ing in cotton fields and studied their everyday movements, and on Sundays
she participated in black Christian worship services to document elements of
West African cultural retention in rural black devotional practices. Such "participant observation" provided primary source material from which Primus
choreographed and danced numerous pieces exploring themes of racial and
class oppression. She based her choreography to the song "Hard Time Blues"
on this anthropological research.

"Hard Time Blues" is Primus's working-class manifesto based on a song
about southern sharecroppers by folksinger Josh White. Primus and Josh
White's creative partnership was a natural one. Both were regular performers
at Café Society, where they intermingled with a wide array of radical black
and white artists, activists, and appreciators of art as participants in the progressive, interracial gatherings at the forefront of New York bohemia. When
White released "Hard Times Blues" in 1941, Primus was still dancing with the
New Dance Group, and Josh White's class consciousness resonated with her.
White and Primus shared an interest in the plight of black sharecroppers,
which is exemplified by the third stanza of the song "Hard Time Blues":

Now the sun a-shinin' fourteen days and no rain.
Hoein' and plantin' was all in vain.
They had hard, hard times, Lord, all around,
Meal barrel's empty, crops burned to the ground.[47]

When Primus performed "Hard Time Blues" throughout the mid-1940s, postwar prosperity was on the horizon but Depression era hardships lingered,
especially for black Americans. This modern dance piece captured the spirits

of hard-pressed black American sharecroppers in its staccato and frenzied movements.[48]

Thankfully, the documentary film *Free to Dance* includes rare footage of Primus performing "Hard Time Blues."[49] She began the dance at center stage with one hand out and her head bowed. Although Primus performed "Hard Time Blues" as a solo, she conveyed the presence of uncompromising elites who rebuffed sharecroppers' requests for aid. As the music and lyrics rose toward a crescendo, she spun in circles. With one arm behind her back and her right hand extended in supplication, her fierce twirling conjuring the frustrations of sharecroppers struggling through "hard times," and denied help by those more fortunate. While the guitar chords and vocals increased in speed and intensity, Primus executed high jumps and hanging leaps, and her pounding fist connotes the physical brawn and political power of the working class. Although Primus's political activism centered on racial justice and she did not explicitly discuss women's rights, her strong arm and pounding fist evoke contemporaneous images of "Rosie the Riveter," a symbol of working-class women's rights. In contrast to the polyrhythmic movement that dominated "African Ceremonial," "Hard Time Blues" is stripped down. Although Primus's jumps electrified audiences, she maintained gravity in tone, fitting the subject matter. Even the staging underscores the political importance of Primus's work. American flags surrounded her as she danced. This visual image illustrates the power of Primus's political voice, which especially appealed to advocates for the rights of working class people.[50]

I describe the choreographic elements of Primus's work in detail, because I contend that her use of dance as a mode of political protest is especially powerful in the context of class oppression as experienced through the body in hard labor. By using her own body to articulate the frustrations and hopes of over-worked, physically and emotionally tired working-class Americans, she gave such marginalized peoples a political voice and platform. This kinesthetic and rhetorical strategy was rooted in Primus's conception that dance is a language—capable of conveying not only emotion but also intellectual ideas, when words fail. "Hard Time Blues" illustrates this point.

Although Primus was leery about facing the "ugliness" of Jim Crow head on, she believed her anthropological research in the South was necessary to the development of her own voice as an artist-activist. In a 1944 interview, when asked how she would deal with racism during her travels throughout the south, Primus compared Jim Crow to Hitler's Nazi regime. She also declared that she would not allow racism to thwart her work. Primus said, "I'm militant and I don't tolerate racial abuse, but there is food for me in the South and I'm not going to let my personal scruples stand in the way this time. I'm going to comply with their Nazi-like rules because I'd hate to let people know who I am."[51] [The last sentence refers to the fact that Primus was traveling as an anonymous migrant worker.] Once again, Primus used her first-hand experience in the South as a kind of moral ammunition to challenge Jim Crow racism. In doing so, she inserted herself into the black intellectual discourse of the time regarding the fight for justice on two fronts: fascism abroad and racism at home.

Africa on Primus's Mind

Because Primus used education and cultural exposure as ammunition to challenge societal notions of black inferiority, she deliberately carved out a space for herself, in the public sphere, as a powerful artist-educator. Primus described the impetus behind her first visit to western Africa as a mission to "find material not only to enrich our theatre but to add to our knowledge of people little understood."[52] It might be a cliché, but for Primus's purposes, it still rang true: Knowledge is power. The bold and dramatic way in which Primus declared her appreciation of African diasporic cultures from an insider perspective as a "participant observant" and trained anthropologist allowed her to move beyond the romanticized depictions of blackness of her artistic predecessors. As an inheritor of celebratory yet exoticized images of the African diaspora rendered by Harlem Renaissance artists, from poet Claude Mckay's "Bananas ripe and green, and ginger root" in his nostalgic recollection of his homeland Jamaica in "The Tropics of New York"[53] to the iconic images of Egyptian pyramids and pharaohs in Aaron Douglas's complex, multilayered, and even ethereal renderings of black civilizations past, Primus embraced these positive depictions of blackness and moved beyond them. By basing her choreography on thorough, detailed anthropological research of specific African diaporic dances and cultures, Primus added a greater degree of nuance to academic and popular understandings of blackness.

In Primus's world, the souls of black folk were beautiful, brilliant, and diverse. Her's was a radical portrait of blackness to present to mainstream America at a time when the country was still reeling from the ravages of white supremacy and racial violence. I contend that Primus's style of artistic activism, especially her celebration of West African cultures, was shaped by her family history and immigrant cultural identity. Pearl Primus's fundamental mission to redefine blackness in positive terms, genealogically and philosophically, began with her own African roots. Africa dominated Primus's artistic imagination, so much so, that in 1943, she titled her professional debut,

"African Ceremonial," which opened on Broadway to critical acclaim. "African Ceremonial" featured West African and Central African dances performed as part of wedding celebratory rituals. Although Primus had not yet traveled to the continent, she based the choreography on oral history, secondary literature, and African visual art. For Primus, "African Ceremonial" became a sort of figurative "roots pilgrimage" to uncover hitherto unknown history, as most black Americans could not trace their lineage beyond three generations given the chaos and destruction of familial bonds wrought by slavery. Primus's 1943 debut was a variation of prevalent primitivist artistic themes, but it was also a bold—albeit romantic—declaration of pride in African cultures. Primus's work rebutted claims of black American cultural paucity or erasure at a time when historians were suggesting that black Americans had been stripped of their cultural history, that they were tabula rasa, irrevocably devastated by the psychic rupture of racialized slavery.

Primus argued that Africa did not need uplifting but was just fine *as is*. At the beginning of her career, her notion of racial uplift clashed with prevailing "race leaders'" strategies. One dance critic would later observe: "When she began doing African dances in the 1940s, she encountered resistance from black audiences who, she said, 'had been taught,' to be ashamed of their heritage as 'primitive.'"[54] Primus's approach was completely Africa-centered while most black leaders believed blacks would be uplifted through the adoption of Victorian mores. African American social, political, and religious leaders in the late nineteenth and early twentieth centuries argued that African Americans needed to travel to Africa to share Western civilization with their African brothers and sisters. Even influential black consciousness leaders such as Marcus Garvey and Ethelred Brown, still adhered to Western notions of civilization and progress. Although Garvey espoused a metaphysical and political return to Africa, he preached that Africa would be redeemed through modernization and industrialization.

"Omowale": Daughter Returned Home

In 1949, Primus visited Monrovia, Liberia, for the first time, sponsored by the Julius Rosenwald Fellowship. Her goal was to study dance throughout Africa. On the very first day of her diary entries documenting her travels to western Africa, Primus wrote:

Things I must do
keep notes daily—

keep up with technique
Jot down notes on new movements
write up dances & musical instruments
French Visa
Visa for Accra.
Letters to contacts—
Press articles—Nigeria—itinerary to paper[55]

Always observant, studious, and forward-thinking, Primus juggled the double-burden of logistical administration—her passport, visas, letters of introduction, and so on, along with carving out time for the creative practice required to make her sojourn successful. She remained committed to honing her crafts as choreographer and dancer while taking in all of the sights and sounds of western Africa as fresh primary sources for future work. She was comfortable in the role of artist-anthropologist, and she thoroughly enjoyed studying this new cultural context as well as crafting a position of power for herself in this new space.

Following in the footsteps of contemporaneous anthropologist and choreographer Katherine Dunham, Primus was among the last cohort of artists to receive a Rosenwald grant. At a dance performance earlier that year at Fisk University, Primus had impressed one of the members of the prize's selection committee so much that when he learned that she had never visited Africa, he insisted that the Rosenwald Foundation sponsor her sojourn. Primus made a second trip to Liberia in 1952, and from 1959 until 1961 she spent a third stay in Liberia to help establish a Performing Arts Center there. From 1962 through 1963, Primus studied in Liberia for the fourth time; the Rebekah Harkness Foundation funded that trip.

Primus's diary entries reflect an almost giddy excitement about her travels throughout the continent that she deemed her "motherland." In her characteristic style of listing mundane daily activities such as doing laundry, washing hair, and so on, intertwined with monumental events, Primus wrote:

> Rose early—wash—hang wash on trees—and bars of wood—found in bathroom—Rest house large but cold in appearance—Visit Oni to meet wives—not available—He tells me true history of Orangun—I now have both myth and reality—Oni gives me new name—Omawale—child returns home—pictures of Oni and self—will stop in to record message to America.[56]

Primus's diary entries are both poetic and impressionistic. One might think she'd list the most important, existential development first—the honor of

Nigerian elders bestowing her with a new Igbo name, Omowale—meaning daughter returned home, but she saved that detail for last. Primus's diary entries hint at an obsessive-compulsive desire to document every minute detail of her time in Africa. This reflected her excitement about her travels, but it also provides useful insights regarding her personality. Compulsive tendencies are common among artists who perform at a high level because attention to details is part of a spirit of perfectionism that made performance artists like Primus shine. Although her diary entries sometimes preface monumental accomplishments with mundane details, Primus undoubtedly considered the honor of receiving the Nigerian name "Omowale" an important event because she repeatedly recounted this story in interviews with journalists in the United States and abroad after her initial life-changing visit to West Africa.[57] Primus said it best when she declared in her diary, "I now have both myth and reality." Although it's possible to argue that a degree of romanticism might cloud the vision of any African diasporic person who makes a "roots pilgrimage" to the most likely home of her ancestors for the first time, 1949 was a turning point in Primus's understanding of her own African diasporic cultural identity. She now possessed first-hand knowledge to complement and challenge her prior, distant studies of African cultures and people.

Before Primus won the Rosenwald grant, her performance art took shape along points of a diverse cultural and spiritual constellation. To create African-based choreographies, she drew upon her imagination, her cultural participation in Caribbean New York communities, and her family-informed Africa-centered cosmologies. In her early career, Primus's notions of African cultural authenticity were skewed toward a romanticized vision of Africa, but dance critics still found her performances powerful and convincing. Her intellectual curiosity, creativity, and theatrical skill brought rave reviews, but such praise often sprang from the white reviewers' own distorted understandings of African art and culture.

A number of prominent dance critics based their assessments of Primus's early work as "authentically" African on her Caribbean and West African familial heritage. One reviewer reflected on the role of imagination and family folklore in Primus's development as a dancer by declaring, "When Pearl Primus says she was taught the dances of Africa in her dreams by *her grandfather, a mighty spiritual leader*, no one can dispute her. Performing them as a young girl at Fisk, they were so *authentically* African that an astounded foundation director gave her a grant to go study her cultural heritage at the source."[58] On one hand, the open-mindedness of this critic is noteworthy; she respected Primus's beliefs in ancestor guidance and worship, but on the other hand, the reviewer writing in the late 1960s might have discussed Primus's real-life anthropological research in the Caribbean and in Central and West Africa. Sally Hammond's critique illuminates the delicate cultural and political scales that Primus attempted to balance and that dance critics essayed to understand. Primus did not see any conflict in being an intellectual and a spiritualist, embracing West African cosmologies while pursuing academic studies of Caribbean and African dance and culture. Hammond failed to grasp fully the sophistication of Primus's craft. Hammond employed familiar, facile notions of African-based dance as intuitive and spiritual, while Western dance forms like ballet and even American modern dance, were intellectual. For Primus, this was a false dichotomy. Primus's intellectual and spiritual selves enjoyed a symbiotic relationship; she felt no tension between her scholarly and theatrical endeavors to educate readers and audiences about Caribbean and African cultures, but she did feel intense frustration when critics failed to understand the complexity of her craft and intentions.

Dance critics often expressed negative stereotypes of African artistic production—depicting it as unsophisticated and backwards, which Primus countered by insisting that Africa-based performance art was universal and forward-looking, not merely parochial and entertainingly backward. Again, reviewers' critiques of Primus's work were double-edged. Critics frequently used the word "authentic" or grammatical variations of that word, along with supposed synonyms such as "unadulterated," "true," "sincere," "pure," "genuine," "rooted," and "innate" to describe Primus's "primitivist" dances. These reviews were usually laudatory in tone, but they still confined Primus in a socially constructed box marked "other" and "inferior." One critic posed the dichotomy of city versus country in terms of contamination and purity to describe Primus's research in West Africa: "The farther away from cities she journeyed, the *purer* were the dances. For on the coast and in the more urban areas, the native dance has lost its *dignity* through *contamination* by jitter-bugging and certain unfortunate commercial influences."[59] Although this critic voiced a somewhat positive view of African dance as "dignified," the reader is left with the image of a noble savage, whose "dignity" was separate and unequal from the European. Although Primus would take umbrage at the insinuation that African diasporic dances were not equally respectable.

Many critics framed Primus's first sojourn to West Africa as a cultural "roots pilgrimage"—a long-awaited way to repair cultural and psychic ruptures caused by forced migration during the Slave Trade. Doris Hering interviewed Primus after her first trip to West Africa and described her participation in Orisha-based dance rituals: "As the ceremonies went far into the night, the little American girl could *feel her identity with her African people* growing deeper and stronger, and she knew that when she returned to America, she would dance as never before."[60] In December 1951, one critic wrote, "Pearl Primus, after many spurts, all of which have been interesting but inconclusive, has *finally found her roots*. She has become an eloquent and *inspired vessel of transmission*, bringing to us the *dignity* and *universality* of the dance of Africa in a subtly theatrical setting."[61] This critic echoed the sentiments of many colleagues by maintaining that Primus floundered in modern "nonprimitive" dance but excelled in performances of African-based dances—especially after her sojourn to the continent that she deemed her "motherland."

From the late 1940s through the early 1960s, in Primus's four trips to Liberia she was embraced by top-ranking officials as well everyday people as a member of the community. She chose the role of masks as an educational tool in Mano culture as a dissertation topic because it provided an apt subject to combine her expertise in dance and interest in African culture. She decided upon the "hinterlands of Liberia" as a field site because in a self-ruled nation "she was free to seek understanding of the cultures of the indigenous people without having to avoid the suspicion of colonial officials." She limited the chronology of her dissertation from 1948 through 1963 to study a time "when," as she noted, "the Mano people still followed their traditional way of life."[62] She focused on seven "spirit masks" in her dissertation: Gbini Ge, Long Ge, Gbetu, Bundu, Klua Ge, Zi, and Pia Se. Primus acknowledged cultural conflicts between African American settlers and indigenous Liberians, but the story she tells has a happy ending. She wrote, "Gradually the new settlers and the indigenous people recognized their future depended on working together and eventually becoming a united nation,"[63] and she credited the declaration of the Republic of Liberia as a free nation on July 26, 1847 to this spirit of cooperation.

Eventually Primus lived and studied in Nigeria, Ghana, the Cameroons, Togo, Angola, Zaire, Rhodesia, Tanzania, Central African Republic, Rwanda, Burundi, Fernando Po, and Republic of Benin. She also visited the Ivory Coast, Senegal, Mali, Guinea, Sierra Leone and Gambia prior to embarking upon her in-depth study of the Mano. In later visits to Trinidad, Primus would suggest that the sojourn confirmed that she was already on the right track regarding her pursuit of authenticity in Afro-Caribbean dance, just as her Rosenwald-sponsored travels throughout West Africa and Central Africa had confirmed. "My only assignment was to go to the parts of Africa where I could find material not only to enrich our theatre but to add to our knowledge of people little understood," Primus recalled.[64] After her travels, Primus spoke with a renewed authority regarding the authenticity of her work. In a 1951 interview, Primus declared, "Everything I do is consistent with what I saw in Africa—except for wearing a bra. I have to make that concession to our modern standards."[65]

In numerous interviews, Primus emphasized the intense training and technical precision required to successfully execute African diasporic dance forms. Comparable to any formal European dance technique like ballet, Primus depicted the African dancer's apprenticeship as a grueling process that required dedication on the parts of both student and mentor: "Not only is strict emphasis placed upon the technique, sequence, timing and execution of the dance, but the student is drilled in perfection for years before the actual test of strength. When he has passed through the period of Initiation, the perfect dance he has learned in the bush schools 'becomes a vehicle in which his soul can soar to the heavens.'"[66] Primus also forcefully made the distinction between dancers and non-dancers among African people and black Americans, disproving popular racial stereotypes that suggested that rhythm and musical ability was genetically innate, instead of a culturally constructed and acquired skill.

Primus's Personality

Sources indicate that Pearl Primus's personal style and temperament might easily earn her the moniker of "diva," or, more euphemistically, "force of nature." Her diary entries during her travels throughout western Africa provide vibrant glimpses into her personality, and above all else, her humanity. Even Primus's unconventional style of diary recordings—her succinct listing of tasks, people, places, events, and perceptions strung together by a series of hyphens, reflected her own sense of creativity and the busyness of her mind. The reader is left with the impression that she was too consumed with immersing herself in the indigenous cultures and her grand educational mission to take the precious time to abide by the standard format of diary entries—writing in complete sentences. So, how do we understand this style of writing? One scholar observed, "The diary is best read not as a book with a beginning and end, but as a process. We should ask not what can be learned from the text of the diary, but what can be learned from the individual diarist's work of recounting his/her life, in private, on a continuous basis within a calendar grid."[67] I understand Primus's process of diary writing as serving multiple functions; the diary worked as a planner that allowed Primus to keep track of personal and professional priorities, it served as a research document that Primus could later reference, and it provided a psychological and creative outlet to help Primus manage her chaotic schedule and inevitable interpersonal conflicts that arise when traveling to so many different locales in a foreign land. Should we read Primus's diary as a reliable reflection of historical events? Regarding the believability of diaries as a source of "truth," historian Jochen Hellbeck has observed that the diary's "'uncertain' nature between literary and historical writing, between fictional and documentary, spontaneous and reflected narrative, has frustrated many a literary specialist in search for canonical clarity."[68] This is true. In turn, we should understand Primus's diary as a reflection of her personal "truth"—a documentation of her unique "life witness." From her accounts of standard carsickness and nausea[69] to the emotional drama of interpersonal conflicts,[70] the details that Primus decided to include and her omissions provide insights into her unique personality.

If we put ourselves in her shoes, we also could conclude that living a life as hectic as her own—especially considering the physical of strain of travel during her visits to western Africa from the late 1940s through the 1950s, would make even the most even-keeled person feel irritable. And, of course, Primus was no exception. In one diary entry, she wrote, "Farewells to Yaba . . . tired—irritable."[71] Months later, in another diary entry, Primus wrote, "1½ [hrs of] sleep then chauffeur arrives—helps me pack—I am too exhausted to think."[72] I appreciate Primus's admission of her own physical and emotional fatigue, because in contrast to some dance critics' renderings of her undeniable athleticism in terms that made her seem more like a superhero than a human being, Primus's diary attests to the fact that she was indeed human. Primus's diary provides an intimate account of her psychological, emotional, and spiritual state—beyond the stage lights on Broadway and the flashing cameras of the international media.

As a self-aware, creative, and sensitive soul, Primus developed strong attachments to people she met during her travels; so, when the time came to travel to the next city or to finally return to the United States, saying goodbye to new friends was not easy. After one departure, Primus wrote in her diary, "more farewells . . . tears blistering eyes—hardest part of travel—leaving the friends one meets and learns to love."[73] In this passage, Primus progressed from a sentimental recollection of the emotional strain of saying goodbye to an account of the physical discomforts of transportation in subpar automobiles along unpaved roads in Western Africa. She wrote, "Car too small. . . . We're off—bumping—decide I'll be able to produce no children at end of trip."[74] Primus's use of hyperbole is amusing and revelatory. On one hand it revealed the hardships of travel, on the other hand it revealed Primus's wry sense of humor and grit. Primus's mentor Langston Hughes would have appreciated this diary entry. Primus's comical description of her "road weariness" calls to mind Hughes's brilliantly humorous autobiographical account of his around-the-world trip during the height of the Great Depression, *I Wonder as I Wander*, in which he relays tales of cramped car trips, blisteringly cold train rides, and turbulent excursions by ship.[75] In this regard, Primus's bumpy car ride was par for the course for any adventurous soul traveling on a limited budget at the time.

Primus sometimes deployed her ironic sense of humor as a weapon to disarm potential racists. She detested white supremacy to the core of her being and was occasionally incensed to the point of irreverence in face-to-face confrontation with treatment she perceived to be racist. In her personal diary on May 5, 1949, she recalled snubbing several Belgian women whom she met during one of her sojourns to the Congo: "We arrived at Boma today— some Belgian women stared me up and down—I looked them in the eye and laughed—silly fools."[76] Primus's flippant behavior suggests that although she loved to bask in the limelight, she only desired attention on her own terms.

Primus was used to receiving a lot of attention; her bigger-than-life personality, intellect, and talent often drew stares. She also was keenly aware of white people's fascination with her physical appearance—her thick, natural hair, often coifed in a manner that emphasized its volume, long before the afro was *en vogue*, as well as her ample bosom and muscular legs. Sometimes she leveraged this fascination from white male and female admirers to her advantage to attract monetary donations to her dance mission. But this kind of attention from the Belgian women in West Africa, who conjured memories of Jim Crow racism and colonial enterprise, was unwanted. Challenging the Belgian colonial notion of white supremacy and black servility, Primus's laughter, and her boldness in looking the Belgium women in the eye, was an assertion of power.

It is impossible to retrace the exact facial expressions and intentions behind the countenances of the women. Indeed, it is possible that Primus's sensitive and capricious personality projected unwarranted conclusions; nonetheless, this interaction is telling because it reveals Primus's own sense of self, racial pride, and place as a black American and "Afrocentrist" near the midcentury mark. Primus's tone is reminiscent of the speaker in Langston Hughes's poem "I, Too," who revises the racial hierarchy within the household in which he is employed as a domestic by eating well and enjoying himself, despite his forced segregation to the kitchen and his white employer's attempt to make him feel less than human.[77] Both Primus and the speaker in Hughes's poem point to the fundamental, existential absurdity of white supremacy. Primus's laughter suggests that she was in on the secret; the hollowness of white supremacy had been revealed. As if the encounter with the Belgian women were a mere cobweb brushing across her cheek, Primus turns her attention to loftier landscapes and ideals as the next line in her diary reads: "My thoughts go home tonite—for I have seen many skies like these above our Central Park or Brooklyn."[78] Always the Pan-Africanist looking for connections between black people on the continent of Africa and peoples of African descent living in America and the Caribbean, Primus poetically finds a sense of shared meaning in the sky above that reminds her of skies that she has seen in her beloved New York.[79]

"They Just Don't Understand"

Although Primus's travels throughout the Caribbean and the continent of Africa reinforced her fundamental respect for African diasporic peoples and cultures, many American critics did not share her sentiments. They surveyed Primus's stage performances through the tint of white supremacist politics, and their reviews conspired to constrain her in a double bind. In one instance, an exasperated Primus lamented after newspaper journalists took photos of her group in London, "They just don't understand what we're trying to do. We're trying to show the heritage and dignity of the Negro through his dancing and music—not pander to the lower kind of public taste."[80] When some reviewers described Primus's performance art in terms of raw athleticism and passion, Primus complained, "They don't understand." Primus intended her work to serve grand humanitarian goals of interracial dialogue and mutual cultural respect. She did not perform for the sake of voyeuristic titillation. Sometimes her idealism carried the day, but in many instances, constructionist interpretations of her work prevailed.

On one hand, critics suggested that modern dance required intellectual acumen as well as physical dexterity, while "primitivism" called for raw athleticism and enthusiasm—the former genre being more difficult, sophisticated, and respectable than the latter. This derogatory view seeped through newspaper and journal reviews of Primus's work. Critics frequently alleged that "it is unfortunate that [Primus] has not progressed ideologically or artistically since her initial and brilliant success,"[81] (Ezra Goodman 1948). On the other hand, when Primus choreographed and performed modern dance pieces that better fit critics' definitions of intellectually based "high art," they still insisted that she came up short and urged Primus to stick to what she knew best—"primitivism." In July 1948, well-known dance critic Doris Hering wrote that Primus's "best work is without a doubt among the primitives, where vigor and a feeling of dedication rightfully outweigh choreographic variety and sustained phrasing."[82] Hering attributed Primus's success in African-based dance to her undeniable athletic ability and sheer charisma. This compliment is double-edged: Herring's focus on "vigor" and "dedication" obscured Primus's intellectualism and relegated both African dance as a genre and Primus as a black woman performer as "inferior."

Comparisons always require an explicit or implicit benchmark. The tacitly understood standard in this critic's review is modern, "nonprimitive" theatrical art—mainly performed by white dancers. By labeling the dance and dancer passionate but subpar, Hering did a disservice not only to Primus but also to dance audiences because she overlooked the intellectual underpinnings of Primus's performance pursuits as well as the fundamental complexity of African-based dance styles. Hering never mentioned the library and museum research that Primus had conducted to inform her choreography nor the difficulty in executing polyrhythmic movement of the upper versus the lower body.

Tensions between the cerebral and the emotional self, mind and body, and city and countryside recurred throughout Primus's performance and academic work. For Primus, the mind and body—academic research and the discipline of dance—worked together in a symbiotic relationship. Each fueled the other. She challenged critic's suggestions that intellectualism and kinesthetic expertise were mutually exclusive. In a 1943 review, Robert Lawrence wrote, "This Negro girl, who is said to be working at present on her master's degree in psychology at Hunter College, does not dance intellectually. The only trace of the cerebral to be found in her performance lies in the beautiful control of movement, the tastefulness of her African, Haitian, and jazz dances which are arousing without ever getting out of hand." He also noted, "everything in the Primus act goes first-classly."[83]

Pearl Primus challenged dance critics' racially essentialist interpretations of her work. She tried to convince white and black audiences alike that African civilizations were as sophisticated and intelligent as any Western nation. John Martin was perhaps Primus's most sympathetic critic. Yet sympathy is an understatement when considering Martin's reviews that depicted Primus more as a superhero than a terrestrial being. In 1944, Martin described her choreography and execution as follows: "She can jump over the Brooklyn Bridge, and when in her impassioned dance to the poem 'Strange Fruit' she throws herself down and rolls across the floor at forty miles an hour it makes your hair curl with excitement."[84] Without question, Martin had a penchant for hyperbole, but one fact remains: Primus was athletically gifted, and many memorable moments in her performance career sprung from this natural and practiced physical ability.

Primus credited her teen-aged track and field extracurricular pursuits with providing the training for her signature jumps and hanging leaps in modern dance. Just as she churned her legs to gain height and distance as a high school long jumper, she consciously "climbed in the air" during her choreography for "African Ceremonial" and "Hard Time Blues."

Most white dance critics viewed Primus's athleticism through a lens of racial essentialism. One *Boston Globe* reporter also depicted Primus in myth-ological terms in a 1947 article by calling her "lightning-limbed."[85] This allit-erative compliment was juxtaposed with her thwarted wishes to become a medical doctor: "The dancing doctor from Trinidad, lightning-limbed Pearl Primus, made her Boston debut at Jordan Hall last night and a sold-out house was well-rewarded."[86] Another 1947 article expressed similar amazement regarding Primus's ability to combine her intellectual and artistic pursuits: "Bouncing like a rubber ball, Pearl Primus, one of the world's foremost danc-ers, is whirling her way to a doctor's degree." This critic described Primus as so athletic and energetic that she could rebound like a rubber ball. The writer continued, "Pearl Primus can bounce in the air like a rubber ball, an achievement found rarely in young girls on their way to their master's degree at Hunter College . . . odd combination of intellectualized choreography and free emotional drive."[87]

Popular perceptions of black art as "lowbrow" clashed with Primus's cam-paigns to promote awareness of its beauty and sophistication. And when critics praised her mastery of "primitivist" dance styles by calling her gifts "racially rooted"[88] and labeled her "a dancer and choreographer of whom the Negro race can be justly proud,"[89] she exploded these rigid categories of race in her insistence that her work was human—universal. Primus experi-enced the coincident blessing and curse of being a black artist in America that scholar Paul Gilroy has observed: "Perhaps black artists experience com-munity through a special paradox. It affords them certain protections and compensations yet it is also a source of constraint. It provides them with an imaginative entitlement to elaborate the consciousness of racial adversity while limiting them as artists to the exploration of that adversity."[90] African diasporic cultures struggling against white supremacy provided a broad can-vas upon which Primus created new masterpieces, but she also found popular understandings of this canvas too narrow. She constantly reminded audi-ences that "Negro" artistic production was American and human.

Dance critics often cast Primus as the exoticized "other" as is illustrated by Doris Hering's description of Primus dancing as if she were a "creature pos-sessed."[91] Primus would not object to the metaphysical connotations because she embraced long-standing West African cosmologies, especially belief in ancestor worship, rebirth, and spirit possession; however, she would take umbrage at the use of the word "creature," because it implied an animalistic nature. Dance critics also frequently remarked upon Primus's physical stature, using words like "stocky," "sturdy," and "squat." They found it difficult to reconcile Primus's muscular physique and intellect with her subject matter. In July 1948, one dance critic wrote, "If you look at Pearl Primus with a Broadway eye, you see a short, pudgy young woman bursting with *animal energy* and bounce."[92] Such derogatory descriptions of Primus's body, coupled with critics' insistence that she thrived in "primitivist" dance forms while her attempts at modern choreography were "at best naïve," revealed the cultural biases of white dance critics. Still, Primus worked tirelessly, from the start of her career as a dancer in the late 1920s until her death in 1994, to revise negative stereotypes of blackness. She leveraged her unique cultural identity as a black woman born in the Caribbean and living in America while traveling to Africa to spread her message of Africa-centered humanism.

To her critics, a black woman choreographer and dancer who held a PhD in anthropology from a premier American institution seemed to be a walking oxymoron. Twenty-first-century dance critics are knowledgeable enough or at least adequately politically correct to accept African diasporic art forms as "high art," as developed and sophisticated as any European dance style, but this idea was quite new when Primus started dancing seriously in the early 1940s. Thus, Primus inspired a new generation of black American artists. Her work and very presence inspired black female dancers and creative writers, who upended dance critics' views of Primus by embracing her message and physical blackness as affirmations of themselves. In 1975, Audre Lorde reminisced about Primus's visit to her classroom as a student at Hunter High School. "Primus—beautiful, fat, Black, gorgeous! She talked about Blackness, and she talked to us about beauty. . . . I sat there and ate it up! I couldn't believe what this womin [sic] was saying to me!"[93] For Lorde, Primus's presence was right on time. More than a decade before the release of James Brown's Black Power anthem "Say it Loud—I'm Black and I'm Proud," Primus personified this very ideal. Thus it is not surprising that Audre Lorde, the daughter of immigrants from Grenada who would soon become one of the most outspoken black lesbian intellectuals that America has seen, was inspired by Primus. Similarly, contemporary dancer and choreographer Jawole Willa Jo Zollar has echoed this sentiment. She states, "I have been in awe of Ms. Primus's legacy ever since I heard her speak years ago. . . . She talked of the great legacy of African dance and how as African Americans we should continue to study it, but not at the expense of dance traditions we have evolved on American soil."[94] As founder and director of the professional dance group Urban Bush

Women, Zollar was so inspired by Primus that she choreographed an entire performance art suite in her honor titled *Walking with Pearl . . Africa Diaries* and *Walking with Pearl . . . Southern Diaries.* When I asked Zollar about Pearl Primus's impact on her work, she said, "Urban Bush Women owes a lot to Dr. Primus. She brought power, athleticism and politics to the middle of the aesthetics of the newly developing field of modern dance. She envisioned the Black dancing body in ways that are still reflected in UBW's work and beyond."[95] Similar to Haitian novelist Edwidge Danticat's profound apprecia-tion for the black immigrant women characters in Paule Marshall's fiction, Lorde and Zollar also cherished Primus's work, life, and legacy as they saw themselves reflected in her work and gleaned validation.

In addition to Primus's significance in the worlds of modern dance and mid-twentieth-century civil rights activism, her story is of great cultural import because her personal identity broadens our understanding of the hopes and struggles of a first-generation Caribbean American. Pearl was only three years old when she arrived in New York, but her family's folklore combined with anthropological research and travel experiences forged her strong sense of translocal identity. At the start of her professional career in the early 1940s, Primus was one of few dancers who pursued African diasporic rhythmic expression on the stage. She danced with a purpose as she criticized racism in the United States, introduced American audiences to "authentic" African and Caribbean dance, and promoted mutual cultural respect as an effective educational tool in kindergarten through twelfth-grade classrooms.

Like Trinidadian-born Jazz pianist Hazel Scott, Pearl Primus took Café Society by storm and mingled with both black and white power brokers throughout the city. Both Scott and Primus leveraged their Caribbean cul-tural identities and their artistic talent to win over the hearts and minds of black and white Americans, and their deep-rooted confidence and tal-ent attracted an international following. Like Barbadian-American novelist Paule Marshall, Primus was also a self-proclaimed daughter of the diaspora. She seized every opportunity to speak, write, and dance out her African, Caribbean, black and American cultural identities. American-born black intellectual Harold Cruse might have taken issue with Primus's emphasis on her Caribbean heritage—deeming her guilty of promoting cultural superior-ity as he did with Marshall, but Primus would have retorted that her embrace of her African and Caribbean roots was intended to bring people together instead of pushing them apart. Primus, like Barbadian politician Richard B. Moore, always looked for commonalities. Her message was one of unity and celebration—celebration of African diasporic cultures and unity among African diasporic peoples. Her close personal and professional relationships with other white dancers and intellectuals demonstrates the intense, cross-cultural synergy of bohemian, artistic New York, which overlapped nicely with Primus's broader message of mutual cultural respect. She espoused her own unique brand of cross-cultural humanism throughout her career as a dancer and as an educator at the Five Colleges dance consortium in Massachusetts and as a guest lecturer in K-12 public schools in New York City. Primus believed in the power of art and imagination, and dance was a vehicle to challenge bigotry and even transcend race.

"Afrocentricity," Mutual Cultural Respect, and K-12 Education

During the latter part of her career, Primus turned to the classroom, as dancers often do after their prime athletic years, and wide-eyed, elementary school children at New York public schools as well as college-aged co-eds became her principal audience. Primus presented the idea of dance as a cross-cultural educational tool in a 1966 article in *American Education,* in which she stressed the pedagogical value of dance as a means to promote empathy and mutual cultural respect among students in primary and secondary schools. She wrote, "The basic concepts, principles, and symbolism of dance apply to all people. The child will be able to identify with children in other areas of the world through an understanding of and creative participation in their dance."[96] According to Primus, the sheer experience of performing the quotidian movements of someone from a distant culture could metaphysically transport the "mover" across the expanse of land and ocean into the body and environment of formerly unknown people and cultures. Thus, the desired outcome of incorporating African dance into the school curriculum was to foster a greater degree of open-mindedness, respect, and acceptance, which is quite different from the popular term "tolerance," for people from diverse cultures, near and far.

Primus based her pedagogical approach upon the values of mutual cultural respect and inclusion—suggesting that all cultures possessed a distinctive voice that deserved to be heard. In the expression and reception of this voice, both the speaker and hearer were uplifted; the former was validated by tacit or active presence of the witness and the latter through an expanded worldview. In the introduction to her dissertation, Primus wrote, "The dances, sculpture, music and dramatic folklore of Africa must *speak* for [Africa] in all other lands. They must speak for her in the classroom [sic] of the world without losing their power or their authenticity. They must help explain the heritage of the people of Africa and those of African ancestry. They are her *cultural ambassadors."*[97] Primus believed dance was a particularly effective way to educate Western students about African cultures because early African art forms were usually more functional than western art. West African dance incorporated real-life movements like planting crops or performing wedding celebratory rituals. In this regard, artistic form followed function.

Primus endorsed the educational value of not only African dance, but other art forms as well—including sculpture. She found intrinsic worth in elements of material culture, and her reverence for such items was bound up in her in her own ideas of "authenticity." Primus's appreciation of western African masks, drums, and fabric inspired her writing while she pursued her PhD in anthropology at New York University. In the introduction to her dissertation, Primus wrote, as Jennifer Dunning summarizes, that she "became involved in the study of ancestral masks through identification with African sculpture in order to better understand herself and the heritage of peoples of African ancestry.[98]" Or as Primus herself put it, "[I] present *authentic* pieces of dances created to exhibit the masks or the staff or the drum or the fabric."[99]

Conclusion

If Primus's life were a novel, the motif would be magical realism. In her world, terrestrial beings, ancestor spirits, family folklore, and literal and metaphoric travel experiences as well as intuition intermingled in a dynamic display onstage—a veritable "moveable feast" of identity in motion. While dance critics tried to pin her down by categorizing her work as "primitive" or "Negro," Primus knocked such categories off-kilter. Dance critics tried to ground Primus's work, but the beauty and brilliance of her oeuvre sprang from its multidimensionality and its restless quality—akin to the polyrhythmic nature of the dance itself. In many ways, her personal biography and choreographic style capture the unique sense of temporality and synchronicity that characterizes African diasporic identities. Primus's life epitomized Black Atlantic "flows, exchanges, and in-between elements that call the very desire to be centered into question."[100]

In this regard, Primus was both maven and maverick. She taught and inspired a long line of black dancers from New Dance Group member and solo artist Donald McKayle and Judith Jamison of the famed Alvin Ailey American Dance Theater to Jawole Willa Jo Zollar, founder and director of Urban Bush Women.[101] More than a half century after attending a Pearl Primus performance that motivated him to become a dancer, McKayle remembered the visceral effect that Primus's presence had on him:

I was in high school when I first saw her dance. She was like a vision, a beautiful sculpture. When she began to move her shoulders, her legs and her bracelets began to jangle, my reaction was like a chemical explosion. After that I just knew I had to dance and choreograph. If I hadn't gone to her concert that night I might have had an entirely different career.[102]

In an interview in Harlem during the twilight years of her life, Pearl Primus reflected on her fifty-year career as choreographer and dancer. Her mouth could barely keep pace with her mind.[103] She was adorned in West African garb—a brightly colored batik dress with embroidered collar, layers of cowry shells, coral beads, silver strung about her neck, gold rings on *every* finger, and crowned in an elaborately tied *gele* (head wrap) in contrasting colors. For Primus, the personal was political, and she conveyed her faith in "Afrocentrism" and mutual cultural respect through her attire. Explaining her development as a dancer and scholar, she quickly moved among the realms of the historical, political, and metaphysical. She gleaned inspiration from texts on African and African American history, black visual art, and her own anthropological research in the southern United States, West and Central Africa, and the Caribbean. Echoing Paul Gilroy's observations regarding the carnivalesque nature of African diasporic temporality, Primus also found the "nighttime is the right time" for artistic imagination because she stated that familiar and unknown ancestors taught her dance rituals in her dreams. Pearl Primus drew upon her biography as a source of power rooted in Trinidadian upbringing, Africa-centered family folklore, the vernacular culture of American-born blacks, and the avant-garde swagger of New York bohemia.

One might consider Primus an evangelist for the arts. She encouraged all students, black and white alike, to embrace the transcendent power of their own imaginations. In the latter years of her life, Pearl Primus delivered a commencement speech at Hampshire College in Amherst, Massachusetts, in which she recalled the house that she lived in on 117th Street in East Harlem as a child. She said although she lived among dirt and squalor, her imagination took her to marvelous places. Primus triumphantly declared, "I faced prejudice, hatred, anger, defeat of all kinds, yet I made it to the top. This is my message to you."[104] Thus, imagination was the path to redemption and freedom. All of these political and philosophical worldviews—humanism, Africa-centered consciousness, mutual cultural respect, and high self-esteem—were undergirded by Primus's unwavering faith in West African cosmologies such as ancestor and Orisha worship. "The dead are still with us," Primus would remind her audience during performances and in interviews as she believed that the ancestors who came before her remained in direct communication with all those who were willing to listen—leading and guiding us into a more just society.

While the public face of Caribbean intellectualism during the early twentieth century was noticeably ecumenical in nature and overwhelmingly male, Primus was a forerunner in a second wave of Caribbean intellectualism that was remarkably artistic in nature and noticeably female. Primus's style of activism was embodied and multidimensional. Instead of shouting political speeches atop a stepladder on a Harlem street corner like communist activist Richard B. Moore, or lobbying for legislative change in the case of Shirley Chisholm, I argue that the theatrical and literary production by Caribbean women artists played an equally important role in the battle for racial equality. While Ethelred Brown focused on religious racial uplift, and Richard B. Moore on working-class solidarity and Caribbean Federation, the performing arts allowed Caribbean women artist-activists to use their intellects, talents, and cultural identities in the cause of civil rights. Primus was a forerunner of the artistic expression of an Africa-centered consciousness in America and her work set the stage for the literary expression of African diasporic cultural identity by creative writers such as Barbadian-American novelist Paule Marshall. Primus's celebration of her unique cultural heritage also may be seen as a precursor to the multicultural identity politics of the Black Power and post-civil rights era in which Brooklyn-born, Barbadian-American politician Shirley Chisholm made a name for herself and built a culturally inclusive, feminist legacy.

CHAPTER 5

Shirley Chisholm and the Style of Multicultural Democracy

I am not the candidate of black America, although I am black and proud. I am
not the candidate of the women's movement, although I am a woman and I
am equally proud of that.... I am the candidate of the *people of America*.[1]
—SHIRLEY CHISHOLM

While Trinidadian-born choreographer and dancer Pearl Primus embraced
dance as a "weapon for social change," Barbadian-American politician Shirley
Chisholm used the arena of American electoral politics—including her position in the United States House of Representatives and her 1972 presidential
candidacy, to advance the cause of civil rights and women's rights. Chisholm's
personal identity, as a woman, as a black American, and as a descendent of
immigrants, provides unique insights into the cultural and political landscape
of late 1960s and early 1970s New York. At the height of the cultural wars, in
a nation undergoing dramatic social and ideological transformations, Shirley
Chisholm, the daughter of a mother from Barbados and a father born in British Guiana and raised in Cuba and Barbados, was a remarkable woman who
occupied a unique historical moment. She claimed that her keen intellect and
no-nonsense attitude were positive attributes of her Caribbean heritage, and
she spoke with such boldness and persuasive power that a broad spectrum of
progressive Americans supported her campaign to become the first black and
the first female president of the United States.

In January 1972, Shirley Chisholm stood before a congregation of seven hundred supporters at the Concord Baptist Church in Brooklyn and announced
her bid to become the Democratic Party candidate for the presidency of the
United States of America. "My presence before you now symbolizes a *new
era* in American political history," Chisholm triumphantly declared, "Americans all over are demanding a new sensibility, a new philosophy."[2] Well aware
that the majority of her constituents had reached a tipping point regarding

Tammy L. Brown, *A New Era in American Democracy: Shirley Chisholm*,
Mixed Media, 2014.

the drawn-out war in Vietnam, President Lyndon B. Johnson's blind acceptance of counsel from foreign policy aides inherited from John F. Kennedy,
and Richard Nixon's dishonesty in spreading the war to neutral Cambodia,
Chisholm—a Brooklyn-born black woman with working-class and immigrant roots—presented a new face and a refreshingly candid voice in contrast
to the well-heeled white men she was up against. As Chisholm addressed
the crowd at Concord Baptist Church, her optimism and authoritative voice

met with great applause as she defined this new era in American politics as one of "freedom from violence and war at home and abroad"; "freedom from poverty"; and "medical care, employment, and decent housing" for all Americans. Drawing upon values of the antiwar movement and tenets of the Great Society, Chisholm proclaimed her commitment to rebuilding a "strong and just society."[3]

Chisholm had already made history in 1968 as the first black woman elected to Congress, representing the Bedford-Stuyvesant section of Brooklyn in the United States House of Representatives. Less than four years later, Chisholm continued to rock the proverbial boat by throwing her "hat, rather bonnet," as CBS News anchor Walter Cronkite put it, into the Democratic presidential race, thus becoming the first black person to run for "the highest office in the land." As is evident in Cronkite's self-correction and gendered language, a black woman's formidable presence in the United States political arena was so new that many contemporary commentators lacked the language to adequately discuss and make sense of the political phenomenon. Chisholm's political voice grew out of and represented broader contestations over gender roles within the private sphere as well as feminists' demands for women's equal representation in local and federal political institutions.

Chisholm's success in the political arena was a product of her adept ability to tap into the ethos of the time in which the personal was political and the political was personal. She leveraged her immigrant cultural identity in creative ways to effectively reconcile seemingly contradictory philosophies of racial, ethnic, and feminist pride with humanist and universalist ideals to win over a broad spectrum of voters. She also leveraged her identity as a woman, as a black American, and as a descendant of working-class immigrants to gain support from constituents with similar backgrounds, but she also made efforts to transcend these categories of race, class, and gender by emphasizing the common desire of *all* Americans to lead healthy and productive lives, equally protected by the laws of the land. Chisholm's simultaneous focus on the particular and the universal helped her galvanize support from women, antiwar advocates, young voters, and working-class citizens from diverse racial and cultural backgrounds. Chisholm's construction of her own selfhood was deliberate and complex.

"Being Translocal"

Chisholm's articulation of her Caribbean cultural identity was a central part of her definition of selfhood. While most academic and journalistic treatments of Chisholm's career have put her femaleness and blackness in the foreground, I want to broaden the discourse by highlighting her Caribbean immigrant identity and her family's working-class background to reveal the moral foundation that contributed to the efficacy of Chisholm's appeal to working-class citizens of all racial and ethnic backgrounds, who were often second-generation immigrants like herself. I also emphasize Brooklyn as a place unique in allowing Chisholm to use her transcultural status and dynamic personality to appeal to a broad constituency.

Shirley Chisholm, like many Caribbean New Yorkers, simultaneously held island-specific, regional, racial, and class identities. She privileged one identity over the others depending on the political context; this balancing of diverse thoughts and ideas constituted her "translocal consciousness." Chisholm inhabited a unique historical moment that motivated progressive citizens to embrace her "crossroads" status. Harnessing momentum from the civil rights movement, third-wave feminism, the peace movement, and the Great Society's push for a stronger welfare state, black Americans, immigrants and descendants of immigrants, young people, pacifists, and women of all races welcomed Chisholm's presence.

Chisholm's monumental 1972 presidential campaign provides an apt case study to better understand the dramatic transformations in black political leadership and the discourse over black identity from the 1920s through the 1970s. Even Chisholm's intellectual biography suggests the recursive nature of black identity politics, since her father was a dedicated Garveyite whose accounts of the "great Marcus Garvey of Jamaica"[4] and President Franklin Delano Roosevelt piqued young Shirley's interest in politics. Garvey promoted racial uplift through his ill-fated Black Star Steamship Lines, intended at least in theory to repatriate black Americans to West Africa, and Chisholm assumed steerage of the political machine in the Twelfth District of New York and within the US House of Representatives.

Caribbean Heritage and Cultural Clashes

Shirley Anita St. Hill was born in Brooklyn on November 30, 1924. Her father, Charles St. Hill, was born in British Guiana but grew up in Cuba and Barbados. Her mother, Ruby Seale, was born and raised in Barbados and moved to New York as a teenager. Charles and Ruby met and married in Brooklyn. Ruby worked as a domestic and Charles worked as "a helper in a big cake bakery." Like Brooklyn-born Barbadian-American novelist Paule Marshall, Chisholm grew up in a predominantly Caribbean neighborhood. "There was a large colony of Barbadians in Brooklyn," she recalled.[5] Like Silla Boyce and members of the Barbadian American Association in Marshall's *Brown Girl, Brownstones* (1959), Chisholm's parents strove to purchase a brownstone in Brooklyn. This part of their "American Dream" was actualized when the St. Hill family moved into a brownstone in 1935 and later relocated to a larger "solid three-story [brownstone] on Prospect Place" in 1945. Chisholm's father earned the $10,000 to purchase their new home from working at a bag factory. As an adult, Chisholm depicted her parents' home ownership as a shining example of an intensely immigrant work ethic and discipline as she called the real estate purchase a "really remarkable achievement for parents of four children, who started with nothing and lived through the depression on a laborer's and domestic's wages."[6]

Chisholm made numerous sojourns to her mother's birthplace throughout her youth, and she suggested that being raised by a strict grandmother in Barbados instilled in her an unshakable sense of self-esteem. Shirley was three years old when she and her siblings moved to Barbados, doing so because her mother Ruby preferred the British colonial model of education on the small island to New York public schools. For Barbadian immigrants of Ruby's generation, this pro-British sentiment was not uncommon. Chisholm described her mother as "thoroughly British in her ideas, her manners and her plans for her daughters." In her mother's opinion, Chisholm and her sisters "were to become young ladies—poised, modest, accomplished, educated, and graceful, prepared to take [their] places in the world."[7] These values also overlapped with the aspirations of American-born black intellectuals committed to the cause of racial uplift around the time that Chisholm was born. Still, as an immigrant from Barbados, Ruby's desire for a dignified and successful future for her daughters entailed an education that she deemed proper in the British Caribbean.

In this regard, comparable to Ethelred Brown's appeals for British financial aid for his Unitarian ministry in Jamaica, Chisholm's family also leveraged the British colonial connection to their advantage. Young Shirley and her siblings spent the next six years in Barbados and were reared by their maternal grandmother. Throughout her political career, Chisholm repeatedly attributed her success to her foundational development in the rigorous British-styled primary and secondary school that she attended during her formative years in Barbados. During her twilight years, Chisholm would later recall this experience in idyllic terms. She stated:

> Oh, my childhood, I can remember it. It was a sight! We lived on a great big farm, and we had to take care of all of the animals on the farm—the chickens, the goats,

the sheep.... I grew up with my maternal grandmother, and my maternal aunt, and my maternal uncle. Yes, I went there at the age of three and I went to the elementary schools in the islands. I did not return to the United States until nine years of age. That's six years of upbringing in the island of Barbados.... I'm the oldest of four girls, and all of us received our elementary school [education] in the islands... [T]here of us got scholarships because we were so bright; we had very high IQ's. And that is attributable to my rearing in the British West Indies.... The school system was fantastic—really fantastic.[8]

Chisholm's sister, Muriel Forde, echoed this point. Muriel would later recall, "When you started school in Barbados, you went right into reading, writing, and arithmetic. There was no such thing as kindergarten and playing around with paper. You came to learn how to read and write and 'do sums' as they said."[9] Muriel's description of their primary school education suggests an environment of seriousness and keen discipline in which studies were undertaken in Barbados. Chisholm also would later state, "Years later I would know what an important gift my parents had given me by seeing to it that I had my early education in the strict, traditional, British-style schools. If I speak and write easily now, that early education is the main reason."[10]

Trinidadian-born Black Power political activist Stokely Carmichael also noted stark differences in the quality of primary and secondary education in the English-speaking Caribbean compared to New York. When he started school at PS 39 on Longwood Avenue, the same elementary school that Jamaican-American politician Colin Powell attended, young Stokely was most surprised by the lack of decorum in the classroom as well as the facility in which he breezed through the curriculum. In his autobiography, *Ready for Revolution*, Carmichael wrote, "My biggest surprise, in that regard, was the discovery that not only could I compete academically, but that I was actually much better prepared than the American kids. . . . They knew little in math, while I *knew* my times tables. They couldn't write. Could barely compose or phrase sentences. . . . So I was just soaring through school."[11] While this is a dismal assessment of the quality of education at the New York public school that Carmichael attended, the larger point remains that Carmichael, like Chisholm, also rooted his sense of selfhood and intellectual pride in his education in the British Caribbean. I have yet to find a reliable empirical study that compares the quality of education in the English-speaking Caribbean to New York public schools during the time of Chisholm and Carmichael's youth; so it is impossible to objectively determine the superiority of either educational system. In this context, what matters most is Chisholm and

Carmichael's *perceptions* of their own Caribbean educational experiences as superior to that of New York public schools.

Carmichael, like Chisholm, also attributed his success to his family upbringing and his ability to take advantage of the best educational opportunities afforded him after his immigration to the United States. At home, he enjoyed a warm upbringing by his female relatives and felt a sense of security among his close-knit family and African Caribbean friends. His strict schooling in Trinidad, high quality education at Bronx High School of Science, and his experience with black diversity during his undergraduate studies at historically black Howard University in Washington, DC, helped nourish his intellect and political consciousness.[12] Although he was unimpressed with the quality of his New York public school education in junior high, the older Carmichael credited his admission into the Bronx High School of Science as a major stepping-stone in his intellectual development. When he entered the school in 1956, he mingled with a motley crew of high achievers from affluent, middle- and working-class backgrounds. Perhaps a nascent sense of black pride and commitment to racial equality was ignited when Stokely realized that in the fields of math, science, and language arts, he could go toe-to-toe with—or even surpass—his white classmates, "the majority [of whom] were just middle-class kids of college-educated parents, WASP, Jewish, Irish, [and] Italian."[13] According to Carmichael, such exceptional educational experiences in Trinidad and New York empowered him to become one of the most dynamic spokespersons for the cause of civil rights in the US and anticolonialism abroad.

In contrast, in 1939, Shirley Chisholm graduated from junior high and then attended an all-girls high school in the Brooklyn neighborhood Bedford-Stuyvesant. According to Chisholm, half of the students were white.[14] By the time she graduated from Girls High in 1942, Chisholm's academic acumen had earned her scholarships to several prestigious universities, of which she hoped to attend Oberlin College in Ohio or Vassar College in Poughkeepsie, New York; but she settled on Brooklyn College, because her parents could not afford room and board for the others.[15] Brooklyn College proved to be fertile ground for the Chisholm's maturation, both intellectually and psychologically. So much so, that Chisholm stated, "Brooklyn College changed my life.... My fiercely protective parents had given me a sheltered upbringing that was incredible.... In school, my intelligence had put me in a special category"; but, at Brooklyn College, Chisholm "began to bump up against more of the world."[16]

Chisholm majored in sociology and minored in Spanish. She joined the debate team and excelled, in spite of her lisp. She chose a career in education, and worked first as daycare instructor and later as a supervisor and consultant, because, according to Chisholm, "There was no other road open to a young black woman. Law, medicine, even nursing were too expensive, and few schools would admit black men, much less a black woman. Social work was not yet open to blacks in the early 1940s . . . No matter how well I prepared myself, society wasn't going to give me a chance to do much of anything else."[17] Just as Pearl Primus's dream to become a doctor was thwarted by the racism of her time, and Paule Marshall's mother would later urge her to reign in her ambition of becoming a writer to pursue a more practical vocation—working for the phone company—Chisholm also felt the constraints of her race, gender, and class during her college years. In spite of these pernicious forces, Chisholm graduated *cum laude* from Brooklyn College in 1946. She then worked as a teacher's aide at Mt. Calvary Childcare Center in Harlem and earned her master's degree in early childhood education from Columbia University in 1951. What was the source of Chisholm's mental and emotional fortitude as she persevered, forging ahead with her career in the face of racism and sexism? She attributed her educational and professional accomplishments to the formative years that she spent with her siblings, maternal grandmother, and other extended family in Barbados. Chisholm stated,

> Those early years of my life on the island of Barbados gave me the spirit, gave me the spunk that was necessary to challenge all of these age-old traditions. I was never afraid of anything; I was never afraid of anybody. And the same thing today; you're going to hear from me.[18]

On one hand, Carmichael and Chisholm's celebration of their British colonial educational experiences is ironic, considering the radical, antiracist politics that both intellectuals endorsed throughout their political careers. On the other hand, their emphasis on the value of discipline rather than the racist underpinnings of their primary educational experiences is characteristic of immigrant constructions of selfhood in America. It resonated with the widespread belief in the infinite possibilities of America as a meritocracy. Their nostalgic recollections also demonstrate the complexity of their personal and social identities because Chisholm also recognized the irony of the ways of her compatriots' who identified themselves as more British than black. In her autobiography *Unbought and Unbossed*, Chisholm wrote, "The Barbadians are almost more British than the British and are very proud of their heritage. For instance, they brag that on Barbados the slaves were freed before they were on the other islands. Barbados has the highest literacy rate in the Caribbean—94 percent."[19] While Chisholm acknowledged the irony in black Barbadian celebration of British values, she still defined her own personal success as an outgrowth of the British colonial, no-nonsense approach to reading, writing, and arithmetic.

Victor Robles, a district office administrator for Chisholm, also believed that her Caribbean cultural heritage positively influenced her intellectual and political development. "Shirley Chisholm was a typical West Indian," Robles observed, "I was impressed with this woman—the way she carried herself, her intelligence."[20] Chisholm undoubtedly had a way about herself—a certain savoir faire, which she attributed to her Caribbean-ness, and those around her took note. I, however, interpret Chisholm's intellect and boldness as a personal characteristic cultivated within the context of her family and educational experiences. Still, other members of Chisholm's 1972 campaign bought into positive and negative stereotypes of her Caribbean identity. Comparable to Adam Clayton Powell III's description of his mother Hazel Scott, one of Chisholm's assistants, Bevan Dufty, described Chisholm's sense of pride and even stubbornness as a uniquely West Indian characteristic. In addressing Chisholm's reaction (or lack thereof) to white women colleagues whom she had expected to support her presidential campaign but failed to do so, Dufty stated, "It was kind of a West Indian quality where she really didn't like to ask. She would look at the equation and say, 'Well, Barbara and I are friends; so, she should support me.' It doesn't work that way; it really doesn't."[21] Thus, although Chisholm was undoubtedly outspoken and persuasive, she was too proud to beg for support from some key players. Whether there's any truth to Dufty's claim that the source of Chisholm's pride was her Caribbean-ness or if the attribute was unique to her individual personality, pride did not prevent Chisholm's disappointment when key members of the National Organization of Women waivered in their support for her, and the Congressional Black Caucus failed to endorse her 1972 presidential campaign.[22] This historical context is important. Chisholm's legendary campaign took place only three years before cconomist Thomas Sowell published his controversial thesis about the alleged superior work ethic of Caribbean immigrants compared to American-born blacks; thus, Chisholm's aides' positive assessment of her Caribbean cultural identity foreshadowed scholarly discussions to come.

Chisholm also suggested that Caribbean cultural mores predisposed some immigrants to assume leadership roles in politics and the realm of artistic production. "A surprising number of successful black politicians of our time are of West Indian descent," Chisholm proudly noted, "Thomas Jones, Ruth Goring, William Thompson, and I were all of Barbadian descent. State Senator Walter Stewart of Brooklyn is a Panamanian. So are many prominent blacks elsewhere in politics and the arts."[23] Given her love of literature and music,

Chisholm may have been thinking of Jamaican-born Harlem Renaissance poet Claude McKay, Trinidadian-born pianist Hazel Scott, or contemporaneous Hollywood heartthrobs Sidney Poitier (Bahamas) and Harry Belafonte (Jamaica). Although Chisholm made concerted efforts to bridge cultural and racial gaps during her political campaigns, she still was not immune from ethnocentric pride.

Chisholm was well aware of cultural clashes among foreign-born and American-born blacks as she recalled overhearing American-born black New Yorkers "grumbling for years, 'They're taking over everything,'" and some even employed cultural slurs: "Why don't those monkeys get back on a banana boat?"[24] Chisholm believed that American-born black resentment against Caribbean immigrants was especially pronounced in New York, since they had immigrated in largest numbers to the metropolis.

Like Richard B. Moore, Shirley Chisholm battled negative stereotypes of Caribbean immigrants who were thought to be pushy and arrogant. But unlike Moore, Chisholm provided some fodder to fan the flames of dissent as she suggested a degree of Barbadian superiority in her autobiography titled *Unbought and Unbossed*. Chisholm wrote, "The Barbadians' drive to achieve and excel is almost an obsession and is a characteristic that other islanders do not share to the same degree. The Barbadians who came to Brooklyn all wanted, and most of them got, the same two things: a brownstone house and a college education for their children."[25] The late-twentieth-century Jamaican-born military leader Colin Powell, former Chairman of the Joint Chiefs of Staff as well as Secretary of State, also suggested a sense of Caribbean superiority in his autobiography as he maintained that his parents' coming of age in Jamaica—a county where black people are the majority—fostered an unparalleled self-esteem and racial pride. Although Powell was born in Harlem, he believed that his parents, Maud and Luther Powell, possessed attributes that were uniquely Jamaican that had a positive impact on him.[26] Being surrounded by so many professional black Jamaicans served as role models of success. In contrast, Richard B. Moore was a unifier to the core. There is no record of his ever portraying Caribbean people as superior to American-born blacks or of his presenting Barbadians as more intellectually advanced than his counterparts from other islands in the Caribbean. He may have easily succumbed to the temptation to discriminate in view of the widespread positive stereotypes of Barbadians.

But just as the early-twentieth-century assessment of Caribbean immigrants as the "Jews of the Black Race" was a double-edged compliment, so was the positive stereotype of Barbadians as particularly literate and intellectual as when some other islander suggested that Barbadian scholastic aptitude was obtained at the expense of indigenous pride and self-respect. Stokely Carmichael observed in his autobiography that sometimes other islanders interpreted Barbadian intellectual achievement as a sign of their docility and full-scale acceptance of British mores: "Among Caribbean people, the popular, slightly ironic name for Barbados is 'Little Britain,' a title that, however mocking in its inspiration, was accepted by the Bajans with no little pride."[27]

Like Caribbean intellectuals Richard B. Moore, Pearl Primus, and Paule Marshall, Chisholm also underscored a common African heritage to discourage anti–Caribbean sentiments harbored among American-born blacks. Chisholm stated, "It is wrong, because the accident that my ancestors were brought as slaves to the islands while black mainland natives' ancestors were brought as slaves to the States is really not important, compared to the common heritage of *black brotherhood and unity* in the face of oppression that we have."[28] Although Chisholm capitalized on popular notions of black racial solidarity, she still intensely criticized her contemporaries who spoke the language of unity but failed to apply proactive political action to such ideals. Such analysis demonstrates the power that Chisholm's translocal status afforded her. Chisholm's translocal cultural identities allowed her to both assume and criticize numerous social and political cross-sections, which included the interests of participants in the civil rights movement, Black Power, and third-wave feminism.

Civil Rights, Black Power, and Women's Rights

Chisholm understood the struggle for racial equality and women's rights as inextricably linked. She compared American women's struggles to overcome sexism to the previous political activism that black Americans had waged in attempts to dismantle racial oppression. "It is true that women are second-class citizens, just as black people are," Chisholm suggested, "I want the time to come when we can be as blind to sex as we are to color."[29] Chisholm was not the first to draw this comparison; antebellum white female intellectuals had found much food for thought in exploring similarities between white women's political disenfranchisement and the subaltern position of African slaves in America. But in 1970s New York, Chisholm singularly linked the long-standing political battles against racism and sexism as her personal identity as a black, educated, and outspoken woman was a political statement within itself. Contrary to antebellum eras in which white feminists manipulated the image and words of a black feminist such as Sojourner Truth, the march of time and the evolution toward political inclusion allowed Chisholm to better control her public image and intellectual legacy.

Chisholm faced the double challenge of sexism and racism throughout her political career, but when weighing the detriment of the two, she deemed sexism to be a greater obstacle to overcome. She experienced a unique type of intraracial sexism from black male constituents and political opponents. As scholar Valerie Smith has shrewdly noted, racism and sexism often interact in complex ways and conspire to restrain black women's social and political agency.[30] "To the black men—even some of those supposedly supporting me—sensitive about female domination," Chisholm recalled, "they were running me down as a bossy female, a would-be matriarch."[31] For Chisholm, this accusation was not only political, but it was also personal. Although she was usually taciturn regarding private matters such as her marriage to Jamaican immigrant Conrad Chisholm, in her autobiography she opened up a bit as she wrote:

> Thoughtless people have suggested that my husband would have to be a weak man who enjoys having me dominate him. They are wrong on both counts. Conrad is a strong, self-sufficient personality, and I do not dominate him. As a matter of fact, a weak man's feelings of insecurity would long since have wrecked a marriage like ours.[32]

On one hand, Chisholm's description of Conrad's persistence in courtship, in spite of her aloofness, and her defense of his honor as a strong man is kind of sweet. On the other hand, as I read her words, I imagine the face of an angry, conservative "gender dictator" perched on Chisholm's shoulder—goading her to write these words. And then I think, "Fight the patriarchy," because it's a shame that she felt like she needed to justify herself.

For some black men, Chisholm's assertiveness brought to mind the negative stereotypes of overbearing black women who populated the pages of prevalent "Culture of Poverty" social scientific literature.[33] At the first National Black Feminist Organization (NBFO) conference in 1974, Chisholm observed, "Black women used to be asked, what are you being educated for? You're emasculating the black man. Because of historical circumstances, black women had to develop perseverance and strength—and her reward was to be labeled 'matriarch' by white sociologists. . . . This rhetoric keeps black women hopelessly retarded. Our men are coming forward but our race needs the collective power of black men and black women. We can't be divided by the 'enemy' who tells us black women are keeping black men back. The black women [*sic*] must work side by side with her man."[34] While acknowledging sexism, Chisholm still aimed to bridge the gender gap to press forward with her progressive political agenda. She was a shrewd and pragmatic politician who knew the language of unity is much more appealing than harping on elements of division.

Although Chisholm enjoyed a greater degree of political freedom than her early twentieth-century counterparts who tried to find a voice within Marcus Garvey's pronatal and hypermasculine regime, Chisholm still battled a new form of black political machismo that grew out of Black Power stylistic models. Chisholm recalled that her Republican opponent and former national chairperson of the Congress of Racial Equality (CORE), an American-born black man named James Farmer, leveraged such Black Power masculine iconography to his advantage during his congressional campaign. "Farmer's campaign was well oiled; it had money dripping all over it," Chisholm recalled, "He toured the district with sound trucks manned by young dudes with Afros, beating tom-toms: the big, black, male image. He drew the television cameramen like flies, a big national figure, winding up to become New York City's second black congressman (after Adam Clayton Powell II)."[35] This is quite a stunning scene of black male power—replete with romanticized African diasporic demonstrations of physical strength and subsequent public authority. But Farmer's money and masculine political iconography proved to be no match for Chisholm, who became an icon within her own right, coming to represent 1970s women's political empowerment.

Feminism

Chisholm urged American women of diverse cultural and racial backgrounds to rise up and assert their political voices. Her promotion of women's political empowerment and multiracial political coalitions drastically differed from Jamaican-born Marcus Garvey's Universal Negro Improvement Association, which epitomized black masculinity and industrialized empowerment as its members aimed to carve out a piece of a capitalistic pie for black Americans. In contrast, Chisholm's constituency included women of all races, as she gained a considerable following among white women feminists and successfully secured the institutional support of the National Organization of Women (NOW). While Paule Marshall focused on the need for black women's voices to be heard and for black women to see reflections of themselves in literature,[36] Chisholm's political appeal was much broader as she encouraged all women, regardless of race, to speak up and to become more politically empowered. She was relentlessly optimistic in her assessment of the future of cross-cultural feminist politics in America. "We—American women—are beginning to respond to our oppression," Chisholm observed, "While most of us are not yet revolutionaries, we are getting in tune with the cry of the liberation groups."[37]

Chisholm's understanding of women's intellectual and political character, however, was somewhat romanticized, for she suggested that women held a monopoly on good sense and good will. She believed that women's approach to political issues was more sincere, intuitive, and holistic than that of their male counterparts. Chisholm emphasized the need for women to assume steerage of an American political ship that had veered off course by employing nautical metaphors—terms usually considered masculine—and turned them on their head. "Our country is in deep trouble," she admonished, "And we need women; yes, we need women . . . to make their voices heard in policy making and decision-making processes of this nation so as to be able to get this ship of state guided clearly again on a path of sanity."[38] Chisholm's emphatic tone and effective use of repetition inspired pride and pulled at the heartstrings of female constituents as she underscored women's central role in ushering the United States into a brighter and moralistic future.

While Chisholm's use of nautical metaphors, especially her ordination of women captains of America's brighter future, somewhat challenged prevalent stereotypes of women as passive and subservient, she still extended popular definitions of women's work—rearing children and keeping a clean house—into the realm of politics. Chisholm also urged women to run for political office to "start cleaning . . . up" an unjust and corrupt political system, as an extension of her belief in perceptions of the female gender as exceptionally moral and upstanding human beings. In a 1972 publication geared toward young female readers, Chisholm deemed women politicians to be "much more apt to act for the sake of a principle or moral purpose,"[39] than their male counterparts. For Chisholm, "cleaning-up" American politics and steering the nation onto a "path of sanity" would require a reassessment of the United States role in foreign affairs and a revision of government spending—prioritizing American citizens. In a 1973 speech, Chisholm observed, "Our government called off the 'war on poverty' at home while its war abroad went on at an enormous cost in lives and resources."[40] This criticism of the irony in government spending also harked back to Chisholm's arguments about the moral economy of the nation and the need for women to employ their common sense and good will to help the nation.

Chisholm focused on the nurture of children as another woman's role that had political and social utility and gave foundation for the necessary presence of women in government. She linked a profound democratic hope to the image of America's children—its next generation of leaders, and the proper nurturing of these children by upstanding women citizens. She declared, "I say unequivocally that there is a need for women in America to move out politically to save America's children—to save our children."[41] For Chisholm, "saving America's children" entailed improving daycare services, primary and secondary schools, and healthcare. Chisholm's voice reached a crescendo and was met with great applause. As a former primary school teacher and day care facility administrator, Chisholm spoke from personal convictions and experiential knowledge. The content and delivery of her message emphasized the need for a new era in American politics as she urged women voters to exercise their citizenship rights and fully participate in the experiment in American democracy to right the wrongs committed by war-hungry and elitist male politicians.

In stark contrast to the bellicose and bombastic politics of the war-torn late 1960s and early 1970s, Chisholm proposed a kinder and gentler approach to governing. In numerous speeches, she linked the nonviolent philosophies of Jesus Christ, Mahatma Gandhi, and Martin Luther King to the true character of most women. "The warmth, gentleness, and compassion that are part of the female stereotype are positive human values," Chisholm proposed, "values that are becoming more and more important as the values of our world begin to shatter and fall from our grasp." This passage was a prayer of sorts—that the next generation of young women would use their "female strength"[42] for the greater good of society as a whole. Although Chisholm's celebration of the virtues of female citizens grew out of her own gender essentialist notions, it also was rooted in historical realities. Pacifism was a longstanding tradition among female political activists—from Progressive Era reformist Jane Addams opposing World War I as the first president of the United States Women's International League for Peace and Freedom in 1915, to Manhattan US Representative Bella S. Abzug's vehement opposition to the war in Vietnam.

Although Chisholm's feminist appeal transcended race and attracted a culturally diverse constituency of women, Chisholm still acknowledged the enduring overlap of race and class, and how this social reality shaped white women's political concerns differently than it shaped those of their black counterparts. "It has been generally true that the women's movement has been a white middle-class phenomenon," Chisholm observed. "Black women share many of the same concerns as white ones, including the need for a national day care system and a guarantee of equal pay for equal work, but they have different priorities from white women."[43] Given the disproportionate number of poor black women compared to their white counterparts, Chisholm characterized black women's concerns as pragmatic and white women's as more ideological.

Chisholm drew upon diverse old and new political philosophies to construct her political identity: feminism, black racial consciousness, post-civil rights multiculturalism, American democracy, humanism, and universalism. She inhabited a unique historical moment, in which the idea that the personal is political and the political is personal resonated with participants in political movements ranging from civil rights and women's rights to gay rights. In this cultural landscape, even the self-presentation of political activists took on new meaning.

Personal Style and Visual Politics

Shirley Chisholm was meticulous about her physical appearance, she spoke Spanish fluently, and contrary to her prim and proper schoolmarm image, she knew how to tell a bawdy joke and she could dance.[44] Politician Bevan Dufty recalled:

> She was a great dancer. My analogy is she would have been the perfect dance partner to Dr. Huxtable on the *Cosby Show* because she did that very interpretive kind of mood dancing, and she'd have her eyes closed, and would really get into her groove, and she was just a lot of fun. Behind closed doors she could really cuss, and tell salty stories, but at the same time she had a regality about her and a formality about her where we never called her Shirley. We always called her Ms. C or Mrs. C. . . . And her office was wild.[45]

For Chisholm, dancing functioned as a release from the pressures of her political office. She encountered a great deal of racism and sexism—including an assassination attempt that she tried to push to the margins of her memory.[46] Like Adam Clayton Powell II, Chisholm was a celebrity politician in her own right. So, when she went out socially with friends and colleagues, Chisholm would don a wide-brimmed hat and oversized sunglasses to disguise herself to avoid being recognized. But, on the dance floor, she felt free. Pearl Primus would certainly identity with this point: given the pressures of public intellectualism, all activists should practice some form of creative release. Chisholm achieved this release and exhibited the multifaceted nature of her personality on the dance floor. Even at age sixty-one when she retired, *Jet* magazine published a short article titled "Chisholm Tells Retirees She Still Boogies at

61."[47] Chisholm based her sense of self worth on her exceptional intellect and on her vim and vigor. Upon her retirement, she proudly declared, "Very few people can keep up with me."[48]

In addition to her physical vitality and flare on the dance floor, Chisholm also defined her selfhood through her style of dress. She devoted deliberate attention to her physical appearance because she understood that the personal is political and the political is personal. In turn, Chisholm wore smart cat-eyed glasses, Fashion Fair makeup, tailored below-the-knew dresses, fur coats, and occasionally donned a fedora. Her attire mirrored her confidence, intelligence, liveliness, and likeability.

Chisholm's clothing, accessories, and demeanor also reflected her betwixt and between cultural identities and marked her as a participant in a unique moment in American political history. Her eyeglasses resembled those worn by the slain militant civil rights activist Malcolm X, one of her political role models, and she sported chic and neatly tailored dresses often made of fabric with bold geometric-shaped prints, echoing the mod styles of the time. She was remarkably poised, well spoken, and self-assured. Even her omnipresent wigs hint at her multi-layered cultural identity. She did not wear an Afro or the manufactured coif popularized by the predominantly younger prominent "Black Power" activists engaged in radical identity politics, such as Angela Davis, Kathleen Cleaver, or Assata Shakur. Nor did she wear the longer, straighter, flowing hairstyles that were prevalent in the 1970s. Chisholm's wigs most often consisted of large, piled-high curls resembling 1950s bouffant hairdos and conveying a sense of wholesomeness that was reinforced by her daycare center and schoolteacher professional roots.

Chisholm's carefully chosen attire, signature wigs, and slender physique rendered an image of the quintessential lady, perhaps to salve the reception of her aggressive rhetorical style and hardline pragmatism. Chisholm stood—historically and existentially—as a bridge between previous and present eras of hypermasculine black racial uplift agendas posed by other Caribbean–born men like Garvey and Carmichael of the Black Panthers and a new age of cross-cultural and multivocal politics. According to congressional aide, administrative assistant, and friend Joyce Bolden, Chisholm loved for her to apply makeup and assist in the selection of wigs. Caribbean New Yorker Wesley "Mac" Holder, Chisholm's mentor and adviser, was not enthusiastic about the level of care that Chisholm took regarding her physical appearance.[49] Perhaps Holder believed that Chisholm's ample wigs and glamorous jewelry might detract from her formidable intellect and the seriousness of the political issues at hand. Chisholm disagreed. She combined the political influence of her father Charles, a true organic intellectual, with the fashion sense of her mother Ruby, an excellent seamstress, and presented herself as a smart, mature, and politically savvy woman.

Chisholm's political debut occurred when personal style was increasingly political. Her fashion sense echoed broader aesthetic trends even in the media. Black American female sitcom characters such as the title role of *Julia*, the elegant and competent nurse played by Diahann Carroll; Louise (or "Weezie"), wife of George Jefferson in *The Jeffersons*; and even project-dwelling Wilona of *Good Times* all wore similar wigs. These characters were African American women of various social and economic backgrounds who all represented a more mature generation of the "New Black Woman," being in their late thirties and older and balancing outspoken personalities with style and grace.

The fullness and height of Chisholm's wigs evoked glamorous images of Motown "girl groups," recalling the elaborate wigs worn by Diana Ross and the Supremes. Keeping with this theme, Chisholm appeared on the cover of *Jet* magazine in 1972.[50] She wore a salt-and-pepper wig with large curls, enhanced eyebrows, cat-eye frames, subtle blush, mauve lipstick, dangly gold earrings, a coat with a fur collar, and a slight smile. Chisholm looked directly into the camera, engaging the viewer head-on, conveying an image of refinement and seriousness, but also approachability. In numerous issues of *Ebony* magazine throughout the 1970s, Chisholm appeared in similar attire. Often standing beside or shaking hands with young black inner-city potential constituents, Chisholm's fur collars and coats—whether faux or real, herringbone print poncho, large wigs, and church-lady hats sometimes struck a stark contrast with the casual dress of those around her. Chisholm was forty-eight years old when she campaigned to become the Democratic Party's presidential candidate, and even her self-presentation characterized her as part of a slightly older generation's approach to black consciousness and feminism at the time.

Although Chisholm's physical appearance and pragmatic politics sharply contrasted with the more Africa-centered and militant stylized politics of the Black Panther Party, the organization still strongly endorsed her. The national chairperson Bobby Seale considered Chisholm to be "the best social critic of America's injustices to run for President from whatever party." And when some of Chisholm's supporters encouraged her to shun any association with the group's radicalism and to renounce the Black Panther's backing, she "flatly refused," because as American citizens the party members were free to support whomever they chose. Chisholm had intimate knowledge of intraracial sexism prevalent among black public and private communities at the time; she was especially "gratified . . . that the Panthers succeeded in rising above sex prejudice, something that many blacks find difficult," for they supported Chisholm based on the integrity of her "positions and [her] programs, without regard to [her] being female."[51]

Chisholm's self-presentation conveyed her personal pride and demonstrated her broader participation in a significant historical moment. Her political presence represented a highpoint and merger of civil rights activism for racial equality and social justice and American feminist struggles against institutional and quotidian sexism, replete with the accompanying generational and cultural clashes. In many ways, Chisholm stood at a political and existential crossroads during the 1970s, as she articulated her identity as a feminist, as a black American, and as a progressive politician and human being—committed to improving the plight of everyday working-class Americans, of all races and cultural backgrounds, whom she often referred to as simply "the people."

"Multiculturalism"

Shirley Chisholm's translocal status allowed her to speak from a position of experience and power to a broad ranging group of constituents. Chisholm's intense intellect, gumption, and political savvy combined to draw a broad range of constituents including women and young first-time voters of all races as well as members of the working classes and black Americans in general. Shirley Downs, a white feminist who served as a legislative aide during Chisholm's 1972 campaign, would later recall Chisholm's deliberate efforts to bridge cultural differences as she appealed to a somewhat eclectic constituency from diverse cultural backgrounds. "She would talk to any group. She didn't care if you were old, if you were young, if you were black, if you were white, if you were Hispanic. This was a maiden voyage."[52] Like Chisholm, Downs highlighted the newness of Chisholm's presence in the political arena. While Garvey's early twentieth-century campaign focused on racial uplift through black-nationalist forms of cooperative economics and social segregation, the political momentum of and identity politics associated with the civil rights and feminist movements allowed Chisholm to engage with a fundamentally integrationist mission and find a degree of success as she gained the most delegates for a female presidential until Hilary Clinton's 2008 campaign to represent the Democratic Party.

Chisholm's political success lay in her grassroots appeal as she launched a variegated, no-frills approach to New York politics and drew an extremely culturally diverse constituency. In her 1970 autobiography titled *Unbought and Unbossed,* Chisholm recalled, "During the week I went to endless little house parties and teas given by women. In the black neighborhood I ate chitlins, in the Jewish neighborhood bagels and lox, in the Puerto Rican neighborhood *arroz con pollo.* . . . Sometimes a woman would tell me that she would like to have a party for me, but she couldn't afford it, and I would provide the money. I went to all kinds of homes. I wasn't interested in style."[53] Chisholm welcomed such encounters as she, in many ways, epitomized Brooklyn residents' polyglot political voices throughout her Congressional campaign. In her 1973 autobiography, *The Good Fight,* Chisholm recalled, "There were ordinary black and white, Jewish, WASP, and Spanish-surnamed citizens here and there who kept telling me, 'You're what this country needs.'"[54] Again, an extremely culturally diverse group of supporters embraced Chisholm because the newness of her political presence and voice was particularly refreshing at a time of upheaval. The United States was still reeling from the cultural wars of the 1960s, issues of inner-city poverty, and the catastrophes of Vietnam. Chisholm's straightforward speech and commitment to everyday people served as a counterpoint to many of her contemporaries who seemed to be out of touch with "the people."

Like Jamaican-born Unitarian minister Ethelred Brown, Shirley Chisholm presented herself as an extremely dignified and competent intellectual who just happened to be a member of a socially constructed racial group that was deemed inferior. She advanced humanist and universalist notions of the fundamental equality of all human beings, but her rhetoric of egalitarianism focused on shared biological traits, common desires, and democratic ideals instead of Unitarian theology. Chisholm suggested that underneath the epidermis, all human beings possess the same organs and biological systems, and these biological commonalities demonstrate broader existential and political equalities. Although Chisholm capitalized on the burgeoning rhetoric of multiculturalism, mainly the emphasis on mutual cultural respect, she also employed arguments of biological essentialism to underscore the basic commonalities of all human beings, regardless of race. "Take away an accident of pigmentation of a thin layer of our outer skin," Chisholm intellectualized, "and there is no difference between me and anyone else. All we want is for that trivial difference to make no difference."[55] Chisholm echoed the wish of Martin Luther King's famous 1963 "I Have a Dream" speech, for they both hoped for a day when everyone would be judged by the "content of their character" instead of the "color of their skin."

Chisholm's cross-cultural understanding of "the people" also included broader appeals that transcended race and cultural differences and were rooted in humanist and universalist philosophies. When contemplating racial bias and sexism, she posed the rhetorical question: "My God, what do we want? What does any human being want?"[56] Chisholm recognized that Americans of color were disproportionately poor in comparison to their white counterparts, but she emphasized their common desires for quality healthcare and public schools. She called for unity among American citizens in order to realize these common goals: "All of us in this country today regardless of our particular sex realize that we've got to come together in order to make the republic work for everyone regardless of race, creed, or color."[57]

Chisholm also tapped into language and concepts of intelligence and equality based in the modern human sciences and universalist understandings of spirituality to further her arguments for political equality. To cover all bases, Chisholm made intellectual and moral appeals to her constituents, urging them to recognize the unique abilities and fundamental equalities of their fellow citizens. "There is no psychological test as yet that indicates that man has a superior brain to women or vice versa," Chisholm proposed. "The fact of the matter is moralistically that the talents that we have are talents that have been given to us, if you will, by God and that it is our responsibility to utilize these talents ... in a creative and constructive manner."[58] Chisholm relied on Christian liberalism to prove that women citizens possessed valuable skills, which could be put to good use for the greater good of their local communities and the nation.

Although Chisholm expressed pride in her cultural, racial, and gendered identity, she also employed humanist and universalist speech to transcend these socially constructed categories. While appropriating political rhetoric from the very recent civil rights movement and ongoing feminist activism, Chisholm self-consciously presented herself as a spokesperson for all working-class people, regardless of race and gender. "I am not the candidate of black America, although I am black and proud. I am not the candidate of the women's movement, although I am a woman and I am equally proud of that," Chisholm pronounced in 1972 at the Concord Baptist Church. "I am the candidate of the *people of America*."[59]

Chisholm pursued the politically astute path of celebrating her multidimensional identities as a child of immigrants, as a black American, and as a woman, while emphasizing her American-ness to appeal to the broadest constituency possible. In contrast, fellow Brooklyn-born, Barbadian-American intellectual Paule Marshall also embraced her multilayered identities as a child of immigrants, as a black American, and as a woman, but throughout her career she has emphasized her African-ness in her literature and interviews. While Chisholm's political presence signaled a new era in American democracy, Paule Marshall's focus on Barbadian vernacular in her writing may be seen as a continuation of artistic activism within the same tradition of Pearl Primus's use of dance to promote mutual cultural respect.

CHAPTER 6

Paule Marshall and the Voice of Black Immigrant Women

Soully-gal, talk yuh talk! . . . In this man world
you got to take yuh mouth and make a gun!'
—PAULE MARSHALL

While Barbadian-American politician Shirley Chisholm used her exceptional public speaking skills and political office in the fight for civil rights and women's rights, novelist Paule Marshall emphasized the written and spoken word, especially the unique cadences of Barbadian immigrant women's speech, as a source of personal and political power. Born in Brooklyn to parents from Barbados, Marshall based her fictional characters on her lived experience. The characters in her novels and the women in her life deployed fiery speech to confront racism in America and to remind themselves of the beauty and struggles of the homeland they had left behind. Like other pioneering performance artists such as Pearl Primus and Hazel Scott, Marshall took great pride in her Caribbean heritage as she used her work to give voice to an often overlooked demographic: black immigrant women.

Marshall adds a unique perspective to the broader study of Caribbean immigrants in New York City because she is second-generation American—and the only subject of this book who was still living as I was writing it. While Ethelred Brown, Richard B. Moore, and Pearl Primus emigrated respectively from Jamaica, Barbados, and Trinidad to New York during various stages of childhood, adolescence, and young adulthood, Marshall was born Valenza Pauline Burke in Brooklyn on April 9, 1929, and the city's densely packed blocks of brownstones were among her first sights. She did not see her ancestral island until the age of six.

As a child of immigrants who came of age during post-World War I Brooklyn, Marshall witnessed firsthand the failures and triumphs of American democracy. Her writing reflects the mind of a brilliant black woman of

Tammy L. Brown, *Talk That Talk: Paule Marshall*, Mixed Media, 2014.

Caribbean descent who entered the literary limelight at a unique historical moment. During the height of the civil rights movement and third-wave feminism, she published novels, short stories, and essays that reflected these culture wars.

In this chapter, I use Paule Marshall's life and writing to explore the meanings of American democracy and the history of black women's personal and political empowerment. I provide close readings of her life story, novels, and essays—mainly *Brown Girl, Brownstones*, *The Chosen Place, the Timeless People*, *Praisesong for the Widow*, and "The Poets in the Kitchen"— to reveal how Marshall's Caribbean identity shaped her black consciousness and feminist politics. In this regard, I embrace the advice of biographer Arnold Rampersad, who argues that biographies of creative writers should "suggest an intimate relationship to the art of the writer."[2] This underscores the fact that most fiction is autobiographical to some extent. Writers write what they know and the details of their lived experience reflected in historical context are paramount.

To show how Marshall's life story and creative writing reflect the lived experiences of Caribbean New Yorkers, I juxtapose original interviews that I conducted with Caribbean women immigrants with my analysis of Marshall's work. In no way am I suggesting that fictional characters are interchangeable with the lives of real human beings; however, because Marshall's writing is historically based, her work serves as a window into the cultural landscape of Caribbean New York. Marshall's writing indeed reveals the complex intersections of race, ethnicity, class, gender, and geographic identities at the time as well as a broader trend regarding the shifting demographics of New York, especially the expansion of the Caribbean intelligentsia from Harlem to the borough of Brooklyn.

Marshall provides a much-needed insider's view of ethnic diversity within black New York. Scholars writing during the opening decades of the century discussed the social, cultural, and political milieu of New York as an industrializing city that produced alienation and crime, but ethnic diversity among black New Yorkers received little attention. At the end of the twentieth century, historian Winston James recognized the academic focus on European immigrants that overlooked their Caribbean counterparts as a type of "intellectual apartheid."[3] Decades before James reprimanded historians who ignore black immigrants, Panama-born sociologist Roy Bryce-Laporte invoked Ralph Ellison's classic novel *Invisible Man* to describe the lack of analysis regarding intraracial black cultural diversity. He wrote, "Caribbean immigrants suffer multiple levels of Ellisonian-like invisibility."[4] Although black immigrants were indeed an understudied topic, Bryce-Laporte's assertion raises the question: Invisible to whom? Bryce-Laporte's notion of invisibility privileges the white gaze, while I explore American-born and foreign-born blacks' vivid perceptions of self and each other in relation to lines between insider and outsider status that have been drawn, erased, and redrawn. Paule Marshall's oeuvre underscores these points by delving into African diasporic communities and focusing especially on black immigrant women on their own terms.[5]

Marshall's constructions of African diasporic identities and her insistence that black immigrant women be "seen and heard" allows her characters and readers to take ownership of their pasts to carve out a more confident place in the present. Privileging black women's voices in her work, Paule Marshall demonstrates that those often thought of as subaltern can speak effectively for themselves.[6] This idea of "giving voice" is integrally tied to democratic notions of representation, which imply visibility and necessitate a critique of notions of black American invisibility as articulated by black intellectuals.

By the time scholar Harold Cruse published *The Crisis of the Negro Intellectual* in 1967, cultural clashes between Caribbean immigrants and American-born blacks had been in full swing for over forty years. Cruse stood at the center of such conflicts among black intellectuals. For instance, in an attempt to cast Paule Marshall as a confused woman suffering from an identity crisis, Cruse called Marshall "neither fish nor fowl"—referring to her mixed Caribbean and black American heritage. Reading Marshall's short stories and novels, one is left with a sense of the author's existential angst as she repeatedly attempts to reconcile her multiple identities as a woman, Barbadian-American, Pan-Africanist, and politically conscious human being keenly cognizant of the myriad ways in which capitalism contributed to the social and economic oppression of blacks in the United States and abroad. Countering arguments by sociologists in the 1980s and 1990s who predicted that second-generation Caribbean Americans would lose their island-specific cultural heritage and seamlessly assimilate into American-born black culture, Marshall's life and work demonstrate that Caribbean immigrant identities during an era of cultural pluralism and post-structuralism have been much more complicated.[11] Marshall's persistent concern with "reconciling" her multiple identities reflects the cultural clashes among American-born and foreign-born blacks. If black American and Caribbean cultures were similar and harmonious, there would be nothing to "reconcile."

Paule Marshall's visions and revisions of blackness were shaped by the unique interaction of intraracial cultural clashes, the construction of a somewhat romanticized African diaspora, anticapitalist sensibilities, power struggles between men and women, and generational conflicts. So it is not surprising that binaries abound in her work. Marshall effectively captures the tension of old versus new, countryside versus city, and an agricultural colonial economy versus an American industrial one. In an autobiographical essay titled "To Da-duh in Memoriam," Marshall recalled the manifestation of these tensions when she visited Barbados as a child: young Pauline boasted about the grandeur of New York skyscrapers in the fast-paced city, while her physically slight yet mentally strong grandmother adamantly emphasized the natural beauty of Barbados's rural landscape. For Marshall's grandmother, whom she affectionately called "Da-duh," the island's tall, thick-trunked trees dwarfed New York's skyscrapers.[7] Thus, the emergence of a Caribbean American identity was marked not only by conflicts among inter-island ethnic communities and tensions between Caribbean immigrants and American-born blacks, but also by inter-generational struggles within families.

My discussion of Paule Marshall's attempts to reconcile these binaries builds on biographical interviews with the author and analysis of her novels, short stories, and essays. Marshall published her first short story in 1954, but even her more recent work lends understanding to earlier periods, her characters and constructed narratives based on memories of her own coming of age while living in a tightly knit, Caribbean community in Brooklyn. Her literary corpus and interviews paint a complex cityscape—replete with the sights, sounds, smells, and textures of Caribbean New York.[8] Marshall's early writing focuses on Barbadian immigrant identities in New York and on issues of feminism. The short stories of her next period explore black male subjects grappling with the limitations rigid notions of masculinity in various locales throughout the African diaspora. Later novels critique European colonialism and American imperialism. And her most recent work draws concrete interpersonal, cultural, and political linkages among members in her carefully constructed, albeit somewhat romanticized African diaspora, one that only begins to address the cleavages and conflicts among people of African descent in America and around the world. In a 2004 interview, Marshall claimed that over her lifetime her work changed only in style—her later work is quite succinct compared to her earlier work—but not in content.[9] But I contend that Marshall's concerns have broadened in thematic and geographic scope, and this expansion grows from historical realities surrounding each work. To understand Marshall's intellectual and artistic evolution, we must begin with the push and pull factors that motivated her parents to move from Barbados to Brooklyn.

"From Barbados to Brooklyn": Push and Pull Factors

Abstract qualities such as "drive," "hope," and "ambition" propelled black immigrants to build new lives in New York City. In many ways, the stakes were higher for a person who traveled far to become a success. One woman who emigrated from Jamaica to New York in the 1960s recalled a visit to Jamaica after spending a few years in the United States; when she discovered her former classmates had surpassed her in educational training and professional experience in the nursing field, she vowed, "I'd rather die than return to Jamaica before reaching a similar or higher level of success."[10] Mary Phillips's immigrant status compounded her sense of professional rivalry; she measured her success against her peers in New York City and in Jamaica.

Limited opportunities in their homelands motivated many Caribbean immigrants to endure short-term sacrifice in the interest of long-term gains. Paule Marshall's parents, Samuel and Ada (Clement) Burke, emigrated from Barbados to New York during World War I. They were among the 13,019 Caribbean immigrants who moved to the United States between 1914 and 1918.[11] The few jobs in Barbados and the many more in New York motivated their relocation. Sugar production was the primary source of income for most of the Caribbean at the time; between 1900 and 1929 the British Caribbean alone exported 802,000 tons of sugar.[12] From the 1910s through the 1930s, sugarcane remained the major product of the colonial economy of Barbados. This agricultural, colonial economy provided limited employment opportunities for educated Barbadian professionals, skilled workers, and laborers hoping to become social and economically upwardly mobile. Between 1908 and 1924, most black immigrants who moved to the United States were skilled workers; they numbered 33,233.[13] These newcomers were seamstresses, dressmakers, carpenters, and accountants. During the same time frame, 22,204 black immigrant "servants," 12,338 farm laborers, and 12,449 manual laborers also arrived in the United States.[14] Marshall's parents were among this group of working-class peoples who hoped to carve out a more financially secure existence in a new place.

Marshall's parents found low-wage jobs in New York factories and as housekeepers for whites living in the wealthier sections of Brooklyn. Samuel worked in a mattress factory and Ada worked as a domestic, mainly in Jewish homes.[15] Ada and her sturdy collective of Barbadian women friends called this work "scrubbing Jew floor."[16] The relationship between Caribbean immigrants and Jewish New Yorkers was markedly conflicted. On one hand, Marshall's mother and friends criticized their Jewish employers and landlords for being exploitive, but they also respected Jewish New Yorkers' work ethic and social and economic success. Some black immigrants considered Jews "model immigrants" and aimed to duplicate their systems of cooperative economics and entrepreneurial drive. Shirley Chisholm used this cultural comparison in praise of her parents who worked hard to earn enough money to purchase a brownstone home in Brooklyn. Chisholm stated, "It is important to notice that they never questioned they had to do these things: Barbadians are like that. They are bright, thrifty, ambitious people. The other islanders call them 'Black Jews.'"[17]

This Caribbean American emphasis on entrepreneurship as a means to achieve their American dreams is reflected in Marshall's first novel. In *Brown*

Girl, Brownstones, the main mother figure, Silla Boyce, urges her husband Deighton to follow the entrepreneurial example of other Barbadian and Jewish immigrants by joining the Barbadian American Association to pool resources to take advantage of the real estate business as a means to achieve upward social and economic mobility. She says, "They got this Business Association going good now and 'nough people joining. Even I gon join. Every West Indian out here taking a lesson from the Jew landlord and converting these old houses into rooming houses—making the closets-self into rooms some them—and pulling down plenty-plenty money by the week."[18] Silla's use of hyperbole and repetition underscores the potential profitability of property ownership. Closets are obviously too small to sleep in, but her point is clear. The more tenants that a landlord packs into a brownstone, the larger the profit. Her repetition of the adjective "plenty" to describe how much money they stand to make connotes the literal stacking of coins and dollar bills.

Delayed gratification possessed a unique tenor for Caribbean immigrants. Like their Irish, Italian, and Polish counterparts, they were willing to work menial jobs because the pay was so much higher than what they made in their countries of origin. New York life was hard, but life in Barbados was worse. Although the Barbadian women in Marshall's Brooklyn community often recalled the good times they shared in Barbados, Marshall recognized that "mixed in with those memories, tempering the nostalgia were the bitter, angry recollections of the poverty and the peculiar brand of colonial oppression and exploitation they had known on the island."[19] The balance of power in Barbados's British-run agricultural economy was so skewed that in 1929 the white elite owned ninety thousand acres of tillable land, while the black farmers owned only seventeen thousand acres total.[20] The average land holding for the approximately eighteen thousand small farmers was a mere 0.94 acres per person.

Such colonial exploitation pushed ambitious blacks out of the islands in search of better opportunities in cities such New York, Miami, and Philadelphia, as well as later London and various Canadian cities later. Most scholars have emphasized the importance of Caribbean immigrants' majority status in their homelands as a key component in self-esteem after arrival in the United States. Many scholars have misread Caribbean immigrants' tolerance of racial injustices in the United States as superior self-esteem in contrast to American-born blacks. Winston James and Joyce Moore Turner propose that Caribbean immigrants possessed less damaged psyches regarding racism, since slavery in the Caribbean allowed for more individual autonomy and was abolished earlier; such less-bruised spirits were better equipped to navigate the pitfalls of Jim and Jane Crow than their American-born black counterparts. I propose that Caribbean immigrants like Marshall's parents were willing to endure racism in the United States because of the material benefits that New York City offered, which sharply contrasted with the paltry possibilities in their islands of origin.

Paule Marshall's characters add texture to this observation. One of the first binaries that the reader encounters in *Brown Girl, Brownstones* is in descriptions of life in rural Barbados versus urban New York, also known as "home" versus "this man's country." The mother figure, Silla, details the perniciousness of race-based oppression in Barbados and the futility of trying to advance in such an unjust society: "you know what it is to work hard and still never made a head-way? That's Bimshire. One crop. People having to work for next skin to nothing. The white people treating we like slaves still and we taking it."[21] Although Silla's immigration to New York City proves that she refuses to "take it," she still speaks in solidarity with Barbadians who remain oppressed on the island by using the pronoun "we." She paints a portrait of economic stasis by underscoring that *one* agricultural crop fuels Bimshire's meager economy. She also suggests that liquor stores and organized religion conspire to "keep we pacify and in ignorance," and ends her tirade with a tone of resignation: "That's Barbados."[22] Marshall based this fictional account of destitution in Barbados on the stark reality that her parents and their friends knew too well.

Such a grim depiction of the poverty and limited opportunities in Barbados strengthens the backdrop that explains why families like Paule Marshall's immigrated to New York City, which they considered culturally and climatically cold. Again, Marshall's family struggled financially in New York, but they still believed their opportunities for social and economic advancement were greater in the new cosmopolitan locale versus the small island. Because American dollars could stretch further in Barbados than in New York, in 1959 Marshall spent eight months in Barbados writing and revising drafts of *Brown Girl*. During her sojourn, she lamented the destitution that still plagued her parents' birthplace thirty years after they had left. She observed, "The road to the airport lined with board and shingle houses weathered by the sun gives a picture of abject poverty." Marshall blamed this destitution on class schisms and neocolonialism, continuing, "The tragedy of Barbados [is that] the middle class tends to forget the ills of the lower classes and become British oriented. This is even more tragic since the real economic power lies in a few 'white' British families."[23] This observation is poignant and provocative. Like Caribbean New Negro leaders Ethelred Brown and Richard B. Moore, Marshall urged solidarity among African Caribbeans across class lines. She admonished middle- and upper-class black Barbadians to relinquish their false sense of superiority (to members of Barbados's lower classes) and refocus their attention on the main culprit—the white minority that controlled the island's wealth.

"American Dreams"

In contrast to the destitution of Barbados, the United States held out material hope. However, Marshall is quite critical of immigrant American Dreams that entailed the endless acquisition of consumer products and even the pursuit of property ownership by any means necessary. In turn, as a cautionary tale, many of Marshall's characters' unbridled greed hinders their self-actualization. This prevalent theme calls to mind the Biblical verse, "What does it profit a [wo]man to gain the whole world and lose [her] soul?"[24] Marshall's black women characters frequently pursue power via material possessions, but find that the fulfillment of their materialistic American Dreams yields false power, which ultimately hinders "being seen and heard." Or if one is "seen and heard," the presentation is not the true self. In contrast, Marshall often frames the true self in terms of a black woman character whose soul-journey requires an awakened understanding of a somewhat amorphous African heritage. This Africa-centered return to self then wins out over prior materialistic values that had been obstructing the true self.

The issue of property ownership was at the center of Marshall's critique of Barbadian immigrants' materialistic American Dreams; however, I maintain that the quest for home ownership also should be seen as an outgrowth of immigrants' prior experiences with property ownership in their islands of origin. It is true that buying a home was a major goal for most Caribbean New Yorkers. However, one surprising element in my interviews counters popular notions of immigrants in pursuit of the American Dream defined as home ownership and the trappings of comfortable suburban life. During numerous oral histories that I recorded from 2004 through 2006, Caribbean New Yorkers emphasized that their families and friends pursued property ownership as a natural extension of values held before their arrival in the United States. This drive was more pragmatic than idealistic—rooted in their previous experiences of owning homes in rural, Caribbean environments, which made them view paying high rent in New York City as "throwing money out the window."

Though Caribbean immigrants' experiences of prior property ownership and self-sufficiency practiced by growing food and keeping farm animals fueled their drive to "buy house" in New York City, some immigrants still considered home ownership to be a uniquely American ambition. Most of the characters in *Brown Girl, Brownstones* aggressively pursue their American Dreams mainly defined in capitalistic terms like conspicuous consumption and property ownership; however, not all of the Barbadian immigrants in the novel obtain material success. In *Brown Girl, Brownstones,* the Boyces work hard but never earn enough money to rent out their Brooklyn brownstone and move to Crown Heights like their successful Barbadian immigrant neighbors. The Boyces' narrative of immigrant struggle and social and economic failure parallels Marshall's own family's financial woes. Marshall recognized her parents' frustration:

> They were not able to progress in terms of the larger Barbadian community, West Indian community; so, that was very difficult for them. They never actually owned a house, even though we lived in the traditional brownstone house, we were *only leasing.* That was such a tragedy for my mother—the Barbadians, her friends, neighbors and so on, they were buying. So, not every Barbadian, not every West Indian owned a house. *Not every one of them fulfilled the American Dream.*[25]

Marshall's witnessing her parents' financial struggles and disappointment undoubtedly influenced the self-reflective themes she has pursued in her novels; her critiques of capitalism often involve a character striving to obtain material wealth at the expense of one's soul, integrity, love, or the like. In *Brown Girl, Brownstones,* Silla's unbridled ambition to buy a brownstone destroys her marriage, and Avey Johnson in *Praisesong for the Widow* epitomizes black American middle-class success, but she still remains unfulfilled until she returns to her "roots" by rediscovering her African heritage. Marshall's critique of capitalism is compelling, but her process of exorcizing the demons of capitalistic desire run amok is flawed. Looking for answers in a premodern past does not always help one's adjustment to a postmodern present and future.

In addition to home ownership, many of the Barbadian immigrants in Marshall's world measured their success by the achievements of their children. For black immigrant women in particular, being seen and heard within Caribbean New York was indeed tied to the educational and professional success of one's children. Paule Marshall's mother promoted a fairly modest "American Dream" compared to their Barbadian neighbors who pushed their children to pursue professional careers as teachers and social workers. Ada encouraged Paule to find a practical job. Marshall recalled, "When I said I wanted to go to college, my mother suggested that the telephone company had just started hiring colored, and maybe I should go downtown."[26] In contrast, her father, Samuel, favored spiritual commitment over a secular, American-brand of progress—measured in property ownership, the company one keeps, and the career status of one's children.[27] The main parental figures in *Brown Girl, Brownstones* reflect similar conflicts regarding Caribbean immigrants' differing attitudes toward success in America.

Samuel Burke's membership in Father Divine's religious organization required him to forsake all secular possessions and affiliations. Divine's Peace Mission attracted a significant number of Caribbean immigrants. Statistics on Divine's membership are somewhat contradictory, and it is difficult to calculate the number of Caribbean congregants since a central tenet of Divine's message was the restructuring of familial relationships, which included name changes—as the spiritual family of Divinites supplanted the importance of the nuclear family. Nonetheless, a 1931 Peace Mission rally in New York City attracted between five and ten thousand participants.[28] During the same year, Divine was arrested at his Long Island commune for "disturbing the peace" with Peace Mission worship services. Other estimates of Divine's membership during the height of the Great Depression were as high as two million.[29] Divine's brand of "New Thought" theology which maintained that God would prosper Divinites appealed to Marshall's father as it was epitomized by the lavish banquets that Father Divine hosted, even in the midst of economic depression.

For such immigrants, participation in Divine's Peace Mission allowed for radical refashioning of self—and how one is seen and heard in his or her community. This redefinition of community lifted the pressure to social and economically succeed as immigrants. This value of "being seen and heard" was related to Caribbean male immigrants' sense of masculinity and community respect. When Samuel left his family during the latter years of the Depression to join Father Divine's religious commune in Harlem, his departure placed an enormous financial and emotional strain on the family.[30] Later Marshall recognized her father's angst as a non-practicing artist and musician and as a black man frustrated by daily battles against northern-style Jim Crow as he struggled to find a decent-paying job. She said, "his desire to find a position that he felt was of some worth was defeated at every turn; so, his involvement with Father Divine came out of a sense of almost giving up on his part. That in Father Divine's kingdom that you were no longer mother and father, but rather sister and brother to everyone; so, that the responsibility to family was not the central thing, and so on."[31]

The American Dream also entailed a reorientation toward gender roles. After arrival in New York, many Caribbean immigrants realized that the more rigid gender roles to which they adhered in the islands would not work in

New York. The higher cost of living required a double income. Also, many Caribbean women observed the financial independence of their American counterparts, and decided to follow suit.

Marshall's father's failure to support his family most likely was exacerbated by prevailing notions of masculinity and manhood. Deighton, the father figure in *Brown Girl, Brownstones*, resembles Marshall's own father as he becomes so frustrated with his unemployment that he abandons his role as husband and father and joins a Harlem-based religious commune led by a character called Father Peace. He studies hard to become an accountant, but every time he shows up at a job interview, he is denied the job because of the color of his skin. Even so Deighton prefers his homeland to the city, because he feels more like a man in Barbados than in New York; "'Pon a Sat'day I would walk 'bout town like I was a full-full man," he says, "all up Broad Street and Swan Street like I did own the damn place."[32] His higher social and economic status on the island made him a "full-full man," whereas his material failure in New York disrupts traditional gender roles as his wife, Silla, the primary breadwinner, becomes the more "masculine" figure in the household. She repeatedly calls Deighton a "piece of man" and compares his social and economic failure to other Barbadian immigrant men's success. Just as Deighton retreated to Father Peace's religious commune because he felt overwhelmed by racism and the fast pace of cosmopolitan New York, Marshall says, her father resigned from his familial and community obligations in similar fashion. Another woman who emigrated from Jamaica to Brooklyn in 1970 recalled how gender roles shifted in her own family, after arriving in the United States:

> Mom was the primary cook; my dad helped out too, here that is, but in Jamaica it was just mom who cooked. . . . Oh yeah—oh absolutely. In Jamaica, the woman's role is definitely in the house—cook, clean, and take care of the children. And the man's role is to go out to make money to take care of the family. That meant you didn't find many women going out to college to further their education. My mother didn't start working outside of the home until they came to New York.
>
> When my mom came here and saw how other women were liberated [i.e., they were driving and shopping] my mom had to wait for my dad to give her money to go shopping; so, when she came here and saw other women and how liberated they were, she decided to join the club. Back then, my mom went to school and became a nurse's aid.
>
> Yeah, it was really hard for him to adjust because dad was used to, in Jamaica, coming home to a hot meal and clothes being clean. When he came here, he had

to help out. He wasn't one to argue, he did whatever needed to keep the peace, but I don't think he liked it very much.[33]

Such shifts in family structure combined with the economic downturn of the 1920s proved to be too much for some to bear, and some Caribbean New Yorkers' American Dreams turned into nightmares. Jamaican-born Unitarian minister Ethelred Brown blamed the Great Depression for his son's emotional depression, which compelled the young man to commit suicide in 1929.[34] Marshall has recalled how women in her community found strength in Barbadian folklore and colloquialisms as they attributed suicides on Wall Street to the failure to "bind up one's belly," a Barbadian idiom that means one must draw on the strength within to endure hardships. These women had experienced so much hardship in Barbados that they reasoned they could survive the economic depression in the United States. Some Caribbean immigrants dealt with the economic decline by returning to their islands of origin; between 1928 and 1931, 1,135 black men and 1,592 black women left the United States.[35] For the Caribbean intellectuals who remained in New York, they continued to fight for racial equality—a cause that was inextricably connected to the democratic value of being seen and heard as a contributor to American society.

Representation: Giving Voice

Paule Marshall embraced this notion of "equal recognition" as a value inherent in democratic societies. In nearly every interview, Marshall has stated that her main motivation to become a writer stemmed from her desire to capture the rich oral tradition of Barbadian immigrant women who surrounded her as a youth. Marshall also has noted that a substantial negative motivation propelled her to become a writer—the absence of black female voices in American literature. Consistent with W. E. B. Du Bois's classic construction of double-consciousness, growing up in the Western world, Marshall voraciously read white male writers like Mark Twain, William Faulkner, and Charles Dickens, but she always felt something missing. It was not until she stumbled upon the early twentieth-century African American poet Paul Lawrence Dunbar that she learned of black writers. Marshall recalled,

The library was a retreat, a wonderful way to discover new worlds. . . . I remember feeling there was something missing, and then I came across Paul Laurence Dunbar, and learned that there was a black poet who had produced a thick volume of poems. Although I couldn't have said it consciously back then, he in a sense *validated black experience for me.* I went to school in Brooklyn during the '40s and '50s, and the black poets and writers—even the great writers of the Harlem Renaissance of the '20s—just weren't taught in the schools. Ironically, they *were* taught in the segregated schools in the South at that time.[36]

This writer's nagging sense, even as a child, that "there was *something*" missing in American literature, broaches the concept of recognition and cross-cultural inclusion in democratic societies. It is not surprising that work by early African American poets like Dunbar, who used black American dialect in his poems, influenced Marshall's work. The speaker in Dunbar's famous poem, "A Negro Love Song," praises his love's beauty and coyness:

> Hyeahd huh sigh a little sigh,
> Seen a light gleam f'om huh eye,
> An' a smile go flittin' by.

Dunbar's embrace of African American vernacular speech was a welcome and inspiring example of black literature for Marshall. She also savored Gwendolyn Brook's novel *Maud Martha.* The similarities between Brooks's work and Marshall's first novel, *Brown Girl, Brownstones,* are striking. Brooks's novel is semi-autobiographical and captures the triumphs and trials of a young black girl, born into a working-class family in 1940s Chicago. Gwendolyn Brooks was born and raised in Chicago and like Maud, she was shaped by the beauty and struggles of everyday people, most brilliantly captured in black American vernacular English.[37] Such acclaimed literature written in black vernacular by American-born black authors such as Dunbar, Langston Hughes, Zora Neale Hurston, and Gwendolyn Brooks encouraged Marshall to record the unique cadence of her Barbadian-American world in Brooklyn.

The importance of black authors as role models for future generations of black writers is a principle that still reverberates throughout the African diaspora. Novelist Chimamanda Adichie raised a similar point in her humorous confession that as a child growing up in eastern Nigeria, she only wrote stories about blue-eyed, white characters who ate apples and played in the snow because those were the only characters that she knew through reading British and American literature. It was not until she encountered the writing of African authors, whose work validated her own "life witness," that she felt free to write about her own lived experiences. Adichie stated, "Because of writers like Chinua Achebe and Camara Laye I went through a mental shift in my perception of literature. I realized that people like me, girls with skin the color of chocolate, whose kinky hair could not form ponytails, could also exist in literature. I started to write about things I recognized."[38] Notwithstanding Adichie's unfortunate use of the familiar trope of "edible blackness" when describing her own skin,[39] the fact remains that Adichie gleaned inspiration and validation from African writers who came before her. Like Paule Marshall's admiration for and emulation of Harlem Renaissance writers Langston Hughes and Gwendolyn Brooks, Adichie felt emboldened by the work of author Camara Laye, who is best known for his autobiography *L'Enfant Noir* (published in America as *The Dark Child*, 1953)—a nostalgic documentation of his youth in Kouroussa, French Guinea, and the writing of distinguished Nigerian novelist Chinua Achebe, whose compelling account of the cultural clashes between the indigenous Igbo people and British missionaries in *Things Fall Apart* (1958) is considered a classic text throughout the world. For Adichie and Marshall, the psychological import of seeing reflections of themselves in literature, especially given the respective histories of racial oppression in the United States, the Caribbean, and Nigeria, cannot be understated.

The idea of being recognized as a member of a culturally discrete group and possessing a distinctive voice that deserves to be heard is integrally linked to democratic ideals and postmodern constructions of the self in the United States. From the height of immigration in the 1920s to the post–civil rights spike in immigration after 1965, popular notions of ethnicity and American identity have changed from the "melting pot" model to the "mosaic." Jewish writer Israel Zangwill ("Melting Pot," 1908) and automobile mogul Henry Ford's views of progress during the 1920s entailed immigrant assimilation into a homogenous (white) American culture.[40] Zangwill popularized the "melting pot" as a metaphor for identity formation in his 1908 play. Zangwill stated, "America is the crucible of God. It is the melting pot where all the races are fusing and reforming . . . these are the fires of God you've come to. . . . Into the crucible with you all. God is making the American."[41] Zangwill's crucible did not include black immigrants. Thus, Marshall's drive to ensure that black women are seen and heard is a response to previous omissions.

This idealization of homogeneity as the new American identity drastically differs from 1960s African American cultural production by artists such as James Brown, who declared, "Say it loud—I'm black and I'm proud!"[42] Marshall's work expresses a comparable sense of confidence in cultural identity. This revisionist impulse is deeply rooted in the history of civil rights activism and identity politics in the United States, especially from the 1950s through the 1960s. Philosopher Charles Taylor rightfully recognizes the notion of "equal citizenship" as a product of the 1960s civil rights movement in the

United States. According to Taylor, "Equal recognition is not just the appropriate mode for a healthy democratic society. Its refusal can inflict damage on those who are denied it, according to a widespread modern view."[43]

The main difference between Marshall's celebration of black women's voices and the multiculturalism preached by other Caribbean immigrant women and contemporary philosophers is that Marshall has delimited her ideal audience to black women, as the reader should be a reflection of her favorite fictive characters, who are also black women of various cultural backgrounds throughout the African diaspora. While Trinidadian-American choreographer Pearl Primus suggested that recognition of the greatness of African cultures benefits people of all cultures as they are edified by learning something new that might even be applicable to their own lives, Marshall has promoted the inclusion of black and women's voices in literature as a way to empower black women, by validating their experiences. This sense of "equal recognition" privileges a self-reflective gaze, instead of preoccupation with an omnipresent white gaze. Because she published her early work more than a decade before the debut of Brown's black pride anthem in 1969, Marshall prefigured Black Power identity politics and the advent of cultural pluralism in the late 1970s and early 1980s.

Liberal activists' arguments for "equal recognition" in post–civil rights America have changed over time from an emphasis on reparations for marginalized communities to the cultural pluralist model of equal representation for the good of all. From the 1960s through the 1970s, advocates for African American civil rights and women's empowerment suggested that the omission of experiences of peoples of color and women did harm to such groups underrepresented in literature, media, academe, and so on. By the 1980s, liberal activists began to promote cultural diversity in education and the workplace as a value that benefited whole communities as white Americans could become enlightened through knowledge of diverse cultural practices. Marshall's notion of cultural pluralism falls within the former category; she has focused on the value of telling black women's stories to affirm black women readers that their lives and experiences are valid. Marshall has stressed the importance of young black women seeing reflections of themselves in literature. She described her ideal reader:

> She's a young woman, oh, maybe in her late teens, early '20s, and she goes to the library, maybe a bookstore, and she sees some work there by this person called Paule Marshall and she sees works by other black women writers. And we provide that young woman who's looking for herself a picture, a portrayal of characters who are being treated with complexity and depth and truth. And I really see that as a very empowering kind of act.[44]

Marshall's mission to inspire confidence in young black women readers by validating their experiences has inspired other black women writers, among them Haitian American novelist Edwidge Danticat, who has expressed the transformative power of reading Marshall's novels while coming into her own right as a fiction writer. *Brown Girl, Brownstones* was the first novel that Danticat ever read. She recalled, "It's a very powerful novel . . . that I've read many times over the years. But I remember when I first read it . . . as a girl, just *something* that spoke so strongly because it was the *first* time I saw in a book . . . some of what was happening around me—people who work in factories, who are really *struggling to fulfill a dream*. And to see that . . . *reflection* of sort of what's happening in your surroundings in a book was the most extraordinary feeling for me."[45]

Marshall's drive to document black women's voices has stemmed from her childhood experiences listening to Barbadian immigrant women's conversations at her mother's kitchen table.[46] Nearly two decades before the explosion of television as a primary source of family entertainment in the 1950s, these Barbadian women gleaned their news from the radio and word of mouth. Marshall wrote an essay titled "The Making of a Writer: From the Poets in the Kitchen" to pay homage formally to the Barbadian immigrant women who have influenced her own voice and craft. Marshall has noted that these women's gatherings were filled with much more than gossip; they vigorously discussed local and global politics and produced speech acts of defiance to counter the daily indignities they experienced as black immigrant domestics working in white people's homes. Marshall recalled the political content of such discussions, "F.D.R. was their hero; Marcus Garvey was their God."[47] President Franklin Delano Roosevelt's New Deal lent hope to Caribbean immigrants just as it did to American-born blacks who were tired of suffering through the economic depression of the 1930s. Roosevelt's Works Progress Administration provided jobs during a time of record-high unemployment. Garvey also provided inspiration through his rhetoric and business plans to uplift the black race as a whole.

While Marcus Garvey's message of racial uplift in the United States and industrialized progress in African countries attracted both American-born and foreign-born blacks, Garvey's leadership particularly inspired Barbadian immigrants in Marshall's Brooklyn community because of his Caribbean roots. Marshall's mother and friends often discussed Garveyism during their kitchen conversations. Marshall recalled, "The name of the fiery, Jamaican-born black nationalist of the 20's was constantly invoked around the table. For he had been their leader when they first came to the United States from the West Indies shortly after World War One. They had contributed to his organization, the Universal Negro Improvement Association (UNIA), out of their meager salaries, bought shares in his ill-fated Black Star Shipping Line, and at the height of the movement they had marched as members of his 'nurses' brigade; in their white uniforms up Seventh Avenue in Harlem during the great Garvey Day parades."[48] Between 1921 and 1933, nineteen branches of Garvey's UNIA flourished in New York.[49] Garvey offered hope by presenting an alternate vision of power and uplift—a world in which black people have dignity through racial solidarity.

Redeeming Africa through industrialization and cooperative econom-ics was an integral part of this mission, which these Barbadian immigrant women also embraced. They marched in UNIA parades—the ultimate dem-onstration of racial uplift—consistent with contemporary notions of order and progress promoted by advocates of progressive politics like Jane Addams and Florence Kelley. Marshall acknowledged the symbolic importance of Garvey's parades and the Black Star Line for her mother's friends, "If he had succeeded in that project, not that any of those women in the community or at that kitchen table would have gone to Africa, but there was that support of Garvey which was very much in the air for me growing up."[50]

Marshall has remembered these sessions around the kitchen table as a ritual of spiritual rejuvenation—similar to scholars' discussions of the impor-tant role of religion for native-born black Americans in combating institu-tionalized racism in the United States—from slavery to the 1960s civil rights movement.[51] These Barbadian immigrant women labored as domestics in white households; they experienced the degradation that accompanied 1930s politics of race, class, and gender in the United States. In a 1973 article titled "Shaping the World of my Art," Marshall called her mother's kitchen a "sanc-tuary" and observed, "those long afternoon rap sessions were highly func-tional, therapeutic; they were . . . a kind of magic rite, a form of juju, for it was their way to exorcise the day's humiliations and restore them to themselves."[52] The characters in the novel vent about how their employers annoy them; they also dream out loud as they reason that the current sacrifice is worth a more financially secure future—usually exemplified by owning property and pav-ing the way for professional careers for their children as teachers or social workers. Silla's friends echo the same defiance that Marshall heard in real life: "Soully-gal, talk yuh talk! . . . In this man world you got to take yuh mouth and make a gun!"[53] These speech acts were weapons, helping Barbadian women not only cope with racialized oppression but even dismantle it.[54]

Marshall has recognized these speech acts and the unique dialect of Bar-badian-American English as such significant vehicles of quotidian empow-erment that she borrows poet Czeslaw Milosz's notion of language as a homeland. Marshall wrote, "Confronted therefore by a world they could not encompass, which even limited their rights as parents, and at the same time finding themselves permanently separated from the world they had known, *they took refuge in language.* 'Language is the only homeland,' Czeslaw Milosz, the émigré Polish writer and Nobel Laureate, has said. This is what it became for the women at the kitchen table."[55] This concept of language as a homeland is particularly compelling considering the speakers were immigrants status. A sense of displacement is central to the notion of language as homeland. The impulse to implement a portable practice of national identity demonstrates these Caribbean immigrants' sense of dual identities and dual citizenship as they hoped to take advantage of social and economic opportunities in their new home, New York City, while holding on to the cultural familiarity of their birthplace, Barbados.

It is not surprising that these Barbadian women emphasized language as an important vehicle to express cultural and national identity. In contrast to scholar Benedict Anderson's well-known discussion of print culture as a key component in national identity,[56] Marshall has suggested that oral culture is an integral part of Caribbean American identity and is an extension of African traditions. Because the Barbadian immigrant characters in Marshall's novels speak English in a Barbadian dialect and black American vernacular, Marshall aimed to articulate the existence of nations within a nation. Caribbean New York was a subpart of black New York but still connected to broader spheres of belonging, which included city, region, and nation. Caribbean New Yorkers' housing patterns have reflected this sense of ethnic identity as they maintained cultural ties to home by establishing "Little Jamaica," "Little Barbados," and "Little Trinidad" in the city.

Numerous scholars and creative writers have explored the topic of language, one's ability or inability to speak standard English, as a marker of social and political inclusion or marginality. Henry Louis Gates has posed the question, "How can the black subject posit a full and sufficient self in a language in which blackness is a sign of absence? Can writing, with the very difference it makes and marks, mask the blackness of the black face that addresses the text of Western letters, in a voice that speaks English through an idiom which contains the irreducible element of cultural difference that will always separate the white voice from the black?"[57] Marshall never attempted to "mask the blackness of the black face" in her writing because she embraced Barbadian and black New Yorkers' dialects in the recorded word. What Gates terms "the irreducible element of cultural difference," black English, is the very soil upon which Marshall builds her world of Caribbean American nationalism.

"Sister Outsider"[58]

Marshall is most insistent on recognition when she discusses black women. Her earliest work reflects this concern. *Brown Girl, Brownstones*, first published by Random House in 1959 and later reissued by the Feminist Press in 1981, remains a groundbreaking text in feminist, African American, and American literature, the first novel to depict a black American girl's coming of age.[59] Marshall's account of the Barbadian-American protagonist, Selina Boyce, from age seven until age fifteen is a true bildungsroman, and its publication places Marshall about a decade ahead of her time as texts with comparable themes proliferated in the late 1960s and throughout the 1970s. *Brown Girl's* exploration of racial and ethnic identity and advancement of strong feminist themes precedes the civil rights movement, Black Power, and third-wave feminism. In a 1992 interview, even Marshall recognized her own foresight regarding the feminist themes she tackled in *Brown Girl, Brownstones*:

> Even then I was on the right track in terms of what I was trying to say, even if technical things were a little off and my theme was a bit overstated. Still and all, it was firmly grounded in what are some of my main preoccupations as a writer: a woman's need for self-fulfillment, her reaching out for another self and the kinds of opposition and resistance that she runs into. These are themes that really only came into their own in the early 1970s, when there was a flowering of writing by women. But way back then in the '50s I was aware of all the constraints placed upon women, and in particular upon women writers, and I felt so strongly about this that I began writing about it then.[60]

Once again, the principle of giving voice to underrepresented peoples has pervaded Marshall's work, and in this context she stressed femaleness and literature that explores women's experiences.

Marshall felt the sting of prevalent racist and sexist notions of what constituted good literature early on in her career. Just after an influential editor at Random House in New York City agreed to publish Marshall's first novel, she had a "devastating" run-in with another Random House executive. In numerous interviews Marshall reflected on Bennett Cerf's cynical assessment of her work. After welcoming her as a new writer, Marshall recalled, "He ended our polite exchange with words that were just devastating to me. He said: 'Well, you know, nothing usually happens with *this kind of book*,' and made a kind of dismissing sweeping motion with his hand."[61] Marshall interpreted Cerf's words and gestures to mean a novel about black immigrant women would not attract a broad readership. Marshall continued, "I found what it meant to be a woman in that society, and also of course what it meant to be black: that even though my book was going to be published and the publisher found some literary merit in it, I was not really a part of the literary community."[62]

Marshall's creative and intellectual maturation produced a progressive confidence to stage this intervention in American letters as she decided that Caribbean women's experiences were valuable and deserved to be heard. She has noted that her first short story, "The Valley Between," first published in 1954 included only white characters.[63] Although she was not ready to write about the community she knew best, Caribbean women in New York, "The Valley Between" still contains strong feminist themes. The main character is an intelligent, ambitious, and college-educated young woman, but her husband disapproves of her desire to further her education. His chauvinistic attitude is the root of conflict in their marriage. Marshall wrote that the main character in this short story was based on a composite of classmates she met while attending "an all women's, predominantly Jewish, free city college in New York" (Hunter College) as an undergraduate. On one hand, she envied the blinding diamond engagement rings that her classmates gregariously displayed, but on the other hand, she felt sorry for them because she considered them "doomed to become housewives in Brooklyn or Queens." For Marshall, Cassie, the main character, represents "the stifled, unfulfilled woman" that Marshall believed some of her classmates became.[64]

Marshall has grappled with the limitations imposed by the social constructions of gender as well as race in both her life and her writing. Because Marshall was intelligent, ambitious, and college-educated, like Cassie, she also struggled against sexism as she forged her career as a writer. Marshall noted that in addition to the strong, dynamic Barbadian women who influenced her writing, her "own personal struggle to have a life and a career that had a measure of independence" also informed stories like "The Valley Between."[65] In this respect, Marshall found common ground with other women writers and readers, regardless of cultural background.

Marshall came into her own as a writer amid the culture wars of the 1960s and her literary voice reflects the dynamic intersections of civil rights activism and feminism of the time. Although the cadence of her characters might appear much less radical than the bombastic poetry of Black Arts Movement poets such as Amiri Baraka and Ethelridge Knight, the voice and imagery of black women poets such as Nikki Giovanni and Sonia Sanchez and the political rhetoric of outspoken Black Panther Party leader Angela Davis had to influence Marshall's thought to a certain extent. While the early twentieth century might be seen as an era of the black male writer—Claude McKay, Langston Hughes, Richard Wright, Ralph Ellison—Marshall's literary voice and example paved the way for the "golden age" of black women writers such as Maya Angelou, Toni Cade Bambara, Toni Morrison, Alice Walker, and Audre Lorde during the latter half of the century.

Daughter of the Diaspora

Beyond her powerful role as a black feminist writer who paved the way for brilliant black women authors to come, Marshall should be seen as a "daughter of the diaspora" through and through. Marshall's writing and interviews position her as a proud black woman who strongly identifies with the cultures and people of black America, the Caribbean, and West Africa. Even her favorite novels by other authors reflect Marshall's African diasporic identity. When an interviewer asked Marshall which books had been foundational to her intellectual development, she said,

> The three books that have sustained me over the years and that I reread on a regular basis reflect the three great wings of the Black Diaspora. They are *Ake* by the Nobel laureate in Literature Wole Soyinka, a memoir of his childhood in Nigeria. *The Dragon Can't Dance* by Earl Lovelace, a West Indian writer, and *All God's Dangers*, the memoir of a sharecropper in the Deep South, which speaks volumes about the African-American experience.[66]

In a 1988 interview, Marshall stated, "When I say African-American, I'm talking about blacks from Brazil to Brooklyn."[67] Marshall's understanding of cultural identity is never static. The African diaspora that she constructs, through her work and life, is ever evolving to address current political realities in conversation with historical context. The personal and political power that Marshall has derived from her own African diasporic identity is rooted in her own travel experiences throughout the United States, Africa, and the Caribbean. In the late 1960s and early 1970s, Africa-centered scholars borrowed the notion of diaspora from Jewish studies to describe a similar phenomenon of cultural scattering and connectedness for peoples of African descent around the world. Marshall draws upon this notion of diaspora in her writing.[68]

Marshall was in her late forties when she traveled to Africa for the first time. She went to Nigeria in 1977 for the Festac Black Arts Festival, and followed up with a trip to Kenya and Uganda in 1980. Marshall found her interactions with native-born Nigerians, Ghanaians, Kenyans, and so on extremely positive. In 1986, Marshall recalled, "What was extraordinary for me was the way Africans adopted me."[69] In later interviews she also would laughingly recall how various West African Festac participants whom she met would try to *read* her physical features; they would point to her eyes, her nose or lips and proclaim her lineage in whichever ethnic group was known by such features. Marshall's experiences greatly resembled that of Trinidadian-American choreographer and dancer Pearl Primus. In different contexts during separate visits to West African countries, both Primus and Marshall were given the title "Omowale"—an Ibo phrase meaning "a native daughter has returned."[70] As a writer, Marshall has assumed the role of facilitator in such "family reunions," which grew out of fundamentally modern, post–civil rights notions of kinship. Marshall wrote, "As the history of people of African descent in the United States and the diaspora is fragmented and interrupted, I consider it my task as a writer to initiate readers to the challenges this journey entails."[71]

Individual and group identity understood in terms of race and ethnicity is a profoundly modern phenomenon, rooted in the historical and political realities of the Enlightenment, colonialism, slavery, and imperialism. The clashing of cultures inherent in such colonial and neocolonial encounters has produced a sense of cultural hybridity, non-presence, and identity-in-motion that characterizes postmodern constructions of the self. Marshall has acknowledged tensions between self-identity versus the identities that outsiders try to place upon you. Her work grapples with the insolubility of identity the sense of identity in motion that Derrida explores. Marshall noted, "I don't see it so much as a burden. . . . But it is true that at the end of my novels my characters are often moving off in a continuous search for self. It might come off sounding like a burden, but that's not really how it was designed. What I want to suggest is the continuing need to define self."[72]

Marshall embodies this historical dissonance because she considers herself to be both Caribbean and African American. Homi K. Bhabha has noted that "to turn the presumption of equal cultural respect into the recognition of equal cultural worth, it does not recognize the disjunctive, 'borderline' temporalities of partial minority cultures."[73] I agree. Like Pearl Primus, constructions of African diasporic identities are at the center of Paule Marshall's work. Marshall echoes Primus's discussion of transnational identities as a person of African descent via the Caribbean living in America. Marshall stated, "Well, I was once accused by, I think it was Harold Cruse, in *Crisis of the Negro Intellectual* of being neither fish nor fowl, of fallen between two stools as a writer because of my background. . . . And I like to think of myself, my work—especially the work—as a kind of bridge that joins the great wings of the black diaspora in this part of the world."[74] Marshall agreed with fellow scholar and creative writer Edward Braithwaite, when she declared, "perhaps there is a certain advantage in being neither fish nor fowl; perhaps it gives me a unique angle from which to view the two communities."

Marshall's discussion of diaspora in her fiction stems from a very personal sense of cultural hybridity: "I'm always trying to, at a personal level, reconcile my sort of mixed bag of a background— the fact that I'm Afro-American, was born and raised in Brooklyn but, I'm also Afro-West Indian through my parents who were born and raised in the West Indies and so I've always had this *dual culture which I see as one culture.*[75] Similarly, the main character, Sonny, in Marshall's most recent novel, *The Fisher King*, represents the reconciliation of multiple cultures. Marshall has noted, "here is this little boy, eight and a half years old, who embodies, in a sense, all wings of the black diaspora. He is African through his father. He is African-American through his grandmother. He is West Indian through his grandfather. So he brings together in his person this unity and this reconciliation, which is one of the themes of my work."[76] Because Sonny is a child, he is able to fluidly move among black American, Caribbean, and European cultures; he does not carry the historical baggage that prevents the adults from doing the same.

Similarly, perhaps Marshall's second-generation American status facilitated the reconciliation of her "mixed bag of a background." Marshall's mother arrived in New York as an adult, and limited her sphere of friends to Barbadian New Yorkers, but young Paule's daily interactions at school and at play facilitated her friendships with native-born African Americans. She straddled multiple cultures in her daily life as she interacted with Caribbean communities in New York that maintained close ties to their islands of origin and as she interfaced with African American culture and American culture writ large. Marshall recalled, "My world was Brooklyn, my allegiance was to the African-American community of which I was very much a part—my friends, my school, my playground, just up and down the street there on Hancock Street, that was my world, as well as the house which was West Indian."[77] In another interview she stated, "As a child I moved with the utmost ease between these cultures; it was the way the world was for me. With this double exposure, there was the desire in me from early on to play with a variety of voices, to always be stretching and exploring the English language. It has to do with the fact that I come from people for whom language is an art form."[78]

Marshall's coming of age among Caribbean New Yorkers who were adamant Garvey supporters nurtured her own black consciousness and African diasporic identity. In addition to strongly feeling Caribbean and African, Marshall has stated that her mother's kitchen table discussions about Garvey fostered a symbolic and cultural association with people on the continent of Africa: "But there also was this world which I was made aware of—this larger world of Africa—through the talk that went on at that table, and the type of militarism that was part of that talk. The sense of the whole need for black people whether in America, the West Indies, or Africa—the sense that our strength as a people had to do with bringing the forces together."[79] This sense of Pan-Africanism dominates Marshall's writing, especially her latter work. The radicalizing black nationalist conversations that Marshall heard during her childhood in the 1930s informed her writing from 1954 to the present, demonstrating the long history of intellectual engagement in the cause of black empowerment in the United States among Caribbean immigrants as well as American-born blacks.

Marshall's Africa-centered consciousness grew out of a long tradition of black radicalism, which she witnessed firsthand. From her mother's participation in Marcus Garvey's UNIA parades throughout the streets of Harlem in the 1920s to "Afrocentric" scholars' declarations of black genius on college campuses across the nation in the 1960s, Marshall's work was shaped by the black radicalism of the time. The 1960s incarnation of "Afrocentricity" in black American communities encouraged a cultural "return" to the continent of Africa—to reclaim the knowledge, beauty, and dignity that their ancestors had lost in the TransAtlantic Slave Trade. In one interview, Marshall reflected on this Africa-centered identity:

> There was this larger world of darker peoples so these were the strands that I see as forming my perception of the world and my perception of the world as I'm dealing with it in the work. . . . For me Africa is a part of my way of seeing the world, of defining myself. . . . When I talk about the importance of Africa in my work and the necessity of dealing with it or responding to it of having it resonate in the work . . . I'm not talking about physical journeys to Africa . . . I'm talking about something which is true for most Americans. . . . I was in Europe this summer and there was a number of Euro-Americans going home—Americans are always seeking to more closely define self—and part of that definition for Euro-Americans has to do with Europe—for me as a black American, it has to do with Africa.[80]

Marshall has identified Africa as an equally important part of her identity as the Caribbean. She said, "Africa is an extension of the West Indies for me . . . that kind of completion of the self." Marshall has stressed the importance of Africa, both mythic and real, in her worldview by consciously using African imagery in her novels. In *The Chosen Place, the Timeless People*, Marshall uses a Benin mask as a metaphor to describe a cane worker's striking facial structure, and she compares a shopkeeper on the fictitious Caribbean island to a "tribal African chief seated behind a counter as he makes libations to the gods."[81]

Marshall read a great deal of literature on the history of the slave trade as well as African history, which encouraged her to pursue themes pertaining to African diasporic cultural identity in novels such as *The Chosen Place, The Timeless People* (1969). This is her longest novel, and many literary critics consider it her magnum opus. Marshall has stated that she made a very self-conscious effort "to give voice to that whole need not only to retrace the triangular passage—but of *reaching out* to Africa because [she] saw that as a part of [her] shaping and as part of the shaping of black people." When readers and literary critics question her more recent publications—perhaps as a departure from earlier, overtly feminist themes, Marshall insists on highlighting the thematic unity of her work. Marshall stated, "The diaspora has always been part of my work. In fact, with this book [*The Fisher King*], people say this doesn't sound like you—it doesn't read like you. Who is this little boy? What's his background? His father's African, and his mother is Caribbean and African American; so, he embodies the diaspora. So, that's always there in the work if you look closely."[82]

Conclusion

Because Paule Marshall is the only living biographical subject in this book, her continued publications invite us to ponder the contours of immigrant and African diasporic cultural identities in twenty-first century America. For instance, in March 2009, Marshall sat with a *New York Times* reporter at the Helmsley Park Lane hotel in midtown Manhattan, sipping herbal tea while reflecting on her most recent publication, *Triangular Road: A Memoir* (2009). Perhaps the expectant curiosity that alights the eyes of the young girl on the book's cover—ankles crossed, hands clasped atop an open book, chin tilted upward—toward the viewer, and brows slightly raised, is the same spirit that animated her conversation with the journalist, decades later. The child in the photograph, Paule Marshall around age six, looks angelic—dressed in all white, with a white bow and thick curls haloing her face. She also appears precociously astute; her calm, watchful eyes, her mouth inquisitively set, her small, assured hands resting at the center of the open book, give the impression that this young girl has been reading (and thinking) for years. The graphic design of the dust jacket not only reflects the author's personality, but it also illustrates her literal and figurative African diasporic journeys. This photograph of young Paule forms sharp angles with a juxtaposed map of west

Africa and the Atlantic Ocean, and the map is set against a letter written in the author's own lilting cursive; these artifacts form an undeniable triangle.

In the same interview, Marshall explained her own autobiographical, cultural map that inspired the title of her memoir: "Africa, Barbados, Brooklyn—that's the triangle that defines me and my work."[83] Always mindful of the synergistic effects of geographic location, migration, and history in shaping individual identity, Marshall has consciously lived her life and produced inventive literature as a "daughter of the diaspora." She has described her exploration of African diasporic history in all of her novels as a "personal quest for a truer definition of self," which lends "richness, texture, and resonance" to her work.[84] Born in 1929 in Brooklyn, NY, to parents from Barbados, Marshall draws parallels between her own African diasporic heritage and that of President Barack Obama, born in 1961 in Honolulu, HI, to a black Kenyan father and a white mother from Kansas, to underscore her point. "We need to see the *triangular nature* of our inheritance and our place in the world," Marshall declared and observed, "I think that's what Obama suggests in his person and what people saw in him."[85]

From the start of her publication career in 1954 through the present, Paule Marshall has embraced her African diasporic cultural identity as a source of personal and political power; hence, the African diaspora is central to her writing.[86] The legacy of black folk's resistance to racialized oppression throughout the Transatlantic Slave Trade from the 1600s through the late 1880s, colonialism in the Caribbean and throughout the continent of Africa as well as Jim Crow racism in the United States throughout the twentieth century represent a rich "inheritance" from which African diasporic peoples, including President Obama, draw unique moral authority and political power. Knowing the history of one's African diasporic heritage translates into personal power as the knowledge that President Obama and Paule Marshall have acquired regarding the branches of their family trees that respectively extend to Kenya in eastern Africa—scientifically accepted as the birthplace of all humankind, and Barbados, the southeastern-most outpost of the Caribbean during the Transatlantic slave trade, is grounding and self-affirming, but this is only part of the equation. An even greater sense of political power is gained through public declarations of one's cultural identity, especially the triumphs and trials of one's ancestors, because such speech acts are rooted in a fundamental belief in the highest ideals of American democracy—that every voice deserves to be heard, regardless of race, ethnicity, social and economic class, or gender. Marshall learned this principle at an early age.

As a young girl growing up amid the fiery speech of black immigrant women in Brooklyn, NY, Marshall was made aware of the power of words, which her Barbadian-born mother and her mother's friends used as a type of verbal graffiti that. This rendering of the self, the expression of one's deepest fears, frustrations, and hopes in the vernacular English of one's homeland, grew out of an existential impulse—a desire to declare: *I am here.* In a January 2009 *Publishers Weekly* interview, Marshall reminisced about the distinctive power of the voices of Barbadian immigrants that filled the soundscape of her youth. "I knew that the way they spoke English was different from the English that I spoke in school," Marshall recalled, "but it was so full of color, it was so full of their *own authority* that I had a sense that they were on to something."[87]

Marshall's fiction centers on the dialect of black immigrant women, replete with culturally unique metaphors (*i.e.* The sea ain't got no back door) and Barbadian-inflected grammatical structures that drastically diverge from forms of standard British English taught in colonial schools in Barbados and American grammar taught in New York public schools, because she understands language as a vehicle of power. In Marshall's novels, which have become important works on cultural studies syllabi in academe, Marshall's characters wield Caribbean patois as a weapon to challenge elements of white supremacy that permeate Caribbean and American public education curricula and broader society. The language and accent in which black immigrants and descendants of immigrants express themselves—Caribbean patois in the case of Paule Marshall compared to President Obama's deliberate Baptist minister's drawl and use of American vernacular and humor rooted in African American comedic traditions—conveys a sense of self confidence that audiences find profoundly compelling.

Paule Marshall's fiction broadens our understanding of Caribbean immigrants as immigrants and signals the self-reflective importance of "being seen and heard"—especially for black immigrant women. This discussion of ethnic diversity within blackness is rooted in an insider perspective versus outsider perspective that shrouds Caribbean visibility. This insider perspective demonstrates intraethnic and intraracial class conflicts, as in the case of middle and upper class Caribbean immigrant landlords who exploited American-born and foreign-born black tenants from lower social and economic classes. Though educational and job opportunities in New York surpassed the limited opportunities in the agricultural economies of their countries of origin, Caribbean immigrants' social and economic success was still predicated upon someone else's disadvantage.

Paule Marshall's observant personality, literary talent, and deliberate intention to bridge African, Caribbean and black American cultures provide us with complex, and compelling insights into the lives of black immigrants in New York as well as people of African descent throughout the diaspora. Just as Marshall uses the history, culture, and people of Africa, especially western Africa, as a unifying force in her novels and short stories, the life and legacy of black consciousness leader Marcus Garvey served as a unifying force for the Barbadian immigrant women in Marshall's world. For Marshall's mother and friends, whom she affectionately called the "poets in the kitchen," Garvey's bold intellect and strong example of black pride was a major source of inspiration. Even after his exile in to England and death over a decade later, "Garvey: He lived on through the power of their memories."[88]

"Garvey's Ghost": Life after Death[1]

> Belief in the existence and power of ancestors creates a sense of conti-
> nuity in the living, the dead and the unborn. The cycle does not begin
> with physical birth nor end with death. The spirits of the ancestors are
> all around, never wandering too far to return either to help or punish
> the living. They have a spiritual existence in the invisible world.[2]
>
> **—PEARL PRIMUS**

From Marcus Garvey's black nationalist, racial uplift movement in 1920s
Harlem to Paule Marshall's literary insistence that black immigrant women's
voices be heard in 1960s Brooklyn and beyond, Caribbean intellectuals have
shaped and continue to inform our understandings of blackness and the
struggle for racial equality in modern America. Their lives and work deepen
our understanding of the meanings of American democracy, the history of
black intellectualism, and the power of the written, spoken, and performed
word as weapons for social change. They also reveal shifting gender dynamics
among Caribbean thought leaders—from the overwhelmingly male leadership during the early-twentieth century to the advent of Caribbean women's
artistic activism at mid-century. Their lives serve as windows into the long
history of political collaborations and cultural clashes between Caribbean
immigrants and American-born blacks, and the ever-changing political landscape of Caribbean New York.

The cosmopolitan, polyglot demographics of New York have long made it
an ideal locale in which black intellectuals can leverage their cultural experiences in the cause of social justice. The biographies of Jamaican-born Unitarian minister Ethelred Brown; Barbadian-born activist Richard B. Moore;
Trinidadian-born choreographer and dancer Pearl Primus; Barbadian American politician Shirley Chisholm; and novelist Paule Marshall, who was born
in Brooklyn to parents from Barbados, prove this point. From racial uplift,
Pan-Caribbean consciousness, anti-imperialism, civil rights activism, and
feminism to post–civil rights era struggles for cultural inclusion in primary

Tammy L. Brown, *Blackstar (Return): Marcus Garvey*, Mixed Media, 2014.

school education, on college campuses, and in American electoral politics, their modes of resistance to racism were diverse and far-reaching. My
attention to the written, spoken, and performed word—including sermons,
speeches, novels, and choreography—demonstrate the creative ways in which
leaders leveraged their cultural identities in the cause of racial equality. Their
life stories function as windows into the personal and political meanings of
blackness in the United States and around the world.

In any conversation about the political impact of Caribbean intellectuals in
New York, the first name that usually comes to mind is Jamaican-born, black
nationalist leader Marcus Mosiah Garvey. Nineteen-twenties New York City

was the intellectual environment in which Garvey's Universal Negro Improvement Association (UNIA) attracted its largest following worldwide—thirty-five thousand members at its height.[3] The UNIA's ambitious scope, theatrical symbolism, and pragmatic cooperative economics mission still looms large in academic discussions of black nationalism and in the popular imagination. So, it is not surprising that many of my colleagues have asked why Garvey is not a central figure in this book.

Because Marcus Garvey continues to be the most extensively documented Caribbean intellectual to transform the consciousness of black New Yorkers and people of African descent throughout the diaspora, I deliberately selected lesser-known public intellectuals and historical figures whose Caribbean heritage has attracted less attention to show there were "other games in town" than Garvey. In an effort to expand scholarly and popular discussions of the long history of collaborative activism and antagonism between Caribbean immigrants and American-born blacks, I selected the life stories of Ethelred Brown, Richard B. Moore, Pearl Primus, Shirley Chisholm, and Paule Marshall to develop my overarching argument that understanding the cultural background, family upbringing, and individual personalities of intellectuals is crucial to understanding resistance in the long battle for racial equality in modern America. Still, I conclude with a discussion of Garvey because I cannot understate the magnitude of his black consciousness legacy, which influenced my historical actors' understandings of their own black racial identities.

Garvey's ghost haunts the cultural landscape of black thought and artistic production from the 1920s to the present. In turn, Pearl Primus's belief in ancestor worship, epitomized by the phrase "Those who are dead are never gone,"[4] is particularly apt when considering this phenomenon. According to Primus, "The spirits of the ancestors are all around, never wandering too far to return either to help or punish the living."[5] Likewise, for the protagonists in this study, Garvey was an omnipresent intellectual ally or foe. He literally and figuratively stood at the center of debates over black racial identity and uplift strategies as each historical actor participated in significant political movements ranging from communism, socialism, anti-colonialism, civil rights activism, and feminism to pragmatic humanism. Although Garvey's deportation and death preceded the political and intellectual prime of most of the actors on whom I have focused, these intellectuals continued to contest his legacy, arguing with or gleaning inspiration from Garvey's bold intellect and charismatic personality.

As the title of jazz drummer Max Roach's celebratory 1961 composition, "Garvey's Ghost,"[6] suggests, African diasporic artists were inspired by Garvey's black consciousness political movement more than three decades after the fall of his modest empire. Born in North Carolina and raised in Brooklyn,

Roach appropriated the symbolic grandeur of Garvey's legacy as an expression of his own radical, black consciousness during the height of the civil rights movement. In Roach's elegy for Garvey, the insistent snare of the drums combined with the tinny clang of the cowbell harken back to a polyrhythmic West African beat to which Pearl Primus would have loved to dance. The dramatic swing of the piano and horns makes the song sound grand enough to accompany the pomp and circumstance of a UNIA parade through the streets of Harlem. Lastly, the haunting tone of jazz vocalist Abbey Lincoln's rendering of the abstract lyrics, "Aaahhh ah ahhhh" and "Oooohhh ooh oooohh," gives the song a spooky and hallowed sound.[7] Abbey Lincoln, an American-born, radical artist-activist whom Roach would marry in 1962, also epitomized the recursive nature of black identity politics—from Garvey's 1920s racial uplift mission to the 1960s Black Power movement, as she collaborated with Max Roach on significant albums protesting racial inequality.[8]

Although Marcus Garvey particularly appealed to Caribbean New Yorkers because of his own Caribbean lineage and his prominence as a "race man" in early twentieth–century Harlem, Garvey's larger-than-life persona is so far-reaching that his image and words have been featured in music, poetry, plays, paintings, films, and even cartoons by black artists around the globe.[9] Fifteen years after Max Roach released "Garvey's Ghost," Jamaican, roots reggae singer Burning Spear released an album by the same title.[10] *Garvey's Ghost* by Burning Spear opens with a song titled "The Ghost" in which he chants, "Marcus Garvey's words come to pass," and "Can't get no food to eat / Can't get no money to spend." More than a decade after Jamaica gained independence from British colonial rule, Burning Spear observed that the economic ravages of colonialism endured. Still, he urged his compatriots to find strength in the historic example of Marcus Garvey. One year before the production of this album, Burning Spear released a record simply titled *Marcus Garvey*.[11] Both albums include songs with stripped down lyrics—with Burning Spear repeating the name "Mr. Garvey, oh Marcus Mosiah Garvey" in a plaintive tone. The act of invoking Marcus Garvey, whom Burning Spear called a prophet, functions as a praise poem and a prayer.

From America to the Caribbean to Europe to Africa and back again, Garvey's ghost possessed black artists throughout the African diaspora. In 1981, reggae band Steel Pulse of Birmingham, England, eulogized Garvey in the upbeat ode "Worth His Weight in Gold." They urged their listeners to:

Rally round the flag
Red, gold, black and green
A bright shining star—Africa
Catch a star liner right now—Africa.[12]

Thus, Garvey lives on as a source of black pride as Steel Pulse celebrated Garvey's ambitious but ill-fated *Black Star Line* of steamships designed to transport black Americans to western Africa. Steel Pulse also hailed the Pan-African flag that Garvey created as a symbol of black solidarity and political unity. In this flag, the color black represents all people of African descent, red stands for the bloodshed of black people who endured slavery and colonialism, green represents the land of Africa, and gold symbolizes the continent's abundance of natural resources—especially diamonds and precious metals.

From the 1980s through the 1990s, during a time known as the golden age of hip hop, rap groups such as X Clan and Public Enemy prominently featured the red, black, and green Pan-African flag in their politically conscious lyrics and music videos. They displayed images of their black nationalist hero as a visual refrain to accompany the booming beat. In X Clan's video for "Heed the Word of the Brother,"[13] the camera pans across a wall of paintings of esteemed black activists. Marcus Garvey is included in this lineup; he looks dignified, standing erect in a crisp black suit and firmly holding a black cane against the backdrop of the red, black, and green Pan-African flag. This austere portrait of Garvey is deliberately placed on the right-hand side of a close-up rendering of radical, Muslim, black-consciousness leader Malcolm X in his famous thinking-man pose—with left index finger touching his temple. Malcolm X's father, Earl Little—a Baptist minister and devout Garveyite who was murdered by whites who opposed his message of black empowerment—would appreciate Malcolm's revered place in history alongside venerated black leaders including Marcus Garvey.

In addition, rapper Chuck D of Public Enemy lyrically celebrates Marcus Garvey in the poetic tirade "Prophets of Rage." Born and raised in Queens, New York, Chuck D gained first-hand knowledge of Caribbean culture through conversations with his neighbors who had emigrated from various islands.[14] In a September 2014 lecture at Miami University of Ohio–Hamilton, Chuck D, dressed in a natty Bob Marley T-shirt in the colors of the Pan-African flag and a black baseball cap turned backward, commanded the attention of the auditorium. He talked about his interpretation of the Caribbean roots of hip hop, saying, "DJ culture has roots in the Caribbean—dub and overdubbing. . . . Kingston parties introduced two turntables because the music can't stop because there might be a problem."[15] He then referenced the long history of racial oppression in Jamaica—slavery centering on the back-breaking work of harvesting sugarcane, British colonialism, and postcolonial poverty—to describe a social climate so intense that the "party had to be right," because if the music stopped, "there might be a problem." Chuck D said he witnessed a "similar intensity in the Bronx after it was leveled and [communities were] destroyed." In response, New York DJs adopted a similar turntable technique to "keep the party going because if the party stopped, it might be a problem."[16] Chuck D's use of repetition is amusing and profound. Although scholars do not all agree on the Caribbean roots of hip hop in America,[17] what matters most, in this context, is Chuck D's personal experience and poetic interpretation of the synergy between American-born black and Caribbean artistic production. When I interviewed Chuck D after his lecture, he proudly declared that he was the first hip-hop artist to mention Marcus Garvey in rap lyrics.[18] And I said, "Really? Even before X Clan?" And he said, "Yes."

This might well be true, considering Public Enemy's song "Prophets of Rage" was released two years before X Clan's "Heed the Word of the Brother." In "Prophets of Rage," Chuck D proclaims, in a booming baritone voice,

I'm like Garvey
So you can see B
It's like that, I'm like Nat [Turner].[19]

According to Public Enemy, the issues of inner-city poverty compounded by antagonisms between black citizens and white police officers throughout the nation during the 1980s and 1990s called for revolutionary action akin to historical events such as Marcus Garvey's "Back to Africa" movement or Nat Turner's famous slave rebellion. Likewise, one year later in the music video for Public Enemy's battle cry "Fight the Power"[20] written for filmmaker Spike Lee's provocative depiction of racial tensions in Brooklyn in *Do the Right Thing*,[21] one member of a radicalized black crowd carries a poster-sized placard of Marcus Garvey while protestors shout the refrain "Fight the Power!" along with front man Chuck D.[22] In the classic video for this hip-hop anthem, the colors of the Pan-African flag provide a backdrop to the stage where the group performs dressed in the colors of the flag: Chuck D in a red baseball cap, red sweatshirt, black pants, and black leather jacket; Flava Flav in a green leather baseball cap, green sweatshirt, red oversized clock necklace, and green pants. Garvey's image and the Pan-African colors function as a visual refrain—reinforcing the lyrical message of black empowerment. In this video, Public Enemy's nod to Marcus Garvey is apt because the political rally-style footage shot in late 1980s Brooklyn harkens back to the days in which Marcus Garvey "moved the crowd" in Harlem—from street-corner orations to the grandeur and pageantry of his UNIA parades.

More than a decade after the release of Public Enemy's "Fight the Power" video, Garvey's ghost lingered in the lyrics and imagery of premier hip-hop artists. The Brooklyn-born rap duo, Mos Def and Talib Kweli, paid homage to Marcus Garvey by adopting the stage name *Black Star*, again adapted from the name of Garvey's Black Star Line steamships, and they released a critically acclaimed album by the same title in 1998.[23] The spirit of this album is joyful and reflective—a meditation on the struggles of the past while striving toward a better future. The album is an extended praise poem to the residents of black New York—with songs ranging from a celebration of black beauty in "Brown Skin Lady" to an ode to the beautiful-ugly city of New York in "Definition." For these African diasporic artists, it does not matter that while Garvey was big on vision, he came up short in the realm of logistical execution. What matters most is Garvey was the author and communicator of such grand ideals of black empowerment that his racial uplift message still resonates with politically oppressed people—from the anti-colonial and civil rights struggles of the 1960s through the present-day battle against racial profiling and police brutality in the United States.

Personality Politics and Life after Death

Why does Marcus Garvey dominate discussions of Caribbean contributions to the development of black consciousness in New York and throughout the African diaspora? I contend that, much like the main historical actors in this book, Garvey's intellectual personality, epitomized by his mastery of the written, spoken, and performed word, was more important than his Caribbean identity in determining his enduring legacy as a political leader. He was in the right place at the right time; Garvey's uplifting message of black empowerment underscored by his undeniable charisma allowed him to seize the historical moment. Garvey was proactive, creative, dynamic, and prolific. He also possessed a penchant for the theatrical flair that inspired the politically oppressed black masses. Garvey's principal biographer, historian Tony Martin has described Garvey's triumph and enduring appeal as follows:

> The time was ripe for Garvey, but the time alone cannot explain his success. . . .
> Long before [Garvey] burst on the scene, he was already imbued with a powerful
> sense of mission. This gave his life a singleness of purpose that allowed him to
> keep bouncing back after the most punishing setbacks. For those who heard him,
> his oratorical skill exercised a spellbinding influence. Yet many followed him who
> never saw him. For them his writings, especially his *Negro World* editorials, exer-
> cised the same fascination.[24]

Although Martin's assessment of Garvey borders on hagiography, his point is still well taken. As a singular leader, Garvey's vision and stick-to-itiveness combined with his exceptional oratorical and writing skills fueled his emergence as a heroic figure.

There are no shortcuts to success. Garvey understood this truth, and was, in turn, a workaholic through and through. In documentary-filmmaker Stanley Nelson's powerful portrait of Garvey as a man and leader, *Look for Me in the Whirlwind*, Garvey's son Marcus Garvey Jr. recalled, "My father was committed totally to the struggle and that's why he never seemed to relax. He never seemed to take a day off.... He was always dressed ready to work. And he was working at home; he was working at the office. He kept tremendous hours."[25] Many Caribbean immigrants and scholars of Caribbean history have described this intense work ethic as innately Caribbean, but I disagree. We must view immigrants as individuals and not as a monolithic group. I contend that hard work, perseverance, and intellect are qualities cultivated within the individual and shaped by personality and family upbringing. My conclusion is bolstered by the fact that countless American-born black artists, activists, and intellectuals shared similar qualities that fueled their own personal and political success.

This brings us to a meta-discussion about Caribbean intellectuals' *perceptions* that their Caribbean-ness predisposed them toward professional success. In response to this prevalent perception, I contend that the issue is not whether Caribbean immigrants were actually culturally superior to American-born blacks, but what matters most is many Caribbean immigrants *believed* their Caribbean heritage was a major factor in their success. In many ways, this belief becomes a self-fulfilling prophecy. This is especially true for intellectuals such as W. A. Domingo, Ethelred Brown, Hazel Scott, Pearl Primus, Shirley Chisholm, and Stokely Carmichael, who leveraged their Caribbean cultural identity as a source of spiritual strength and optimism which allowed them to overcome setbacks in their careers and persevere in the cause of social justice.

Considering the boldness, wit, and *savoir faire* displayed by each of the protagonists in this book juxtaposed with Marcus Garvey's larger-than-life persona, I've concluded that personality was more important than Caribbean identity in determining the influence of each intellectual. Just as Garvey's courageous refusal to cancel a speaking engagement the day after being shot by an assailant in his Harlem office lent him a kind of street credibility akin to the machismo that Jamaican-American rapper the Notorious B.I.G. displayed in the albums *Ready to Die* and *Life after Death*, Marcus Garvey took on mythical proportions in the wake of the attempted assassination.[26] So what did the Notorious B.I.G. and Marcus Garvey have in common with the historical actors in this book? What they had in common was a love for the written, spoken, and performed word and a boldness to share their creative thoughts and political ideas with not only black New Yorkers but with people of African descent around the world.

Word Power

To say Marcus Garvey was a powerful speaker would be an understatement. He was one among many black intellectuals who drew upon their Caribbean cultural experiences and the progressive cultural milieu of New York to raise their voices in the cause of black empowerment. And through the expression of this translocal black identity they gained a sense of personal and political power. The spoken word, especially sermons and political speeches, were an important part of this cultural production. Verbal sparring among black intellectuals took place on street corners in Harlem, around kitchen tables in Brooklyn, in cigar shops in Queens and in Manhattan cafés. Marcus Garvey's platform of choice was a stepladder at the corner of 135th Street and Lennox Avenue or alternately the stage of Lafayette Hall on 131st Street and Seventh Avenue in Harlem. Garvey's passion and oratorical finesse infused his July 8, 1917, speech in response to the horrendous East St. Louis race riot that had begun six days earlier, during which more than one hundred black people lost their lives. Garvey called the riot a "massacre" and declared, "This is no time for fine words, but a time to lift one's voice against the savagery of a people who claim to be the dispensers of democracy."[27] As a devout follower of Marcus Garvey, Shirley Chisholm's father, Charles St. Hill, was most likely aware of this famous speech. He was an ardent Garveyite and would often recall the fiery words of his political hero when he recounted stories of black greatness to young Shirley as a child. Perhaps the telling and retelling of Garvey's bravely vigorous speeches helped Chisholm realize the power of her own voice.

Likewise, Chisholm felt equally at home arguing her point among colleagues at the New York state legislature in Albany or enjoying a potluck dinner with housewives and working-class women at a volunteer's brownstone in Brooklyn. I evoke these names because Garvey and Chisholm were among the most charismatic Caribbean intellectuals to capture the hearts and minds of black New Yorkers during the early- and late-twentieth century, and their mastery of the spoken word helped to grow their respective constituencies. Both Garvey and Chisholm employed the hermeneutics of war to mobilize their followers, painting a portrait of valiant soldiers attacking systems of white supremacy. Their fast-talking, forceful, no-holds-barred oratorical style brings to mind the quick fire of military combat. In Chisholm's first political memoir, *Unbought and Unbossed*, she admonished readers, "Unless we start to fight and defeat the enemies in our own country, poverty and racism, and make our talk of equality and opportunity ring true, we are exposed in the eyes of the world as hypocrites when we talk about making people free."[28] This passage and Chisholm's aptly titled second political memoir, *The Good Fight* (1973), demonstrate the fierceness of spirit and rhetorical sharpness in which Chisholm waged her battle against racism, sexism, and poverty. Although Garvey's wives, Amy Ashwood and Amy Jacques, represented a type of early-twentieth century black women's empowerment, Garvey's segregationist and overwhelmingly masculine racial uplift enterprise contrasts starkly with Chisholm's feminist and integrationist approach to political empowerment for black Americans, women, and working-class Americans from diverse racial and cultural backgrounds.

Garvey's ghost hovered over Caribbean New York and influenced the cultural production of black intellectuals for decades. Novelist Paule Marshall emphasized Garvey's tremendous impact on the development of black pride among Caribbean New Yorkers.[29] She also used the hermeneutics of war in her creative writing. Marshall wrote "Soully-gal, talk yuh talk! . . . In this man world you got to take yuh mouth and make a gun!"[30] In her novel *Brown Girl, Brownstones* (1959), she drew upon the unique language of her mother's birthplace, Barbados, and the brutal realities of racism experienced by domestic workers in Depression-era Brooklyn. The characters in Marshall's fiction used their words to tear down systems of oppression and build up their own self-confidence. Thus the written, spoken, and performed word were powerful vehicles for Caribbean intellectuals to battle racism and create their own psychologically affirmative enclaves—a type of island within the city of New York.

City of Islands

The individual life stories in this book prove my argument that there is no such thing as an archetypal immigrant experience. Each life story is distinctive—singularly shaped by the place, time, and experiences inhabited.

Moreover, the expression of each individual's personal and political identity changed throughout each individual's lifetime to suit the historical moment. I call this sense of individualized and ever-evolving political selfhood, "life witness."

Among the changing elements of historical moments were gender relations and identities. While black male religious and political leaders dominated black intellectualism during the early twentieth century, black women literary and performance artists assumed center stage from the 1940s onward. This shift was enabled by a convergence of ideas and political movements such as the birth of the New Woman and the New Negro in the 1920s, the artistic innovation of the Harlem Renaissance, the empowerment women experienced as they took up industrial jobs in war-time America, and the rise of third-wave feminism in the 1970s.

The lives of the Caribbean intellectuals discussed in this book also reflect the change in black New York's seat of power from Harlem to Brooklyn throughout the twentieth century. From the height of Marcus Garvey's black consciousness movement in 1920s Harlem to the depths of Shirley Chisholm's cross-cultural, grassroots political campaigns in 1960s Brooklyn, intellectuals reflected the changing demographics of New York City. While the majority of blacks resided in Harlem, the Tenderloin, and San Juan Hill during the early decades of the twentieth century, fair housing activism, civil rights legislation, and the sheer volume of black immigrants led Caribbean New Yorkers to move to Brooklyn and Queens from the midcentury onward. Today, Brooklyn is the borough most densely populated by Caribbean immigrants.

By placing the heart, soul, minds, and feet of African diasporic intellectuals on New York pavement, we gain a better understanding of the major role that Caribbean immigrants have played in their cultural battle for racial equality in modern America. Throughout the chronological expanse of this project, the 1920s to the present, black racial identity has undergone numerous constructions and contestations as Caribbean and American-born black political and religious leaders as well as artists attempted to shape more politically empowered futures. Caribbean intellectuals used their foreign-born status and prior travel experience to provide alternative views of blackness with important ramifications for racial uplift, anticolonialism, and civil rights advancement.

Their history is American history. As the Brooklyn-born son of Russian-Jewish immigrants, historian Oscar Handlin stated in his Pulitzer Prize-winning book *The Uprooted*, "Once I thought to write a history of the immigrants in America. Then I discovered that the immigrants *were* American History."[31]

The Struggle Continues . . .

Cultural diversity is still on the rise in America. Today, three million people of Caribbean descent live in the United States and comprise more than one percent of the country's population. In contrast to the largely Anglophone first wave of black immigrants during the early twentieth century, today's Caribbean immigrants are overwhelmingly Spanish-speaking and come from islands such as Cuba, the Dominican Republic, and Puerto Rico. More than 686,814 Caribbean immigrants live in New York, and constitute one third of its black population. According to the 2010 census, black New Yorkers make up 27 percent of the city's population, a significant figure compared to the much lower national average of 13 percent. Counting the children of Caribbean immigrants, first- and second-generation Caribbean New Yorkers make up more than half of New York's total black population.

A new generation of Caribbean intellectuals is alive and well and producing compelling work in New York City. Mixed media artist Terry Boddie exemplifies this cohort. Terry contributed to an iPhone App that I curated for Black History Month 2013 titled *Black Arts Live!* This digital anthology features the biographies and creative work of eight up-and-coming, literary visual, and performance artists who illustrate the profound cultural diversity, creativity, and intellectual accomplishments of contemporary artists throughout the African diaspora. Thus, like the new immigrants at the dawn of the twentieth century, current-day Caribbean New Yorkers continue to collaborate with American-born blacks on intellectual and artistic production. In Terry Boddie's interview for *Black Arts Live!*, he stated:

> I spent the first fifteen years of my life in Nevis—a small island in the eastern Caribbean about halfway between Venezuela in the south and Miami in the north. . . . I came [to New York] and went to school in the south Bronx at William Howard Taft. And then went on to college, first at New York University and then at Hunter College. . . . On the advice of [a] friend, I went to Hunter College for graduate school. In retrospect, I'm very fortunate to have made that decision because what graduate school essentially gave me was first the technical skills but also the conceptual and intellectual skills to execute and talk about the work I do as a visual artist.[32]

Just as Pearl Primus developed her talent as a dancer and choreographer during her undergraduate studies at Hunter College, Terry Boddie honed his artistic skills at the same institution more than a half-century later. Terry draws upon his Caribbean cultural heritage by using iconography rooted in his upbringing in the islands—flying kites, Caribbean proverbs, and even his own dreadlocks—in his mixed media meditations on memory, migration and globalization. Recently his work has been exhibited in "KREYOL Factory" at the Parc La Villette in Paris, France and in the show "Infinite Island: Contemporary Caribbean Art" at the Brooklyn Museum.[33] Terry's work is complex, compelling, and insightful.

Another one of my favorite current-day Caribbean American intellectuals is civil rights attorney Kristen Clarke. I met Kristen during my freshman year at Harvard and she quickly became an intellectual mentor and friend. Kristen was born in Brooklyn and raised in the East New York section of Brooklyn. Kristen's parents are from Jamaica and she grew up listening to the politically conscious reggae rhythms of Jamaican-born musicians such as Bob Marley and Peter Tosh.[34] In contrast to my negative encounters with African and Caribbean immigrants during my undergraduate and graduate studies (see Introduction), my friendship with Kristen is a prime example of cultural collaboration between Caribbean American and American-born blacks. Consistent with my argument that the personal is political and the political is personal, I attribute this positive interaction to our similar artistic, self-assured, and adventurous personalities. Although both of us have gained a great deal of pride and confidence from our respective families, our individual sense of self does not preclude the brilliance of other cultural perspectives. This is not blind admiration but is instead eyes-wide-open mutual respect. Pearl Primus would appreciate this point. I also attribute our positive interactions to a shared interest in expansive definitions of blackness and cultural belonging and in the intersections of art and politics—Kristen is a photographer inspired by the dynamic evolution of rap and hip-hop culture and I'm a creative writer, mixed-media visual artist, and historian. Kristen has stated, "I have always viewed Blackness through a broad lens—seeing the connections that tie individuals of African descent across the Diaspora."[35] In turn, as politically conscious college students, both of us found common ground with anti-apartheid activists. While Kristen used photography to document her travels throughout South Africa the summer after her junior year, I traveled to Johannesburg, Durban, and Cape Town to conduct research on the history of black women's political activism the following summer.

Similarly, my broad sense of African diasporic identity during my high school years inspired me to travel to St. Croix to learn about the culture and document this experience through poetry. Thanks to the positive energy and generosity of family friends, Nellie and Toyia Bess, who were born in

Cincinnati but relocated to St. Croix to run a daycare center (which Shirley Chisholm would appreciate), I spent two weeks in the United States Virgin Islands during spring break of my senior year—conducting interviews and writing poetry. I recall discussing topics ranging from how to make *callaloo* soup to Emperor Haile Selassie I's symbolic significance to Rastafarians. For my senior project to graduate from Cincinnati Country Day School, I self-published a book of poetry titled *I Ain't Chicken* in which I documented my St. Croix experience in a section called "Wading Carib Waters." In the poem "Island Fever," I paint a portrait of a young man who longed to leave St. Croix to pursue his American dreams on the mainland. I wrote,

Osmand say he be fiendin' for
Highway river currents runnin' swift
Osmand say he fiendin' be
Wherever the American liner drift.[36]

Just as Caribbean immigrants flocked to New York at the turn of the twentieth century, inhabitants of the English-speaking islands desired to try their luck in the United States near the turn of the twenty-first century.

My visit to St. Croix is picture-perfect in my mind. On one hand, this is true because the family friends with whom I stayed and the people I met were sincerely nice. On the other hand, my first visit to the Caribbean stands out because it presents a stark contrast to interactions that I had years later with Caribbean immigrants in the United States who harbored negative stereotypes of American-born blacks.

Such cultural clashes and collaborations between Caribbean immigrants and American-born blacks run deep. When I asked Caribbean American civil rights attorney Kristen Clarke if she has observed such inter-cultural conflicts, she said:

> While I did not witness tensions growing up, I did observe a pattern later in life in which Black people of Caribbean descent appeared to be disproportionately represented among, for example, the incoming class of Black students at Harvard University. Many of my friends of Caribbean descent have parents who were extremely strict and placed great value on striving for academic excellence. I also fully recognize that many of these same parents are a self-selected group who left the Caribbean in search of greater opportunities for their children.[37]

Like scholars who compare the educational and occupational success of Caribbean immigrants to the success of American-born black migrants moving within American borders, Kristen understands the variable of self-selection. However, Kristen also echoes a sentiment expressed by Pearl Primus, Shirley Chisholm, Paule Marshall, and several Caribbean American women I interviewed, about the formative influence of strict parents who value education. I'd like to underscore the gender dynamics that are built into this phenomenon. While Trinidadian-born Black Power activist Stokely Carmichael and Jamaican-American politician Colin Powell also discussed their parents' high regard for education, for the women in my study, their parents' protectiveness took on an added dimension. Shirley Chisholm's description of her mother's parenting style is a case in point. In Chisholm's autobiography, she stated:

> My family kept me on a tight rein in high school years. Mother knew the minute when I should get home from school, and I had to be there on the dot or face a barrage of questions. My father remonstrated with Mother sometimes: 'Ruby, you must remember these are American kids, not island kids. You are here in America.' Mother was not impressed. We girls were allowed to go to school programs and occasional parties, but I never had a date, a regular date in high school. In fact, I never had one in college.[38]

Although Chisholm understood her mother's strictness as a particularly West Indian characteristic, I suggest that comparable practices of strict parenting also existed among American-born blacks during the same time Chisholm came of age in New York and still exist today. Literature on black American Christian women's practice of racial uplift by adhering to conservative styles of dress and behavior at the time that Chisholm was born supports this point.[39] Furthermore, as the daughter of an American-born black Christian pastor, I also can testify to the truth of the existence of strict parenting styles among American-born blacks. Because my argument is qualitative and anecdotal, more research needs to be conducted on this topic. I leave that challenge to my colleagues in the social sciences for now.

Still, Kristen's point regarding family values is well taken. I understand Kristen's bold intellect and mastery of the written and spoken word as characteristics distinctively developed in her personality and cultivated within the context of her family and educational training as an undergraduate at Harvard and as a graduate student at Columbia University's Law School. Mix in a healthy dose of hip hop infused social awareness nurtured in the vibrant cultures of Brooklyn and the result is an outspoken activist committed to the cause of social justice. To this day, one of the most memorable experiences from my undergraduate career is when, as the president of the Black Student Association (BSA), Kristen Clarke organized a protest in response to the publication of *The Bell Curve* by political scientist Charles Murray and psychologist Richard Herrnstein.[40] In this infamous text, the authors argue that black Americans' scores on Intelligent Quotient (IQ) tests are lower than whites because blacks are genetically inferior to whites. I was among the more than 80 students who stood on the steps of Widener Library in protest. Some BSA members held signs that read "Break the Bell Curve" and "Embrace Truth, Not Hate."[41] Kristen opened the rally by stating: "We are here today united, Black, Latino, Asian, Jewish and white. . . . The real issue at hand is not IQ. . . . [The authors'] hidden agenda is aimed at eliminating welfare and hurting the poor."[42] Later, as I stood at the microphone, reciting poetry, I caught a glimpse of what the architects of the Black Arts Movement might have felt during their poetic protest of the continuation of white supremacy. Kristen, a sophomore at the time, spoke with such clarity, authority, and wisdom beyond her years. Perhaps the spirit of Marcus Garvey was guiding her on that brisk, November day.

Not only does Garvey's legacy continue to animate the activism and creative work of black intellectuals today, but Barbadian American politician Shirley Chisholm also serves as an enduring inspiration for generations of Caribbean and American-born black writers and artists. New York–born and bred graphic designer Jennifer Cruté is a case in point. In her hilarious, autobiographical comic book titled *Jennifer's Journal: The Life of a Suburban Girl*, Jennifer relays an account of her coming-of-age in New York. When she delivered a guest lecture for my students at Miami University of Ohio-Oxford in Spring 2014, she credited one of the major historical figures in my book— Shirley Chisholm, for helping her take a leap of faith to leave the lucrative commercial, graphic design industry to embark upon a career as an independent artist.[43] Jennifer said Shirley Chisholm appeared to her in a dream and told her that she must pursue the important work of depicting the world through her own eyes. The autobiographical nature of Jennifer's work and the self-affirming advice that Chisholm's ghost gave Jennifer in her dream calls to mind Paule Marshall's mission to document the diversity of black women's experiences so that her readers might be empowered through seeing reflections of themselves in the literature. Thus, just as Garvey's ghost continues to haunt black artistic production today, Shirley Chisholm's encouraging, feminist spirit is also alive and well. (Perhaps I should ask reggae artist Burning Spear or the musical descendants of Jazz drummer Max Roach to create a praise song for Shirley Chisholm—akin to the odes that they created for Marcus Garvey).

Jennifer Cruté's art and writing capture the brilliant diversity of cultures and experiences that make New York a cultural capital of the world. Jennifer especially devotes careful attention to the nuanced accents—literal and meta-phorical, that constitute black New York. When I asked her about an amusing anecdote in her book about a Trinidadian wedding that she attended as a child where she ate a gigantic piece of black rum cake, which she had mistaken for chocolate cake, Jennifer discussed the high points of New York. She said:

> The diversity of New York City is always going to be in my artwork, because it's there.... I'm doing a section in my comics about New York. Some of it is just the things I love about New York City, like the drummers who get on the A train and ride from Brooklyn into Manhattan. When I get on the train and realize that they're there, I'm like, "Yes!" It just makes the ride so much better. Everyone I've talked to knows who I'm talking about, it doesn't matter what background. They just sit down in the middle of the train and drum, then they walk around and collect money and sell CDs. So I'm actually going to be working on a painting of them, because I don't know if they realize how touching they are to so many New Yorkers. And that's just a little piece of that diversity. And that's why I love New York City. The art comes from so many different directions.[44]

Jennifer's appreciation of cultural and artistic diversity within blackness reso-nates with the historical actors in this book and current-day New Yorkers.

New York continues to be the home of America's largest Caribbean immi-grant population, but cities such as Boston, Washington, DC, Miami, and Minneapolis also boast a significant number of black immigrants from the continent of Africa and from the Caribbean. My own personal biography reflects this experience of the drastically increasing cultural diversity within the black population. When I was an undergraduate at Harvard, I observed the significant number of Haitian immigrants who happened to be taxicab drivers. When I interned at *TransAfrica Forum* in Dupont Circle in Washing-ton, DC, the summer after my sophomore year, I dined at Ethiopian restau-rants near U Street and met numerous immigrants from eastern Africa. After completing my undergraduate studies, I lived in Minneapolis and worked in St. Paul, MN, where I witnessed the quickly growing Latino and Somali immi-grant populations. Even my hometown of Cincinnati, Ohio, is experiencing a surge in diversity within blackness, as immigrants from northern and western Africa, especially Mauritania and Senegal, have flocked to the Queen City in the past decade.

These black immigrant populations continue to collaborate and clash with American-born blacks. My recent conversation with a young woman immigrant from Mauritania is a case in point. I ordered takeout from a Sen-egalese restaurant on Vine Street in the Carthage area of Cincinnati that my brother raved about. The menu of curried chicken, lamb, and goat reminded me of Caribbean restaurants in which I dined when I lived in the Bronx for a year while teaching at Lehman College, and in numerous subsequent visits with friends in Brooklyn. As my niece, who happens to be my mini-me, and I waited for our order of jerk chicken wings, savory shrimp kabobs, and curried chicken, rice, and beans, I struck up a conversation with the friendly young woman cashier, Rahma Athie.[45]

Rahma told me that she emigrated from Mauritania to Cincinnati with her mom, dad and five siblings in 2006. She looked at my twelve-year-old niece and said, "I was around her size," and we smiled. Rahma attended Withrow High School—a public school that is historically populated by American-born blacks. She quickly recalled the sting of negative stereotypes of Africa that her American-born black classmates hurled at her. Rahma said, "When I came here it was hard because there was a lot of racism and we weren't used to the racism. People would say 'You are African monkeys; go back to your home!'" When she relayed this experience my jaw dropped, and I said, "What?! Isn't this the twenty-first century?" Such insults call to mind the derogatory term "monkey chaser" that American-born blacks used to insult Caribbean immigrants with during the early twentieth century.[46] Unfortunately, intraracial cultural conflicts still exist and persist.

Sadly, black-white racism also still exists in the United States. With the election of America's first black president, Barack Obama, there have been academic and popular discussions of America as a post-racial society—where Dr. Martin Luther King's dream that we all be judged by the content of our character, and not by the color of our skin, has finally been achieved. To such color-blind utopians, I say: I hate to burst your bubble, but we aren't *there* yet. I expressed a similar sentiment in a February 2013 interview, "Are we post-racial? To that question I say, 'No.' We're not post-racial, but we are evolving as a democracy."[47] And even as we confront current-day racial tensions exemplified by the August 2014 protests and riots in Ferguson, Missouri, over the tragedy of Michael Brown—an unarmed, black male teenager shot and killed by a white police officer—we should look toward the examples of Ethelred Brown, Richard B. Moore, Pearl Primus, Shirley Chisholm, and Paule Marshall, who wielded the written, spoken, and performed word as a weapon in the battle against racism, especially against negative stereotypes of blackness. The drama of Ferguson unfurled before my eyes as I watched the news coverage. Then, on MSNBC, I saw a familiar face, a fellow professor, born and raised in St. Louis, who described the celebratory tone of black residents as one of "release" after the militarized police retreated and curfew was lifted. This young scholar wore slacks, a dress shirt, and a tie, but prominently draped across his back was a t-shirt emblazoned with the image of Marcus Garvey.[48] Just as Garvey vexed and inspired the historical actors in this book and countless other Caribbean immigrants and American-born black intellectuals, Garvey's ghost continues to encourage contemporary activists and scholars to raise their voices in the cause of social justice. The struggle continues.

Acknowledgments

As I sit at the kitchen table in my sister's home in Houston, Texas, at a quarter till two in the morning, this is the ideal time and place to meditate on gratitude. This book would not be the book that it became without the unconditional love, faith, and positive energy of my family. So, as I write these words, I think of my youngest nephews, Corey and Cayden, ages 5 and 7, fast asleep in their cozy room. I picture their faces, so much like the face of their mother— my sister and best friend, Charnée. I think of the countless trips I've made to Houston in winter, spring, and summer breaks. During a writing process that sometimes felt unending, the funny conversations, Xbox challenges, and movie breaks that I've enjoyed with all of my nieces and nephews were indeed priceless. Last year's excursion to see *Frozen* with Cayden and Corey is a case in point. My nephews grudgingly admitted that they enjoyed the film even though they thought it was "for girls," but I said the movie was perfect for them because it was about the power of sibling love. My nephews are too young to fully comprehend that the sisterly bond between me and their mom, fourteen months my senior, was the very thing that urged her to pray for boys close in age who would be the best of friends. So as a professorial, feminist aunty, I was thrilled by the unconventional ending of *Frozen*—unconventional, at least, for a Disney movie. Instead of a charming medieval knight with chiseled features atop a white stallion who saves the helpless heroine, it is an act of bravery and love by one sister for the other that saves the day. In real life, the same has been true for me. It has not been the fine, dreadlocked man in the black, drop-top Corvette of my imagination that rescues me, but the strength and profound love of my big sister, which never fails to lift me higher. Charnée Brown: for this immeasurable gift, I express my wholehearted gratitude.

My family—our synergy is greater than the sum of our individual selves. To my parents, Pastor Stephen F. and Marion J. Brown: your faith grounds me. Dad, I sometimes tease you, saying you're auditioning to become a saint, but I appreciate your setting the bar so high because your wisdom and compassion are qualities that I strive to emulate. As a self-taught pastor, carpenter, and entrepreneur, your intellect, work ethic, and creativity have been foundational to my sense of self—especially my ability to dream of new things to create with my own mind and hands. Mom, your encouraging spirit, conscientiousness, and impeccably healthy lifestyle help to keep us dreamers on track. From my elementary school days to the present, your love of history and sharp commentary on the politics of race in America have been cornerstones in my intellectual growth. It has also been a privilege to watch you develop as a writer over the years. So even when you ask me to review one of your essays in record time, I am grateful to give back to you what you have so freely given to me. To my brothers Darren and Lamont: much like our father, you possess the uncanny ability to say the simplest and funniest thing that is so profound that it shifts my consciousness in that very moment. Darren, your drive inspires me. Lamont, thank you for shining the light. Charnée, despite your own hectic schedule, you are the one who gets this team into shape and makes sure no one comes undone.

To my grandmother Clementine Dowdell, and in memory of my grandmother Clara Wills: thank you for your perseverance and encouragement, because without you, there would be no me. To my great aunt Paralee Wilmer: for letting me know you're proud of me and for deepening my knowledge of my own family history. To my sister-in-law Lynette: Charnée and I like to call you a "ride or die" friend who knows how to get the job done; thank you for the no-nonsense help with my many moves (from New York to Cincy to North Carolina and back). To all of my nieces and nephews: Darius, Simone, Brianna, Cidnei, Darren Jr., Tamara, Payton, Paige, Darian, Cayden, and Corey; I often say, "When the revolution comes, we'll have our own army." In Aunt Tammy's world, this revolution is rooted in organic intellectual debate, good humor, profound creativity, and generosity of spirit. I am grateful to be your aunty because all of you exemplify these qualities. To my mini-me Ms. Paige LaKenya Brown—born the same year that I began research for this book and talking early—your phone calls were the perfect way to end a long day of research, writing, and revising. Your precociousness never fails to remind me that this is indeed a beautiful world.

To my extended family—biological and spiritual, thank you. Shirley Broadnax, I am grateful for your unconditional love and encouragement. To this day, I relish your compliment that when I talk about history, I "break it down so everyday people will understand." That is my primary goal; so, thank you for confirming that I am on track! Aima Ahonkhai Nottidge, for over two decades, conversations with you always help me return to my higher self. Thank you for being a true friend. Dana Hughes-Moorehead, Erika Singleton-Wilson, Courtney Griffin, LaVerne Davis and family, Felicia and Edrick Felix, and the rest of "The African Village," Jameze Latrail, Shawntee Brown,

Dora and Todd Dawson, and members of Abundant Life Faith Fellowship Church, I bow to you with love, respect, and gratitude—always.

As I write these words, I am halfway through a 2,283-mile road trip from my hometown Cincinnati to my sister's home in Houston. On the return leg, I'll spend one night in Mississippi and one night in Tennessee, site-seeing and catching up with old friends. I used to hate road trips, especially if I was the driver. Anywhere farther than a three-hour drive, I booked a plane. But while I was in graduate school, something changed. It started with three-hour drives from Princeton, New Jersey, to Maryland and Washington, DC, where my sister and several good friends lived at the time. Then it stretched to five-hour drives between Cincinnati and Nashville, Tennessee, where I lived while on a writing fellowship thanks to the generosity of historian Elizabeth Lunbeck and the history department at Vanderbilt University. I then graduated to eight-hour drives between Cincinnati and Chapel Hill, where I lived for two years while completing a writing fellowship at the University of North Carolina. Then I took on my first eighteen-hour road trip, from Chapel Hill to Houston and back again. On the outbound leg, I spent one night in Atlanta with a childhood friend, I spontaneously stopped to visit my nephew who is an undergraduate at Tuskegee University, and I spent a night in New Orleans with extended family. On the return leg, I spent one night in Montgomery, Alabama, at the house of my sister's college roommate, and then drove back to Chapel Hill. I admit, I was proud of myself for finishing that thirty-six-hour round trip drive by myself.

Have you noticed a pattern? If I wrote it as an equation, it would look something like this: (me + travel + writing) x (family + friends) = Happiness. I believe writing is one of the best vehicles for intellectual exploration, and to do this well, you must feel happy and free. For me, driving by myself on the wide-open road is freedom.

So it is not surprising that the process of writing this book has been very much like taking a long road trip. This metaphor percolated in my subconscious so much that before starting my current road trip to Houston, I had to get my hands on Langston Hughes's classic autobiography *I Wonder as I Wonder*. This brilliantly funny account of Hughes's travels through the southern United States, Europe, Russia, and Asia has been the perfect travel companion. Just as the places Hughes visited and the conversations he had while traveling shaped his consciousness as a writer, the cities I've called home and the awesome intellectual dialogues I've had with family, friends, and colleagues have been crucial to this book.

To my friends and colleagues at Princeton University, thank you. My sincere thanks to historian Elizabeth Lunbeck for showing me that it is possible to do good work, find time for bike rides, and still have a good sense of humor. Your sincere encouragement of independent thought, your depth of knowledge and your practice of compassionate professionalism inspire me to be the best teacher I can be. Likewise, Stanley Katz, your calm, positive energy is a rare find in academe and is wholeheartedly appreciated. I am still benefitting from your Phil Jackson style of coaching—a Zen-like engaged intellectualism and pursuit of excellence which I strive to achieve when teaching and advising my own students.

Cornel West, thank you for the genuine encouragement and the delightful intellectual dialogues over meals at the Annex. Dan Rodgers, I'm very grateful for your general intellectual guidance and your advice to stick to the chapter-by-chapter biographical format. I especially appreciate the encouragement to follow through with my initial methodological approach, because the process helped me realize how much I love writing biographies. Thanks to Valerie Smith for drawing my attention to Paule Marshall and for her intellectual encouragement, and to Nell Painter for urging my interest in Caribbean immigration history. Thanks to Colin Palmer, Albert Raboteau, Marie Griffith, Howard Taylor, and Eddie Glaude for your intellectual presence and moral support. Carolyn Rouse, thank you for the encouragement, by word and example, to pursue my artistic interests as well as my scholarship.

To all Princeton people who study-buddied or generally sent positive energy, thank you: Chad Williams, Anastasia Curwood, Joe Conley, Jolie Dyl, Chris Garces, Nicholas Guyatt, Keith Mayes, Ann Morning, and Sarah Igo. Malinda Lindquist, your intellect, generosity, and humility are remarkable. Thanks to Lyndon Dominique for the hilariously enjoyable intellectual banter and for all positive vibes. Thanks to Sam Roberts for reminding me to keep my game face on and for kindly answering all sophomoric questions. To Temitayo Ogunbiyi for being a creative/ artistic sounding board and intellectual ally. For friends who harbored me—literally provided a place for me to stay while conducting research in New York, thank you: Nneka Offor, Erika Singleton, and LeShane Lindsey. To all Princeton administrators who generously provided good conversation and moral support: Joy Montero, David Redman, and Maryann Rodriguez. To Dana Hughes and the Madden family, many thanks for the home-cooked meals and hospitality; you made Princeton feel like home.

To my colleagues at Miami University of Ohio: thank you. It is such a pleasure and privilege to teach and write alongside such dedicated, creative and intellectually astute colleagues. My sincere gratitude to those who read early drafts of this manuscript and generously offered suggestions for revision: Drew Cayton, Carla Pestana, Daniel Cobb, and Allan Winkler. Drew, I especially appreciate your positive and pragmatic approach to writing; your sage advice has rung in my ears throughout the process of writing this book. To all colleagues who imparted positive energy and intellectual insights throughout the evolution of this project, thank you: Madelyn Detloff, Gaile Pohlhaus, Peggy Schaffer, Steve Norris, Lisa Weems, Adrian Gaskins, Sheila Croucher, Tammy Kernodle, Denise McCoskey and Helane Adams Androne. Madelyn and Peggy, I especially appreciate all of the encouraging words and generous assistance with navigating the bureaucracy of academe. Nishani Frazier, thank you for being a comrade on this intellectual journey. Gwendolyn Etter-Lewis, your graciousness and wisdom are so keen that you've earned the title of the oracle in this odyssey.

The University of North Carolina at Chapel Hill (UNC) provided the ideal intellectual environment to push through the final revisions of this book. My sincere thanks to Bill and Marcie Ferris; I know good people when I see them, and you stood out the moment I arrived in Chapel Hill. Bill, I reserve my deepest gratitude for you for introducing me to editor Craig Gill at the University Press of Mississippi, which granted me the freedom to write the book that I wanted to write. To my colleagues at UNC and Duke University who offered advice throughout the writing process, thank you: Vincent Brown, Priscilla Wald, Mark Anthony Neal, Charles Price, Bernie Herman, Michelle Robinson, Reginald Hildebrand, Benjamin Filene, Mosi Ifantiji, Sharon Holland, Joy Kasson, Barbara Entwisle and Sibby Anderson-Thompkins. To Edward Vargas, Brittney Cofield-Poole, Thomas Hunter, Dare Kumolu-Johnson, and the rest of the crew, thank you for the good food, great conversations, and good times.

To my colleagues at Vanderbilt University, thank you: Richard Blackett, Lucius Outlaw, and Victor Anderson. Richard, thank you for advising me to deepen my biographical methodological approach and for encouraging me to just tell the story. To my Nashville housemates and friends, thanks for the good food and great conversations—Jamie Moffitt, Joon Powell, and Garrett Stark, please kindly notify me at least one week in advance before The Revolution comes; I want to be on time.

In the New York City Archives: Thanks to André Elizée at the Schomburg Center for Research in Black Culture for introducing me to the Richard B. Moore Papers, and to Nurah Jeter for making sure I was properly dressed for the Commandment Keepers' Shabbat. Thanks to Steven Fullwood and all Schomburg archivists for sharing your expertise and for the thought-provoking conversations. To Irma Watkins-Owens at Fordham University, for so thoroughly and kindly answering my numerous e-mail inquiries and for being a generous reservoir of knowledge on Caribbean New York.

To the intellectual role models and comrades that I've met along the way, especially through the Association for the Study of African American Life and History, thank you: Randal Jelks, Shannon King, Minkah Makalani, Cheryl Hicks, and Robyn Spencer. I am inspired by your work and your scholarly example. I am grateful for conversations with authors whose work overlaps with my own: Farah Jasmine Griffin, Barbara Winslow, Zinga Fraser, and Peggy Schwartz. I also sincerely thank John Guess and the entire staff at the Houston Museum of African American Culture for providing me with a dynamic platform to share my research and writing.

To my Harvard classmates and friends, thank you for your brilliance, encouragement, and overall "super-flyness." Imani Perry, thanks for the awesome conversations about engaging with the subject at hand for the sheer *love* of pursuing a life of the mind. Alvin Tillery, thank you for being an intellectual role model. Abena Osseo Asare, thanks for the great discussions about the quirks of academe and for the solid intellectual support, from our Harvard Freshman Seminar days to the present. Joshua Powe, thanks for the overall positive energy; also, thank you for your commitment to improving the quality of K-12 education—much respect. Kristen Clarke: your keen intellect, creativity and lifelong commitment to engaged intellectualism and social justice continue to inspire me.

Funding: all road trips require gas money, lodging, and square meals. Thanks to the Altman Faculty Fellowship at Miami University of Ohio, The University of North Carolina at Chapel Hill Carolina Postdoctoral Program for Faculty Diversity, Vanderbilt University's Department of History, the Mellon Foundation, and Princeton University's Graduate School, Department of History, Center for Arts and Cultural Policy Studies, Center for the Study of Religion, Center for African American Studies, and Policy Research Institute for the Region for funding this intellectual endeavor.

Thanks to everybody and all good energy that helped bring this project to fruition. It takes a universe to raise a book, and my cosmos has been filled with very kind and generous souls. May all of the good karma boomerang.

Notes

Prologue

1. Jill Lepore, "Historians Who Love Too Much: Reflections on Microhistory and Biography." *The Journal of American History* 88, no. 1 (June 2001): 129.

2. Edward Hallett Carr, *What is History?* (New York: Vintage Books, 1967) 24.

3. David Levering Lewis, "The Autobiography of Biography," Public Lecture, City University of New York, September 18, 2013. Lewis also published this speech as a short article of the same name in *American Scholar* 83, no. 3 (Summer 2014): 94–102; Lewis, David Levering, "The Dialectics of History: An Interview with David Levering Lewis," *Political Affairs*, 2004. http://www.politicalaffairs.net/the-dialectics-of-history-an -interview-with-david-levering-lewis/.

4. Barbara Ransby, *Ella Baker and the Black Freedom Movement: A Radical Democratic Vision* (Chapel Hill: University of North Carolina Press, 2005).

5. Because Cornel West served on my dissertation committee and is energetically interested in the life of the mind, I enjoyed many conversations with him while completing my graduate studies at Princeton University. Dr. West used the term "post-Negroes" on numerous occasions in our conversations to describe American-born blacks who were descendants of slaves.

6. Other scholars note the significance of the term "JB" as an abbreviation for "just black," or American-born black. See Christina M. Greer's dissertation *Black Ethnicity: Identity, Participation, and Policy*, Columbia University, 2008; and Christina M. Greer, *Black Ethnics: Race, Immigration and the Pursuit of the American Dream* (Oxford: Oxford University Press, 2013), 2.

7. Sara Rimer and Karen W. Arenson, "Top Colleges Take More Blacks, but Which Ones?" *New York Times*, June 24, 2004.

8. Thanks to the Hickman Humanities Award, founded by retired English teacher Sara Hickman at Cincinnati Country Day School, I was awarded a grant for my proposal to travel to St. Croix, learn about its culture, and record my experience in the form of poetry. This trip was possible thanks to the generosity of family friends Nellie and Toyia Bess, who lived in St. Croix and allowed me to stay with them during spring break of my senior year in high school. When I returned I gave a public lecture at CCDS, where I presented the poetry based on my experience.

9. In Summer 1997, I traveled to Johannesburg, Durban, and Cape Town, South Africa, to conduct research for my undergraduate honors thesis, titled *From Bullets to Ballots: Black Women, Activism, and Violence in South Africa, 1920s-Present*, which I completed in May

1998. I graduated *magna cum laude* with a bachelors degree in history and international relations from Harvard University in 1998.

10. This language regarding the process of intellectual and emotional maturation is borrowed from the titles of English poet William Blake's books *Songs of Innocence*, first published in 1789, and *Songs of Experience*, published in 1804.

11. Milton Vickerman, "Attitudes toward African Americans," *Crosscurrents: West Indian Immigrants and Race* (New York: Oxford University Press, 1999), 137–164; Mary C. Waters, "West Indians at Work," in *Black Identities: West Indian Immigrant Dreams and American Realities* (Cambridge, MA: Harvard University Press, 1999), 94–139; Waters, "Encountering American Race Relations," in *Black Identities: West Indian Immigrant Dreams and American Realities*, 140–191; Regine O. Jackson, "Black Immigrants and the Rhetoric of Social Distancing," *Sociology Compass* 4 (2010):193–206.

12. This forty-eight-year-old Guyanese teacher was quoted in Mary C. Waters, "West Indians at Work," in *Black Identities: West Indian Immigrant Dreams and American Realities*, 68.

13. Milton Vickerman, "Jamaicans: Balancing Race and Ethnicity," in *New Immigrants in New York* (New York: Columbia University Press, 2001), 213.

14. David Roediger, *Wages of Whiteness: Race and the Making of the American Working Class* (London: Verso, 1991); Noel Ignatiev, *How the Irish Became White* (New York: Routledge, 1995); Matthew Frye Jacobson, *Whiteness of a Different Color: European Immigrants and the Alchemy of Race* (Cambridge: Harvard University Press, 1998).

Introduction

1. Historian and biographer David Levering Lewis often describes biography as a window into specific historical and cultural contexts. See David Levering Lewis, "The Dialectics of History," 2004.

2. David Levering Lewis, "The Dialectics of History," 2004

3. I embrace the work of biographers such as David Levering Lewis, Arnold Rampersad, Annette Gordon-Reed, and Wil Haygood as benchmarks in this regard.

4. Book-length biographies of Ethelred Brown, Pearl Primus, Hazel Scott, and Shirley Chisholm were published while I revised this manuscript. See Juan M. Floyd-Thomas, *The Origins of Black Humanism in America: Reverend Ethelred Brown and the Unitarian Church* (New York: Palgrave MacMillan, 2008); Karen Chilton, *Hazel Scott: The Pioneering Journey of a Jazz Pianist from Café Society to Hollywood to HUAC* (Ann Arbor: University of Michigan Press, 2010); Barbara Winslow, *Shirley Chisholm: Catalyst for Change* (Philadelphia: Westview Press, 2014); and Peggy and Murray Schwartz, *The Dance Claimed Me: A Biography of Pearl Primus* (New Haven: Yale University Press, 2011). Pearl Primus was also the topic of a book chapter in Farah Jasmine Griffin, *Harlem Nocturne: Women Artists and Progressive Politics During World War II* (New York: Basic Civitas Books, 2013).

5. Ziggy Marley and the Melody Makers, "What's True?" *Conscious Party* (Virgin Records, 1988).

6. Ibid.

7. Chimamanda Ngozi Adichie, "The Danger of a Single Story," TED Global Conference, March 15, 2009.

8. Ibid.

9. Kimberlé Crenshaw, often called the founder of critical race theory, effectively writes about how racism *intersects* with sexism to make black women's experiences of sociopolitical oppression pronouncedly unique; Kimberlé Crenshaw, "Mapping the Margins: Intersectionality, Identity Politics, and Violence against Women of Color," *Stanford Law Review* 43, no. 6 (Jul., 1991), 1241–1299. English and Literature scholar Valerie Smith also suggests that one must consider the synergistic multi-facets of identity, instead of studying race in isolation; Valerie Smith, *Not Just Race, Not Just Gender: Black Feminist Readings* (New York: Routledge, 1998). In contrast to historian James Barrett and David Roediger's discussion of how European immigrants *became* white, Ronald Takaki's analysis of Asian immigrants' multi-generational, *full-circle* identity construction, and Sarah Deutsch's discussion of Anglo-Hispanic borderlands, this dissertation demonstrates the blurring of class, racial, ethnic, and religious parameters in the very unique location—Harlem. For discussions of generational differences regarding Asian-American cultural assimilation see Ronald Takaki, *Strangers from a Different Shore: A History of Asian Americans* (Boston: Little, Brown, c1989).

10. Mary Jo Maynes, Jennifer L. Pierce, and Barbara Laslett, *Telling Stories: The Use of Personal Narratives in the Social Sciences and History* (Ithica, NY: Cornell Unversity Press, 2008) Kindle file.

11. Annette Gordon-Reed, *The Hemingses of Monticello: An American Family*, 290.

12. Arnold Rampersad, "Design and Truth in Biography," *South Central Modern Language Association Review* 9, no. 2 (Summer 1992), 2.

13. Alice Kessler-Harris, "Why Biography?" *American Historical Review* 114, no. 3 June 2009, 626.

14. David Levering Lewis, "Failing to Know Martin Luther King, Jr.," *The Journal of American History* 78, no. 1 (June 1991): 81–85.

15. Jochen Hellbeck, *Revolution on my Mind: Writing a Diary Under Stalin* (Cambridge, MA: Harvard University Press, 2009),12-13.

16. Lepore, Jill. "Historians Who Love Too Much: Reflections on Microhistory and Biography." *The Journal of American History* 88, no. 1 (June 2001): 129–144. JSTOR.

17. See Laurel Thatcher Ulrich, *A Midwife's Tale: The Life of Martha Ballard, Based on Her Diary, 1785–1812* (New York: Vintage Books, 1990); Nell Irvin Painter,*Sojourner Truth: A Life, a Symbol* (New York: W. W. Norton & Company, 1996); Annette Gordon-Reed, *The Hemingses of Monticello: An American Family* (New York: W. W. Norton & Company, 2008).

18. David Levering Lewis, "The Autobiography of Biography," Public Lecture, City University of New York, New York, NY, September 18, 2013.

19. The "Great Man Theory" of history was popularized by Scottish writer Thomas Carlyle in the 1840s.

20. Blanche Wiesen Cook, "Outing History," *The Seductions of Biography* (London, UK: Routledge), 1996, 85–86.

21. American-born black authors such as James Weldon Johnson, Ira De Augustine Reid, and Roi Ottley surveyed black immigrants to better understand their cultural acclimation

process, or lack thereof. Johnson was a poet, diplomat, and leading cultural critic who had a personal interest in Caribbean culture as his mother had been born free in Nassau, Bahamas and spent a major portion of her childhood years in New York City. Johnson estimated that Harlem's Caribbean population totaled approximately fifty thousand. James Weldon Johnson, *Black Manhattan* (New York: Knopf, 1930). For a detailed discussion of race and place in the context of Harlem, see Alaine Locke, ed. *The New Negro* (New York: Boni, 1925); Ira DeAugustine Reid, *The Negro Immigrant: His Background, Characteristics and Social Adjustment, 1899–1937* (New York: Columbia University Press, 1939); David L. Lewis, *When Harlem Was in Vogue* (New York: Knopf, 1981); Roi Ottley, *New World A-Coming: Inside Black America* (Boston: Houghton Mifflin, 1943); Gilbert Osofsky, *Harlem: The Making of a Ghetto: Negro New York, 1890–1930* (New York: Harper Torchbook, 1964). Ira De Augustine Reid's *The Negro Immigrant: His Background, Characteristics and Social Adjustment, 1899–1937* was a ground-breaking tour de force as Reid keenly analyzed the differences between racism experienced in British colonial possessions and Jim Crow New York during the early twentieth century. De Augustine Reid was a professor of sociology at Atlanta University when he published the first book-length study of black immigrants. "The Negro immigrant undergoes a reorganization of status involving adjustment to an intra-racial situation and to an inter-racial one," Reid observed, "Leaving communities where he was part of the numerical majority, he moves into one where he is part of the numerical and social minority." Ira DeAugustine Reid, *The Negro Immigrant: His Background, Characteristics and Social Adjustment, 1899–1937* (New York: Columbia University Press, 1939), 26.

22. Historian Winston James lists the total number of black immigrants living in the US during the early twentieth century as 150,000 in *Holding Aloft the Banner of Ethiopia: Caribbean Radicalism in Early Twentieth-Century America* (London; New York: Verso, 1998), 7.

23. W. E. B. Du Bois, *The Souls of Black Folk* (New York: Random House, 2003), xli.

24. Irma Watkins-Owens, *Blood Relations: Caribbean Immigrants and the Harlem Community, 1900–1903* (Bloomington: Indiana University Press, 1996); Winston James, *Holding Aloft the Banner of Ethiopia* (London; New York: Verso, 1998); Joyce Moore Turner, *Caribbean Crusaders and the Harlem Renaissance* (Urbana; Chicago: University of Illinois Press, 2005).

25. The small cadre of intellectuals writing about black immigrants diminished after the 1940s until the culture wars of the 1970s roused scholarly interest in Caribbean immigrants to the US. The proliferation of African American studies and ethnic studies departments as well as popular political debates regarding the urban poor brought attention to the social and economic success of black immigrants as compared to alleged native-born black American lag. The majority of sociological scholarship focuses on Caribbean immigrants living in New York City. As the numbers of immigrants from the Spanish-speaking Caribbean increases, studies are appearing on Cuban, Puerto Rican, and Dominican immigrants living in New York City, Chicago, Miami, and so. Princeton University sociologist Alexandro Portes wrote an important study on Haitian and Cuban immigrants in Miami, Florida. Alejandro Portes and Alex Stepick, *City on the Edge: the Transformation of Miami* (Berkeley: University of California Press, c1993).

26. Current scholarship on Caribbean New York is still addressing, for the most part, the thesis of Caribbean-immigrant success proposed by economist Thomas Sowell in 1975.

Sowell contends that Caribbean immigrants excelled their American-born black counterparts because of a superior work ethic. Although some aspects of Sowell's study remain compelling, Sowell did not construct Caribbean immigrants as immigrants; instead he focused primarily on racial identity. He compared African Caribbean immigrants to American-born blacks, but did not explore how the cultural assimilation of Caribbean immigrants compared to that of European immigrants. See Thomas Sowell, *Ethnic America: A History* (New York: Basic Books, 1981); Philip Kasinitz, *Caribbean New York: Black Immigrants and the Politics of Race* (Ithaca, NY: Cornell University Press, 1992); Mary C. Waters, *Black Identities: West Indian Immigrant Dreams and American Realities*, 1999; Nancy Foner, ed., *Islands in the City: West Indian Migration to New York* (Berkeley and Los Angeles: University of California Press, 2001); Milton Vickerman, *Crosscurrents: West Indian Immigrants and Race* (New York: Oxford University Press, 1998).

27. See Herbert Gans, "Second-Generation Decline: Scenarios for the Economic and Ethnic Futures of the Post-1965 American Immigrants." *Ethnic and Racial Studies* 15: 173–192, 1992; Sheri-Ann Butterfield, "Something in Between: Locating Identity among Second Generation West Indians in New York City," in *Mighty Change, Tall Within: Black Identity in the Hudson Valley*, edited by M. B. Young Armstead (Albany, New York: State University of New York Press, 2003), 233–261. Some contemporary scholarship, especially in the field of sociology, has debunked the myth of a Caribbean model minority, especially with respect to the second and third generations. See Suzanne Model, *West Indian Immigrants: A Black Success Story?* (New York: Russell Sage Foundation, 2011).

28. Irma Watkins-Owens, *Blood Relations*, 1.

29. Roi Ottley, *New World A-Coming: Inside Black America* (Boston: Houghton Mifflin, 1943), 46–47.

30. For detailed accounts of the formation and politics of "whiteness," see: James R. Barrett, "Americanization from the Bottom Up: Immigration and the Remaking of the Working Class in the United States, 1880-1930," *Journal of American History*, 79, no. 3 (December 1992), 996–1020; James R. Barrett and David Roediger, "Inbetween Peoples: Race, Nationality and the 'New Immigrant' Working Class," *Journal of Ethnic History* 16 (Spring 1997): 2–44; Lizabeth Cohen, *Making a New Deal: Industrial Workers in Chicago, 1919-1939* (Cambridge, 1990); David Roediger, *Wages of Whiteness: Race and the Making of the American Working Class* (London: Verso, 1991); Noel Ignatiev, *How the Irish Became White* (New York: Routledge, 1995); Matthew Frye Jacobson, *Whiteness of a Different Color: European Immigrants and the Alchemy of Race* (Cambridge: Harvard University Press, 1998); and Nell Irvin Painter, *The History of White People* (New York: W. W. Norton & Company, 2010).

31. A few historians have criticized whiteness studies scholars who focus on European "New Immigrants" as such studies have failed to discuss the complex identity constructions of African Caribbean immigrants who arrived in the United States during the same era. See Barbara J. Fields, "Whiteness, Racism, and Identity," *International Labor and Working-Class History* 60, (2001): 48–56; historian Winston James called whiteness studies scholars' discussions of European immigrants and oversight of black immigrants a kind of "intellectual apartheid." Winston James, "Explaining Afro-Caribbean Social Mobility in the United

States: Beyond the Sowell Thesis," *Comparative Studies in Society and History* 4, no. 2 (2002): 218–262.

32. For further discussion of the "process and condition" of the creation of the African diaspora, see Robin D. G. Kelley and Tiffany Ruby Patterson, "Unfinished Migrations: Reflections on the African Diaspora and the Makings of the Modern World," *African Studies Review* 43, no. 1, special issue on the diaspora (April 2000): 11–45.

33. For a fuller discussion of black religious organizations, movements and leaders in New York, see Arthur Huff Fauset, *Black Gods of the Metropolis: Negro Religious Cults of the Urban North* (Philadelphia: University of Pennsylvania Press, 1944); Robert Orsi, *Gods of the City: Religion and the American Urban Landscape* (Bloomington: Indiana University Press, 1999); Robert Orsi, *The Madonna of 115th Street: Faith and Community in Italian Harlem, 1880–1950* (New Haven: Yale University Press, 1985); Jill Watts, *God, Harlem, U.S.A.* (Berkeley: University of California Press, 1995). My study of Unitarian minister Ethelred Brown and Rabbi Wentworth Matthew is also intended to be a corrective to biased, negative depictions of black religious sects such as Howard Brotz, *The Black Jews of Harlem: Negro Nationalism and the Dilemmas of Negro Leadership* (New York: Schocken Books, 1970).

34. Unitarianism and Judaism were uncommon religious and denominational practices in black America. Most religion-based racial uplift missions were Christian denominations: Baptist, Pentecostal or part of the African Methodist Episcopal Church movement. For a fuller discussion of the diversity of black intellectuals' racial uplift projects, see See Evelyn Brooks Higginbotham, *Righteous Discontent: The Women's Movement in the Black Baptist Church, 1880–1920* (Cambridge, MA: Harvard University Press, 1993); Kevin Gaines, *Uplifting the Race: Black Leadership, Politics, and Culture in the Twentieth Century* (Chapel Hill: University of North Carolina Press, 1996); Victoria W. Wolcott, *Remaking Respectability: African American Women in Inter-War Detroit* (Chapel Hill: University of North Carolina Press, 2000); E. Frances White, *Dark Continent of our Bodies: Black Feminism & Politics of Respectability* (Philadelphia: Temple University Press, 2001); Martin Summers, *Manliness and Discontents: The Black Middle Class and the Transformation of Masculinity, 1900–1930* (Chapel Hill: University of North Carolina Press, 2003); Whaley, Deborah Elizabeth. *Discipling Women: Alpha Kappa Alpha, Black Counterpublics, and the Cultural Politics of Black Sororities* (Albany: State University of New York, 2010).

35. W. Burghardt Turner and Joyce Moore Turner, eds., *Caribbean Militant in Harlem: Collected Writings, 1920–1972* (Bloomington: Indiana University Press, 1988). Also see discussions of Richard B. Moore's participation in the African Blood Brotherhood in Winston James, *Holding Aloft the Banner of Ethiopia* (London; New York: Verso, 1998); Joyce Moore Turner, *Caribbean Crusaders and the Harlem Renaissance* (Urbana; Chicago: University of Illinois Press, 2005); and Minkah Makalani, *In the Cause of Freedom: Radical Black Internationalism from Harlem to London, 1917–1939* (Chapel Hill: University of North Carolina Press, 2011).

36. There were some exceptions to this rule. Caribbean women intellectuals such as Amy Ashwood Garvey (Jamaica), Amy Jacques Garvey (Jamaica), Claudia Jones (Trinidad), and Grace Campbell (Caribbean American), also contributed to early-twentieth century black intellectualism in New York City. See Ula Y. Taylor, *The Veiled Garvey: The Life and Times*

of Amy Jacques Garvey (Chapel Hill: University of North Carolina Press, 2002) and Carol Boyce Davies, *Left of Karl Marx: The Political Life of Black Communist Claudia Jones* (Durham: Duke University Press, 2008).

37. Shirley Chisholm, quoted in *Chisholm '72—Unbought and Unbossed*, DVD, directed by Shola Lynch (Beverly Hills: Twentieth Century Fox Home Entertainment, 2004).

38. Scholars such as Tamara Mose Brown, Lara Putnam, Minkah Makalani, and Joyce Moore Turner use the term "Caribbean" in their work. Historian Lara Putnam uses the term "British Caribbeans" to refer to immigrants from the English-speaking Caribbean. See Lara Putnam, *Radical Moves: Caribbean Migrants and the Politics of Race in the Jazz Age* (Chapel Hill: University of North Carolina Press), 2013.

39. Oneka LaBennett, conversation with author, July 24, 2014. Also see Oneka LaBennett, *She's Mad Real: Popular Culture and West Indian Girls in Brooklyn* (New York: New York University Press, 2011); Alvin Tillery and Michelle Chresfield, "Model Blacks or 'Ras the Exhorter': A Quantitative Content Analysis of Black Newspapers' Coverage of the First Wave of Afro-Caribbean Immigration to the United States," *Journal of Black Studies* 43, no. 5 (July 2012), 545–570; Nancy Foner, "Gender and Migration: West Indians in Comparative Perspective," *International Migration* 47, no.1 (2009): 3–29.

Chapter 1

1. Claude McKay quoted in James, *Holding Aloft the Banner*, pg. 5.

2. *New York Amsterdam News,* August 11, 1945, 1; Barney Josephson and Terry Trilling-Josephson, *Café Society: The Wrong Place for the Right People* (Champaign: University of Illinois Press, 2009), 191.

3. Harlem Renaissance writer Alaine Locke observed that the "Negro of the North and the Negro of the South, the man from the city and the man from the town and village," all contributed to Harlem's dynamic social and political milieu. Locke's "New Negro" was inextricably rooted in Harlem's complex intercultural exchange, and he suggested that this collaboration among foreign-born and American-born black Americans was the main element that made this burgeoning black metropolis so distinctive. Locke held that their "greatest experience has been the finding of one another." Alain Locke also acknowledged "the peasant, the student, the business man, the professional man, artist, poet, musician, adventurer and worker, preacher and criminal, exploiter and social outcast." Locke, *The New Negro* (New York: Atheneum, 1992 [1925]), 6.

4. See Table 16-1, based on statistics from the US Department of Commerce, Darlene Clark Hine, ed., *The African American Odyssey*, 5th edition (Upper Saddle River, NJ: Prentice Hall, 2010), 438.

5. Joe William Trotter, *The Great Migration in Historical Perspective: New Dimensions of Race, Class, and Gender* (Bloomington: Indian University Press, 1991), 128.

6. For a full discussion of the importance of the Exodus narrative in African American religious thought, see Eddie Glaude, *Exodus! Religion, Race, and Nation in Early Nineteenth-Century Black America* (Chicago: University of Chicago Press, 2000).

7. Jacob Lawrence's famous sixty-one panel series, *The Migration of the Negro*, was semi-autobiographical—documenting the triumphs and trials of blacks who made the trek from the South to the North from the 1910s through the 1930s. For a fuller discussion of Jacob Lawrence's *Migration Series*, first displayed in 1941, see Farah Jasmine Griffin, *Who Set You Flowin'? The African-American Migration Narrative* (New York: Oxford University Press, 1995); Elizabeth Hutton Turner, *et al.*, *Over the Line: The Art and Life of Jacob Lawrence* (Seattle: University of Washington Press, 2001); Jutta Lorensen, "Between Image and Word, Color and Time/ Jacob Lawrence's 'The Migration Series,'" *African American Review* 40, no. 3 (Fall 2006), 571–586.

8. For a discussion of natural disasters as a push factor for Caribbean immigration to New York and other cities, see Winston James, *Holding Aloft the Banner of Ethiopia* (London; New York: Verso, 1998), 33–35.

9. For a thorough treatment of Caribbean immigrant women's work experiences during the early twentieth century, see Irma Watkins-Owens, "Early-Twentieth-Century Caribbean Women: Migration and Social Networks in New York City," in Nancy Foner, ed., *Islands in the City: West Indian Migration to New York* (Berkeley and Los Angeles: University of California Press, 2001), 35.

10. Irma Watkins-Owens, *Blood Relations: Caribbean Immigrants and the Harlem Community, 1900–1903* (Bloomington: Indiana University Press, 1996), 18.

11. After Marcus Garvey and Amy Ashwood divorced in 1922, Ashwood traveled extensively and lived in London for a stint, but returned often to New York to produce plays and musicals with her new companion Sam Manning, a Trinidadian-born Calypso performer and composer. A full page advertisement for Amy Ashwood Garvey and Sam Manning's production "Black Magic" appeared in the November 1927 issue of the *West Indian American* newspaper. A glamor shot of Ashwood's three-quarter profile and Manning looking handsome and resolute are prominently featured in the announcement, which mentions the couple's prior theatrical collaborations including "Hey! Hey!" and "Brown Sugar." The performance of "Black Magic" took place during the week of November 21, 1927, at the Lafayette Theater on 7th Avenue at 132nd Street. "The Theatrical World," *West Indian American*, November 1927, 17. Stokely Carmichael's father Adolphus also was moved by the heart to emigrate from Trinidad to New York. Adolphus's wife Mabel left Trinidad in 1944 because she could no longer stand living in the same household with her domineering in-laws, especially Adolphus's strong-minded sisters. Mabel gave Adolphus an ultimatum; she told him that he would have to decide between her and his family. Adolphus decided he could not live without Mabel; so, he followed her to New York in 1946. Other members of his family would join them in New York over the course of the decade, but by then Mabel had already established her own household, outside of the purview of her in-laws and felt comfortable in her authority as the matriarch of the house. Kwame Ture with Ekwueme Michael Thelwell, *Ready for Revolution: The Life and Struggles of Stokely Carmichael (Kwame Ture)* (New York: Scribner, 2003), 20–21.

12. Winston James, *Holding Aloft the Banner of Ethiopia* (London; New York: Verso, 1998), 8.

13. An even larger group, 240,000 laborers, migrated to Panama to work on the Panama Canal. Many used the money earned from the backbreaking labor to sponsor family members'

immigration to New York and other US cities or their own eventual migration to the US. Other Caribbean workers moved to Costa Rica, Guatemala, and Honduras to work on banana plantations or to Cuba to work sugar fields. Historian Irma Watkins Owens underscores the importance of "Panama silver" in providing the financial backing for Caribbean immigrants to move to the United States. Although Caribbean immigrants found work on the Panama Canal to be lucrative, they still struggled through rampant disease such as malaria and yellow fever and they endured American-style Jim Crow by way of differential wages. White workers were paid in gold and black workers were paid in Silver. For a fuller discussion of racist politics and the building the Panama Canal see Irma Watkins-Owens, *Blood Relations: Caribbean Immigrants and the Harlem Community, 1900–1903* (Bloomington: Indiana University Press, 1996), 14; *American Experience: Panama Canal*, documentary film (PBS, 2010).

14. Gilbert Osofsky, *Harlem: The Making of a Ghetto—Negro New York, 1890–1930* (New York: Harper Torchbook, 1964, 1971), 131.

15. Numerous scholars have lamented the dearth of scholarship on the topic of African Caribbean immigrants in the US. Roy Bryce-Laporte, "Introduction: New York City and the New Caribbean Immigration: A Contextual Statement," *International Migration Review* 13, no. 2 (Summer 1979): 229. Historian Winston James has also made a similar comparison and called whiteness studies scholars who solely write about white European immigrants, without any mention of Afro-Caribbean immigrants, a type of "intellectual apartheid." Winston James, "Explaining Afro-Caribbean Social Mobility in the United States: Beyond the Sowell Thesis" *Comparative Studies in Society and History* 44, no. 2 (2002): 218–62.

16. Emma Lazarus, "The New Colossus," in John Hollander, ed., *Emma Lazarus: Selected Poems* (Library of America, 2005), 58.

17. Winston James, "Explaining Afro-Caribbean Social Mobility," 226.

18. Roi Ottley, *New World A-Coming* (1943), 46.

19. "Harlem Pastor Founder of Community Church Works Seven Days a Week as Elevator Boy," *New York Home News*, October 1, 1922.

20. See Paule Marshall's depiction of the father figure in *Brown Girl, Brownstones*, Deighton Boyce—a very intelligent immigrant from Barbados who hopes to become an accountant in New York, but when he was turned away from every accounting job that he pursued, he became so frustrated that he gave up on his nuclear family and joined Father Peace's religious commune. This story mirrors the Marshall's own biography because her father also felt so exasperated by racism that he joined Father Divine's religious sect in Harlem. See Paule Marshall, *Brown Girl, Brownstones* (Mineola, NY: Dover Publications, 2009), 138–150.

21. Richard Plunz, *A History of Housing in New York City* (New York: Columbia University Press, 1990), 30.

22. Of course there were exceptions to this rule of geographic division of black and white New York. For example Greenwich Village, especially Café Society, was a site of multicultural exchange. It also was common practice for white New Yorkers to travel uptown to Harlem on quests for entertainment that considered exotic. Such interracial taboos fueled the nightclub industry and prostitution in Harlem. See Andrea Barnet, *All-Night Party: The Women of Bohemian Greenwich Village and Harlem, 1913–1930* (Chapel Hill, NC: Algonquin Books, 2004); .

23. The New Negro movement was not limited to New York City. New Negro movements flourished in cities such as Chicago, Philadelphia, Washington DC, and locales outside of the US. For a fuller discussion of the New Negro movements in Chicago and other major metropoles throughout the United States, see Davarian Baldwin, *Chicago's New Negroes: Modernity, the Great Migration, and Black Urban Life* (Chapel Hill: University of North Carolina Press, 2007), and Davarian Baldwin and Minkah Makalani, eds., *Escape from New York: The 'Harlem Renaissance' Reconsidered* (Minneapolis: University of Minnesota Press, 2013).

24. James Weldon Johnson, "Harlem," Alain Locke, ed., *New Negro* (New York: Touchstone, 1925, 1997), 301.

25. Alain Locke also acknowledged "the peasant, the student, the business man, the professional man, artist, poet, musician, adventurer and worker, preacher and criminal, exploiter and social outcast." Locke, *The New Negro* (New York: Atheneum, 1992 [1925]), 6.

26. Alain Locke also acknowledged "the peasant, the student, the business man, the professional man, artist, poet, musician, adventurer and worker, preacher and criminal, exploiter and social outcast." Locke, *The New Negro* (New York: Atheneum, 1992 [1925]), 6.

27. Joshua Bruce Guild, "You can't go home again: Migration, citizenship, and black community in postwar New York and London (England)," PhD dissertation, Yale University, 2007.

28. The annual West Indian Day Parade, which takes place in Brooklyn during Labor Day weekend, is one of the most dramatic demonstrations of Caribbean cultural nationalism outside of the Caribbean. Percy Hintzen astutely observes how Caribbean immigrants' practice of carnival also represents broader ethnic tensions between Jewish communities and Caribbean immigrants in New York. In the Crown Heights section of Brooklyn, Hasidic Jews and black immigrants have struggled to coexist peacefully, and they have battled for control of real estate and public space. For a fuller discussion of the history of carnival and the West Indian Day Parade in New York, see Percy Hintzen, *West Indian in the West: Self Representations in a Migrant Community* (New York: New York University Press, 2001), 38.

29. Marcus Garvey, "The Conspiracy Of The East St. Louis Riots," Robert A. Hill, ed. *The Marcus Garvey and Universal Negro Improvement Association Papers, Volume I, 1826— August 1919.* Berkeley and Los Angeles: University of California Press, 1983. Shirley Chisholm's father, Charles St. Hill, was most likely aware of this famous speech. Mr. St. Hill was an ardent Garveyite and would often recall the fiery words of his political hero when he recounted stories of black greatness to young Shirley as a child. Perhaps the telling and retelling of Garvey's bravely vigorous speech helped Chisholm realize the power of her own voice.

30. Ibid.

31. Caribbean émigrés used the spoken, written and performed word to transform the meanings of blackness in modern America. Philosopher Pierre Bourdieu observed that words gain their meaning from the social and political climate in which they are uttered. "Grammar defines meaning only very partially" Bourdieu suggests, "[I]t is in relation to a market that the complete determination of the signification of discourse occurs." In this context, Caribbean intellectuals used the language of race and place as a type of currency in

a "market of ideas" to gain personal and political power. Pierre Bourdieu *Language and Symbolic Power* (1991), 38.

32. Adam Clayton Powell Jr., *Adam by Adam: The Autobiography of Adam Clayton Powell, Jr.* (New York: Daphina Books) 1971, *Adam by Adam*, 225.

33. Karen Chilton, *Hazel Scott: The Pioneering Journey of a Jazz Pianist from Café Society to Hollywood to HUAC* (Ann Arbor: University of Michigan Press, 2008), 10.

34. Ibid., 11.

35. Adam Clayton Powell Jr., *Adam by Adam: The Autobiography of Adam Clayton Powell, Jr.* (New York: Daphina Books) 1971, 225.

36. Chilton, *Hazel Scott*, 7.

37. Ibid., 9.

38. Hazel Scott, quoted in Chilton, *Hazel Scott*, 18.

39. Irma Watkins-Owens, *Blood Relations: Caribbean Immigrants and the Harlem Community, 1900–1903* (Bloomington: Indiana University Press, 1996), 56.

40. Irma Watkins-Owens, *Blood Relations: Caribbean Immigrants and the Harlem Community, 1900–1903* (Bloomington: Indiana University Press, 1996), 67–68.

41. American West Indian Ladies Society records, New York Public Library Archives and Manuscripts, Sc MG 498, http://www.nypl.org/archives/3446.

42. "Small's Paradise," advertisement in the *West Indian American*, New York, NY, Saturday, October 15, 1927, 5.

43. Sara Edwin Jenkins, "Night Clubs of New York: Moral Turpitude?," *West Indian American*, New York, NY, November 1927, 8.

44. "Sports," *West Indian American*, New York, NY, November 1927, 15.

45. Ibid.

46. In George Edmund Haynes's sample of 330 establishments, 65 businesses were owned by Caribbean immigrants. Haynes's work, *The Negro at Work in New York* (New York: Columbia University, 1912), is referenced in Irma Watkins Owens, *Blood Relations: Caribbean Immigrants and the Harlem Community, 1900–1903* (Bloomington: Indiana University Press, 1996), 127.

47. Irma Watkins Owens, *Blood Relations: Caribbean Immigrants and the Harlem Community, 1900–1903* (Bloomington: Indiana University Press, 1996), 127–28.

48. *West Indian American*, November 1927, 18.

49. Ibid., 5.

50. *West Indian American*, January 1928, 11.

51. The improvement of the lives of individual black immigrants was integrally linked to a broader challenge of the color lines of British colonialism and US racism. This dynamic made the New Negro movement not only a national effort but a transnational phenomenon.

52. W. E. B. Du Bois, *The Crisis*, September 1920, 214.

53. The prevailing discourse of black racial solidarity during the 1920s was distinctly masculine, and Du Bois's statement underscores this point. In this statement, Du Bois suggested that the work of racial uplift would center on Caribbean immigrants helping "12 million black *men* of America." For a full discussion of the masculinist implications of Caribbean political leadership, see Michelle Ann Stephens, *Black Empire: The Masculine*

Global Imaginary of Caribbean Intellectuals in the United States, 1914–1962 (Durham, NC: Duke University Press, 2005).

54. Winston James, *Holding Aloft the Banner*, 292.

55. Ira DeAugustine Reid, *The Negro Immigrant: His Background, Characteristics and Social Adjustment, 1899–1937* (New York: Columbia University Press, 1939), 49.

56. W. A. Domingo, "Gift of the Black Tropics," *The New Negro*, Alain Locke, ed., (New York: Albert & Charles Boni, Inc., 1925), 345.

57. Review of "Who's Who In Colored America," 13.

58. James Weldon Johnson, *Black Manhattan* (New York: Da Capo Press, Inc. 1930, 1958, 1991) 153.

59. "The American Negro," *West Indian American*, October 15, 1927, 6.

60. W. A. Domingo, "Gift of the Black Tropics," 348.

61. Historian Jesse Hoffnung-Garskof suggests that Schomburg "fits uneasily into our contemporary notions of how ethnic history should look—with early colonies of Puerto Ricans or blacks evolving neatly into later 'communities.'" Hoffnung-Garskof argues that many scholars have "gloss[ed] over the ambiguity and shifting identity that are central to [Schomburg's] biography." See Jesse Hoffnung-Garskof, "The Migrations of Arturo Schomburg: On Being Antilliano, Negro, and Puerto Rican in New York 1891–1938," *Journal of American Ethnic History* 21, no. 1 (November 2001): 4. See also Winston James, *Holding Aloft the Banner*, 198; Elinor Des Verney Sinnette, *Arthur Alfonso Schomburg: Black Bibliophile and Collector* (Detroit: Wayne State University Press, 1989), 23.

62. James, *Holding Aloft*, 270.

63. Paule Marshall, *Triangular Road: A Memoir* (New York: Basic Civitas Books, 2009).

64. Haygood, *King of the Cats*, 145.

65. Louis Martin quoted in ibid.

66. Adam Clayton Powell Jr., *Adam by Adam: The Autobiography of Adam Clayton Powell, Jr.* (New York: Daphina Books, 1971), 113.

67. Adam Clayton Powell Jr., *Adam by Adam: The Autobiography of Adam Clayton Powell, Jr.* (New York: Daphina Books 1971), 224; Powell's marriage to his third wife, Yvette Marjorie Flores Diago from San Juan, Puerto Rico, inspired the chapter title "Caribbean Love Affair" in Gil and Ann Chapman, *Adam Clayton Powell: Saint or Sinner* (San Diego: Publishers Export Co. 1967).

68. Interview with Adam Clayton Powell III, August 22, 2011.

69. Ira DeAugustine Reid, *The Negro Immigrant: His Background, Characteristics and Social Adjustment, 1899–1937* (New York: Columbia University Press, 1939), 109.

70. Ibid. Claude McKay also noted the prevalence of the ethnic slur as the term repeatedly appears in his novels. In *Home to Harlem*, when the main character Jake orders Scotch whiskey at a bar, his companion Rose accuses him of being pretentious because she considers it a white man's drink and she has seen the "*monkey-chasers* order it when they want to put on style." In this context, the pejorative term takes on new meaning as the American-born black character Rose paints a picture of Caribbean immigrants straining to hide their alleged primitive nature. In real life, this accusation of Caribbean immigrants "putting on airs" was part and parcel a critique of British colonial history throughout the Caribbean,

which shaped the cultural practices and accents that marked Caribbean immigrants as different from American-born blacks. Claude Mc Kay, *Home to Harlem* (Harper & Brothers and Lebanon, NJ: Northeastern University Press, 1928, 1987), 38.

71. This sing-song rhyme has been analyzed as one of the most glaring folk culture examples of American-born black antagonism toward Caribbean immigrants. See Colin Grant, *Negro with a Hat: The Rise and Fall of Marcus Garvey* (Oxford: Oxford University Press, 2008), 90; R. Clifford Jones, *James K. Humphrey and the Sabbath-Day Adventists* (Jackson, MS: University Press of Mississippi, 2006), 75; Karen De Young, *Soldier: The Life of Colin Powell* (New York: Knopf, 2007), 18; Irma Watkins Owens, *Blood Relations: Caribbean Immigrants and the Harlem Community, 1900–1903* (Bloomington: Indiana University Press, 1996), 28; Clarence Earl Walker, *Deromanticizing Black History: Critical Essays and Reappraisals* (Knoxville: University of Tennessee Press, 1991), 42; Heather Hathaway, *Caribbean Waves: Relocating Claude McKay and Paule Marshall* (Bloomington: Indiana University Press, 1999), 21.

72. A. B. Christa Schwarz, *Gay Voices of the Harlem Renaissance* (Bloomington: Indiana University Press, 2003), 88.

73. W. E. B. Du Bois, "Review of *Home to Harlem*," *Crisis*, September 1928. W. E. B. Du Bois vehement criticism of Claude McKay's *Home to Harlem* appears in the following texts: Wayne F. Cooper, *Claude McKay: Rebel Sojourner in the Harlem Renaissance: A Biography* (Baton Rouge: Louisiana State University Press, 1996), 244; Abby Arthur, Ronald Maberry Johnson, *Propaganda and Aesthetics: The Literary Politics of African-American Magazines in the Twentieth Century* (Amherst, MA: University of Massachusetts Press, 1991), 47; Emily Bernard, *Carl Van Vechten and the Harlem Renaissance: A Portrait in Black and White* (New Haven: Yale University Press, 2012), 165; Louis J. Parascandola, ed., *"Look for me all around you": Anglophone Caribbean Immigrants in the Harlem Renaissance* (Detroit: Wayne State University Press 2005), 27.

74. This excerpt from Claude McKay's June 18, 1928 letter in responses to W. E. B. Du Bois's negative review of *Home to Harlem* is documented in Abby Arthur, Ronald Maberry Johnson, *Propaganda and Aesthetics: The Literary Politics of African-American Magazines in the Twentieth Century* (Amherst, MA: University of Massachusetts Press, 1991), 47.

75. Caribbean intellectuals also criticized Claude McKay's *Home to Harlem*. Marcus Garvey lampooned the novel of his compatriot in a 1928 issue of *Negro World*. Marcus Garvey, "*Home to Harlem*, Claude McKay's Damaging Book Should Earn Wholesale Condemnation of Negroes," *Negro World* (September 29, 1928)np. 1.

76. W. E. B. Du Bois, "Back to Africa," *Century Magazine*, 105 (Feb. 1923).

77. "All For One—One for All," *West Indian American*, October 15, 1927, 6.

78. James H. Hubert, Secretary, New York Urban League, "The Dark Cellar," *West Indian American* 1, no. 4 (January 1928): 4.

79. Makalani, Minkah, *In the Cause of Freedom: Radical Black internationalism from Harlem to London, 1917–1939* (Chapel Hill: University of North Carolina Press, 2011) 139.

80. Martha Biondi, *To Stand and Fight: The Struggle for Civil Rights in Postwar New York* (Cambridge, MA: Harvard University Press, 2006), 19.

81. "The West Indies Must Move Forward—Mr Jack," *West Indian American*, March 1959, 2.

82. Hazel Scott quoted in Karen Chilton, *Hazel Scott: The Pioneering Journey of a Jazz Pianist from Café Society to Hollywood to HUAC* (Ann Arbor: University of Michigan Press, 2008), 147.

83. For a full discussion of the northern vanguard of civil rights activism in New York, see Martha Biondi, *To Stand and Fight: The Struggle for Civil Rights in Postwar New York* (Cambridge, MA: Harvard University Press, 2006).

84. "Powell Weds Scott," 30.

85. "Powell and Hazel Scott Buy on Riverside Drive," *New York Times*, March 27, 1946, 45.

86. Chilton, *Hazel Scott*, photographic insert.

87. *Jet*, November 26, 1953, 41.

88. Hazel Scott's unpublished autobiography. Powell hinted at the volatile nature of his relationship with Scott when he described her formidable intellect and their shared capriciousness: "She is never anywhere without a book by her side, usually the heavy, challenging, demanding type. And as she reads she grasps that one phrase or sentence that is the thesis of the whole book. She has the worst temper of anyone I know, except myself." Powell and Scott divorced in 1961. Weeks after the divorce was finalized, Scott married Swiss comedian Edzio Bedin whom she met while playing concerts in Europe; Powell married his Puerto Rican secretary Yvette Dagio. "Hazel Scott is Married Here," *New York Times*, January 21, 1961, pg. 18; Powell, *Adam by Adam*, pg. 225.

Chapter 2

1. "Rev. Ethelred Brown is Symbol of Radicalism in Pulpits in Harlem," *Daily Gleaner*, January 20, 1934; Brown quoted in *Black Pioneers*, 94.

2. Mark Morrison-Reed, *Black Pioneers*, 90–91.

3. "Harlem Preacher Hit on Head at Sunday Service: Man Assaults Community Church Pastor," newspaper clipping, E. E. Brown Papers, AUA, Cambridge, Massachusetts. See appendix.

4. Ethelred Brown, Letter to Mr. McAfee, New York, January 9, 1928.

5. For a more detailed discussion of the "politics of respectability" among African American leaders, see: Evelyn Brooks Higginbotham, *Righteous Discontent: The Women's Movement in the Black Baptist Church, 1880–1920* (Cambridge, MA: Harvard University Press, 1993). Anthropologist Peter Wilson has also written at length regarding the importance of reputation and respectability in the context of Caribbean cultures; see *Crab Antics: A Caribbean Study of the Conflict between Reputation and Respectability* (Long Grove, IL: Waveland Press, Inc, 1995).

6. Richard B. Moore, "The Critics and Opponents of Marcus Garvey," in John Henrik Clarke, ed., *Marcus Garvey and the Vision of Africa* (New York: Vintage Books, 1973), 230. In the same essay, Moore recounted the details of several opponents of Garvey who were not as fortunate as Brown and himself, as their criticism of Garvey ended in death at the hand of the UNIA's "secret police."

7. W. E. B. Du Bois, "Opinion of W. E. B. Du Bois," *The Crisis* 28, no. 1 (May 1924): 9.

8. Historians Irma Watkins-Owens, Winston James, Joyce Moore Turner, and Minkah Makalani have all noted Brown's participation in black radical politics during the age of the New Negro.

9. Irma Watkins-Owens, *Blood Relations: Caribbean Immigrants and the Harlem Community, 1900–1930* (Bloomington: Indiana University Press, 1996), 62.

10. Ethelred Brown, letter to the American Unitarian Association, November 15, 1926, E. Brown papers, AUA, (Cambridge, MA).

11. Ethelred Brown, letter to the American Unitarian Association, November 15, 1926, E. Brown papers, AUA, (Cambridge, MA). Italics added for emphasis.

12. Shortly after their arrival in New York in 1920, Brown's wife, Ella suffered an emotional and mental breakdown. In a 1928 letter, Brown appealed unsuccessfully to AUA leadership for financial assistance to cover Ella's medical care. "A woman's mentality is in the balance. You have it in your power to tilt it either back to normal or into the darkness of insanity. In spite of the risk of insulting your official dignity I must again appeal to you to give the sign which will mean life." Ethelred Brown, "Letter to Louis C. Cornish," January 1, 1928, E. E. Brown papers, UUA; In the wake of both his wife's depression and the suicide of his unemployed eldest son, AUA leaders continued to deny his requests for financial support. To add insult to injury, the AUA removed Brown's name from the roster of recognized Unitarian ministers on May 23, 1929. In November of the same year, Brown expressed his intense grief over the loss of his son: "I wonder if as a man and a Christian minister you can forget for a minute the attitude of the hard boiled official and think as a man of the pain you have inflicted on me and of the time you chose to inflict it . . . when my heart lay bleeding with the wound caused by the tragic death of my eldest son." Ethelred Brown, Letter to A.U.A., November 1929, E. E. Brown Papers, UUA.

13. Anthropologist Peter Wilson has noted the importance patriarchal nature of family structure in Jamaica throughout the first half of the twentieth century in which the male head of the household was expected to make enough money to support the entire family. See Peter Wilson, "Reputation and Respectability: Suggestion for Caribbean Ethnology," *Man*, New Series 4, no. 1 (March 1969): 74.

14. I intentionally borrow the language from Harlem Renaissance writer Langston Hughes's famous poem "Harlem," *Montage of a Dream Deferred* (1951): "What happens to a dream deferred? Does it dry up like a raisin in the sun? Or fester like a sore—And then run? Does it stink like rotten meat? Or crust and sugar over—like a syrupy sweet? Maybe it just sags like a heavy load. *Or does it explode?*"

15. Brown included details regarding Walter Brown's missionary work on a flyer announcing an upcoming service in 1929. Brown composed the leaflet to serve a dual function—to advertise a specific event as well as to promote himself as a bonafide religious leader as his younger brother's career choice proved that the Brown family approached ecclesiastical affairs with clarity and commitment. The Hubert Harrison Memorial Church Flyer announcing a service titled "The Warfare of Moral Ideals" to take place on Sunday, September 22, 1929.

16. "Harlem Pastor Founder of Community Church Works Seven Days a Week as Elevator Boy," *New York Home News*, October 1, 1922, 5.

17. Egbert Ethelred Brown, "A Brief History of the Harlem Unitarian Church," sermon delivered on September 11, 1949, E. E. Brown Papers, Unitarian Universalist Association Archives (UUA), Boston.

18. Ethelred Brown quoted in Morrison-Reed, *Black Pioneers in a White Denomination*, 33.

19. Brown, "An Easter Sermon," February 2, year not specified, 12.

20. Brown, "A Brief History," 2.

21. Brown, "A Brief History," 2–3.

22. Ethelred Brown, "A Story and an Appeal," *Christian Register*, May 4, 1911, 493 (emphasis added).

23. For a more detailed, compelling discussion of the religious and political significance of the Exodus narrative for African Americans, see Michael Walzer, *Exodus and Revolution* (New York: Basic Books, 1986); Eddie Glaude, *Exodus!: Religion, Race, and Nation in Early Nineteenth-Century Black America* (Chicago: University of Chicago Press, 2000). This pro-black interpretation of the Bible is also linked to the, is most famously evidenced in David Walker's *Appeal* (1829) denouncing slavery, in which he warned white slave masters that God would destroy them if they did not turn from their wicked ways.

24. James H. Cone, *A Black Theology of Liberation* (Maryknoll, NY: Orbis Books, 1986, 1990, 2010) ix.

25. Floyd-Thomas observed, "Brown felt himself called to be a apostle of Black humanism to attack white supremacy, economic exploitation, and bore the mark of the agnostic who deeply despised the perpetuation of theological doctrines and traditions that worked to oppress individuals." Juan M. Floyd-Thomas, *Black Humanism*, 21.

26. Juan M. Floyd-Thomas, *Black Humanism*, 5.

27. Juan M. Floyd-Thomas, *Black Humanism*, 6.

28. Excerpted from Rudyard Kipling's poem "The White Man's Burden."

29. Audre Lorde, "The Masters Tools Will Never Dismantle the Master's House," *Sister Outsider: Essays and Speeches* (New York: Crossing Press, 1984, 2007).

30. Ethelred Brown, "For A Liberal Church," *The New Leader*, New York, December 4, 1928, E. Brown papers, AUA, (Cambridge, MA).

31. Louis C. Cornish to Kenneth McDougall, October 26, 1921, E. E. Brown, Papers, UUA.

32. Brown, "Montego Bay to Harlem," 24.

33. Another black minister, Walker, wanted to start a Unitarian congregation in Alexandria, a more rural area in Jamaica, but Bygrave discouraged him because he considered non-city dwellers too parochial to accept a liberal theology like Unitarianism. Hilary Bygrave, "Report in regard to Montego Bay, etc. Jamaica B.W.I.," April 24, 1913, in Samuel A. Eliot, Papers, Andover-Harvard Theological Library, Harvard Divinity School, American Unitarian Association (AUA).

34. Hilary Bygrave, "Report in Regard to Montego Bay, etc., Jamaica B.W.I.," April 24, 1913, in Samuel A. Eliot Papers. This report predates Alfred Kinsey's surveys on the varieties of "normal" sexual behavior among white Americans by almost half a century. Perhaps the racism laced throughout Bygrave's accusations would have been tempered after reading surveys of mainstream white Americans.

35. Ibid.

36. Dorice Brown, "To the Members of the Unitarian Association, Boston," August 9, 1918, E. E. Brown papers, UUA.

37. Ethelred Brown, "A Statement Presented to the Special Committee Appointed by the American Unitarian Association to Inquire into the Circumstances Leading to the Removal of My Name from the Official List of Unitarian Ministers," December 14, 1931, E. E. Brown Papers, UUA Archives.

38. Dorice Brown, "To the Members of the Unitarian Association, Boston," August 9, 1918, E. E. Brown papers, UUA (emphasis added).

39. Brown, "Letter to Louis C. Cornish," January 12, 1920, E. E. Brown Papers, UUA.

40. The nine charter members included Martin Luther Campbell, Grace Campbell, Hayward Shovington, Ella Matilda Brown (Reverend Brown's wife), Wilfred A. Domingo, Frank A. Crosswaithe, Thomas A Potter, Richard B. Moore, and Lucille E. Ward. Brown, "The Harlem Unitarian Church," 4–5.

41. While local white Unitarian leadership in Cincinnati were familiar with Carter's church, the American Unitarian Association was not made aware of its existence until 1938. This lag in update may be explained in two ways: Brown's zeal and desire to be recognized as a legitimate institution may have surpassed Carter's interest in or need for financial support from the national Unitarian association; or perhaps Carter's American-born status and greater familiarity with American racism made him more reluctant to appeal to the leaders of the white-run organization for support. In contrast, Brown's appeals to the AUA seemed to be a natural extension of his earlier missionary appeals to the British Unitarian Association. *Black Pioneers* (3rd ed., 1994), 187–88.

42. Mark D. Morrison-Reed, *Darkening the Doorways: Black Trailblazers and Missed Opportunities in Unitarian Universalism* (Boston, MA: Skinner House, 2011), 50.

43. Ibid. Brown did not specify whether the members were official members of the Socialist Party in New York or simply upheld socialist principles.

44. Staff writer, "The Resolution which changed the name of 'The Harlem Community Church' to the 'Hubert Harrison Memorial Church,'" *Harrison Memorial Church Bulletin,* September 15, 1929, E. E Brown Papers, UUA, 5.

45. Brown, "The Harlem Unitarian Church," September 11, 1949, 6; *Black Pioneers*, 82. Brown wrote that changing the name of his congregation to the Hubert Harrison Memorial Church in 1928 was a major mistake. He explained that he and his small congregation believed that the name change would attract followers of Harrison's "Outdoor University" after his death, but the name drew criticism instead. Members of the Outdoor University objected to the use of Harrison's name for a religious congregation, even considering its liberal theology, because Harrison was a self-professed agnostic. "The Harlem Unitarian Church," 6.

46. Staff writer, "A Statement and an Invitation," *Harrison Memorial Church Bulletin,* September 15, 1929, E. E. Brown Papers, UUA, 7.

47. Brown, "From Montego Bay to Harlem," 39.

48. According to historian Noel Ignatiev, white workers grouped foreign-born blacks into the same broad category with American-born blacks.

49. Brown quoted in Mark D. Morrison-Reed's *Black Pioneers in a White Denomination* (1984), 94.

50. Domingo, "Gift of the Black Tropics," 347.

51. Ethelred Brown, letter to American Unitarian Association, November 13, 1926, E. E. Brown papers, UUA (emphasis added).

52. "Rev. Ethelred Brown is Symbol of Radicalism in Pulpits in Harlem," *Daily Gleaner*, January 20, 1934; Brown quoted in *Black Pioneers*, 94.

53. Mark D. Morrison-Reed, *Black Pioneers in White Denomination* (Boston, MA: Skinner Books, 1980), 93.

54. Ethelred Brown quoted in *The World Tomorrow* in Juan M. Floyd-Thomas, *The Origins of Black Humanism in America: Reverend Ethelred Brown and the Unitarian Church* (New York: Palgrave Macmillan, 2008), 1.

55. *Black Pioneers*, 97.

56. A. Powell Davies quoted in *Black Pioneers*, 93.

57. Brown, "The Harlem Unitarian Church," 7.

58. Ibid.

59. *Black Pioneers*, 84.

60. Mark Morrison-Reed, *Black Pioneers*, 85.

61. This song appeared on the back of the brochure distributed to all who attended the Jamaica Progressive League's thirtieth anniversary celebration, January 17, 1937 (emphasis added).

62. The sheet music and lyrics for "Lift Every Voice and Sing" are included in Brown's papers at the UUA.

63. Roberts's song also appeared on the back of the JPL thirtieth-anniversary brochure (emphasis added).

64. E. E. Brown, "The Dreamer Dreameth," November 15, 1944, 9–11.

65. Ibid.

66. Ibid.

67. Ethelred Brown, "Anniversary Sermon," October 5, 1947, 7. (Celebrating the thirtieth anniversary of the Jamaica Benevolent Association).

68. Ibid., 8.

69. Ibid., 13.

70. Ibid.

71. At first glance, these divergent visions of progress might appear to be part of totally separate philosophical projects, but in reality both black nationalist and integrationist visions of racial uplift were part of a much broader political terrain of early twentieth-century progressive politics. Like white progressives, black intellectuals such as Reverend Brown were also working to bring order to a city in flux—teeming with the arrival of new immigrants in conversation with American-born blacks. While white progressives like President Woodrow Wilson endorsed racial segregation as a way to bring order to the nation's increasingly culturally diverse cities, Reverend Brown's pro-integrationist stance was in step with the mission of many black progressives whose visions of racial equality challenged the

Plessey v. Ferguson "separate but equal" verdict in 1896. The plight of black progressives was uniquely shaped by this issue of race.

72. W. E. B. Du Bois, "Back to Africa," *Century Magazine* (February 1923), 105.

73. W. A. Domingo, W. A. Domingo, "Gift of the Black Tropics," in *The New Negro*, Alain Locke, ed. (New York: Albert & Charles Boni, Inc., 1925), 348.

74. Ibid.

75. All of the sources in this chapter can be found in the Egbert Ethelred Brown Papers at the Schomburg Research Center in Harlem, NY, and the American Unitarian Association papers at the Harvard Andover Library in Cambridge, MA.

76. Ethelred Brown is a surprisingly understudied figure in academic disciplines like history and religious studies. The most substantial scholarship on Brown is a chapter-length article in Mark D. Morrison-Reed's *Black Pioneers in a White Denomination* and is the topic of one book-length biography, *The Origins of Black Humanism in America: Reverend Ethelred Brown and the Unitarian Church*, by Juan M. Floyd-Thomas. Morrison-Reed's essay details Brown's struggles to develop a Unitarian congregation in Jamaica during the 1910s, and his encounters with racism within the church with white British and American Unitarian leaders, after his emigration from Kingston, Jamaica, to Harlem from the 1920s through the 1950s. Ethelred Brown has been mentioned in a few paragraphs in current social and political historical studies of Caribbean New Yorkers like *Blood Relations* and *Holding Aloft the Banner of Ethiopia* as well as early sociological studies from the 1920s through the 1940s like Ira Reid's *The Negro Immigrant*, but all of these studies only briefly mention Brown's work to enrich the political backdrop for historical actors deemed more prominent. In contrast, this study centers on Brown and his work. See Mark D. Morrison-Reed, *Black Pioneers in a White Denomination* (Beacon Press: Boston, 1984); Ira De Augustine Reid, *The Negro Immigrant, His Background, Characteristics and Social Adjustment, 1899-1937*, 1939; Irma Watkins-Owens, *Blood Relations: Caribbean Immigrants and the Harlem Community, 1900-1930* (Bloomington: Indiana University Press, 1996); Winston James, *Holding Aloft the Banner of Ethiopia* (London; New York: Verso, 1998).

Chapter 3

1. Turner and Turner, *Caribbean Militant in Harlem*, 7.

2. For a discussion of Community Party criticism of Moore's membership in Ethelred Brown's Harlem Community Church see Minkah Makalani, *In the Cause of Freedom: Radical Black Internationalism from Harlem to London, 1917-1939* (Chapel Hill: University of North Carolina Press, 2011) 153.

3. For a discussion of Richard B. Moore's contribution to the Harlem Community Church as a political forum, see Joyce Moore Turner, Joyce Moore Turner, *Caribbean Crusaders and the Harlem Renaissance* (Urbana: University of Illinois Press, 2005), 69, 70, 165-167.

4. Turner and Turner, *Caribbean Militant in Harlem*, 7.

5. See, for instance, Joyce Moore Turner, *Caribbean Crusaders and the Harlem Renaissance* (Urbana; Chicago: University of Illinois Press, 2005).

6. I am analyzing a photograph of Richard B. Moore as a school-aged boy, which is included in Turner and Turner, *Caribbean Militant in Harlem*, 109.

7. Turner and Turner, *Caribbean Militant in Harlem*, 20.

8. See Winston James, *Holding Aloft the Banner of Ethiopia: Caribbean Radicalism in Early Twentieth-Century America* (London; New York: Verso, 1998), 123; Turner, *Caribbean Crusaders*, 11.

9. Tammy Brown, interview with Joyce Moore Turner, October 9, 2006.

10. This library is not yet open to the public. Based on conversations between historian Richard Blackett and the author, September 2006 through June 2007, Vanderbilt University, Nashville, TN.

11. Frederick Douglass, *The Life and Times of Frederick Douglass* (London: Christian Age Office, St. Bide Street, 1882), 53.

12. Ibid.

13. Turner and Turner, *Caribbean Militant in Harlem*, 69.

14. Arturo Schomburg, "The Negro Digs Up His Past," in *The New Negro*, Alain Locke, ed. (New York: Simon & Schuster., 1925, 1992), 231.

15. Richard B. Moore, "Carib 'Cannibalism': A Study in Anthropological Stereotyping," *Caribbean Studies* 13, no. 3, 117.

16. Mark Naison, *Communists in Harlem during the Depression* (Urbana: University of Illinois Press, 1983), 5.

17. Turner and Turner, *Caribbean Militant in Harlem*, 152.

18. Moore, "Housing and the Negro Masses," *The Negro Champion*, September 8, 1928, 8.

19. Hermina Huiswood quoted in Turner, *Caribbean Crusaders*, 25.

20. Turner and Turner, *Caribbean Militant in Harlem*, 52.

21. Ibid., 96.

22. Ibid.

23. Richard B. Moore, "Statement at the Congress of the League against Imperialism and for National Independence," *Proceedings of the Congress* (Berlin, 1927), 126–30; *The Crisis*, July 1927, 165–66; Turner and Turner, *Caribbean Militant in Harlem*, 143.

24. African American political activist Ida B. Wells employed a similar rhetorical strategy during her anti-lynching campaigns. See Gail Bederman, "'The White Man's Civilization on Trial': Ida B. Wells, Representations of Lynching, and Northern Middle-Class Manhood," in *Manliness and Civilization: A Cultural History of Gender and Race in the United States, 1880–1917* (Chicago: University of Chicago Press, 1995).

25. Turner and Turner, *Caribbean Militant in Harlem*, 269 (emphasis added).

26. Ibid., 263; Richard B. Moore, "Declaration of Rights of The Caribbean Peoples to Self-Determination and Self-Government," West Indies National Emergency Committee, submitted to the Pan-American Foreign Ministers' Conference (Havana, Cuba), 1940.

27. Richard B. Moore, "Statement at the Congress of the League against Imperialism and for National Independence," *Proceedings of the Congress* (Berlin, 1927), 126–30; *The Crisis*, July 1927, 165–66; Turner and Turner, *Caribbean Militant in Harlem*, 143 (emphasis added).

28. C. L. R. James, "'My Friends': A Fireside Chat on the War by Native Son" (1940), in Scott McLemee, ed., *C. L. R. James on the "Negro Question"* (Jackson: University Press of Mississippi, 1996), 19.

29. American Committee for West Indian Federation, "Memorandum of Federation and Self-Government of the West Indies" submitted to the Caribbean Labour Congress, Coke Hall, Kingston, Jamaica, September 2–9, 1947.

30. Richard B. Moore, "Reply to Mr. Sabben-Claire," in "Memorandum of Federation and Self-Government," Appendix II. See also Turner and Turner, *Caribbean Militant in Harlem*, 277.

31. Richard B. Moore, "Statement before the Platform Committee of the New Party," July 21, 1948; Turner and Turner, *Caribbean Militant in Harlem*, 248.

32. Richard B. Moore, "Bicentennial Reflections on Afro-Americans in the Revolutionary Period 1770–1831," 1.

33. Ibid.

34. Claudia Jones, *Jim Crow in Uniform* (New York: New Age Publishers, 1940), 6, 14. Paule Marshall also used the image of black mothers who mourned the loss of their sons' mental stability and lives during World War II. See *Brown Girl, Brownstones*, 235, 242.

35. Thomas R. Bowen, "We Are Welcomed by Leading Citizens," *West Indian American* 1, no. 2 (November 1927): 11. This section featured a series of short articles by notable Caribbean intellectuals, which all appeared under the same title.

36. W. A. Domingo, "We Are Welcomed by Leading Citizens," *West Indian American* 1, no. 2 (November 1927): 11.

37. See Benedict Anderson, *Imagined Communities: Reflections on the Origin and Spread of Nationalism* (London: Verso, 1983).

38. "A Federated West Indies," *West Indian American* 1, no. 2 (November 1927): 10.

39. William E. Pace, "We Are Welcomed by Leading Citizens," *West Indian American* 1, no. 2 (November 1927), 11.

40. American Committee for West Indian Federation, "Memorandum of Federation" (emphasis added).

41. Richard B. Moore, "Caribbean Unity and Freedom," *Freedomways*, Third Quarter, 1964; Turner and Turner, *Caribbean Militant in Harlem*, 123 (emphasis added).

42. Ibid., 136.

43. Quotations from Moore, "Caribbean Unity and Freedom."

44. Ibid., 123.

45. Ibid.

46. Claude McKay, "If We Must Die," *Harlem Shadows: The Poems of Claude McKay* (New York: Harcourt, Brace and Co., 1922).

47. Ida B. Wells, *Crusade for Justice: The Autobiography of Ida B. Wells* (Chicago: University of Chicago Press, 1970), Kindle file, 411.

48. "Negroes Appeal to Wilson," *New York Times*, August 1, 1919.

49. *West Indian American* 1, no. 4 (May 1959), 4.

50. Ibid.

51. Ibid., 1.

52. Ibid.

53. *West Indian American* 1, no. 3 (April 1959), 1.

54. Harold Cruse, Letter to Richard B. Moore, February 28, 1963.

55. Ethelred Brown, "Who Provides 'Father Divine' with Money?" December 30, 1934.

56. Shirley Chisholm, *Unbought and Unbossed*, 76.

57. Brown, Joyce Moore Turner interview.

58. Harold Cruse, Letter to Richard B. Moore, February 28, 1963.

59. Ibid.

60. Quotations from Cruse, *The Crisis of the Negro Intellectual*, 255–56.

61. Richard B. Moore, "The Critics and Opponents of Marcus Garvey," *Marcus Garvey and the Vision of Africa*, ed. John Henrik Clarke (New York: Random House, 1974), 222.

62. Turner and Turner, *Caribbean Militant in Harlem*, 1, 4–5.

63. Ibid., 4.

64. Turner and Turner, *Caribbean Militant in Harlem*, 7.

65. Ibid., 6.

66. Chimamanda Ngozi Adichie, "The Danger of a Single Story," TED Global, July 2009.

67. Moore spent a great deal of his political career arguing that the term "Afro-American" should replace the term "Negro," which he perceived to be pejorative. See ibid., 223–39.

68. All of the documentary sources in this chapter may be found in the Richard B. Moore Papers at the Schomburg Center for Research in Black Culture in Harlem.

69. Turner and Turner, *Caribbean Militant in Harlem*, 224 (emphasis added).

70. Richard B. Moore, "African Culture and Dr. Leakey's Development: White African by L. S. B. Leakey," manuscript, 11 (emphasis added).

71. Stokely Carmichael (Kwame Ture) with Michael Thelwell, *Ready for Revolution: The Life and Struggles of Stokely Carmichael* (New York: Scribner, 2003), 14.

72. "Dancer," *The Washington Post*, no date, Pearl Primus Papers, New York Public Library—Lincoln Center.

Chapter 4

1. Pearl Primus, "Pearl Primus Thrills Broadway," *Daily Worker*, New York, Saturday 7, 1944, 11.

2. In *The Norton Anthology of African American Literature*, this era is categorized as "Realism, Naturalism, Modernism, 1940–1960," Henry Louis Gates, ed., *The Norton Anthology of African American Literature*, 2nd edition (New York: W. W. Norton & Company, 2003). Also see Edwin Morgan, "American Art at Mid-Century," *American Quarterly* 1, no. 4 (Winter, 1949), 326–30.

3. Lisa D. Cook, "Converging to a National Lynching Data Base: Recent Developments," East Lansing, MI: Department of Economics, Michigan State University, 2011, 22.

4. Ida B. Wells, *Southern Horrors: Lynch Law in all its Phases*, pamphlet, 1892; Crystal Feimster, *Southern Horrors: Women and the Politics of Rape and Lynching* (Cambridge, MA: Harvard University Press, 2011).

5. Toni Morrison, "Unspeakable Things Unspoken: The Afro-American Presence in Literature, *The Tanner Lectures on Human Values* (Ann Arbor: University of Michigan, October 7, 1988).

6. Houston A. Baker Jr., "The Point of Entanglement: Modernism, Diaspora, and Toni Morrison's *Love*," *African and Black Diaspora: An International Journal* 4, no.1 (January 2011): 1–18.

7. Dance Announcement by Theatre of the Riverside Church, February 24, 1981.

8. For a more detailed description of the New Dance Group's philosophy and radical political mission, see Peggy and Murray Schwartz, *The Dance Claimed Me: A Biography of Pearl Primus* (New Haven: Yale University Press, 2011), 29–30; Susan Manning, *Modern Dance, Negro Dance: Race in Motion* (Minneapolis, MN: University of Minnesota, 2004), 62–63.

9. For a discussion of the Haitian dance Yanvaloo, also known as *yanvalu* see Yvonne Daniel, *Dancing Wisdom: Embodied Knowledge in Haitian Vodou, Cuban Yoruba, and Bahian Candomble* (Urbana & Chicago: University of Illinois Press, 2005), 8–9.

10. Pearl Primus, "Pearl Primus Thrills Broadway," *Daily Worker*, New York, Saturday 7, 1944, 11.

11. Farah Jasmine Griffin, *Harlem Nocturne: Women Artists and Progressive Politics During World War II* (New York: Basic Civitas Books, 2013), ebook, 24.

12. Primus diary, Monday, January 19, 1949, American Dance Festival Archives, Pearl Primus Collection, 1920–1994, Box 3.

13. Peggy and Murray Schwartz, *The Dance Claimed Me: A Biography of Pearl Primus* (New Haven: Yale University Press, 2011), 130–31.

14. Ibid., p 73.

15. Ibid.

16. "Pearl Primus," Schomburg Research Center Oral History Project, Saturday June 19, 1993, New York; Pearl Primus, "The New Dance Group Gala Concert: A Historic Retrospective of New Dance Group Presentations, 1930s–1970s," American Dance Guild, 1994.

17. "Pearl Primus," Schomburg Research Center Oral History Project, Saturday June 19, 1993, New York, NY.

18. Peggy and Murray Schwartz, *The Dance Claimed Me: A Biography of Pearl Primus* (New Haven: Yale University Press, 2011) p 14.

19. Pearl Eileene Primus, "An Anthropological Study of Masks as Teaching Aids in the Enculturation of Mano Children," PhD dissertation, New York University, 1978, 25–26.

20. Ann Pellegrini, *Performance Anxieties: Staging Psychoanalysis, Staging Race* (New York: Routledge, 1997), 7.

21. Pearl Eileene Primus, "An Anthropological Study of Masks as Teaching Aids in the Enculturation of Mano Children," PhD dissertation, New York University, 1978.

22. "Profile," *Ebony*, January 1951, 54.

23. See Matthew Frye Jacobson, *Whiteness of a Different Color: European Immigrants and the Alchemy of Race* (Cambridge, MA: Harvard University Press, 1998); Robert W. Rydell, *All the World's a Fair: Visions of Empire at American International Expositions, 1876–1916* (Chicago: University of Chicago Press, 1984).

24. Primus, "An Anthropological Study of Masks as Teaching Aids in the Enculturation of Mano Children." PhD dissertation, New York University, 1978, 25–26 (emphasis added).

25. Pearl Primus quoted in Ezra Goodman, "Hard Time Blues," *Dance*, April 1946, 31.

26. Ibid.

27. Ibid.

28. Ibid., 55.

29. Ibid.

30. Jennifer Dunning, "Lincoln Center Scene Moves Outdoors: Pearl Primus Dancing Indoors and Out," *New York Times*, August 17, 1979, C1.

31. Countee Cullen, "Heritage," in *Color* (New York: Harper & Brothers, 1925).

32. Dunning, "Pearl Primus Dancing Indoors and Out."

33. Langston Hughes quoted in Farah Jasmine Griffin, *Harlem Nocturne*, ebook, 23.

34. Pearl Primus, "Pearl Primus Thrills Broadway," *Daily Worker*, New York, October, 7, 1944, 11.

35. John Martin, "Brilliant Dancing by Pearl Primus," *New York Times*, October 5, 1944, 18.

36. Very little scholarship exists on Primus's work, especially her focus on African diasporic dance. John Martin's *The Modern Dance* (1936) and Doris Hering's *25 Years of American Dance* (1954) discuss Primus's explosive entrance on the New York dance scene in the early 1940's, but they do not take a long-view of her life and work, placing them in historical context.

37. Billie Holiday, "Strange Fruit," (New York, NY: Commodore, 1939); *Anthology*. CD. (Marina del Ray, FL: Stardust Records, 2000).

38. Billie Holiday, "Strange Fruit," (New York, NY: Commodore, 1939); Primus's interpretation of "Strange Fruit" drew government scrutiny as she was investigated by the Committee of Un-American Activity, but she was not convicted. After thorough searches, no transcript has been found of Pearl's hearing.

39. Farah Jasmine Griffin, *Harlem Nocturne*, ebook, 64.

40. "Steps of the Gods, *Free to Dance*, DVD, directed by Madison D. Lacy (New York: National Black Programming Consortium, 2001).

41. See Nell Irvin Painter, "Soul Murder," *Southern History across the Color Line* (Chapel Hill: University of North Carolina Press, 2002). Painter suggests that racialized violence during slavery not only physically and psychologically harmed African slaves, but also damaged its white perpetrators as well as the people related to them. Painter specifically highlights the prevalence of domestic violence in the master's house; it was not uncommon for masters to beat their wives. Even Thomas Jefferson expressed concern regarding the detrimental effects of slavery on the psyches of white masters. Jefferson wrote, "The man must be a prodigy who can retain his manners and morals undepraved by such circumstances." Thomas Jefferson quoted in Painter, *Southern History across the Color Line*, 36.

42. Pearl Primus quoted in Michael Carter, "Pearl Primus Dances Out Social Problems: Entertainer Attempts to Contribute to Interracial Understanding; Tours South to Study Actions in Church," *Afro-American Baltimore*, July 22, 1944, 6.

43. Yael Woll quoted in *The Dance Claimed Me*, 61.

44. *The Dance Claimed Me*, 12.

45. Michael Carter, "Pearl Primus Dances Out Social Problems" *Afro-American Baltimore* July 22, 19445

46. In Spring 2000 I participated in a community advisory meeting with dancer Bill T. Jones at the Walker Art Center in Minneapolis, MN. During this meeting, Jones discussed how he conducted informal anthropological research of crop harvesters throughout the southern United States as case studies to inform his own choreography.

47. Josh White, *Hard Times Blues*

48. Ibid.

49. "Steps of the Gods, *Free to Dance*, DVD, directed by Madison D. Lacy (New York: National Black Programming Consortium, 2001).

50. Ibid.

51. Michael Carter, "Pearl Primus Dances Out Social Problems," 6.

52. Vernon Rice, "A Real Pearl," *New York Post* August 13, 1950.

53. Claude McKay, "The Tropics in New York," *Harlem Shadows* (New York: Harcourt, Brace and Company, Inc., 1922) 8.

54. Anna Kisselgoff, "Pearl Primus Rejoices in the Black Tradition," *New York Times*, June 19, 1988.

55. Pearl Primus, Diary Entry, Tuesday, January 4, 1949, American Dance Festival Archive, Duke University.

56. Primus diary, Monday, January 28, 1949, American Dance Festival Archives, Pearl Primus Collection, 1920–1994, Box 3.

57. Primus talked to journalist Walter Terry about the circumstances in which she was given the name "Omowale," which means "child has returned home," during a visit to western Nigeria in the late 1940s. Walter Terry, *New York Herald Tribune*, New York Public Library Performance Arts Pearl Primus Clippings File, no date.

58. Sally Hammond, "Spreading the Heritage," *New York Post*, March 27, 1969 (Dance Clipping File, NYPL Lincoln Center). Emphasis added.

59. Doris Hering, "'Little Fast Feet:' The Story of a Pilgrimage of Pearl Primus to Africa," *Dance*, July 1950, 22 (emphasis added).

60. Ibid. (emphasis added).

61. Unnamed author, "Pearl Primus and Company in 'Dark Rhythms,'" *Dance*, December 1951, 16 (emphasis added).

62. Primus, *Anthropological Study of Masks*, vi, 25.

63. Ibid., xxxiv.

64. Vernon Rice, "A Real Pearl," *New York Post*, August 13, 1950.

65. "Genuine Africa," *Time*, May 21, 1951.

66. Pearl Primus, "Africa," *Dance Magazine*, March 1958, 45–46.

67. Irina Paperno, "What Can Be Done with Diaries?" *Russian Review* 63, no. 4 (Oct 2004): 573.

68. Jochen Hellbeck, "The Diary between Literature and History: A Historian's Critical Response," *Russian Review* 63, no. 4 (Oct 2004):_621.

69. Pearl Primus diary, January 30, 1949, American Dance Festival Archives, Pearl Primus Collection, 1920–1994, Box 3.

70. Pearl Primus diary, January 20, 1949, American Dance Festival Archives, Pearl Primus Collection, 1920–1994, Box 3.

71. Ibid.

72. Ibid.

73. Ibid.

74. Ibid.

75. Langston Hughes, *I Wonder as I Wander: An Autobiographical Journey* (New York: Hill and Wang, 1993).

76. Pearl Primus Diary, May 5, 1949, American Dance Festival Collection, Duke University, Pearl Primus Collection, 1920–1994, Box 3.

77. Langston Hughes,

I, too, I am the darker brother
They send me to eat in the kitchen
When company comes
But I laugh
And eat well
And grow strong.

78. Pearl Primus, Diary entry, May 5, 1949, American Dance Festival Collection, Duke University.

79. Pearl Primus, Diary entry, May 5, 1949, American Dance Festival Collection, Duke University.

80. "Pearl Turns to Africa," *Picture Post*, London November 14, 1951, 40.

81. E. A. G., "Pearl Primus," *Dance Observer*, July 1946, 76. (Emphasis added).

82. Doris Hering, "Pearl Primus YM-YWHA Dance Center, April 11, 1948," *Dance*, July 1948, 41 (emphasis added).

83. *New York Herald Tribune*, April 29, 1943.

84. John Martin, "Pearl Primus," *Current Biography*, 1944, 553.

85. Phyllis Watts, "The Dance," *Boston Globe*, Saturday, January 18, 1947.

86. Ibid. (emphasis added).

87. *Liberty Magazine*, June 3, 1947.

88. Martin, "Pearl Primus."

89. Watts, "The Dance."

90. Gilroy, *Black Atlantic*, 182.

91. Doris Hering, "Percival Borde and Company," *Dance Magazine*, December 1958, 23; "Percival Borde with Pearl Primus, Guest Artist," October 1958, 26.

92. Hering, "Pearl Primus YM-YWHA Dance Center," p. 41 (emphasis added).

93. Audre Lorde quoted in Richard C. Green, "(Up)staging the Primitive" in *Dancing Many Drums: Excavations in African American Dance*, Thomas F. Defrantz (Madison, WI: University of Wisconsin Press, 2002) 129.

94. Jawole Willa Jo Zollar quoted in "Riffing on the Primus Legacy," *Five Colleges: The Consortium Update*, January 2003, 1.

95. Jawole Willa Jo Zollar, email message to author, August 23, 2014.

96. *American Education*, February 1966 (emphasis added).

97. Primus, *Anthropological Study of Masks*, xxxi (emphasis added).

98. Primus, *Anthropological Study of Masks*, 25–26.

99. Dunning, "Pearl Primus Dancing Indoors and Out."

100. Paul Gilroy, *The Black Atlantic: Modernity and Double Consciousness* (Cambridge, MA: Harvard University Press, 1993), 190.

101. "Donald McKayle: Teaching Dancers to Dig Deep," *Dance Magazine*, New York: Mac-Fadden Performing Arts Media, LLC., August 2008; Schwartz, *The Dance Claimed Me*, 184.

102. "Donald McKayle: Teaching Dancers to Dig Deep," 79.

103. "Pearl Primus," Schomburg Research Center Oral History Project, Saturday June 19, 1993, New York, NY.

104. Pearl Primus quoted in *The Dance Claimed Me*, 15.

Chapter 5

1. Shirley Chisholm in Lynch, *Chisholm '72*.

2. Shirley Chisholm, quoted in *Chisholm '72—Unbought and Unbossed*, DVD, directed by Shola Lynch (Beverly Hills: Twentieth Century Fox Home Entertainment, 2004).

3. "Statement of Candidacy for the Office of President of the United States by the Honorable Shirley Chisholm," January 25, 1972; Container 3, Shirley Chisholm Papers in Julie Gallagher, "Waging 'The Good Fight': The Political Career of Shirley Chisholm, 1953–1982," *The Journal of African American History* 92, no. 3 (Summer 2007): 3.

4. Shirley Chisholm, quoted in *Chisholm '72—Unbought and Unbossed*, DVD, directed by Shola Lynch (Beverly Hills: Twentieth Century Fox Home Entertainment, 2004).

5. Shirley Chisholm, *Unbought and Unbossed* (Boston: Houghton Mifflin, 1970), 3, 13.

6. Ibid., 26–27.

7. Ibid., 13.

8. Shirley Chisholm, "Growing up in Barbados," National Visionary Leadership Project: Oral History Archive, http://www.visionaryproject.org/chisholmshirley/ accessed August 22, 2014.

9. Muriel Forde quoted in Lynch, *Chisholm '72*.

10. Shirley Chisholm, *Unbought and Unbossed*, 7–8.

11. Stokely Carmichael (Kwame Ture) with Michael Thelwell, *Ready for Revolution: The Life and Struggles of Stokely Carmichael* (New York: Scribner, 2003), 58.

12. Like Barbadian-American politician Shirley Chisholm, Carmichael also believed that the more rigorous, British-styled education that he experienced in the Caribbean prepared him to excel in New York public schools. While Chisholm shone in the field of language arts in high school and throughout her studies as an undergraduate at Brooklyn College, Carmichael excelled in mathematics in junior high and high school and later in oratorical skills and leadership at Howard University.

13. Kwame Ture with Ekwueme Michael Thelwell, *Ready for Revolution: The Life and Struggles of Stokely Carmichael (Kwame Ture)* (New York: Scribner, 2003) 84.

14. Chisholm, *Unbought and Unbossed* (1970), 19.

15. Ibid., 21.

16. Shirley Chisholm, *Unbought and Unbossed* (Take Root Media edition, 2010), 40.

17. Chisholm, *Unbought and Unbossed* (1970), 23.

18. Shirley Chisholm, "Growing up in Barbados," National Visionary Leadership Project: Oral History Archive, http://www.visionaryproject.org/chisholmshirley/ accessed August 22, 2014.

19. Shirley Chisholm, *Unbought and Unbossed* (Boston: Houghton Mifflin Company, 1970), 5.

20. Victor Robles quoted in Lynch, *Chisholm '72*.

21. Bevan Dufty interview, Shirley Chisholm Project archives, Brooklyn College, September 29, 2008.

22. In the documentary film *Chisholm '72*, poet and political actvist Amiri Baraka discussed the Congressional Black Caucus's failure to endorse Chisholm during her presidential campaing. Baraka blamed Chisholm for failing to attend the National Black Political Convention in Gary, Indiana, because he considered it a crucial event to campaign for support from important, black political leaders. In his commentary, Baraka repeadely said, "You have to stay in their faces"—meaning, because Chisholm did not attend the convention, she was somewhat out of sight and out of mind. Lynch, *Chisholm '72*.

23. Chisholm, *Unbought and Unbossed*, 76.

24. Ibid.

25. Chisholm, *Unbought and Unbossed*, 5.

26. Colin Powell, *My American Journey* (New York: Ballantine Books, 2010) Kindle file.

27. Carmichael, *Ready for Revolution*, 15.

28. Ibid. (emphasis added).

29. Ibid., 75.

30. Valerie Smith, *Not Just Race, Not Just Gender: Black Feminist Readings* (New York: Routledge, 1998).

31. Chisholm, *Unbought and Unbossed*, 1970, 74.

32. Ibid., 63–64.

33. See Daniel Patrick Moynihan, *The Negro Family: The Case for National Action* (Washington, DC: US Government Printing Office, 1965).

34. Chisholm quoted in Anne Williams, "Unconquerable," *Off Our Backs* 4, no. 2 (December–January, 1974): 3.

35. Chisholm, *Unbought and Unbossed*, 71.

36. See Chapter 6.

37. Shirley Chisholm, "Economic Justice for Women," *The Good Fight* (New York, NY: Harper & Row, 1973), 191.

38. Shirley Chisholm, "Esteemed Women: Representative Shirley Chisholm urges women to run for office," (North Hollywood: Center for Cassette Studios, Inc.), no date.

39. Shirley Chisholm, "Shirley Chisholm," *Young and Female* (New York: Random House, 1972), 23.

40. Shirley Chisholm, "The Relationship between Religion and Today's Social Issues," *Religious Education* 69, no. 2 (March–April 1974): 117–23.

41. Ibid.

42. Ibid., 23–24.

43. Shirley Chisholm, "Economic Justice for Women," *The Good Fight*, 107–9.

44. Shirley Chisholm, *Unbought and Unbossed*, 26.

45. Bevan Dufty interview, Shirley Chisholm Project archives, Brooklyn College, September 29, 2008.

46. In the documentary film *Chisholm '72*, Shirley Chisholm briefly recalled the attempt to assassinate her, but she said she preferred to not talk about the incident.

47. "Chisholm Tells Retirees She Still Boogies at 61," *Jet*, June 16, 1986, 27.

48. Ibid.

49. Joyce Bolden, "The Life and Legacy of Shirley Chisholm," The Shirley Chisholm Project at Brooklyn College and Medgar Evers College, Brooklyn, May 8, 2008.

50. "Shirley Chisholm kicks off Campaign for U.S. President," *Jet*, February 10, 1972.

51. Bobby Seale quoted in Shirley Chisholm, *The Good Fight*, 107–9.

52. Shirley Downs quoted in Lynch, *Chisholm '72*.

53. Chisholm, *Unbought and Unbossed*, 70.

54. Chisholm, *The Good Fight*, 27.

55. Chisholm, *Unbought and Unbossed*, 135.

56. Ibid.

57. Shirley Chisholm, "Esteemed Women," unpublished speech, no date.

58. Ibid.

59. Shirley Chisholm in Lynch, *Chisholm '72*.

Chapter 6

1. Paule Marshall, "From the Poets in the Kitchen," in *Rena and Other Short Stories* (Old Westbury, NY: Feminist Press, 1983), 7.

2. Arnold Rampersad, "Design and Truth in Biography," *South Central Modern Language Association Review* 9, no. 2 (Summer 1992): 17.

3. Winston James, "Explaining Afro-Caribbean Social Mobility in the United States: Beyond the Sowell Thesis," *Comparative Studies in Society and History* 44, no. 2 (April 2002): 219.

4. Roy Bryce-Laporte, "Introduction: New York City and the New Caribbean Immigration: A Contextual Statement," *International Migration Review* 13, no. 2 (Summer 1979): 229. Historian Winston James has also made a similar comparison and called whiteness studies scholars who solely write about white European immigrants, without any mention of Afro-Caribbean immigrants, a type of "intellectual apartheid." Winston James, "Explaining Afro-Caribbean Social Mobility in the United States: Beyond the Sowell Thesis" *Comparative Studies in Society and History* 44, no. 2 (2002): 218–62.

5. Thankfully, significant scholarship on Caribbean New York has been produced in the three decades since Bryce-Laporte posited his Ellisonian argument. Still, the majority of the

literature on the topic is in the fields of sociology and political science and centers on quantitative and qualitative studies of Caribbean immigrants from 1965 to the present. While several historians—including Irma Watkins Owens, Winston James, Joyce Moore Turner, and Minkah Makalani—have produced seminal studies of African Caribbean immigration during the first half of the twentieth century, more scholarship is needed, especially work drawing attention to the lived experiences of black immigrant women.

6. Gayatri Chakravorty Spivak, "Can the Subaltern Speak?" in *Marxism and the Interpretation of Culture*, ed. Cary Nelson and Lawrence Grossberg (Urbana: University of Illinois Press, 1988) 271.

7. Paule Marshall, "To Da-Duh, in Memorium," *Reena, and Other Stories* (New York: The Feminist Press, 1983) 93-106.

8. See Paule Marshall, *Brown Girl, Brownstones* (New York: Feminist Press, 1981).

9. Tammy L. Brown, interview with Paule Marshall, New York, October 28, 2004.

10. Tammy L. Brown, interview with Mary Phillips, Queens, New York, March 23, 2006.

11. Adapted from Winston James "Immigration Reports, 1899–1932," *Holding Aloft the Banner of Ethiopia: Caribbean Radicalism in Early Twentieth-Century America* (London; New York: Verso, 1998), table 1.2, 356.

12. Adapted from ibid., table 1.4, 359. See also J. R. Ward. *Poverty and Progress in the Caribbean, 1800–1969* (Houndmills, UK: Macmillan, 1985) 27.

13. Ibid., Immigration Reports, 1908-1924, 363.

14. Ibid.

15. Brown, Paule Marshall interview.

16. Paule Marshall, "From the Poets in the Kitchen," in *Rena and Other Short Stories* (Old Westbury, NY: Feminist Press, 1983).

17. Shirley Chisholm, *Unbought and Unbossed* (Boston: Houghton Mifflin Company, 1970), 4.

18. Marshall, *Brown Girl, Brownstones*, 173.

19. Paule Marshall, "Shaping the World of My Art," *New Letters* 40, no. 1 (Autumn 1973):101.

20. James, *Holding Aloft the Banner*, 37.

21. Marshall, *Brown Girl, Brownstones*, 70.

22. Ibid.

23. Constantine Hall, "Paule Marshall Gains Literary Fame," *West Indian-American* 9, no. 1 (October 1959): 4. Marshall lived in Barbados for eight months while writing the first drafts of *Brown Girl, Brownstones*.

24. In the King James Bible, Mark 8:36 reads, "For what shall it profit a man, if he shall gain the whole world, and lose his own soul?" Variations of this scripture also appear in Matthew 16:26 and Luke 9:25.

25. Brown, Paule Marshall interview.

26. Ibid.

27. Despite the emotional pain caused by her father's absence, Marshall excelled academically and professionally, and her Barbadian Brooklyn community celebrated her success.

Daryl Cumber Dance, "An Interview with Paule Marshall," *Southern Review* 28, no. 1 (Winter 92): 1–20.

28. Robert Weisbrot, *Father Divine and the Struggle for Racial Equality* (Urbana: University of Illinois Press, 1983), 49.

29. John Hoshor, *God in a Rolls Royce* (New York: Hillman-Curl, 1936); Weisbrot, *Father Divine and the Struggle for Racial Equality*, 68.

30. Dance, "An Interview with Paule Marshall," 5.

31. Brown, Paule Marshall interview.

32. Marshall, *Brown Girl, Brownstones*, 10.

33. Tammy L. Brown, interview with Maise Henry, Philadelphia, April 25, 2006.

34. Mark D. Morrison-Reed, *Black Pioneers in a White Denomination* (Boston, MA: Skinner House Books, 1994) 78.

35. James, *Holding Aloft the Banner*, 364. The number of black immigrants entering the United States already had been drastically curtailed by the 1924 immigration legislation that implemented strict quotas. By 1928 the number of net arrivals almost equaled departures for black immigrants.

36. Sally Lodge, "Paule Marshall," in *Writing for Your Life*, ed. Sybil Steinberg (New York: Pushcart Press, 1992), 328 (emphasis added).

37. Gwendolyn Brooks, *Maud Martha* (Chicago: Third World Press, 1993).

38. Chimamanda Ngozi Adichie, "The Danger of a Single Story," TED Global Conference, March 15, 2009.

39. For a full discussion of the trope of "edible blackness," see Kyla Wazana Tompkins, *Racial Indigestion: Eating Bodies in the Nineteenth Century* (New York University Press, 2012).

40. See James R. Barrett, "Americanization from the Bottom Up: Immigration and the Remaking of the Working Class in the United States, 1880–1930," *Journal of American History* 79, no. 3 (December 1992): 996–1020; James R. Barrett and David Roediger, "In Between Peoples: Race, Nationality and the 'New Immigrant' Working Class," *Journal of Ethnic History* 16 (Spring 1997): 2–44; David Roediger, *Wages of Whiteness: Race and the Making of the American Working Class* (London: Verso, 1991); Noel Ignatiev, *How the Irish Became White* (New York: Routledge, 1995); Matthew Frye Jacobson, *Whiteness of a Different Color: European Immigrants and the Alchemy of Race* (Cambridge, MA: Harvard University Press, 1998).

41. Israel Zangwill, *The Melting-Pot: Drama in Four Acts* (New York: Macmillan, 1923).

42. James Brown, "Say It Loud—I'm Black and Proud," Vox Studios: Los Angeles, August 7, 1968.

43. Charles Taylor, "The Politics of Recognition," in *Multiculturalism*, ed. Amy Gutman (Princeton: Princeton University Press, 1994), 38.

44. Tom Vitale, "'Daughters': Book about African-American Woman," *Morning Edition*, National Public Radio, January 6, 1992.

45. Edwidge Danticat quoted in Neal Conan, "Analysis: Seeing Our World through Fiction and the Experience of Immigrants," *Talk of the Nation*, July 1, 2004 (emphasis added).

46. Joyce Pettis, "A Melus Interview: Paule Marshall," *Melus* 17, no. 4 (Winter 91–92): 118; Paule Marshall, "From the Poets in the Kitchen."

47. Marshall, "From the Poets in the Kitchen," 5.

48. Ibid.

49. James, *Holding Aloft the Banner*, 365.

50. Brown, Paule Marshall interview.

51. For a fuller discussion, see Albert J. Raboteau, *Slave Religion: The "Invisible Institution" in the Antebellum South* (New York: Oxford University Press, 1978).

52. Paule Marshall, "Shaping the World of My Art," *New Letters* 40, no. 1 (Autumn 1973): 98.

53. Marshall, "From the Poets in the Kitchen," 7.

54. This mode of resistance is consistent with anthropologist James Scott's notion of "weapons of the weak." James C. Scott, *Weapons of the Weak: Everyday Forms of Peasant Resistance* (New Haven: Yale University Press, 1985).

55. Marshall, "From the Poets in the Kitchen," 7 (emphasis added).

56. Benedict Anderson, *Imagined Communities: Reflections on the Origin and Spread of Nationalism* (London: Verso, 1983).

57. Henry Louis Gates, "Writing 'Race' and the Difference It Makes," in *"Race," Writing, and Difference* (Chicago: University of Chicago Press Journals, 1992) 12.

58. This subheading is borrowed from the title of African American woman poet Audre Lorde's *Sister Outside: Essays and Speeches* (Trumansburg: Crossing Press, 1984), in which she discusses experiences of triple-marginality as an African American gay woman.

59. See Barbara Christian, *Black Women Novelists: The Development of a Tradition, 1892–1976* (Westport, Conn.: Greenwood Press, 1980); Susan Stanford Friedman, "Women's Autobiographical Selves: The Theory and Practice," in *The Private Self: Theory and Practice in Women's Autobiographical Writing*, ed. Shari Benstock (Chapel Hill: University of North Carolina Press, 1988), 34–62; Mary Helen Washington, afterword to the first Feminist Press edition of Marshall's *Brown Girl, Brownstones*, 1980; Susan Willis, "Describing Arcs of Recovery: Paule Marshall's Relationship to Afro-American Culture," *Specifying Black Women Writing the American Experience* (Madison: University of Wisconsin Press, 1987), 53–82.

60. Lodge, "Paule Marshall," 327.

61. Ibid., 329 (emphasis added).

62. Ibid.

63. Brown, Paule Marshall interview.

64. The quotations here are from Paule Marshall, introduction to "The Valley Between," in *Rena and Other Stories*, 15.

65. Brown, Paule Marshall interview.

66. Nicole Warren, "Five Questions for Paule Marshall," New Brunswick, NJ, November 17, 2003.

67. Sandi Russell, "Interview with Paule Marshall," *Wasafari* 4 (1988): 15.

68. See Paul Gilroy, *The Black Atlantic: Modernity and Double Consciousness* (Cambridge, MA: Harvard University Press, 1993); Brent Hayes Edwards, *The Practice of Diaspora: Literature, Translation, and the Rise of Black Internationalism* (Cambridge, MA: Harvard University Press, 2003).

69. Paule Marshall and Maryse Condé, "Return of a Native Daughter: An Interview with Paule Marshall and Maryse Condé," *SAGE: A Scholarly Journal on Black Women* 3, no. 2 (Fall 1986): 52.

70. Ibid. Malcolm X also was given the same name "Omowale" when he traveled to western Africa for the first time in the 1960s. This name was conferred by members of the Muslim Students' Society of Nigeria. Manning Marable, *Malcolm X: A Life of Reinvention* (New York: Penguin Books, 2011).

71. Ibid.

72. Paule Marshall interview by Kay Bonetti, March 1994.

73. Homi K. Bhabha, "Culture's In-Between," *Questions of Cultural Identity* (Thousand Oaks, CA: Sage, 1996), 56.

74. Dance, "An Interview with Paule Marshall," 9.

75. Ibid. See also Pettis, "Paule Marshall," 118.

76. Lisa Simeone, "Interview: Paule Marshall Discusses her Book, 'The Fisher King,'" *All Things Considered*, National Public Radio (January 7, 2001).

77. Brown, Paule Marshall interview.

78. Lodge, "Paule Marshall," 330.

79. Brown, Paule Marshall interview.

80. Bonetti, Paule Marshall interview.

81. Ibid.

82. Brown, Paule Marshall interview.

83. Paule Marshall quoted in Felicia R. Lee, "Voyage of a Girl Moored in Brooklyn," *New York Times* http://www.nytimes.com/2009/03/12/books/12paul.html accessed June 9, 2011.

84. Paule Marshall interview with Melody Graulich and Lisa Sisco, "Meditations on Language and the Self: A Conversation with Paule Marshall," *NWSA Journal* 4, no. 4 (Fall 1992): 293.

85. Paule Marshall quoted in Felicia R. Lee, "Voyage of a Girl Moored in Brooklyn," *New York Times* http://www.nytimes.com/2009/03/12/books/12paul.html accessed June 9, 2011. Italics added for emphasis.

86. From the late 1960s through the early 1970s, "Afrocentric" scholars borrowed the notion of diaspora from Jewish studies to describe a similar phenomenon of cultural scattering and connectedness for peoples of African descent around the world. See Molefi Asante and Maulana Karenga. Later scholars like Paul Gilroy have used terms like the "Black Atlantic" to discuss double-consciousness, modernity, and black identity, and scholar Brent Edwards focuses on the importance of translation in building African diasporic identities among peoples of African descent living in France, the Caribbean and the US. See Paul Gilroy, *The Black Atlantic: Modernity and Double Consciousness* (Cambridge, MA: Harvard University Press, 1993); Brent Hayes Edwards, *The Practice of Diaspora: Literature, Translation, and the Rise of Black Internationalism* (Cambridge, MA: Harvard University Press, 2003).

87. Paule Marshall interview with Sarah F. Gold, "To Barbados and Beyond," *Publishers Weekly*, January 26, 2009, 106. Italics added for emphasis.

88. Marshall, "From the Poets in the Kitchen," 5.

Coda

1. Max Roach, "Garvey's Ghost," *Percussion Bittersweet* (New York, NY: Impulse!, 1961, 1993); Steel Pulse, "Worth His Weight in Gold (Rally Round)," *True Democracy* (Arathus, Denmark: "Feedback" Studios, 1981). The subtitle of this chapter, "Life after Death," is taken from the album by rap artist The Notorious B.I.G. by the same title; The Notorious B.I.G., *Life after Death*, New York: Bad Boy, 1997.

2. Pearl Primus dissertation, 10.

3. Tony Martin, *Marcus Garvey, Hero: A First Biography* (Dover, MA: Majority Press, 1983) 96.

4. Primus included this quote in her dissertation: footnote no. 3 in Pearl Primus's dissertation, 45; Birago Diop in Leopold Sidar Senghor's *Hostice Noires* (Paris, 1948), 144, as quoted in Janheinz Jahn's *Muntu* (New York: Grove Press), 108.

5. Pearl Primus dissertation, 10.

6. Max Roach, "Garvey's Ghost," *Percussion Bittersweet*, CD (New York, NY: Impulse!, c1961, 1993); Steel Pulse, "Worth His Weight in Gold (Rally Round)," *True Democracy*, CD (Arathus, Denmark: "Feedback" Studios, 1981.

7. Ibid.

8. For a detailed discussion of the evolution of Abbey Lincoln as an artist, see Farah Jasmine Griffin, *If You Can't be Free, be a Mystery: In Search of Billie Holiday* (New York: The Free Press, 2001), 169–192. The album *We Insist!: Max Roach's Freedom Now Suite* (1960), which included the songs "Freedom Day," "Tear for Johannesburg," and Lincoln's famous rendition of "Driva Man" epitomized Max Roach and Abbey Lincoln's collaboraive artistic activism.

9. One of the most amusing depictions of Marcus Garvey that I've seen to date is the Disney movie finale of the cartoon *The Proud Family*, which features a villain named Dr. Marcus Garvey Carver who is an odd mixture of the historical figures Marcus Garvey and George Washington Carver, founder of Black History Month and agricultural innovator and professor at one of the most prestigious historically-black colleges in the United States, Tuskegee University; Bruce W. Smith, *The Proud Family Movie* (Los Angeles: Disney Enterprises, Inc., 2005). One of the earliest African American filmmakers, Bud Pollard, produced a satire of Marcus Garvey titled *The Black King* in which he depicted Garvey as a scam artist; Bud Pollard, *The Black King*, Bridgeport, CT: Synergy Entertainment, 1932, 2006.

10. Burning Spear, *Garvey's Ghost* (New York: Island Records, 1976).

11. Burning Spear, *Marcus Garvey* (New York: Island Records, 1975).

12. Steel Pulse, "Worth His Weight in Gold (Rally Round)," *True Democracy*, CD (Arathus, Denmark: "Feedback" Studios, 1981.

13. X-Clan, "Heed the Word of the Brother," New York: 4th & Broadway label, 1990.

14. Chuck D interview by the author, September 10, 2014.

15. Chuck D. Lecture, "Race, Rap and Reality," Miami University of Ohio—Hamilton, September 10, 2014.

16. Ibid.

17. For instance, in *Prophets of the Hood*, scholar Imani Perry writes, "[Paul Gilroy] argues that West Coast artists Ice Cube and Tim Dog borrowed substantially from the Caribbean,

an argument I am not yet convinced of. I believe the more compelling story of the music of Ice Cube and many other West Coast MCs is the Current of southern language through their mouths, even in a context in which regional affiliations is deeply important. The question is not, 'Are you black American?' but rather, 'What kind of black American are you?'" Imani Perry, *Prophets of the Hood: Politics and Poetics in Hip Hop* (Durham: Duke University Press, 2004) 21.

18. Ibid.

19. Public Enemy, "Prophets of Rage," *It Takes a Nation of Millions to Hold Us Back* (New York: Def Jam/ Columbia, 1988).

20. Public Enemy, "Fight the Power," *Do the Right Thing*, Movie soundtrack. Detroit: Motown, 1989.

21. Spike Lee, *Do the Right Thing* (New York: 40 Acres and a Mule, 1989).

22. Public Enemy, music video for "Fight the Power," Movie soundtrack. Detroit: Motown, 1989.

23. Mos Def and Talib Kweli (Black Star), *Black Star* (New York: Rawkus, 1998, 2002).

24. Tony Martin, *Marcus Garvey, Hero: A First Biography* (Dover, MA: Majority Press, 1983) 162.

25. Stanley Nelson, *Marcus Garvey: Look for me in the Whirlwind*, (Arlington, VA: Public Broadcasting Station, 2002).

26. In the documentary film *Look for Me in the Whirlwind* produced by Stanley Nelson, scholars describe how Garvey took on mythological proportions after he emerged strong after the shooting; for more details about the attempted assassination of Marcus Garvey see Joseph H. Bonney, "May the Colored Man Realize that Marcus Garvey is Striving for His Betterment!," *Negro World*, October 25, 1919, in Robert A. Hill, ed., *The Marcus Garvey and Universal Negro Improvement Association Papers* (Durham, NC: Duke University, 2011) 402.

27. Marcus Garvey, "The Conspiracy of the East St. Louis Riots," in *The Marcus Garvey and Universal Negro Improvement Association Papers, Volume I, 1826–August 1919*, ed. Robert A. Hill (Berkeley: University of California Press, 1983).

28. Shirley Chisholm, *Unbought and Unbossed* (Boston: Houghton Mifflin, 1970), 97.

29. Paule Marshall interview by Kay Bonetti, March 1994; Interview with Paule Marshall by Tammy L. Brown, October 28, 2004.

30. Paule Marshall, "From the Poets in the Kitchen," in *Rena and Other Short Stories* (Old Westbury, NY: Feminist Press, 1983), 7.

31. Oscar Handlin, *The Uprooted: The Epic Story of the Great Migration that Makes the American People* (New York: Little Brown and Company, 1951, 1973) 3.

32. Terry Boddie interview for *Black Arts Live!*, curated by Tammy L. Brown.

33. Terry Boddie, email exchange with the author, September 12, 2014.

34. Kristen Clarke, email exchange with the author, September 10, 2014.

35. Ibid.

36. Tammy L. Brown, "Island Fever," *I Ain't Chicken*, Cincinnati, OH: self-published, 1994, 89.

37. Ibid.

38. Shirley Chisholm, *Unbought and Unbossed*, (Boston: Houghton Milton, 1970) 38.

39. See Evelyn Brooks Higginbotham, *Righteous Discontent: The Women's Movement in the Black Baptist Church, 1880–1920* (Cambridge, MA: Harvard University Press, 1993); Kevin Gaines, *Uplifting the Race: Black Leadership, Politics, and Culture in the Twentieth Century* (Chapel Hill: University of North Carolina Press, 1996); Victoria W. Wolcott, *Remaking Respectability: African American Women in Inter-War Detroit* (Chapel Hill: University of North Carolina Press, 2000); E. Frances White, *Dark Continent of Our Bodies: Black Feminism & Politics of Respectability* (Philadelphia: Temple University Press, 2001); Martin Summers, *Manliness and Discontents: The Black Middle Class and the Transformation of Masculinity, 1900–1930* (Chapel Hill: University of North Carolina Press, 2003); Whaley, Deborah Elizabeth. *Discipling Women: Alpha Kappa Alpha, Black Counterpublics, and the Cultural Politics of Black Sororities.* Albany: State University of New York, 2010.

40. Richard J. Herrnstein and Charles Murray, *The Bell Curve: Intelligence and Class Structure in American Life* (New York: Free Press, 1994).

41. David L. Greene and Ethan M. Tucker, "BSA Organizes Rall to Protest 'The Bell Curve,'" *The Harvard Crimson*, November 5, 1994.

42. Ibid.

43. Jennifer Cruté, Guest Lecture at Miami University of Ohio—Oxford, March 19, 2014.

44. Jennifer Cruté interviewed by the author, March 22, 2014.

45. Rahma Athie interview by the author, September 2, 2014.

46. A. B. Christa Schwarz, *Gay Voices of the Harlem Renaissance* (Bloomington: Indiana University Press, 2003) 88.

47. Tammy L. Brown quoted in *Black Arts Live!*, iPhone App, February 2013, produced by the author.

48. Dr. Stefan M. Bradley of the St. Louis University spoke on MSNB regarding the riots in Ferguson, MO, after the shooting of Michael Brown, August 2014.

Bibliography

Adichie, Chimamanda Ngozi. *Americanah*. New York: Random House, 2013. Kindle file.

———. "The Danger of a Single Story." TED Global Conference, March 15, 2009.

Akerman, H. "The Apostate Great-Grandfather and the Pious Grandfather of the Negro Girl of Harlem's Talmud Torah." *Daily Forward*, December 13, 1933.

Anderson, Benedict. *Imagined Communities: Reflections on the Origin and Spread of Nationalism*. London: Verso, 1983.

Appiah, Anthony. *Cosmopolitanism: Ethics in a World of Strangers*. New York: Norton, 2006.

———. *Ethics of Identity*. Princeton: Princeton University Press, 2005.

Bailey, Samuel L. *Immigrants in the Lands of Promise: Italians in Buenos Aires and New York City, 1870–1914*. Ithaca, NY: Cornell University Press, 1999.

Baker, Houston A., Jr. *Afro-American Poetics: Revisions of Harlem and the Black Aesthetic*. Madison: University of Wisconsin Press, 1988.

———. "The Point of Entanglement: Modernism, Diaspora, and Toni Morrison's *Love*." *African and Black Diaspora: An International Journal* 4, no. 1 (January 2011): 1–18.

Baldwin, Davarian. *Chicago's New Negroes: Modernity, the Great Migration, and Black Urban Life*. Chapel Hill: University of North Carolina Press, 2007.

———. *Modernism and the Harlem Renaissance*. Chicago: University of Chicago Press, 1987.

Baldwin, James. *Notes of a Native Son*. Boston: Beacon Press, 2012.

Banks, Ingrid. *Hair Matters: Beauty, Power and Black Women's Consciousness*. New York: New York University Press, 2000.

Barber, Beverly Anne Hillsman. "Pearl Primus in Search of Her Roots: 1943–1970." PhD dissertation, Florida State University, 1984.

Barrett, James R., and David Roediger. "Americanization from the Bottom Up: Immigration and the Remaking of the Working Class in the United States, 1880–1930." *Journal of American History* 79, no. 3 (December 1992): 996–1020.

———. "In Between Peoples: Race, Nationality and the 'New Immigrant' Working Class." *Journal of Ethnic History* 16 (Spring 1997): 2–44.

Bederman, Gail. *Manliness and Civilization: A Cultural History of Gender and Race in the United States, 1880–1917*. Chicago: University of Chicago Press, 1995.

Berry, Jacqueline Carol. "Black Jews: A Study of Status Malintegration and (Multi) Marginality." PhD dissertation, Syracuse University, 1977.

Bhabha, Homi K. *Questions of Cultural Identity*. Thousand Oaks, CA: Sage, 1996.

Biondi, Martha. *To Stand and Fight: The Struggle for Civil Rights in Postwar New York*. Cambridge, MA: Harvard University Press, 2006.

Blackett, Richard J. M. *Beating against the Barriers: The Lives of Six Nineteenth-Century Afro-Americans*. Ithaca, NY: Cornell University Press, 1986.

Bowen, Thomas R. "We are Welcomed by Leading Citizens." *West Indian American* 1, November 1927.

Brooks, Gwendolyn. *Maud Martha*. Chicago: Third World Press, 1993.

Brotz, Howard. "The Black Jews of Harlem." AM thesis, University of Chicago, 1947.

——. *The Black Jews of Harlem: Negro Nationalism and the Dilemmas of Negro Leadership*. New York: Schocken Books, 1970.

Brown, Tamara Mose. *Nannies, Childcare and Caribbeans Creating Community*. New York: New York University Press, 2011.

Brown, Tammy. "Re-Visioning Blackness: West Indian Intellectuals and the Discourse of Identity, New York City, 1920–1980." PhD dissertation, Princeton University, 2007.

——. "'A New Era in American Politics': Shirley Chisholm and the Discourse of Identity." *Callaloo* 31, no. 4 (Fall 2008) 1013–1025.

——. *Black Arts Live!* iPhone app, February 2013.

——. "Art Is a Weapon for Social Change." TEDx Talk, Xavier University, Cincinnati, OH, April 11, 2014.

——. "Island Fever." In *I Ain't Chicken*, Cincinnati, OH: self-published, 1994.

Bryce-Laporte, Roy. "Introduction: New York City and the New Caribbean Immigration: A Contextual Statement." *International Migration Review* 13, no. 2 (Summer 1979): 214–234.

——. "Visibility of the New Immigrants." *Society* 14, no. 6 (1977): 18–22.

Burning Spear. *Marcus Garvey*. New York: Island Records, 1975.

——. *Garvey's Ghost*. New York: Island Records, 1976.

Butterfield, Sherri-Ann Patrice. "Big Tings a Gwaan: Constructions of Racial and Ethnic Identity among Second-Generation West Indian Immigrants." PhD dissertation, University of Michigan, 2001.

——. "Something in Between: Locating Identity among Second-Generation West Indians in New York City." In *Mighty Change, Tall Within: Black Identity in the Hudson Valley*, ed. Myra B. Young Armstead. Albany: State University of New York Press, 2003: 232–262.

Campbell, D'Ann. *Women at War with America: Private Lives in a Patriotic Era*. Cambridge, MA: Harvard University Press, 1984.

Carby, Hazel. *Race Men*. Cambridge, MA: Harvard University Press, 1998.

Carmichael, Stokely (Kwame Ture), with Michael Thelwell. *Ready for Revolution: The Life and Struggles of Stokely Carmichael*. New York: Scribner, 2003.

Carr, Edward Hallett. *What is History?* New York: Vintage Books, 1967.

Carter, Michael. "Pearl Primus Dances Out Social Problems." *Afro-American Baltimore*, July 22, 1944.

Chilton, Karen. *Hazel Scott: The Pioneering Journey of a Jazz Pianist from Café Society to Hollywood to HUAC*. Ann Arbor: University of Michigan Press, 2010.

Chisholm, Shirley. "Esteemed Women: Representative Shirley Chisholm Urges Women to Run for Office." North Hollywood: Center for Cassette Studios, n.d.

——. *The Good Fight*. New York: Harper & Row, 1973.

——. *Unbought and Unbossed*. Boston: Houghton Mifflin, 1970.

"Chisholm Tells Retirees She Still Boogies at 61." *Jet*, June 16, 1986, 27.

Christian, Barbara. *Black Women Novelists: The Development of a Tradition, 1892–1976*. Westport, Conn.: Greenwood Press, 1980.

Chuck D. "Race, Rap and Reality." Lecture at Miami University of Ohio–Hamilton, September 10, 2014.

Cohen, Lizabeth. *Making a New Deal: Industrial Workers in Chicago, 1919–1939*. Cambridge, MA: Harvard University Press, 1990.

Cook, Blanche Wiesen. "Outing History." In *The Seductions of Biography*. London, UK: Routledge, 1996.

Cook, Lisa D. "Converging to a National Lynching Data Base: Recent Developments." East Lansing, MI: Department of Economics, Michigan State University, 2011.

Cooper, Michael, Kate Hammer, Karen James and Matthew Sweeney. "Councilwoman Wins Divisive House Primary." *New York Times*, September 13, 2006.

Craig, Maxine Leeds. *Ain't I A Beauty Queen? Black Women, Beauty, and the Politics of Race*. New York: Oxford University Press, 2002.

Crenshaw, Kimberlé. "Mapping the Margins: Intersectionality, Identity Politics, and Violence against Women of Color." *Stanford Law Review* 43, no. 6 (July 1991): 1241–1299. Creque-Harris, Leah. "The Representation of African Dance on the Concert Stage: From the Early Black Musical to Pearl Primus." PhD dissertation, Emory University, 1991.

Cruse, Harold. *The Crisis of the Negro Intellectual*. New York: Morrow, 1967.

———. *Plural but Equal: A Critical Study of Blacks and Minorities and the American Plural Society*. New York: Morrow, 1987.

———. *Rebellion or Revolution?* New York: Morrow, 1968.

Cruté, Jennifer. Guest Lecture at Miami University of Ohio—Oxford, March 19, 2014.

Dance, Daryl Cumber. "An Interview with Paule Marshall." *Southern Review* 28 (Winter 1992): 1–20.

Davies, Carol Boyce. *Left of Karl Marx: The Political Life of Black Communist Claudia Jones*. Durham: Duke University Press, 2008.

Defrantz, Thomas F. *Dancing Many Drums: Excavations in African American Dance*. Madison, WI: University of Wisconsin Press, 2002.

"Donald McKayle: Teaching Dancers to Dig Deep." *Dance Magazine*, New York: MacFadden Performing Arts Media, LLC., August 2008.

Douglass, Frederick. *My Bondage and My Freedom*. New York: Dover, 1969.

Dorman, Jacob S. *Chosen People: The Rise of American Black Israelite Religions*. New York: Oxford University Press, 2012, Kindle file.

Drake, St. Clair, and Horace R. Cayton. *Black Metropolis: A Study of Negro Life in a Northern City*. Chicago: University of Chicago Press, 1942.

Du Bois, W. E. B. *Black Reconstruction: An Essay toward a History of the Part which Black Folk Played in the attempt to Reconstruct Democracy in America, 1860–1880*. New York: Harcourt, Brace and Company, 1935.

Dudziak, Mary. *Cold War Civil Rights: Race and the Image of American Democracy*. Princeton: Princeton University Press, 2000.

Dunning, Jennifer. "Pearl Primus Dancing Indoors and Out." *New York Times*, August 17, 1979. E. A. G. "Pearl Primus." *Dance Observer*, July 1946.

Edwards, Brent Hayes. *The Practice of Diaspora: Literature, Translation, and the Rise of Black Internationalism*. Cambridge, MA: Harvard University Press, 2003.

Elkins, Stanley. *Slavery: A Problem in American Institutional and Intellectual Life*. 2nd ed. Chicago: University of Chicago Press, 1969.

Evans, Jessica, and Stuart Hall, ed. *Visual Culture: The Reader*. Thousand Oaks, CA: Sage Publications, 1999.

Fauset, Arthur Huff. *Black Gods of the Metropolis: Negro Religious Cults of the Urban North*. Philadelphia: University of Pennsylvania Press, 1944.

Feimster, Crystal. *Southern Horrors: Women and the Politics of Rape and Lynching*, Cambridge, MA: Harvard University Press, 2011.

Fields, Barbara J. "Whiteness, Racism, and Identity." *International Labor and Working-Class History* 60 (2001): 48–56.

Floyd-Thomas, Juan M. *The Origins of Black Humanism in America: Reverend Ethelred Brown and the Unitarian Church*. New York: Palgrave MacMillan, 2008.

Foner, Nancy. "West Indian Identity in the Diaspora: Comparative and Historical Perspectives." *Latin American Perspectives* 25, no. 3 (1998): 173–88.

——. *Islands in the City: West Indian Migration to New York*. Berkeley and Los Angeles: University of California Press, 2001.

"For Congress in Brooklyn." *The New York Times*. New York, NY, August 30, 2006.

Friedman, Susan Stanford. "Women's Autobiographical Selves: The Theory and Practice." In *The Private Self: Theory and Practice in Women's Autobiographical Writing*. Edited by Shari Benstock. Chapel Hill: University of North Carolina Press, 1988. 34–63.

Garvey, Marcus. "*Home to Harlem*, Claude McKay's Damaging Book Should Earn Wholesale Condemnation of Negroes." *Negro World*, September 29, 1928.

Gates, Henry Louis. "Writing 'Race' and the Difference It Makes." In *"Race," Writing, and Difference*. Chicago: University of Chicago Press Journals, 1992.

——. *The Norton Anthology of African American Literature*, 2nd edition. New York: W. W. Norton & Company, 2003.

Gordon-Reed, Annette. *The Hemingses of Monticello: An American Family*. New York: W.W. Norton, 2008.

Griffin, Farah Jasmine. *Who Set You Flowin'? The African-American Migration Narrative*. New York: Oxford University Press, 1995.

——. *If You Can't be Free, be a Mystery: In Search of Billie Holiday*. New York: The Free Press, 2001.

——. *Harlem Nocturne: Women Artists and Progressive Politics During World War II*. New York: Basic Civitas Books, 2013.

Gaines, Kevin. *Uplifting the Race: Black Leadership, Politics, and Culture in the Twentieth Century*. Chapel Hill: University of North Carolina Press, 1996.

Gardell, Mattias. *In the Name of Elijah Muhammad: Louis Farrakhan and the Nation of Islam*. Durham, N.C.: Duke University Press, 1996.

Gaynell, Elgie. "The Dance Griots: An Examination of the Dance Pedagogy of Katherine Dunham and Black Pioneering Dancers in Chicago and New York City, from 1931–1946." Ed.D. dissertation, Temple University, 1998.

Genovese, Eugene D. *Roll, Jordan, Roll: The World the Slaves Made*. New York: Pantheon Books, 1974.

Gilman, Sander. *Jewish Frontiers: Essays on Bodies, Histories, and Identities*. New York: Palgrave Macmillan, 2003.

———. *The Jew's Body*. New York: Routledge, 1991.

Gilroy, Paul. *Against Race: Imagining Political Culture beyond the Color Line*. Cambridge, MA: Harvard University Press, 2000.

———. *Between Camps: Nations, Cultures and the Allure of Race*. New York: Routledge, 2000.

———. *The Black Atlantic: Modernity and Double Consciousness*. Cambridge, MA: Harvard University Press, 1993.

Glaude, Eddie. *Exodus! Religion, Race, and Nation in Early Nineteenth-Century Black America*. Chicago: University of Chicago Press, 2000.

Glover, Jean Ruth. "Pearl Primus: Cross-cultural Pioneer of American Dance." M.A. thesis, American University, 1989.

Gold, Michael. *Jews Without Money*. New York: Liveright, 1930.

Goodman, Ezra. "Hard Time Blues." *Dance*, April 1946.

Gorlin, Deborah. "Dance Is the Fist." *UMASSmag Online*, Spring 2003.

Grant, Colin. *Negro with a Hat: The Rise and Fall of Marcus Garvey*. Oxford: Oxford University Press, 2008.

Green, Richard C. "Pearl Primus and 'The Negro Problem' in American Dance." *UCLA Journal of Dance Ethnology*, 19 (1995): 68–76.

Greene, David L. and Ethan M. Tucker, "BSA Organizes Rall to Protest 'The Bell Curve,' *The Harvard Crimson*, November 5, 1994.

Greer, Christina M. "Black Ethnicity: Identity, Participation, and Policy." PhD dissertation, Columbia University, 2008.

Greer, Christina M. *Black Ethnics: Race, Immigration and the Pursuit of the American Dream*. Oxford: Oxford University Press, 2013.

Griffin, Farah Jasmine. *Who Set You Flowin'? The African-American Migration Narrative*. New York: Oxford University Press, 1995.

Griffith, R. Marie. "Body Salvation: New Thought, Father Divine, and the Feast of Material Pleasures." *Religion and American Culture* 11, no. 2 (Summer 2001): 119–53.

———. *Born Again Bodies: Flesh and Spirit in American Christianity*. Berkeley: University of California Press, 2004.

Gross, Ben. "Listening In." *Daily News*, August 30, 1945.

Gore, Dayo F. *Radicalism at the Crossroads: African American Women Activists in the Cold War*. New York: New York University Press, 2011.

Guild, Joshua Bruce. "You can't go home again: Migration, citizenship, and black community in postwar New York and London (England)." PhD dissertation, Yale University, 2007.

Gutierrez, David G. *Walls and Mirrors: Mexican Americans, Mexican Immigrants, and the Politics of Ethnicity*. Berkeley: University of California Press, 1995.

Haley, Alex. *The Autobiography of Malcolm X*. New York: Ballantine Books, 1964.

Hall, Constantine. "Paule Marshall Gains Literary Fame." *West Indian-American*, October 1959.

Hall, Stuart, ed. *Representation: Cultural Representations and Signifying.* Thousand Oaks, CA: Sage Publications, 1997).

Hall, Stuart, and Paul du Gay, eds. *Questions of Cultural Identity.* Thousand Oaks, CA: Sage Publications, 1996.

Hammond, Sally. "Spreading the Heritage." *New York Post*, March 27, 1969.

Handlin, Oscar. *The Uprooted: The Epic Story of the Great Migration that Makes the American People.* New York: Little Brown and Company, 1951, 1973.

"Harlem Pastor Founder of Community Church Works Seven Days a Week as Elevator Boy." *New York Home News*, October 1, 1922.

Haskins, James. *Black Dance in America: A History Through Its People.* New York: Harper Trophy, 1990.

Higashida, Cheryl. *Black Internationalist Feminism.* : Urbana: University of Illinois Press, 2011.

Haygood, Will. *King of the Cats: The Life and Times of Adam Clayton Powell, Jr.* Boston, New York: Houghton Mifflin, 1993.

Haywood, Harry. *Black Bolshevik: Autobiography of an Afro-American Communist.* Chicago: Liberator Press, 1978.

Hellbeck, Jochen. *Revolution on my Mind: Writing a Diary Under Stalin.* Cambridge, MA: Harvard University Press, 2009.

———. "The Diary between Literature and History—A Historian's Critical Response." *Russian Review* 63, no. 4 (Oct 2004): 621.

Hentoff, Nat. "An Inheritance Comes to PS 83." *American Education* 2, no. 2 (1966): 28–32.

Hering, Doris. "'Little Fast Feet': The Story of a Pilgrimage of Pearl Primus to Africa." *Dance,* July 1950, 22.

———. "Pearl Primus and Her Company." *Dance Magazine*, March 1956, 75.

———. "Pearl Primus YM-YWHA Dance Center, April 11, 1948." *Dance*, July 1948, 41.

———. "Percival Borde and Company." *Dance Magazine*, December 1958, 13.

Herrnstein, Richard J. and Charles Murray. *The Bell Curve: Intelligence and Class Structure in American Life.* New York: Free Press, 1994.

Hicks, Cheryl, *Talk with You Like a Woman: African American Women, Justice, and Reform in New York, 1890–1935.* Chapel Hill: University of North Carolina Press, 2010.

Hicks, Jonathan "In Her Mother's Footsteps, Now in Shirley's Chisholm's, Too." *New York Times*, September 14, 2006.

Higginbotham, Evelyn Brooks. *Righteous Discontent: The Women's Movement in the Black Baptist Church, 1880–1920.* Cambridge, MA: Harvard University Press, 1993.

Higham, John. *Strangers in the Land: Patterns of American Nativism, 1860–1925.* New Brunswick, NJ: Rutgers University Press, 1994.

Hill, Robert A., ed. *The Marcus Garvey and Universal Negro Improvement Association Papers.* Durham, NC: Duke University, 2011.

Hoffnung-Garskof, Jesse. "The Migrations of Arturo Schomburg: On Being Antilliano, Negro, and Puerto Rican in New York 1891–1938." *Journal of American Ethnic History* 21, no. 1, November 2001.

Holder, Calvin. "The Causes and Compositions of West Indian Immigration to New York City, 1900–1952." *Afro-Americans in New York Life and History*, January 1987.

Holub, Johannes. *The New Dance Group Gala Concert: An Historic Retrospective of New Dance Group Presentations 1930s–1970s*. New York: American Dance Guild, 1994.

Hoshor, John. *God in a Rolls Royce*. New York: Hillman-Curl, 1936.

Hughes, Langston. *I Wonder as I Wander: An Autobiographical Journey*. New York: Hill and Wang, 1993.

Ifatunji, Mosi Adesina. "Are Black Immigrants A Model Minority?: Race, Ethnicity and Social Inequality in the United States." PhD dissertation, University of Illinois at Chicago, 2011.

Ignatiev, Noel. *How the Irish Became White*. New York: Routledge, 1995.

Isay, David. "I Did Not Join the Hebrew Faith—I Returned." *New York Times Magazine*, September 26, 1999.

Jacobson, Matthew Frye. *Whiteness of a Different Color: European Immigrants and the Alchemy of Race*. Cambridge, MA: Harvard University Press, 1998.

James, C. L. R. *The Black Jacobins: Toussaint L'Ouverture and the San Domingo Revolution*. New York: Dial Press, 1938.

———. "'My Friends': A Fireside Chat on the War by Native Son." In *C. L. R. James on the "Negro Question."* Edited by Scott McLemee. Jackson: University Press of Mississippi, 1996. 17–22.

James, Winston. "Explaining Afro-Caribbean Social Mobility in the United States: Beyond the Sowell Thesis." *Comparative Studies in Society and History* 44, no. 2 (2002): 218–62.

———. *Holding Aloft the Banner of Ethiopia: Caribbean Radicalism in Early Twentieth-Century America*. New York: Verso, 1998.

Jhally, Sut. *Race: The Floating Signifier*. Videocassette. Northampton, MA: Media Education Foundation, 1996.

———. *Representation and the Media*. Videocassette. Northampton, MA: Media Education Foundation, 1997.

Johnson, James Weldon. *Black Manhattan*. New York: Knopf, 1930.

Jones, Claudia. *Jim Crow in Uniform*. New York: New Age Publishers, 1940.

Josephson, Barney and Terry Trilling-Josephson. *Café Society: The Wrong Place for the Right People*. Champaign: University of Illinois Press, 2009.

Kasinitz, Philip. *Caribbean New York: Black Immigrants and the Politics of Race*. Ithaca, NY: Cornell University Press, 1992.

Kelley, Robin D.G. *Hammer and Hoe: Alabama Communists during the Great Depression*. Chapel Hill: University of North Carolina Press, 1990.

Kelley, Robin. *Race Rebels: Culture, Politics, and the Black Working Class*. New York: Free Press, 1994.

Kelly, Robin D.G. and Tiffany Ruby Patterson. "Unfinished Migrations: Reflections on the African Diaspora and the Makings of the Modern World." *African Studies Review* 43, no. 1, Special Issue on the diaspora (April 2000), 11–45.

Kessler-Harris, Alice. "Why Biography?" *American Historical Review* 114, no. 3 (June 2009).

Kirk, Christina. "The Silent Minority." *Sunday News*, April 19, 1970.

Kisselgoff, Anna. "Pearl Primus Rejoices in the Black Tradition." *New York Times*, June 19, 1988.

Knight, Franklin W., and Colin A. Palmer, eds. *The Modern Caribbean*. Chapel Hill: University of North Carolina Press, 1989.

Kronen, H. B. "Five Colleges Praise Primus." *Dance Magazine*, June 2002.

Lacy, Madison D. *Free to Dance*. DVD. New York: National Black Programming Consortium, 2001.

LaBennett, Oneka. *She's Mad Real: Popular Culture and West Indian Girls in Brooklyn*. New York: New York University Press, 2011.

Landing, James E. *Black Judaism: Story of an American Movement*. Durham, N.C.: Carolina Academic Press, 2002.

Law, Robin and Paul E. Lovejoy, eds. *The Biography of Mahommah Gardo Basquaqua: His Passage from Slavery to Freedom in Africa and America*. Princeton, NJ: Markus Wiener Publishers, 2007.

Lears, T. Jackson. *No Place of Grace: Antimodernism and the Transformation of American Culture, 1880–1920*. Chicago: University of Chicago Press, 1981.

Lee, Chang-rae. *Native Speaker*. New York: Riverhead Books, 1995.

Lee, Spike. *Do the Right Thing*. New York: 40 Acres and a Mule, 1989.

Lepore, Jill. "Historians Who Love Too Much: Reflections on Microhistory and Biography" *The Journal of American History* 88, no. 1 (June 2001).

Levering Lewis, David. "The Autobiography of Biography." Public Lecture, City University of New York, New York, NY, September 18, 2013.

———. "The Autobiography of Biography." *American Scholar* 83, no. 3 (Summer 2014).

———. "The Dialectics of History: An Interview with David Levering Lewis." *Political Affairs*, 2004. http://www.politicalaffairs.net/the-dialectics-of-history-an-interview-with-david-levering-lewis/

———. *When Harlem Was in Vogue*. New York: Knopf, 1981.

Locke, Alain. *The New Negro*. New York: Atheneum, 1992.

Locke, Alaine, ed. *The New Negro*. New York: Boni, 1925.

Lodge, Sally. "Paule Marshall." In *Writing for Your Life*, edited by Sybil Steinberg. New York: Pushcart Press, 1992.

Lorde, Audre. *Sister Outside: Essays and Speeches*. Trumansburg, NY: Crossing Press, 1984.

Lounds, Morris, Jr. "Hebrew Israelites/Black Jews: A Case Study in the Formation of Group Identity." PhD dissertation, Massachusetts Institute of Technology, 1976.

Lovejoy, Paul E. "Biography as Source Material: Towards a Biographical Archive of Enslaved African,'" In *Source Material for Studying the Slave Trade and the African Diaspora*, edited by Robin Law. Stirling, 1997.

Luker, Ralph. *The Social Gospel in Black and White: American Radical Reform, 1885–1912*. Chapel Hill: University of North Carolina Press, 1991.

Lurie, Alison. *The Language of Clothes*. New York: Henry Holt, 2001.

Lynch, Shola. *Chisholm '72—Unbought and Unbossed*. DVD. Beverly Hills: Twentieth Century Fox Home Entertainment, 2004.

Makalani, Minkah. *In the Cause of Freedom: Radical Black internationalism from Harlem to London, 1917–1939*. Chapel Hill: University of North Carolina Press, 2011.

Marable, Manning. *Malcolm X: A Life of Reinvention*. New York: Penguin Books, 2011.

Marley, Ziggy and the Melody Makers. "What's True?" *Conscious Party*. Virgin Records, 1988.

Marshall, Paule. *Brown Girl, Brownstones*. New York: Feminist Press, 1959.

——. *The Chosen Place, the Timeless People*. New York: Vintage, 1964.

——. *Daughters*. New York: Athenaeum, 1991.

——. *The Fisher King*. New York: Scribner, 2000.

——. "The Negro Woman in Literature." *Freedomways* 4 (First Quarter 1966), 20–25.

——. *Praisesong for the Widow*. New York: Dutton, 1984.

——. *Rena and Other Short Stories*. Old Westbury, NY: Feminist Press, 1983.

——. "Shaping the World of My Art." *New Letters* 40, no. 1 (October 1973): 97–112

——. *Soul Clap Hands and Sing*. Washington, DC: Howard University Press, 1961.

——. *Triangular Road: A Memoir*. New York: Basic Civitas Books, 2009.

Marshall, Paule, and Maryse Condé. "Return of a Native Daughter: An Interview with Paule Marshall and Maryse Condé." *SAGE: A Scholarly Journal on Black Women* 3, no. 2 (Fall 1986): 52.

Martin, John. "The Dance: Five Artists." *New York Times*, February 21, 1943.

——. "Pearl Primus." *Current Biography*, 1944, 553.

Martin, Tony. *Marcus Garvey, Hero: A First Biography*. Dover, MA: Majority Press, 1983.

——. *The Pan-African Connection*. Dover: Majority Press, 1984.

Matthew, Rabbi Wentworth A. "The Root and Inception of the House of Israel." *Impact*, October 1968.

——. "The Truth about Black Jews and Judaism in America, Part V." *New York Age*, June 14, 1958.

Maynes, Mary Jo, Jennifer L. Pierce, and Barbara Laslett. *Telling Stories: The Use of Personal Narratives in the Social Sciences and History*. Ithica, NY: Cornell Unversity Press, 2008, Kindle file.

McClintock, Anne. *Imperial Leather: Race, Gender and Sexuality in the Colonial Contest*. New York: Routledge, 1995.

McDuffie, Erik S. *Sojourning for Freedom: Black Women, American Communism, and the Making of the Black Left Feminism*. Durham: Duke University Press, 2011.

Mc Kay, Claude. *Home to Harlem*. Harper & Brothers and Lebanon, NJ: Northeastern University Press, 1928, 1987.

——. *Harlem Shadows: The Poems of Claude McKay*. New York: Harcourt, Brace and Co., 1922.

Mercer, Kobena. *Welcome to the Jungle: New Positions in Black Cultural Studies*. New York: Routledge, 1994.

Model, Suzanne. *West Indian Immigrants: A Black Success Story?* New York: Russell Sage Foundation, 2011.

Moore, Richard B. "The Critics and Opponents of Marcus Garvey." In *Marcus Garvey and the Vision of Africa*, edited by John Henrik Clarke. 210–236. New York: Vintage Books, 1973. 210–236.

Morgan, Edwin. "American Art at Mid-Century." *American Quarterly* 1, no. 4 (Winter, 1949): 326–330.

Morrison, Toni. "Nobel Prize Lecture." December 7, 1993.

——. "Unspeakable Things Unspoken: The Afro-American Presence in Literature." In *The Tanner Lectures on Human Values*. Ann Arbor, MI: University of Michigan, October 7, 1988.

———. *Beloved*. New York: Random House, 1987.

Morrison-Reed, Mark D. *Black Pioneers in a White Denomination*. Boston, MA: Skinner House Books, 1994.

Mos Def and Talib Kweli (Black Star), *Black Star*. New York: Rawkus, 1998, 2002.

Moynihan, Daniel. *The Negro Family: The Case for National Action*. Washington, DC: US Government Printing Office, 1965.

Naison, Mark. *Communists in Harlem During the Depression*. Urbana: University of Illinois Press, 1983.

"Negro Sect in Harlem Mixes Jewish and Christian Religions." *New York Sun*, January 29, 1929.

Nelson, Stanley. *Marcus Garvey: Look for me in the Whirlwind*. Arlington, VA: Public Broadcasting Station, 2002.

Nettleford, Rex. *Caribbean Cultural Identity: The Case of Jamaica*. Kingston: Ian Randle, 2003.

———. *Mirror Mirror: Identity, Race and Protest in Jamaica*. Kingston: LMH Publishing, 1998.

"N.Y. Negro Jews Aid Anti-Nazi Drive Abroad." *Philadelphia Tribune*, February 1, 1934.

Orsi, Robert Anthony. *Gods of the City: Religion and the American Urban Landscape*. Bloomington: Indiana University Press, 1999.

———. *The Madonna of 115th Street: Faith and Community in Italian Harlem, 1880–1950*. New Haven: Yale University Press, 1985.

Osofsky, Gilbert. *Harlem: The Making of a Ghetto: Negro New York, 1890–1930*. New York: Harper Torchbook, 1964.

Ottley, Roi. *New World A-Coming: Inside Black America*. Boston: Houghton Mifflin, 1943.

Owens, Irma Watkins. *Blood Relations: Caribbean Immigrants and the Harlem Community, 1900–1903*. Bloomington: Indiana University Press, 1996.

Pace, William E. "We are Welcomed by Leading Citizens." *West Indian American*, November 1927.

Painter, Nell Irvin. *Exodusters: Black Migration to Kansas after Reconstruction*. New York: Norton, 1976.

———. *Sojourner Truth: A Life, A Symbol*. New York: Norton, 1996.

———. "Soul Murder." *Southern History Across the Color Line*. Hapel Hill: University of North Carolina Press, 2002.

Painter, Nell Irvin, ed. *The Narrative of Hosea Hudson: The Life and Times of a Black Radical*. New York: Norton, 1994.

Palmer, Howard. "Mosaic versus Melting Pot? Immigration and Ethnicity in Canada and the United States. *International Journal* 31, no. 3 (1976): 488–528.

Paperno, Irina. "What Can Be Done with Diaries?" *Russian Review* 63, no. 4 (October 2004): 573.

"Pearl Primus and Company in 'Dark Rhythms.'" *Dance*, December 1951.

"Pearl Primus, Ph.D. Returns." *New York Times*, March 18, 1979.

"Pearl Turns to Africa." *Picture Post*, London November 14, 1951.

Peiss, Kathy. *Hope in a Jar: The Making of America's Beauty Culture*. Philadelphia: University of Pennsylvania, 1998.

Pellegrini, Ann. *Performance Anxieties: Staging Psychoanalysis, Staging Race*. New York: Routledge, 1997.

Perpener, John O., III. "The Seminal Years of Black Concert Dance." PhD dissertation, New York University, 1992.

Perry, Imani. *Prophets of the Hood: Politics and Poetics in Hip Hop*. Durham: Duke University Press, 2004.

Pettis, Joyce. "A Melus Interview: Paule Marshall." *Melus*, 17, no. 4 (Winter 1991–92).

Public Enemy. "Prophets of Rage." *It Takes a Nation of Millions to Hold Us Back*. New York: Def Jam/Columbia, 1988.

———. "Fight the Power." *Do the Right Thing*. Film soundtrack. Detroit: Motown, 1989.

Plummer, Brenda Gayle. *Rising Wind: Black Americans and U.S. Foreign Affairs, 1935–1960*. Chapel Hill: University of North Carolina Press, 1996.

Plunz, Richard. *A History of Housing in New York City*. New York: Columbia University Press, 1990.

Pollard, John Bud, *The Black King*, Bridgeport, CT: Synergy Entertainment,1932, 2006.

Portes, Alejandro and Alex Stepick. *City on the Edge: The Transformation of Miami*. Berkeley: University of California Press, 1993.

Powell Jr., Adam Clayton. *Adam by Adam: The Autobiography of Adam Clayton Powell, Jr.* New York: Daphina Books, 1971.

"Powel and Hazel Scott Buy on Riverside Drive." *New York Times*, March 27, 1946, 45.

"Powell Weds Scott: 3,000 New Yorkers Honor the Marriage of Harlem's Preacher-Politician to a Beautiful Hot Piano Player." *Life* magazine, August 13, 1945.

Primus, Pearl. "Africa." *Dance Magazine*, March 1958, 45–46.

———. "An Anthropological Study of Masks as Teaching Aids in the Enculturation of Mano Children." PhD dissertation, New York University, 1978.

———. "The New Dance Group Gala Concert: A Historic Retrospective of New Dance Group Presentations, 1930s–1970s." *American Dance Guild*, 1994.

———. "Pearl Primus Thrills Broadway." *Daily Worker*, New York, Saturday 7, 1944.

———. "Profile." *Ebony*, January 1951, 54.

Lara Putnam, *Radical Moves: Caribbean Migrants and the Politics of Race in the Jazz Age*. Chapel Hill: University of North Carolina Press, 2013.

Raboteau, Albert J. *Fire in the Bones: Reflections on African-American Religious History*. Boston: Beacon Press, 1995.

———. *Slave Religion: The "Invisible Institution" in the Antebellum South*. New York: Oxford University Press, 1978.

Rampersad, Arnold. "Design and Truth in Biography." *South Central Modern Language Association Review* 9, no. 2 (Summer 1992).

Ransby, Barbara. *Ella Baker and the Black Freedom Movement: A Radical Democratic Vision*. Chapel Hill: University of North Carolina Press, 2005.

Reid, Ira DeAugustine. *The Negro Immigrant: His Background, Characteristics and Social Adjustment, 1899–1937*. New York: Columbia University Press, 1939.

"Rev. Ethelred Brown is Symbol of Radicalism in Pulpits in Harlem." *Daily Gleaner*, January 20, 1934.

Rice, Vernon. "A Real Pearl." *New York Post*, August 13, 1950.

"Riffing on the Primus Legacy." *Five Colleges: The Consortium Update*, January 2003.

Rimer, Sara, and Karen W. Arenson. "Top Colleges Take More Blacks, but Which Ones?" *New York Times*, June 24, 2004.

Robinson, Cedrick. *Black Marxism: The Making of the Black Radical Tradition*. London: Zed Press, 1983.

Rodgers, Daniel T. *Atlantic Crossings: Social Politics in a Progressive Age*. Cambridge, MA: Harvard University Press, 1998.

Roediger, David. *Wages of Whiteness: Race and the Making of the American Working Class*. London: Verso, 1991.

Roach, Max. "Garvey's Ghost." *Percussion Bittersweet*. New York, NY: Impulse! 1961, 1993.

Rogers, Reuel. *Afro-Caribbean Immigrants and the Politics of Incorporation: Ethnicity, Exception, or Exit*. Cambridge, UK: Cambridge University Press, 2006.

Rubinstein, Ruth *Dress Codes: Meanings and Messages in American Culture*. Boulder: Westview Press, 1995.

Rushdie, Salman. *Imaginary Homelands: Essays and Criticism 1981–1991*. London: Granta Books, 1991.

Rydell, Robert W. *All the World's a Fair: Visions of Empire at American International Expositions, 1876–1916*. Chicago: University of Chicago Press, 1984.

Safier, Arno. "Dual Minority Status: Group Identification and Membership Conflict—A Study of Black Jews." PhD dissertation, New York University, 1971.

Said, Edward W. *Orientalism*. New York: Pantheon Books, 1978.

Sanchez, George. *Becoming Mexican American: Ethnicity, Culture, and Identity in Chicano Los Angeles, 1900–1945*. Oxford: Oxford University Press, 1993.

Satter, Beryl. "Marcus Garvey, Father Divine and the Gender Politics of Race Difference and Race Neutrality." *American Quarterly* 48, no. 1 (1996): 43–76.

Schwarz, A. B. Christa. *Gay Voices of the Harlem Renaissance*. Bloomington: Indiana University Press, 2003.

Schwartz, Peggy and Murray. *The Dance Claimed Me: A Biography of Pearl Primus*. New Haven: Yale University Press, 2011.

Scott, James C. *Weapons of the Weak: Everyday Forms of Peasant Resistance*. New Haven: Yale University Press, 1985.

Shapiro, Deanne Ruth. "Double Damnation, Double Salvation: The Sources and Varieties of Black Judaism in the United States." PhD dissertation, Columbia University, 1969.

Smith, Anthony D. S. *Nationalism in the Twentieth Century*. Oxford: Martin Robertson, 1979.

Smith, Bruce W. *The Proud Family Movie*. Los Angeles: Disney Enterprises, Inc., 2005.

Smith, Valerie. *Not Race, Not Gender: Black Feminist Readings*. New York: Routledge, 1998.

Spiegel, Lynn. *Make Room for TV: Television and the Family Ideal in Postwar America*. Chicago: University of Chicago Press, 1992.

Spivak, Gayatri Chakravorty. "Can the Subaltern Speak?" In *Marxism and the Interpretation of Culture*, Cary Nelson and Lawrence Grossberg, eds. Urbana: University of Illinois Press, 1988. 271–317.

Stansell, Christine. *American Moderns: Bohemian New York and the Creation of a New Century*. New York: Henry Holt, 2000.

Steel Pulse. "Worth His Weight in Gold (Rally Round)." *True Democracy* (Arathus, Denmark: "Feedback" Studios, 1981).

Steiner, Ralph. "Rare Pictures of N. Y. Ethiopian Hebrews Go on Exhibition." *New York Post*, December 8, 1940.

Takaki, Ronald. *Strangers from a Different Shore: A History of Asian Americans.* Boston: Little, Brown, 1989.

Taylor, Charles. "The Politics of Recognition." In *Multiculturalism*, edited by Amy Gutman. Princeton: Princeton University Press, 1994. 25–75.

Taylor, Ula Y. *The Veiled Garvey: The Life and Times of Amy Jacques Garvey.* Chapel Hill: University of North Carolina Press, 2002.

Terry, Walter. *New York Herald Tribune*, New York Public Library Performance Arts Pearl Primus Clippings File. No date.

Tillery, Alvin and Michelle Chresfield. "Model Blacks or 'Ras the Exhorter': A Quantitative Content Analysis of Black Newspapers' Coverage of the First Wave of Afro-Caribbean Immigration to the United States." *Journal of Black Studies* 43, no. 5 (July 2012): 545–570.

Timothy Tyson. *Radio Free Dixie: Robert F. Williams & the Roots of Black Power.* Chapel Hill: University of North Carolina Press, 1999.

Tuma, Keith. *Fishing by Obstinate Isles: Modern and Postmodern British Poetry and American Readers.* Chicago: Northwestern University Press, 1998.

Turner, Joyce Moore. *Caribbean Crusaders and the Harlem Renaissance.* Urbana: University of Illinois Press, 2005.

Turner, Richard B. *Islam in the African-American Experience.* Bloomington: Indiana University Press, 1997.

Tyson, Timothy B. "Robert F. Williams and the Promise of Southern Biography." Unpublished MS.

Van Deburg, William L. *New Day in Babylon: The Black Power Movement and American Culture, 1965–1975.* Chicago: University of Chicago Press, 1992.

Verdelle, A. J. *The Good Negress.* New York: Harper Perennial, 1996.

Vickerman, Milton. *Crosscurrents: West Indian Immigrants and Race.* New York: Oxford University Press, 1999.

Vincent, Ted. *Keep Cool: The Black Activists Who Built the Jazz Age.* London: Pluto Press, 1995.

Von Eschen, Penny. *Race Against Empire: Black Americans and Anticolonialism, 1937–1957.* Ithaca, NY: Cornell University Press, 1997.

Walters, Ronald. *Pan-Africanism in the African Diaspora: An Analysis of Modern Afro-centric Political Movements.* Detroit: Wayne State University Press, 1993.

Ward, J. R. *Poverty and Progress in the Caribbean, 1800–1969.* Houndmills, UK: Macmillan, 1985.

Waters, Mary C. *Black Identities: West Indian Immigrant Dreams and American Realities.* Cambridge, MA: Harvard University Press, 1999.

Watts, Jill. *God, Harlem U.S.A.: The Father Divine Story.* Berkeley: University of California Press, 1992.

Watts, Phyllis. "The Dance." *Boston Globe*, Saturday, January 18, 1947.

———. "The Dance, Jorand Hall, Pearl Primus." *Boston Daily Globe*, January 20, 1947.

Wells, Ida B. *Southern Horrors: Lynch Law in all its Phases*, pamphlet, 1892.

———. *Crusade for Justice: The Autobiography of Ida B. Wells*, Chicago: University of Chicago Press, 1970, Kindle file, 411.

Weisbrot, Robert. *Father Divine and the Struggle for Racial Equality*. Urbana: University of Illinois Press, 1983.

Williams, Anne. "Unconquerable." *Off Our Backs* 4, no. 2 (December–January, 1974): 3.

Williams, Walter. *Black Americans and the Evangelization of Africa: 1877–1900*. Madison: University of Wisconsin Press, 1982.

Winslow, Barbara. *Shirley Chisholm: Catalyst for Change*. Philadelphia: Westview Press, 2014.

"Women Who Made It." *Off Our Backs*, November 30, 1972.

Wyman, Mark. *Round-Trip to America: The Immigrants Return to Europe, 1880–1930*. Ithaca, NY: Cornell University Press, 1993.

Yuan-yin Hsu, Madeline. *Dreaming of Gold, Dreaming of Home: Transnational Migration between the U.S. and South China, 1882–1943*. Stanford: Stanford University Press, 2000.

X-Clan, "Heed the Word of the Brother." New York: 4th & Broadway, 1990.

Zangwill, Israel. *The Melting-Pot: Drama in Four Acts*. New York: Macmillan, 1923.

Manuscript Sources

Atlanta, Georgia
    Emory University Robert W. Woodruff Library Special Collections
      Father Divine Papers
      Theodore Draper Papers

Brooklyn, New York
    The Shirley Chisholm Project at Brooklyn College, City University of New York

Cambridge, Massachusetts
    Unitarian Universalist Association Archives, Andover-Harvard Theological Library, Harvard Divinity School, Harvard University
      Egbert Ethelred Brown papers
      Samuel A. Elliot papers

Durham, North Carolina
    Duke University Special Collections
      Pearl Primus Papers in the American Dance Festival archive

New Brunswick, New Jersey
    Rutgers University Special Collections
      Shirley Chisholm Papers
New York, New York
    Schomburg Research Center in Black Culture

Beth Ha-Tefilah Ethiopian Hebrew Congregation, Inc. Record
Black Jews Clippings File
Commandment Keepers File
Dowridge Challenor Papers
Egbert Ethelred Brown Papers
Harlem Community Church Papers
Claudia Jones Papers
Richard B. Moore papers
New York Public Library Lincoln Center
Pearl Primus Dance Clipping File

Stanford, California
Stanford University Cecil H. Green Library Special Collections
Stokely Carmichael Papers

Interviews

Bonetti, Kay. Interview with Paule Marshall, March 1994.
Brown, Tammy. Rahma Athie interview by the author, September 2, 2014.
——. Interview with Terry Boddie, February 1, 2013.
——. Email exchange with Terry Boddie, September 12, 2014
——. Interview with Chuck D, September 10, 2014.
——. Interview with George Clarke, April 6, 2006.
——. Email exchange Kristen Clarke, September 10, 2014.
——. Interview with Jennifer Cruté, March 22, 2014.
——. Interview with Rosalie Fletcher, April XX, 2006.
——. Email exchange with Noel Ignatiev, March 23, 2006.
——. Interview with Oneka LaBennet, July 24, 2014.
——. Interview with Daryl McMillan, April 6, 2006.
——. Interview with Ulon McMillan, March 24, 2006.
——. Interview with Maise Henry, April 25, 2006.
——. Interview with Paule Marshall, October 28, 2004.
——. Interview with Mary Phillips, March 23, 2006.
——. Interview with Adam Clayton Powell III, August 22, 2011.
——. Interview with Peggy and Murray Schwartz, September 24, 2012.
——. Interview with Joyce Moore Turner, October 9, 2006.
——. Interview with Rabbi Zechariah Lewi, March 25, 2006.
——. Email exchange with Jawole Willa Jo Zollar, August 23, 2014.
Conan, Neal. "Analysis: Seeing Our World through Fiction and the Experience of Immigrants." Interview with Edwige Danticat. *Talk of the Nation*, July 1, 2004.
Murray, James Briggs. Interview with Pearl Primus. June 19, 1993. Videocassette. New York: Schomburg Research Center in Black Culture.

Nash, Joe. Interview with Marie Brooks. Audiocassette. New York: Dance Collection of the New York Public Library of Performing Arts, 1995.

Perron, Wendy. Inteview with Joe Nash, November 9 and 11, 1999. New York: Dance Collection of the New York Public Library of Performing Arts.

Simeone, Lisa. "Interview: Paule Marshall Discusses her Book, 'The Fisher King.'" *All Things Considered*, January 7, 2001.

Sinnette, Elinor Des Verney. *Arthur Alfonso Schomburg: Black Bibliophile and Collector.* Detroit: Wayne State University Press, 1989.

Swain, Donald. Interview with Paule Marshall. CBS Radio, 1991.

Terry, Walter. Interview with Pearl Primus. February 15, 1953. Audiocassette. New York: Dance Collection of the New York Public Library of Performing Arts.

Vitale, Tom. "'Daughters:' Book about African-American Woman." *Morning Edition*, January 6, 1992.

Warren, Nicole. "Five Questions for Paule Marshall." November 17, 2003.

Whaley, Deborah Elizabeth. *Discipling Women: Alpha Kappa Alpha, Black Counterpublics, and the Cultural Politics of Black Sororities.* Albany: State University of New York, 2010.

White, E. Frances *Dark Continent of our Bodies: Black Feminism & Politics of Respectability.* Philadelphia: Temple University Press, 2001.

Williams, Chad L. *Torchbearers of Democracy: African American Soldiers in the World War I Era.* Chapel Hill: University of North Carolina Press, 2013.

Yocum, Rachel. Interview with Pearl Primus Interview. No date. Audiocassette. New York: Dance Collection of the New York Public Library of Performing Arts.

Newspapers and Official Journals

The Advocate
Afro-American Baltimore
The Crisis
The Crusader
Daily Gleaner
Daily Worker
Dance
Dance Observer
The Emancipator
Jewish Daily Forward
New York Age
New York Amsterdam News
New York Herald Tribune
New York Times
Off Our Backs
Pittsburgh Courier
West Indian-American

Index

CPSIA information can be obtained at www.ICGtesting.com
Printed in the USA
LVOW11*1455010915

452380LV00010B/90/P

9 781628 462265